CompTIA
A+® Complete
Review Guide
Second Edition

CompTIA
A+® Complete
Review Guide
Second Edition

Emmett Dulaney

Troy McMillan

WILEY

John Wiley & Sons, Inc.

Senior Acquisitions Editor: Jeff Kellum
Development Editor: Dick Margulis
Technical Editors: Robin Abernathy, Ian Seaton
Production Editor: Rebecca Anderson
Copy Editor: Elizabeth Welch
Editorial Manager: Pete Gaughan
Production Manager: Tim Tate
Vice President and Executive Group Publisher: Richard Swadley
Vice President and Publisher: Neil Edde
Media Project Manager 1: Laura Moss-Hollister
Media Associate Producer: Doug Kuhn
Media Quality Assurance: Shawn Patrick
Book Designer: Happenstance Type-O-Rama
Compositor: Craig Woods, Happenstance Type-O-Rama
Proofreader: Rebecca Rider
Indexer: Robert Swanson
Project Coordinator, Cover: Katherine Crocker
Cover Designer: Ryan Sneed
Cover Image: © Jeremy Woodhouse / Photodisc / Getty Images

Copyright © 2012 by John Wiley & Sons, Inc., Indianapolis, Indiana

Published simultaneously in Canada

ISBN: 978-1-118-32408-0

ISBN: 978-1-118-46386-4 (ebk.)

ISBN: 978-1-118-42187-1 (ebk.)

ISBN: 978-1-118-43406-2 (ebk.)

For general information on our other products and services or to obtain technical support, please contact our Customer Care Department within the U.S. at (877) 762-2974, outside the U.S. at (317) 572-3993 or fax (317) 572-4002.

Wiley publishes in a variety of print and electronic formats and by print-on-demand. Some material included with standard print versions of this book may not be included in e-books or in print-on-demand. If this book refers to media such as a CD or DVD that is not included in the version you purchased, you may download this material at http://booksupport.wiley.com. For more information about Wiley products, visit www.wiley.com.

Library of Congress Control Number: 2012944685

Dear Reader,

Thank you for choosing *CompTIA A+ Complete Review Guide, Second Edition.* This book is part of a family of premium-quality Sybex books, all of which are written by outstanding authors who combine practical experience with a gift for teaching.

Sybex was founded in 1976. More than 30 years later, we're still committed to producing consistently exceptional books. With each of our titles, we're working hard to set a new standard for the industry. From the paper we print on, to the authors we work with, our goal is to bring you the best books available.

I hope you see all that reflected in these pages. I'd be very interested to hear your comments and get your feedback on how we're doing. Feel free to let me know what you think about this or any other Sybex book by sending me an email at nedde@wiley.com. If you think you've found a technical error in this book, please visit http://sybex.custhelp.com. Customer feedback is critical to our efforts at Sybex.

Best regards,

Neil Edde
Vice President and Publisher
Sybex, an Imprint of Wiley

For Jim and Linda: thank you for always being there.
—Emmett Dulaney

For my dear father, who has always supported me no matter what.
—Troy McMillan

Acknowledgments

There are a great many people without whom this book would not be possible. Among them is Jeff Kellum, who does his job as an acquisitions editor extremely well and pulls you along with him. Thanks must also go to Faithe Wempen and David Groth for their work on earlier editions of this book.

—Emmett Dulaney

Special thanks go out to Jeff Kellum as always, and to Robin Abernathy, who did an incredible job on the technical edit. I also would like thank Dick Margulis, the development editor, who ensured that we kept everything on track and met our deadlines. Finally, thanks to Emmett, who was a pleasure to work with.

—Troy McMillan

About the Authors

Emmett Dulaney holds or has held 18 vendor certifications and is the author of over 30 books. An associate professor at Anderson University, he is the former director of training for Mercury Technical Solutions. He specializes in certification and cross-platform integration, and is a columnist for CertCities and Campus Technology. Emmett can be reached at eadulaney@comcast.net.

Troy McMillan writes practice tests and study guides for Kaplan Cert Prep, while also running his own training and consulting company. Holding over 30 industry certifications in Cisco, CompTIA, Microsoft, and wireless technologies, Troy is also a Cisco Certified trainer, MCT, and author of a number of books on technology-related subjects. Troy can be reached at mcmillantroy@hotmail.com.

Contents at a Glance

Contents

Chapter   7   **Security**   **325**

Introduction

The A+ certification program was developed by the Computing Technology Industry Association (CompTIA) to provide an industry-wide means of certifying the competency of computer service technicians. The A+ certification, which is granted to those who have attained the level of knowledge and troubleshooting skills that are needed to provide capable support in the field of personal computers, is similar to other certifications in the computer industry. The theory behind these certifications is that if you needed to have service performed on any of their products, you would sooner call a technician who has been certified in one of the appropriate programs than you would just call the first so-called "expert" in the phone book.

CompTIA's A+ exam objectives are periodically updated to keep the certification applicable to the most recent hardware and software. This is necessary because a technician must be able to work on the latest equipment. The most recent revisions to the objectives—and to the whole program—were introduced in 2012 and are reflected in this book.

This book and the Sybex *CompTIA A+ Complete Study Guide* (both the Standard and Deluxe Editions) are tools to help you prepare for this certification—and for the new areas of focus of a modern computer technician's job.

What Is A+ Certification?

The A+ certification program was created to offer a wide-ranging certification, in the sense that it's intended to certify competence with personal computers from many different makers and vendors. Everyone must take and pass two exams: 220-801 and 220-802.

 Note that for the new exams, CompTIA did away with the user-friendly naming that existed with previous editions: Essentials and Practical Applications.

You don't have to take the 220-801 exam and the 220-802 exam at the same time. However, the A+ certification isn't awarded until you've passed both tests.

For the latest pricing on the exams and updates to the registration procedures, call Pearson VUE at (877) 551-7587. You can also go to www.pearsonvue.com for additional information or to register online. If you have further questions about the scope of the exams or related CompTIA programs, refer to the CompTIA website at www.comptia.org.

Who Should Buy This Book?

If you want to acquire a solid foundation in personal computer basics, and your goal is to prepare for the exams by filling in any gaps in your knowledge, this book is for you. You'll find clear explanations of the concepts you need to grasp and plenty of help to achieve the high level of professional competency you need in order to succeed in your chosen field.

If you want to become certified as an A+ holder, this book is definitely what you need. However, if you just want to attempt to pass the exam without really understanding the basics of personal computers, this guide isn't for you. It's written for people who want to acquire skills and knowledge of PC basics.

How to Use This Book and the Companion Website

We've included several testing features in the book and on the companion website. These tools will help you retain vital exam content as well as prepare to sit for the actual exams:

Chapter Review Questions   To test your knowledge as you progress through the book, there are review questions at the end of each chapter. As you finish each chapter, answer the review questions and then check your answers—the correct answers appear in Appendix A. You can go back to reread the section that deals with each question you got wrong to ensure that you answer correctly the next time you're tested on the material.

Instructions on how to download the electronic flashcards and the bonus practice exams can be found at www.sybex.com/go/aplusrg2e.

Electronic Flashcards   We've provided electronic flashcard for on-the-go review. These are short questions and answers, just like the flashcards you probably used to study in school.

Test Engine   We've also included the Sybex Test Engine. Using this custom test engine, you can identify weak areas up front and then develop a solid studying strategy using each of these robust testing features. Our thorough readme file will walk you through the quick, easy installation process. There are a total of four practice exams: two for exam 220-801 and two for 220-802. Take these practice exams just as if you were taking the actual exam (without any reference material). When you've finished the first exam, move on to the next one to solidify your test-taking skills. If you get more than 90 percent of the answers correct, you're ready to take the certification exams.

Glossary of Terms in PDF   From the companion website, we have included a very useful glossary of terms in PDF format so you can easily read it on any computer. If you have to travel and brush up on any key terms, you can do so with this useful resource.

Minimum System Requirements

You should have a minimum of 45 MB of disk space, as well as Windows 2000 or higher to use the Sybex Test Engine. You will also need Adobe Reader (downloadable from www.adobe.com) for the Glossary.

Tips for Taking the A+ Exams

Here are some general tips for taking your exams successfully:

- Bring two forms of ID with you. One must be a photo ID, such as a driver's license. The other can be a major credit card or a passport. Both forms must include a signature.

- Arrive early at the exam center so you can relax and review your study materials, particularly tables and lists of exam-related information.

- Read the questions carefully. Don't be tempted to jump to an early conclusion. Make sure you know exactly what the question is asking.

- Don't leave any unanswered questions. Unanswered questions are scored against you.

- There will be questions with multiple correct responses. When there is more than one correct answer, a message at the bottom of the screen will prompt you to either "Choose two." or "Choose all that apply." Be sure to read the messages displayed to know how many correct answers you must choose.

- When answering multiple-choice questions you're not sure about, use a process of elimination to get rid of the obviously incorrect answers first. Doing so will improve your odds if you need to make an educated guess.

- On form-based tests (nonadaptive), because the hard questions will eat up the most time, save them for last. You can move forward and backward through the exam.

- For the latest pricing on the exams and updates to the registration procedures, visit CompTIA's website at www.comptia.org.

Performance-Based Questions

CompTIA has begun to include performance-based questions on their exams. These differ from the traditional multiple-choice questions in that the candidate is expected to perform a task or series of tasks. Don't be surprised if on the exams you are presented with a scenario and asked to complete a task.

Exam Objectives

CompTIA goes to great lengths to ensure that its certification programs accurately reflect the IT industry's best practices. The company does this by establishing Cornerstone Committees for each of its exam programs. Each committee consist of a small group of IT professionals, training providers, and publishers who are responsible for establishing the exam's baseline competency level and who determine the appropriate target audience level.

Once these factors are determined, CompTIA shares this information with a group of hand-selected Subject Matter Experts (SMEs). These folks are the true brainpower behind the certification program. They review the committee's findings, refine them, and shape them into the objectives you see before you. CompTIA calls this process a Job Task Analysis (JTA).

Finally, CompTIA conducts a survey to ensure that the objectives and weightings truly reflect the job requirements. Only then can the SMEs go to work writing the hundreds of questions needed for the exam. And, in many cases, they have to go back to the drawing board for further refinements before the exam is ready to go live in its final state. So, rest assured, the content you're about to learn will serve you long after you take the exam.

 Exam objectives are subject to change at any time without prior notice and at CompTIA's sole discretion. Please visit the certification page of CompTIA's website at www.comptia.org for the most current listing of exam objectives.

CompTIA also publishes relative weightings for each of the exam's objectives. The following tables list the objective domains and the extent to which they're represented on each exam. For example, on the 220-801 exam expect to spend more time answering questions that pertain to PC hardware than to printers.

220-801 Exam Domains	% of Exam
1.0 PC Hardware	40%
2.0 Networking	27%
3.0 Laptops	11%
4.0 Printers	11%
5.0 Operational Procedures	11%
Total	**100%**

220-802 Exam Domains	% of Exam
1.0 Operating Systems	33%
2.0 Security	22%
3.0 Mobile Devices	9%
4.0 Troubleshooting	36%
Total	**100%**

The following sections look at the objectives beneath each of these in more detail.

CompTIA 220-801 Exam Objectives

1.0 PC Hardware

1.1 Configure and apply BIOS settings.

- Install firmware upgrades – flash BIOS
- BIOS component information
  - RAM
  - Hard drive
  - Optical drive
  - CPU
- BIOS configurations
  - Boot sequence
  - Enabling and disabling devices
  - Date/time
  - Clock speeds
  - Virtualization support
  - BIOS security (passwords, drive encryption: TPM, lo-jack)
- Use built-in diagnostics
- Monitoring
  - Temperature monitoring
  - Fan speeds
  - Intrusion detection/notification
  - Voltage
  - Clock
  - Bus speed

1.2 Differentiate between motherboard components, their purposes, and properties.

- Sizes
  - ATX
  - Micro-ATX
  - ILX
- Expansion Slots
  - PCI
  - PCI-X

- PCIe
- miniPCI
- CNR
- AGP2x, 4x, 8x
- RAM slots
- CPU sockets
- Chipsets
  - North Bridge
  - South Bridge
  - CMOS battery
- Jumpers
- Power connections and types
- Fan connectors
- Front panel connectors
  - USB
  - Audio
  - Power button
  - Power light
  - Drive activity lights
  - Reset button
- Bus speeds

1.3 Compare and contrast RAM types and features.

- Types
  - DDR
  - DDR2
  - DDR3
  - SDRAM
  - SODIMM
  - RAMBUS
  - DIMM
  - Parity vs. non-parity
  - ECC vs. non-ECC
  - RAM configurations
    - Single channel vs. dual channel vs. triple channel
  - Single sided vs. double sided
- RAM compatibility and speed

1.4 Install and configure expansion cards.

- Sound cards
- Video cards
- Network cards
- Serial and parallel cards
- USB cards
- FireWire cards
- Storage cards
- Modem cards
- Wireless/cellular cards
- TV tuner cards
- Video capture cards
- Riser cards

1.5 Install and configure storage devices and use appropriate media.

- Optical drives
  - CD-ROM
  - DVD-ROM
  - Blu-Ray
- Combo drives and burners
  - CD-RW
  - DVD-RW
  - Dual Layer DVD-RW
  - BD-R
  - BD-RE
- Connection Types
  - External
    - USB
    - FireWire
    - eSATA
    - Ethernet
  - Internal SATA, IDE and SCSI
    - IDE configuration and setup (Master, Slave, Cable Select)
    - SCSI IDs (0-15)
  - Hot swappable drives

- Hard drives
    - Magnetic
    - 5400 rpm
    - 7200 rpm
    - 10,000 rpm
    - 15,000 rpm
- Solid state/flash drives
    - Compact flash
    - SD
    - Micro-SD
    - Mini-SD
    - *x*D
    - SSD
- RAID Types
    - 0
    - 1
    - 5
    - 10
- Floppy drive
- Tape drive
- Media capacity
    - CD
    - CD-RW
    - DVD-RW
    - DVD
    - Blu-Ray
    - Tape
    - Floppy
    - DL DVD

1.6 Differentiate among various CPU types and features and select the appropriate cooling methods.

- Socket types
    - Intel: LGA, 775, 1155, 1366
    - AMD: 940, AM2, AM2+, AM3, AM3+, FMI, F

- Characteristics
  - Speeds
  - Cores
  - Cache size/type
  - Hyperthreading
  - Virtualization support
  - Architecture (32-bit vs. 64-bit)
  - Integrated GPU
- Cooling
  - Heat sink
  - Fans
  - Thermal paste
  - Liquid-based

1.7 Compare and contrast various connection interfaces and explain their purpose.

- Physical connections
  - USB 1.1 vs. 2.0 vs. 3.0 speed and distance characteristics
    - Connector types: A, B, mini, micro
  - FireWire 400 vs. FireWire 800 speed and distance characteristics
  - SATA1 vs. SATA2 vs. SATA3, eSATA, IDE speeds
  - Other connector types
    - Serial
    - Parallel
    - VGA
    - HDMI
    - DVI
    - Audio
    - RJ-45
    - RJ-11
  - Analog vs. digital transmission
    - VGA vs. HDMI
- Speeds, distances, and frequencies of wireless device connections
  - Bluetooth
  - IR
  - RF

1.8 Install an appropriate power supply based on a given scenario.

- Connector types and their voltages
  - SATA
  - Molex
  - 4/8-pin 12v
  - PCIe 6/8-pin
  - 20-pin
  - 24-pin
  - Floppy
- Specifications
  - Wattage
  - Size
  - Number of connectors
  - ATX
  - Micro-ATX
- Dual voltage options

1.9 Evaluate and select appropriate components for a custom configuration, to meet customer specifications or needs.

- Graphic / CAD / CAM design workstations
  - Powerful processor
  - High-end video
  - Maximum RAM
- Audio/Video editing workstation
  - Specialized audio and video card
  - Large fast hard drive
  - Dual monitors
- Virtualization workstation
  - Maximum RAM and CPU cores
- Gaming PC
  - Powerful processor
  - High-end video/specialized GPU
  - Better sound card
  - High-end cooling
- Home Theater PC
  - Surround sound audio
  - HDMI output

- HTPC compact form factor
- TV tuner
- Standard thick client
  - Desktop applications
  - Meets recommended requirements for running Windows
- Thin client
  - Basic applications
  - Meets minimum requirements for running Windows
- Home Server PC
  - Media streaming
  - File sharing
  - Print sharing
  - Gigabit NIC
  - RAID array

1.10 Given a scenario, evaluate types and features of display devices.

- Types
  - CRT
  - LCD
  - LED
  - Plasma
  - Projector
  - OLED
- Refresh rates
- Resolution
- Native resolution
- Brightness/lumens
- Analog vs. digital
- Privacy/antiglare filters
- Multiple displays

1.11 Identify connector types and associated cables.

- Display connector types
  - DVI-D
  - DVI-I
  - DVI-A

- DisplayPort
- RCA
- HD-15 (i.e. DE15 or DB15)
- BNC
- miniHDMI
- RJ-45
- miniDin-6
- Display cable types
  - HDMI
  - DVI
  - VGA
  - Component
  - Composite
  - S-video
  - RGB
  - Coaxial
  - Ethernet
- Device connectors and pin arrangements
  - SATA
  - eSATA
  - PATA
    - IDE
    - EIDE
  - Floppy
  - USB
  - IEEE1394
  - SCSI
  - PS/2
  - Parallel
  - Serial
  - Audio
  - RJ-45
- Device cable types
  - SATA
  - eSATA

- IDE
- EIDE
- Floppy
- USB
- IEEE1394
- SCSI
  - 68pin vs. 50pin vs. 25pin
- Parallel
- Serial
- Ethernet
- Phone

1.12 Install and configure various peripheral devices.

- Input devices
  - Mouse
  - Keyboard
  - Touch screen
  - Scanner
  - Barcode reader
  - KVM
  - Microphone
  - Biometric devices
  - Game pads
  - Joysticks
  - Digitizer
- Multimedia devices
  - Digital cameras
  - Microphone
  - Webcam
  - Camcorder
  - MIDI enabled devices
- Output devices
  - Printers
  - Speakers
  - Display devices

2.0 Networking

2.1 Identify types of network cables and connectors.

- Fiber
    - Connectors: SC, ST, and LC
- Twisted Pair
    - Connectors: RJ-11, RJ-45
    - Wiring standards: T568A, T568B
- Coaxial
    - Connectors: BNC, F-connector

2.2 Categorize characteristics of connectors and cabling.

- Fiber
    - Types (single-move vs. multi-mode)
    - Speed and transmission limitations
- Twisted Pair
    - Types: STP, UTP, CAT3, CAT5, CAT5e, CAT6, plenum, PVC
    - Speed and transmission limitations
- Coaxial
    - Types: RG-6, RG-59
    - Speed and transmission limitations

2.3 Explain properties and characteristics of TCP/IP.

- IP class
    - Class A
    - Class B
    - Class C
- IPv4 vs. IPv6
- Public vs. private vs. APIPA
- Static vs. dynamic
- Client-side DNS
- DHCP
- Subnet mask
- Gateway

2.4 Explain common TCP and UDP ports, protocols, and their purpose.

- Ports
    - 21 – FTP
    - 23 – Telnet

- 25 – SMTP
- 53 – DNS
- 80 – HTTP
- 110 – POP3
- 143 – IMAP
- 443 – HTTPS
- 3389 - RDP
- Protocols
  - DHCP
  - DNS
  - LDAP
  - SNMP
  - SMB
  - SSH
  - SFTP
- TCP vs. UDP

2.5 Compare and contrast wireless networking standards and encryption types.

- Standards
  - 802.11 a/b/g/n
  - Speeds, distances, and frequencies
- Encryption types
  - WEP, WPA, WPA2, TKIP, AES

2.6 Install, configure, and deploy a SOHO wireless/wired router using appropriate settings.

- MAC filtering
- Channels (1-11)
- Port forwarding, port triggering
- SDID broadcast (on/off)
- Wireless encryption
- Firewall
- DHCP (on/off)
- DMZ
- NAT
- WPS
- Basic QoS

2.7 Compare and contrast Internet connection types and features.
- Cable
- DSL
- Dial-up
- Fiber
- Satellite
- ISDN
- Cellular (mobile hotspot)
- Line of sight wireless internet service
- WiMAX

2.8 Identify various types of networks.
- LAN
- WAN
- PAN
- MAN
- Topologies
  - Mesh
  - Ring
  - Bus
  - Star
  - Hybrid

2.9 Compare and contrast network devices their functions and features.
- Hub
- Switch
- Router
- Access point
- Bridge
- Modem
- NAS
- Firewall
- VoIP phones
- Internet appliance

2.10 Given a scenario, use appropriate networking tools.
- Crimper
- Multimeter

- Toner probe
- Cable tester
- Loopback plug
- Punchdown tool

3.0 Laptops

3.1 Install and configure laptop hardware and components.

- Expansion options
    - ExpressCard/34
    - ExpressCard/54
    - PCMCIA
    - SODIMM
    - Flash
- Hardware/device replacement
    - Keyboard
    - Hard drive (2.5 vs. 3.5)
    - Memory
    - Optical drive
    - Wireless card
    - Mini-PCIe
    - Screen
    - DC jack
    - Battery
    - Touchpad
    - Plastics
    - Speaker
    - System board
    - CPU

3.2 Compare and contrast the components within the display of a laptop.

- Types
    - LCD
    - LED
    - OLED
    - Plasma

- Wi-Fi antenna connector/placement
- Inverter and its function
- Backlight

3.3 Compare and contrast laptop features.

- Special function keys
  - Dual displays
  - Wireless (on/off)
  - Volume settings
  - Screen brightness
  - Bluetooth (on/off)
  - Keyboard backlight
- Docking station vs. port replicator
- Physical laptop lock and cable lock

4.0 Printers

4.1 Explain the differences between the various printer types and summarize the associated imaging process.

- Laser
  - Imaging drum, fuser assembly, transfer belt, transfer roller, pickup rollers, separate pads, duplexing assembly
  - Imaging process: processing, charging, exposing, developing, transferring, fusing, and cleaning
- Inkjet
  - Ink cartridge, print head, roller, feeder, duplexing assembly, carriage and belt
  - Calibration
- Thermal
  - Feed assembly, heating element
  - Special thermal paper
- Impact
  - Print head, ribbon, tractor feed
  - Impact paper

4.2 Given a scenario, install, and configure printers.

- Use appropriate printer drivers for a given operating system
- Print device sharing
  - Wired
    - USB

- Parallel
- Serial
- Ethernet
  - Wireless
    - Bluetooth
    - 802.11x
    - Infrared (IR)
  - Printer hardware print server
- Printer sharing
  - Sharing local/networked printer via Operating System settings

4.3 Given a scenario, perform printer maintenance.

- Laser
  - Replacing toner, applying maintenance kit, calibration, cleaning
- Thermal
  - Replace paper, clean heating element, remove debris
- Impact
  - Replace ribbon, replace print head, replace paper

5.0 Operational Procedures

5.1 Given a scenario, use appropriate safety procedures.

- ESD straps
- ESD mats
- Self-grounding
- Equipment grounding
- Personal safety
  - Disconnect power before repairing PC
  - Remove jewelry
  - Lifting techniques
  - Weight limitations
  - Electrical fire safety
  - CRT safety – proper disposal
  - Cable management
- Compliance with local government regulations

5.2 Explain environmental impacts and the purpose of environmental controls.

- MSDS documentation for handling and disposal
- Temperature, humidity level awareness and proper ventilation
- Power surges, brownouts, blackouts
  - Battery backup
  - Surge suppressor
- Protection from airborne particles
  - Enclosures
  - Air filters
- Dust and debris
  - Compressed air
  - Vacuums
- Component handling and protection
  - Antistatic bags
- Compliance to local government regulations

5.3 Given a scenario, demonstrate proper communication and professionalism.

- Use proper language – avoid jargon, acronyms, slang when applicable
- Maintain a positive attitude
- Listen and do not interrupt the customer
- Be culturally sensitive
- Be on time (if late contact the customer)
- Avoid distractions
  - Personal calls
  - Talking to co-workers while interacting with customers
  - Personal interruptions
- Dealing with difficult customer or situation
  - Avoid arguing with customers and/or being defensive
  - Do not minimize customers' problems
  - Avoid being judgmental
  - Clarify customer statements (ask open ended questions to narrow the scope of the problem, restate the issue or question to verify understanding)
- Set and meet expectations / timeline and communicate status with the customer
  - Offer different repair / replacement options if applicable
  - Provide proper documentation on the services provided
  - Follow up with customer / user at a later date to verify satisfaction

- Deal appropriately with customers confidential materials
  - Located on computer, desktop, printer, etc.

5.4 Explain the fundamentals of dealing with prohibited content/activity.

- First response
  - Identify
  - Report through proper channels
  - Data/device preservation
- Use of documentation/documentation changes
- Chain of custody
  - Tracking of evidence/documenting process

CompTIA A+ 220-802 Exam Objectives

1.0 Operating Systems

1.1 Compare and contrast the features and requirements of various Microsoft Operating Systems.

- Windows XP Home, Windows XP Professional, Windows XP Media Center, Windows XP 64-bit Professional
- Windows Vista Home Basic, Windows Vista Home Premium, Windows Vista Business, Windows Vista Ultimate, Windows Vista Enterprise
- Windows 7 Starter, Windows 7 Home Premium, Windows 7 Professional, Windows 7 Ultimate, Windows 7 Enterprise
- Features:
  - 32-bit vs. 64-bit
  - Aero, gadgets, user account control, bit-locker, shadow copy, system restore, ready boost, sidebar, compatibility mode, XP mode, easy transfer, administrative tools, defender, Windows firewall, security center, event viewer, file structure and paths, category view vs. classic view
- Upgrade paths – differences between in place upgrades, compatibility tools, Windows upgrade OS advisor

1.2 Given a scenario, install, and configure the operating system using the most appropriate method.

- Boot methods
  - USB
  - CD-ROM

- DVD
- PXE
- Types of installations
  - Creating image
  - Unattended installation
  - Upgrade
  - Clean install
  - Repair installation
  - Multiboot
  - Remote network installation
  - Image deployment
- Partitioning
  - Dynamic
  - Basic
  - Primary
  - Extended
  - Logical
- File system types/formatting
  - FAT
  - FAT32
  - NTFS
  - CDFS
  - Quick format vs. full format
- Load alternative third party drivers when necessary
- Workgroup vs. Domain setup
- Time/date/region/language settings
- Driver installation, software and windows updates
- Factory recovery partition

1.3 Given a scenario, use appropriate command line tools.

- Networking
  - PING
  - TRACERT
  - NETSTAT
  - IPCONFIG

- Component services
- Data sources
- Print management
- Windows memory diagnostics
- Windows firewall
- Advanced security
- MSCONFIG
  - General
  - Boot
  - Services
  - Startup
  - Tools
- Task Manager
  - Applications
  - Processes
  - Performance
  - Networking
  - Users
- Disk management
  - Drive status
  - Mounting
  - Extending partitions
  - Splitting partitions
  - Assigning drive letters
  - Adding drives
  - Adding arrays
- Other
  - User State Migration Tool (USMT), File and Settings Transfer Wizard, Windows Easy Transfer
- Run line utilities
  - MSCONFIG
  - REGEDIT
  - CMD
  - SERVICES.MSC

- MMC
- MSTSC
- NOTEPAD
- EXPLORER
- MSINFO32
- DXDIAG

1.5 Given a scenario, use Control Panel utilities (the items are organized by "classic view/ large icons" in Windows).

- Common to all Microsoft Operating Systems
    - Internet options
        - Connections
        - Security
        - General
        - Privacy
        - Programs
        - Advanced
    - Display
        - Resolution
    - User accounts
    - Folder options
        - Sharing
        - View hidden files
        - Hide extensions
        - Layout
    - System
        - Performance (virtual memory)
        - Hardware profiles
        - Remote settings
        - System protection
    - Security center
    - Windows firewall
    - Power options
        - Hibernate
        - Power plans

- Sleep/suspend
- Standby
- Unique to Windows XP
  - Add/remove programs
  - Network connections
  - Printers and faxes
  - Automatic updates
  - Network setup wizard
- Unique to Windows Vista
  - Tablet PC settings
  - Pen and input devices
  - Offline files
  - Problem reports and solutions
  - Printers
- Unique to Windows 7
  - HomeGroup
  - Action center
  - Remote applications and desktop applications
  - Troubleshooting

1.6 Setup and configure Windows networking on a client/desktop.

- HomeGroup, file/print sharing
- WorkGroup vs. domain setup
- Network shares/mapping drives
- Establish networking connections
  - VPN
  - Dialups
  - Wireless
  - Wired
  - WWAN (Cellular)
- Proxy settings
- Remote desktop
- Home vs. Work vs. Public network settings

- Firewall settings
  - Exceptions
  - Configuration
  - Enabling/disabling Windows firewall
- Configuring an alternative IP address in Windows
  - IP addressing
  - Subnet mask
  - DNS
  - Gateway
- Network card properties
  - Half duplex/full duplex/auto
  - Speed
  - Wake-on-LAN
  - PoE
  - QoS

1.7 Perform preventive maintenance procedures using appropriate tools.
- Best practices
  - Scheduled backups
  - Scheduled check disks
  - Scheduled defragmentation
  - Windows updates
  - Patch management
  - Driver/firmware updates
  - Antivirus updates
- Tools
  - Backup
  - System restore
  - Check disk
  - Recovery image
  - Defrag

1.8 Explain the differences among basic OS security settings.
- User and groups
  - Administrator
  - Power user

- Guest
- Standard user

- NTFS vs. Share permissions
  - Allow vs. deny
  - Moving vs. copying folders and files
  - File attributes
- Shared files and folders
  - Administrative shares vs. local shares
  - Permission propagation
  - Inheritance
- System files and folders
- User authentication
  - Single sign-on

1.9 Explain the basics of client-side virtualization.

- Purpose of virtual machines
- Resource requirements
- Emulator requirements
- Security requirements
- Network requirements
- Hypervisor

2.0 Security

2.1 Apply and use common prevention methods.

- Physical security
  - Lock doors
  - Tailgating
  - Securing physical documents/passwords/shredding
  - Biometrics
  - Badges
  - Key fobs
  - RFID badge
  - RSA tokens
  - Privacy filters
  - Retinal

- Digital security
    - Antivirus
    - Firewalls
    - Antispyware
    - User authentication/strong passwords
    - Directory permissions
- User education
- Principle of least privilege

2.2 Compare and contrast common security threats.

- Social engineering
- Malware
- Rootkits
- Phishing
- Shoulder surfing
- Spyware
- Viruses
    - Worms
    - Trojans

2.3 Implement security best practices to secure a workstation.

- Setting strong passwords
- Requiring passwords
- Restricting user permissions
- Changing default user names
- Disabling guest account
- Screensaver required password
- Disable autorun

2.4 Given a scenario, use the appropriate data destruction/disposal method.

- Low level format vs. standard format
- Hard drive sanitation and sanitation methods
    - Overwrite
    - Drive wipe
- Physical destruction
    - Shredder
    - Drill

- Electromagnetic
- Degaussing tool

2.5 Given a scenario, secure a SOHO wireless network.
- Change default user-names and passwords
- Changing SSID
- Setting encryption
- Disabling SSID broadcast
- Enable MAC filtering
- Antenna and access point placement
- Radio power levels
- Assign static IP addresses

2.6 Given a scenario, secure a SOHO wired network.
- Change default usernames and passwords
- Enable MAC filtering
- Assign static IP addresses
- Disabling ports
- Physical security

3.0 Mobile Devices

3.1 Explain the basic features of mobile operating systems.
- Android vs. iOS
  - Open source vs. closed source/vendor specific
  - App source (app store and market)
  - Screen orientation (accelerometer/gyroscope)
  - Screen calibration
  - GPS and geotracking

3.2 Establish basic network connectivity and configure email.
- Wireless/cellular data network (enable/disable)
- Bluetooth
  - Enable Bluetooth
  - Enable pairing
  - Find device for pairing
  - Enter appropriate pin code
  - Test connectivity

- Email configuration
  - Server address
    - POP3
    - IMAP
    - Port and SLLS settings
  - Exchange
  - Gmail

3.3 Compare and contrast methods for securing mobile devices.

- Passcode locks
- Remote wipes
- Locator applications
- Remote backup applications
- Failed login attempts restrictions
- Antivirus
- Patching/OS updates

3.4 Compare and contrast hardware differences in regards to tablets and laptops.

- No field serviceable parts
- Typically not upgradeable
- Touch interface
  - Touch flow
  - Multitouch
- Solid state drives

3.5 Execute and configure mobile device synchronization.

- Types of data to synchronize
  - Contacts
  - Programs
  - Email
  - Pictures
  - Music
  - Videos
- Software requirements to install the application on the PC
- Connection types to enable synchronization

4.0 Troubleshooting

4.1 Given a scenario, explain the troubleshooting theory.

- Identify the problem
    - Question the user and identify user changes to computer and perform backups before making changes
- Establish a theory of probable cause (question the obvious)
- Test the theory to determine cause
    - Once theory is confirmed determine next steps to resolve problem
    - If theory is not confirmed re-establish new theory or escalate
- Establish a plan of action to resolve the problem and implement the solution
- Verify full system functionality and if applicable implement preventive measures
- Document findings, actions, and outcomes

4.2 Given a scenario, troubleshoot common problems related to motherboards, RAM, CPU and power with appropriate tools.

- Common symptoms
    - Unexpected shutdowns
    - System lockups
    - POST code beeps
    - Blank screen on bootup
    - BIOS time and settings resets
    - Attempts to boot to incorrect devices
    - Continuous reboots
    - No power
    - Overheating
    - Loud noise
    - Intermittent device failure
    - Fans spin – no power to other devices
    - Indicator lights
    - Smoke
    - Burning smell
    - BSOD
- Tools
    - Multimeter
    - Power supply tester

- Loopback plugs
- POST card

4.3 Given a scenario, troubleshoot hard drives and RAID arrays with appropriate tools.

- Common symptoms
  - Read/write failure
  - Slow performance
  - Loud clicking noise
  - Failure to boot
  - Drive not recognized
  - OS not found
  - RAID not found
  - RAID stops working
  - BSOD
- Tools
  - Screwdriver
  - External enclosures
  - CHDKS
  - CHKDSK
  - FORMAT
  - FDISK
  - File recovery software

4.4 Given a scenario, troubleshoot common video and display issues.

- Common symptoms
  - VGA mode
  - No image on screen
  - Overheat shutdown
  - Dead pixels
  - Artifacts
  - Color patterns incorrect
  - Dim image
  - Flickering image
  - Distorted image
  - Discoloration (degaussing)
  - BSOD

4.5   Given a scenario, troubleshoot wired and wireless networks with appropriate tools.
- Common symptoms
  - No connectivity
  - APIPA address
  - Limited connectivity
  - Local connectivity
  - Intermittent connectivity
  - IP conflict
  - Slow transfer speeds
  - Low RF signal
- Tools
  - Cable tester
  - Loopback plug
  - Punch down tools
  - Toner probes
  - Wire strippers
  - Crimper
  - PING
  - IPCONFIG
  - TRACERT
  - NETSTAT
  - NBTSTAT
  - NET
  - Wireless locator

4.6   Given a scenario, troubleshoot operating system problems with appropriate tools.
- Common symptoms
  - BSOD
  - Failure to boot
  - Improper shutdown
  - Spontaneous shutdown/restart
  - RAID not detected during installation
  - Device fails to start
  - Missing dll message
  - Services fails to start

- Compatibility error
- Slow system performance
- Boots to safe mode
- File fails to open
- Missing NTLDR
- Missing Boot.ini
- Missing operating system
- Missing Graphical Interface
- Graphical Interface fails to load
- Invalid boot disk

- Tools
  - Fixboot
  - Recovery console
  - Fixmbr
  - Sfc
  - Repair disks
  - Pre-installation environments
  - MSCONFIG
  - DEFRAG
  - REGSRV32
  - REGEDIT
  - Event viewer
  - Safe mode
  - Command prompt
  - Emergency repair disk
  - Automated system recovery

4.7 Given a scenario, troubleshoot common security issues with appropriate tools and best practices.

- Common symptoms
  - Pop-ups
  - Browser redirection
  - Security alerts
  - Slow performance
  - Internet connectivity issues

- PC locks up
- Windows updates failures
- Rogue antivirus
- Spam
- Renamed system files
- Files disappearing
- File permission changes
- Hijacked email
- Access denied
- Tools
  - Anti-virus software
  - Anti-malware software
  - Anti-spyware software
  - Recovery console
  - System restore
  - Pre-installation environments
  - Event viewer
- Best practices for malware removal
  - Identify malware symptoms
  - Quarantine infected system
  - Disable system restore
  - Remediate infected systems
    - Update anti-virus software
    - Scan and removal techniques (safe mode, pre-installation environment)
  - Schedule scans and updates
  - Enable system restore and create restore points
  - Educate end user

4.8 Given a scenario, troubleshoot, and repair common laptop issues while adhering to the appropriate procedures.

- Common symptoms
  - No display
  - Dim display
  - Flickering display
  - Sticking keys
  - Intermittent wireless

- Battery not charging
- Ghost cursor
- No power
- Num lock indicator lights
- No wireless connectivity
- Cannot display to external monitor
- Disassembling processes for proper re-assembly
  - Document and label cable and screw locations
  - Organize parts
  - Refer to manufacturer documentation
  - Use appropriate hand tools

4.9 Given a scenario, troubleshoot printers with appropriate tools.

- Common symptoms
  - Streaks
  - Faded prints
  - Ghost images
  - Toner not fused to the paper
  - Creased paper
  - Paper not feeding
  - Paper jam
  - No connectivity
  - Garbled characters on paper
  - Vertical lines on page
  - Backed up print queue
  - Low memory errors
  - Access denied
  - Printer will not print
  - Color prints in wrong print color
  - Unable to install printer
  - Error codes
- Tools
  - Maintenance kit
  - Toner vacuum
  - Compressed air
  - Printer spooler

CompTIA
A+® Complete
Review Guide
Second Edition

CompTIA A+ 220-801

PART

I

Chapter

1

PC Hardware

COMPTIA A+ ESSENTIALS EXAM OBJECTIVES COVERED IN THIS CHAPTER:

✓ **1.1 Configure and apply BIOS settings.**

- Install firmware upgrades—flash BIOS
- BIOS component information
  - RAM
  - Hard drive
  - Optical drive
  - CPU
- BIOS configurations
  - Boot sequence
  - Enabling and disabling devices
  - Date/time
  - Clock speeds
  - Virtualization support
  - BIOS security (passwords, drive encryption: TPM, lo-jack)
- Use built-in diagnostics
- Monitoring
  - Temperature monitoring
  - Fan speeds
  - Intrusion detection/notification
  - Voltage
  - Clock
  - Bus speed

✓ **1.2 Differentiate between motherboard components, their purposes, and properties.**

- Sizes
  - ATX
  - Micro-ATX
  - ITX
- Expansion Slots
  - PCI
  - PCI-X
  - PCIe
  - miniPCI
  - CNR
  - AGP2x, 4x, 8x
- RAM slots
- CPU sockets
- Chipsets
  - North Bridge
  - South Bridge
  - CMOS battery
- Jumpers
- Power connections and types
- Fan connections
- Front panel connectors
  - USB
  - Audio
  - Power button
  - Power light
  - Drive activity lights
  - Reset button

✓ **1.3 Compare and contrast RAM types and features.**

- Types
  - DDR
  - DDR2
  - DDR3
  - SDRAM
  - SODIMM
  - RAMBUS
  - DIMM
  - Parity vs. non-parity
  - ECC vs. non-ECC
  - RAM configurations
    - Single channel vs. dual channel vs. triple channel
  - Single sided vs. double sided
- RAM compatibility and speed

✓ **1.4 Install and configure expansion cards.**

- Sound cards
- Video cards
- Network cards
- Serial and parallel cards
- USB cards
- Firewire cards
- Storage cards
- Modem cards
- Wireless/cellular cards
- TV tuner cards
- Video capture cards
- Riser cards

✓ **1.5 Install and configure storage devices and use appropriate media.**

- Optical drives
    - CD-ROM
    - DVD-ROM
    - Blu-Ray
- Combo drives and burners
    - CD-RW
    - DVD-RW
    - Dual Layer DVD-RW
    - BD-R
    - BD-RE
- Connection types
    - External
        - USB
        - Firewire
        - eSATA
        - Ethernet
    - Internal SATA, IDE and SCSI
        - IDE configuration and setup (Master, Slave, Cable Select)
        - SCSI IDs (0–15)
    - Hot swappable drives
- Hard drives
    - Magnetic
    - 5400 rpm
    - 7200 rpm
    - 10,000 rpm
    - 15,000 rpm
- Solid state/flash drives
    - Compact flash
    - SD

- Micro-SD
- Mini-SD
- xD
- SSD
- RAID types
  - 0
  - 1
  - 5
  - 10
- Floppy drive
- Tape drive
- Media capacity
  - CD
  - CD-RW
  - DVD-RW
  - DVD
  - Blu-Ray
  - Tape
  - Floppy
  - DL DVD

✓ **1.6 Differentiate among various CPU types and features and select the appropriate cooling method.**

- Socket types
  - Intel: LGA, 775, 1155, 1156, 1366
  - AMD: 940, AM2, AM2+, AM3, AM3+, FM1, F
- Characteristics
  - Speeds
  - Cores
  - Cache size/type
  - Hyperthreading

- Virtualization support
- Architecture (32-bit vs. 64-bit)
- Integrated GPU
- Cooling
  - Heat sink
  - Fans
  - Thermal paste
  - Liquid-based

✓ **1.7 Compare and contrast various connection interfaces and explain their purpose.**

- Physical connections
  - USB 1.1 vs. 2.0 vs. 3.0 speed and distance characteristics
    - Connector types: A, B, mini, micro
  - Firewire 400 vs. Firewire 800 speed and distance characteristics
  - SATA1 vs. SATA2 vs. SATA3, eSATA, IDE speeds
  - Other connector types
    - Serial
    - Parallel
    - VGA
    - HDMI
    - DVI
    - Audio
    - RJ-45
    - RJ-11
  - Analog vs. digital transmission
    - VGA vs. HDMI
- Speeds, distances and frequencies of wireless device connections
  - Bluetooth
  - IR
  - RF

✓ **1.8 Install an appropriate power supply based on a given scenario.**

- Connector types and their voltages
  - SATA
  - Molex
  - 4/8-pin 12v
  - PCIe 6/8-pin
  - 20-pin
  - 24-pin
  - Floppy
- Specifications
  - Wattage
  - Size
  - Number of connectors
  - ATX
  - Micro-ATX
- Dual voltage options

✓ **1.9 Evaluate and select appropriate components for a custom configuration, to meet customer specifications or needs.**

- Graphic/CAD/CAM design workstation
  - Powerful processor
  - High-end video
  - Maximum RAM
- Audio/Video editing workstation
  - Specialized audio and video card
  - Large fast hard drive
  - Dual monitors
- Virtualization workstation
  - Maximum RAM and CPU cores

- Gaming PC
    - Powerful processor
    - High-end video/specialized GPU
    - Better sound card
    - High-end cooling
- Home Theater PC
    - Surround sound audio
    - HDMI output
    - HTPC compact form factor
    - TV tuner
- Standard thick client
    - Desktop applications
    - Meets recommended requirements for running Windows
- Thin client
    - Basic applications
    - Meets minimum requirements for running Windows
- Home Server PC
    - Media streaming
    - File sharing
    - Print sharing
    - Gigabit NIC
    - RAID array

✓ **1.10 Given a scenario, evaluate types and features of display devices.**

- Types
    - CRT
    - LCD
    - LED
    - Plasma
    - Projector
    - OLED

- Refresh rates

- Resolution

- Native resolution

- Brightness/lumens

- Analog vs. digital

- Privacy/antiglare filters

- Multiple displays

✓ **1.11 Identify connector types and associated cables.**

- Display connector types

    - DVI-D

    - DVI-I

    - DVI-A

    - DisplayPort

    - RCA

    - HD-15 (i.e. DE15 or DB15)

    - BNC

    - miniHDMI

    - RJ-45

    - miniDin-6

- Display cable types

    - HDMI

    - DVI

    - VGA

    - Component

    - Composite

    - S-video

    - RGB

    - Coaxial

    - Ethernet

- Device connectors and various connector pin-outs
  - SATA
  - eSATA
  - PATA
    - IDE
    - EIDE
  - Floppy
  - USB
  - IEEE1394
  - SCSI
  - PS/2
  - Parallel
  - Serial
  - Audio
  - RJ-45
- Device cable types
  - SATA
  - eSATA
  - IDE
  - EIDE
  - Floppy
  - USB
  - IEEE1394
  - SCSI
    - 68pin vs. 50pin vs. 25pin
  - Parallel
  - Serial
  - Ethernet
  - Phone

✓ 1.12 Install and configure various peripheral devices.

- Input devices
    - Mouse
    - Keyboard
    - Touch screen
    - Scanner
    - Barcode reader
    - KVM
    - Microphone
    - Biometric devices
    - Game pads
    - Joysticks
    - Digitizer
- Multimedia devices
    - Digital cameras
    - Microphone
    - Webcam
    - Camcorder
    - MIDI enabled devices
- Output devices
    - Printers
    - Speakers
    - Display devices

In this chapter, we will focus on the exam topics related to PC hardware. We will follow the structure of the CompTIA A+ 220-801 exam blueprint, objective 1, and we will explore the 12 subobjectives that the prospective exam taker will need to master before taking the exam.

1.1 Configure and apply BIOS settings

PCs and other devices that use an operating system usually also contain firmware that provides low-level instructions to the device even in the absence of an operating system. This firmware, called the Basic Input/Output System (BIOS), contains settings that can be manipulated and diagnostic utilities that can be used to monitor the device. This section discusses those settings and utilities. The topics addressed in objective 1.1 include:

- Install firmware upgrades—flash BIOS
- BIOS component information
- BIOS configurations
- Use built-in diagnostics
- Monitoring

Install firmware upgrades—flash BIOS

Computer BIOSs don't go bad; they just become out of date or contain bugs. In the case of a bug, an upgrade will correct the problem. An upgrade may also be indicated when the BIOS doesn't support some component that you would like to install—a larger hard drive or a different type of processor, for instance.

Most of today's BIOSs are written to an Electrically Erasable Programmable Read-Only Memory (EEPROM) chip and can be updated through the use of software. Each manufacturer has its own method for accomplishing this. Check out the documentation for complete details. Regardless of the exact procedure, the process is referred to as *flashing* the BIOS. It means the old instructions are erased from the EEPROM chip and the new instructions are written to the chip.

BIOS component information

At startup, the BIOS will attempt to detect the devices and components at its disposal. The information that it gathers, along with the current state of the components, will be available for review in the BIOS settings. Some of the components and the types of information available with respect to these devices and components are covered in this section.

You can view and adjust a computer's base-level settings through the CMOS Setup program, which you access by pressing a certain key at startup, such as F1 or Delete (depending on the system). The most common settings to adjust in CMOS include port settings (parallel, serial, USB), drive types, boot sequence, date and time, and virus/security protections. The variable settings that are made through the CMOS setup program are stored in NVRAM, while the base instructions that cannot be changed (the BIOS) are stored on an EEPROM chip.

RAM

Most systems today detect the RAM amount and speed automatically. Some motherboards can use different types of RAM, such as parity and non-parity, or different speeds, and the CMOS Setup program may provide the opportunity to change those settings. Increasingly, however, RAM settings are becoming a read-only part of CMOS Setup programs, as the system will detect additional memory added or a change in memory type. This does not preclude you from ensuring you are installing the correct type of memory for the system.

Hard drive

Some CMOS Setup programs have a feature that polls the IDE channels and provides information about the IDE devices attached to them. You can use this feature to gather the settings for a hard disk. However, most hard disks these days are fully Plug and Play, so they automatically report themselves to the CMOS Setup.

Hard drives can be auto-detected by most systems if the IDE setting is set to Auto. The settings detected may include the drive's capacity; its geometry—cylinders, heads, and sectors (CHS); and its preferred PIO (Programmed Input/Output), direct memory access (DMA), or UltraDMA operating mode. You can also configure a hard drive by entering its CHS values manually, but doing so is almost never necessary anymore.

CHS is also called the *drive geometry*, because together these three numbers determine how much data the disk can hold. Most CMOS Setup programs are able to automatically detect the CHS values.

Optical Drive

Optical drives, such as CD, CD-R, CD-RW, and DVD players, are also detected and reported by the BIOS. You can even set the computer to boot from one of these drives if desired (see the section "Boot sequence," later in this chapter). When you do that, in most cases the drives will be listed as CD-ROM or CD-ROM/DVD.

CPU

In most modern systems, the BIOS detects the CPU type and speed automatically, so any CPU settings in CMOS Setup are likely to be read-only. Most operating systems provide utilities for gathering information about the CPU in the computer, but if the computer will not boot or there is no operating system, then viewing the CPU information in the BIOS can be a valuable option.

BIOS configurations

When any of the changes listed in the following section are made to any of the BIOS configurations, it is important that the program be exited properly to save the changes. The CMOS Setup program includes an Exit command, with options that include Save Changes and Discard Changes. In most programs, Esc is a shortcut for exiting and discarding changes, and F10 is a common shortcut for exiting and saving changes.

Boot sequence

Each system has a default boot order, which is the order in which it checks the drives for a valid operating system to which it can boot. Usually, this order is set for hard disk, and then CD-ROM, but these components can be placed in any boot order. For example, you might set CD-ROM first to boot from a Windows 7 Setup disk on a system that already contained an operating system. If you receive an error message when booting, always check the CD-ROM, and if a nonsystem disk is present, remove it and reboot.

Enabling and disabling devices

In CMOS Setup, you can enable or disable integrated components, such as built-in video cards, sound cards, or network cards. You may disable them in order to replace them with different models on expansion boards, for example.

You can also disable the on-board I/O ports for the motherboard, including parallel, serial, and USB. Depending on the utility, there may also be settings that enable or disable USB keyboard usage, Wake on LAN, or other special features.

In addition to enabling or disabling legacy parallel ports, you can assign an operational mode to the port. Table 1.1 lists the common modes for a parallel port. When you're troubleshooting parallel port problems, sometimes trying a different mode will help. Some legacy systems do not allow on-board devices to be disabled. If this is the case, the entire motherboard may need to be replaced.

TABLE 1.1   Parallel port settings

Setting	Description	Use
EPP (enhanced parallel port)	Supports bidirectional communication and transfer rates up to 2 Mbps	Newer ink-jet and laser printers that can utilize bidirectional communication and scanners

Setting	Description	Use
ECP (enhanced capabilities port)	Supports bidirectional communication and achieves transfer rates of 2.5 Mbps using Direct Memory Access (DMA)	Newer ink-jet and laser printers that can utilize bidirectional communication, connectivity devices, and scanners
SPP (standard parallel port, also called Centronics)	Supports bidirectional communication using unidirectional data lines	Older ink-jet and laser printers and slower scanners

Date/time

One of the most basic things you can change in CMOS Setup is the system date and time. You can also change this from within the operating system. When the PC is not keeping correct time or date when turned off, it is usually a CMOS battery issue and a warning that the battery is soon going to die. In the absence of the PC receiving time and date updates from a time server such as a Network Time Protocol (NTP) server, the time kept in the CMOS is the time source for the computer.

Clock speeds

Clock speed is a measurement of the rate at which the clock signal oscillates; it is expressed in millions of cycles per second or MHz. The motherboard must be set to utilize the proper clock settings for the CPU installed in the computer. The BIOS usually detects the type of CPU and automatically sets the proper timings. In some older systems you may have to use jumpers to set the correct clock speed and CPU.

External Speed (Clock Speed) The *clock speed*, or *external speed*, usually expressed in MHz or GHz, is the speed at which the motherboard communicates with the CPU. It's determined by the motherboard, and its cadence is set by a quartz crystal (the system crystal) that generates regular electrical pulses.

Internal Speed The *internal speed* is the maximum speed at which the CPU can perform its internal operations. This may be the same as the motherboard's speed (the external speed), but it's more likely to be a multiple of it. For example, a CPU may have an internal speed of 1.3 GHz but an external speed of 133 MHz. That means for every tick of the system crystal's clock, the CPU has 10 internal ticks of its own clock.

When the proper CPU speed is known, you must make sure the relationship between the speed of the CPU and that of the motherboard bus is correct. This is done with a value called the *multiplier*. Although the bus speed can also be manipulated, usually it is set to accommodate the required speed of the memory to be used, and so it is more likely you will be using the multiplier to achieve the proper relationship between the CPU speed and the bus speed.

For example, if you have a processor that has a CPU speed of 1.82 GHz, the proper settings for the BIOS would be a bus speed of 166 MHz and a multiplier of 11 (166 MHz × 11 = 1.826 GHz). So if the bus needed to be 166 MHz, you would set the multiplier for 11. On the other hand, if you changed the bus speed to 332 MHz (just a random example), the closest multiplier would be 5.5 (332 MHz × 5.67 = 1.826 GHz). When setting the speed of either is required, refer to the documentation from the CPU and motherboard.

Virtualization Support

Many computers, especially servers, host virtual machines (VMs). These are fully functional operating systems running in their own environment. In many cases the motherboard and associated BIOS settings need no alteration to provide services to these virtual machines.

However, some of the newer virtualization products, for example Microsoft Hyper-V, require that the motherboard support *hardware-assisted virtualization*. This is because in these cases the virtualization product is not installed on top of a regular operating system, but is installed directly on bare metal—that is, as an integral part of the operating system, as in Windows Server 2008 R2.

The benefit derived from the virtualization product (also called a hypervisor) using hardware-assisted virtualization is it allows the hypervisor to dynamically allocate memory and CPU to the VMs as required. When the motherboard and the BIOS support this technology, you must ensure that it is enabled. Figure 1.1 shows an example of the settings.

FIGURE 1.1   BIOS virtualization

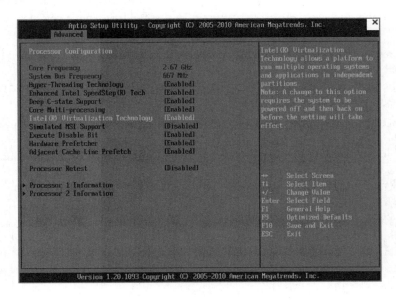

BIOS security (passwords, drive encryption: TPM, lo-jack)

A number of security features are built into most BIOSs. They include BIOS passwords, drive encryption, Trusted Platform Modules (TPM), and lo-jack. These items are discussed in this section.

BIOS passwords   In most CMOS Setup programs, you can set a supervisor password. Doing so requires a password to be entered in order to use the CMOS Setup program, effectively locking out users from making changes to it. You may also be able to set a user password, which restricts the PC from booting unless the password is entered.

To reset a forgotten password, you can remove the CMOS battery to reset everything. There also may be a Reset jumper on the motherboard.

Drive encryption   Many operating systems provide the ability to encrypt an entire volume or drive, protecting a mobile device's data in the event of theft. A good example of this is BitLocker, which is available in Windows Vista and Windows 7. The drives are encrypted with encryption keys, and the proper keys are required to boot the device and access the data.

BitLocker can be used with a TPM chip (discussed in the next section), but it is not required. When this feature is in effect with no TPM chip, the keys are stored on a USB drive that must be presented during startup to allow access to the drives. Without the USB drive holding the key, the device will not boot.

TPM chips   When the device has a Trusted Platform Module (TPM) chip present on the motherboard, additional security and options become available. First the chip contains the keys that unlock the drives. When the computer boots, the TPM chip unlocks the drive only after it compares hashes of the drive to snapshots of the drive taken earlier. If any changes have been made or tampering has been done to the Windows installation, the TPM chip will not unlock the drives.

Moreover, you can (and should) combine this with a PIN entered at startup or a key located in a USB drive. In this scenario the computer will not start unless the hashes pass the test and the PIN or key is provided.

Lo-jack   Lo-jack is a product made by Absolute Software that allows you to remotely locate, lock, and delete the data on a mobile device when it is stolen. It is a small piece of software that embeds itself on the computer and is difficult to detect. Once activated, it stays in contact with a monitoring center, allowing you to send the commands to lock and delete data via the center. Not only can you protect the data in this fashion, but also it will gather forensic data that can help to locate the device and aid in its recovery.

Use built-in diagnostics

Although you may not realize it, every time you start the computer, built-in diagnostics are at work. Every computer has a diagnostic program built into its BIOS called the *power-on self-test* (POST). When you turn on the computer, it executes this set of diagnostics. Many steps are involved in the POST, but they happen very quickly, they're invisible to the user, and they vary among BIOS versions. The steps include checking the CPU, checking the RAM, checking for the presence of a video card, and so on. The main reason to be aware of the POST's existence is that if it encounters a problem, the boot process stops. Being able to determine at what point the problem occurred can help you troubleshoot.

One way to determine the source of a problem is to listen for a *beep code*. This is a series of beeps from the computer's speaker. The number, duration, and pattern of the beeps can sometimes tell you what component is causing the problem. However, the beeps differ depending on the BIOS manufacturer and version, so you must look up the beep code in a chart for your particular BIOS. Different BIOS manufacturers use the beeping differently. AMI BIOS, for example, relies on a raw number of beeps, and uses patterns of short and long beeps.

Another way to determine a problem during the POST routine is to use a *POST card*. This is a circuit board that fits into an Industry Standard Architecture (ISA) or Peripheral Component Interconnect (PCI) expansion slot in the motherboard and reports numeric codes as the boot process progresses. Each of those codes corresponds to a particular component being checked. If the POST card stops at a certain number, you can look up that number in the manual that came with the card to determine the problem.

 BIOS Central is a website containing charts detailing the beep codes and POST error codes for many different BIOS manufacturers.

Monitoring

By viewing the information provided in the BIOS, basic monitoring of the many items can be done with varying degrees of certainty. It is simply a matter of navigating the menu-based BIOS program and locating the proper screen that provides the information. Examples are provided in the following sections.

Temperature monitoring

Temperature is probably the most important item to monitor. When components like the CPU overheat, bad things start to occur, such as repeated reboots. An example of the values shown for the CPU is shown in Figure 1.2. Technicians should retain baseline temperatures for these items. Baseline temperatures should include idle temperature and load temperature baselines. Intel processors tend to run at a higher temperature than AMD.

Fan Speeds

The speed at which various fans are operating can also be displayed in the BIOS. There can be a CPU fan, as well as one or more system fans. See Figure 1.2. Programs are available that monitor this for you and can send alerts. This is particularly important for servers in a data center.

FIGURE 1.2   Temperature monitoring

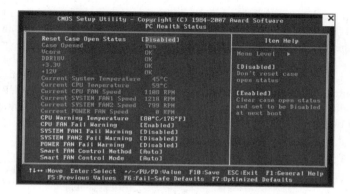

Intrusion detection/notification

It is also possible to enable intrusion detection, which will indicate to you whether the chassis has been opened. This may be referred to as the chassis intrusion detection or possibly the case open status, as shown in Figure 1.2, where this function has been disabled.

Voltage

You can also monitor and change the voltage settings in the BIOS. Be cautious in changing these settings, as improper settings can damage the system or shorten the life of the CPU. Possible settings include:

- CPU voltage
- Memory voltage, which will typically be 1.5V
- Motherboard voltage
- Voltage of the graphics card

These are just a few examples. Figure 1.3 shows an example of these and many more voltage settings.

Clock

The CMOS clock is located on the computer's motherboard and keeps time when the computer is off. The operating system gets its time from the BIOS clock at boot time. This clock can be set using the BIOS if it is not correct. The time setting is shown in Figure 1.4.

Bus speed

The processor's ability to communicate with the rest of the system's components relies on the supporting circuitry. Part of the system board's underlying circuitry is called the *bus*. The computer's bus moves information into and out of the processor and other devices. A bus allows all devices to communicate with one another. The motherboard has several buses. The *external data bus* carries information to and from the CPU and is the fastest bus on the system. The *address bus* typically runs at the same speed as the external data bus and carries data to and from RAM. The address bus gives the address to which the data should go. Data bus uses the address supplied by the address bus and carries the data to the specified location. The PCI, AGP, and ISA interfaces also have their own buses with their own widths and speeds. With newer architectures, the System or front side bus (FSB) connects the CPU to the north bridge (or memory) hub. The back side bus (BSB) connects the CPU with the Level 2 (L2) cache, also called the secondary or external cache; and the memory bus connects the north bridge (or memory) hub to RAM.

FIGURE 1.3   Voltage

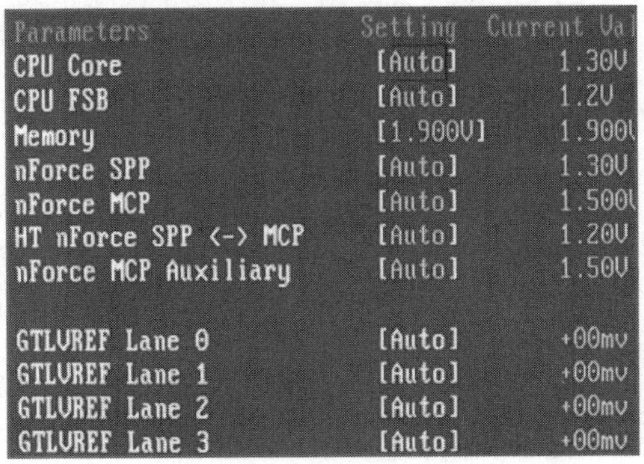

Parameters	Setting	Current Va
CPU Core	[Auto]	1.30V
CPU FSB	[Auto]	1.2V
Memory	[1.900V]	1.900V
nForce SPP	[Auto]	1.30V
nForce MCP	[Auto]	1.500V
HT nForce SPP <-> MCP	[Auto]	1.20V
nForce MCP Auxiliary	[Auto]	1.50V
GTLVREF Lane 0	[Auto]	+00mv
GTLVREF Lane 1	[Auto]	+00mv
GTLVREF Lane 2	[Auto]	+00mv
GTLVREF Lane 3	[Auto]	+00mv

FIGURE 1.4   Clock

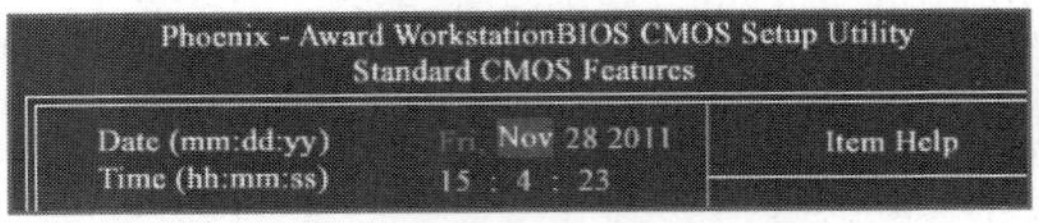

Phoenix - Award WorkstationBIOS CMOS Setup Utility Standard CMOS Features	
Date (mm:dd:yy) Fri, Nov 28 2011	Item Help
Time (hh:mm:ss) 15 : 4 : 23	

The bus speed, like the CPU speed, can also be set. (See the section on the relationship between the bus speed, CPU speed, and the multiplier in the section "Clock speeds.") Usually this should be left alone, as it is normally set to a setting proper for the memory, but it can be changed. In many systems this must be done with jumpers on the motherboard.

Exam Essentials

Flash the BIOS.   Understand the process for upgrading the BIOS. This usually involves running a program from the BIOS vendor that erases the instructions from the EEPROM chip and writes the new instructions to the same chip.

Identify components reported in the BIOS.   These include RAM, hard drives, optical drives, and the CPU. Information is listed for each, and changes can be made to selected settings for each component.

Describe available BIOS configurations.   The setting that can be made using the BIOS include the boot sequence, the enabling and disabling of devices, setting the date and time, adjusting clock speeds, enabling and disabling virtualization features if supported, and setting BIOS passwords.

Identify built-in diagnostic tools in the BIOS.   The power-on self-test is the most important diagnostic testing that occurs. It runs every time the PC is started and will report—either with a displayed error message or with beep tones—any problem components.

Monitor with the BIOS.   Utilize the BIOS display to monitor temperature, fan speeds, intrusion detection messages, voltage settings, the system clock, and the bus speed settings.

1.2 Differentiate between motherboard components, their purposes, and properties

The motherboard is the platform through which all of the connected components communicate. The motherboard provides basic services needed for the machine to operate and provides communication channels through which connected devices such as the processor, memory, disk drives, and expansion devices communicate.

In this section those components will be discussed. The topics addressed in objective 1.2 include:

- Sizes
- Expansion slots
- RAM slots
- CPU sockets
- Chipsets
- Jumpers
- Power connections and types
- Fan connections
- Front Panel connections

The graphics are representative of what can be expected. It all depends on the motherboard manufacturer. Consult the documentation for your motherboard.

Sizes

The spine of the computer is the *system board*, or *motherboard*. This component is made of green or brown fiberglass and is placed in the bottom or side of the case. It's the most important component in the computer because it connects all the other components of a PC together. On the system board you'll find the CPU (central processing unit), underlying circuitry, expansion slots, video components, RAM (random access memory) slots, and a variety of other chips. There are a number of different sizes or *form factors* of motherboards, which will be discussed in this section.

ATX

An older but still used form factor, the ATX (Advanced Technology Extended) provided many design improvements over the previous version, the AT. These improvements include I/O ports built directly into the side of the motherboard, the CPU positioned so that the power-supply fan helps cool it, and the ability for the PC to be turned on and off via software. It uses a PS/2-style connector for the keyboard and mouse, which is rarely used today because USB keyboards are used. Newer ATX models have removed PS/2 connectors. The expansion slots are parallel to the narrow edge of the board. See Figure 1.5.

FIGURE 1.5   An ATX-style motherboard

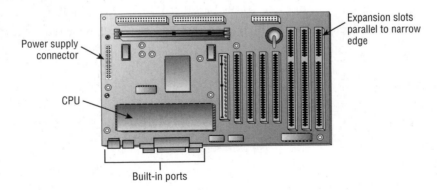

Micro-ATX

The micro-ATX was released in 1997 for smaller—and typically cheaper—systems. It became popular in later years in low-cost PCs. The maximum size of a micro-ATX motherboard is 244 mm square, compared to 305 mm × 244 mm for a standard ATX motherboard. The micro-ATX is backward compatible with the ATX.

ITX

The ITX motherboards—the Mini-ITX, Nano-ITX, and Pico-ITX—were proposed by VIA Technologies. The Mini-ITX fits in the same case as the micro-ATX; uses low power, which means it can be passively cooled (no fan); and has one expansion slot. The Nano-ITX is even smaller; it is used for set-top boxes, media centers, and car computers. The Pico-ITX is even smaller again, half the size of the Nano-ITX. It uses daughter cards to supply additional functionality.

Expansion Slots

Expansion slots exist on a motherboard to allow for the addition of new interfaces to new technologies without replacing the motherboard. If expansions slots did not exist, you would have to buy a new motherboard every time you wanted to add a new device that uses an interface to the board that does not currently exist on the board. In this section various types of expansion slots will be reviewed.

PCI

The Peripheral Component Interconnect (PCI) bus is a fast (33 MHz), wide (32-bit or 64-bit) expansion bus that was a modern standard in motherboards for general-purpose expansion devices. Its slots are typically white. PCI devices can share IRQs and other system resources with one another in some cases. You may see two PCI slots, but most motherboards have gone to newer standards. Figure 1.6 shows some PCI slots.

PCI cards that are 32 bit with 33 MHz operate up to 133 MBps (megabytes per second), whereas 32-bit cards with 64 MHz operate up to 264 MBps. PCI cards that are 64 bit with 33 MHz operate up to 264 MBps, whereas 64-bit cards with 66 MHz operate up to 538 MBps.

FIGURE 1.6   PCI bus connectors

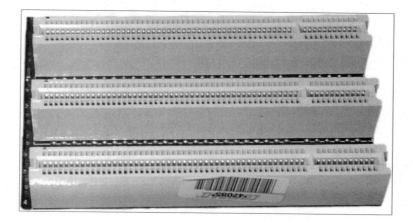

PCI-X

PCI-eXtended (PCI-X) is a double-wide version of the 32-bit PCI local bus. It runs at up to four times the clock speed, achieving higher bandwidth but otherwise uses the same protocol and a similar electrical implementation. It has been replaced by the PCI Express (see the next section), which uses a different connector and a different logical design. There is also a 64-bit PCI specification electrically different but with the same connector as PCI-X.

There are two versions of PCI-X. Version 1 gets up to 1.06 gigabytes per second (GBps) and version 2 gets up to 4.26 GBps.

PCIe

PCI Express (PCIE , PCI-E, or PCIe) uses a network of serial interconnects that operate at high speed. It's based on the PCI system; you can convert a PCIe slot to PCI using an adapter plug-in card, but you cannot convert a PCI slot to PCIe. Intended as a replacement for AGP and PCI, PCIe has the capability of being faster than AGP while maintaining the flexibility of PCI. There are four versions of PCIe: version 1 is up to 8 GBps, version 2 is up to 16 GBps, version 3 is up to 32 GBps, and final specifications for version 4 are still being developed.

miniPCI

Laptops and other portable devices utilize an expansion card called the miniPCI. It has the same functionality as the PCI but has a much smaller form factor. Unlike portable PCM-CIA cards, which are inserted externally into a slot, these are installed inside the case. A miniPCI card alongside a miniPCI Express card is shown in Figure 1.7.

FIGURE 1.7   miniPCI

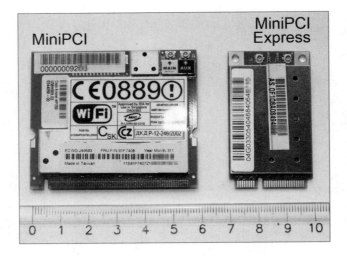

WIKIMEDIA COMMONS/CVDR

CNR

A Communications and Networking Riser (CNR) slot, found on some motherboards, is used for specialized networking, audio, and telephony equipment. The CNR card provides audio, networking, or modem functionality. For the most part, CNR slots have been phased out in favor of on-board or embedded components.

CNR was originally the Audio Modem Riser (AMR), which was originally created to speed manufacturing (and certification) by separating the analog circuitry (modem and analog audio) onto its own card. Over time, this was replaced by CNR, which included the capabilities of AMR and allowed the motherboard chipset to be designed with additional integrated features. A CNR slot is shown in Figure 1.8.

FIGURE 1.8   CNR

WIKIMEDIA
COMMONS/APPALOOSA

AGP2x, 4x, 8x

As systems got faster, PC game players wanted games that had better graphics, more realism, and more speed. However, as the computers got faster, the video technology couldn't seem to keep up, even with the PCI bus. The AGP bus was developed to meet this need. Since 2004 this has been increasingly replaced by PCIe.

The AGP slot is usually brown, and there is only one. It's a 32-bit or 64-bit bus, and it runs very fast (66 MHz or faster). It's used exclusively for the video card. If you use a PCI video card, the AGP slot remains empty. See Figure 1.9.

AGP1x operates at 266 MBps, AGP2x at 533 MBps, AGP4x at 1066 MBps, and AGP8x at 2133 MBps.

RAM slots

RAM slots contain the memory chips. There are many and varied types of memory for PCs today. We'll discuss memory later in this chapter. PCs use memory chips arranged on a small circuit board. These circuit boards are called *single inline memory modules* (SIMMs) or *dual inline memory modules* (DIMMs). DIMMs utilize connectors on both sides of the board, whereas SIMMS utilize single connectors that are mirrored on both sides. DIMM is 64-bit and SIMM is 32-bit. There is also a high-speed type of RAM called *Rambus dynamic RAM* (RDRAM), which comes on circuit boards called *Rambus inline memory modules* (RIMMs).

FIGURE 1.9 An AGP slot on a motherboard

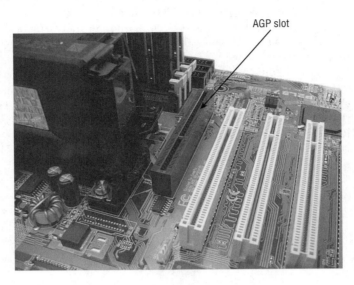

AGP slot

Along with chip placement, memory modules also differ in the number of conductors, or pins, that the particular module uses. The number of pins used directly affects the overall size of the memory slot. Slot sizes include 30-pin, 72-pin, 168-pin, and 184-pin. Laptop memory comes in smaller form factors known as *small outline DIMMs* (SODIMMs). Figure 1.10 shows the form factors for the most popular memory chips. Notice that they basically look the same, but the memory module sizes are different.

FIGURE 1.10 Various memory module form factors

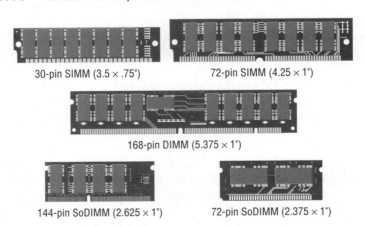

30-pin SIMM (3.5 × .75")

72-pin SIMM (4.25 × 1")

168-pin DIMM (5.375 × 1")

144-pin SoDIMM (2.625 × 1")

72-pin SoDIMM (2.375 × 1")

Memory slots are easy to identify on a motherboard. They're usually white and placed very close together. The number of memory slots varies from motherboard to motherboard, but the appearance of the different slots is similar. Metal pins in the bottom make contact with the soldered tabs on each memory module. Small metal or plastic tabs on each side of the slot keep the memory module securely in its slot.

CPU sockets

The CPU slot permits the attachment of the CPU to the motherboard, allowing the CPU to use the other components of the system. There are many different types of processors, meaning there are many types of CPU connectors.

The CPU slot can take on several different forms. In the past, the CPU slot was a rectangular box called a PGA socket, with many small holes to accommodate the pins on the bottom of the chip. With the release of new and more powerful chips, additional holes were added, changing the configuration of the slot and its designator or number. Figure 1.11 shows a typical PGA-type CPU socket.

FIGURE 1.11   A PGA CPU socket

With the release of the Pentium II, the architecture of the slot went from a rectangle to more of an expansion-slot style of interface called an SECC. This style of CPU slot includes Slot 1 and Slot 2 for Intel CPUs, and Slot A for Athlon (AMD) CPUs. This type of slot looks much like an expansion slot, but it's located in a different place on the motherboard from the other expansion slots.

To see which socket type is used for which processors, examine Table 1.2. This list is not exhaustive. Some of the slots may fit processors that are not specifically listed.

TABLE 1.2   Socket types and the processors they support

Connector type	Processor	Package type
Slot 1	Pentium II and III, All SECC and SECC2	Slot
Slot 2	Pentium II Xeon, Pentium III Xeon (server)	Slot

TABLE 1.2 Socket types and the processors they support *(continued)*

Connector type	Processor	Package type
Socket 370	Pentium III	PGA
Socket 423	Pentium 4	PGA
Socket 478	Pentium 4 and Celeron 4	PGA
SECC (Type I), Slot 1	Pentium II	Slot
SECC2 (Type II), Slot 2	Pentium III	Slot
Slot A	Athlon	Slot
Socket 603	Xeon	PGA
Socket 754	AMD Athlon 64	PGA
Socket 939	Some versions of Athlon 64	PGA
Socket 940	Some versions of Athlon 64 and Opteron	PGA
Socket LGA775 (T)	Core 2 Duo/Quad	LGA
Socket AM2	Athlon 64 family (replacing earlier socket usage)	PGA
Socket F	Opteron	LGA
	AMD Athlon64, X2, Phenom and Phenom II	
	Intel Core2	
	Intel Atom	
	Intel Core i7, Xeon (35xx, 36xx, 55xx, 56xx series)	
Socket AM2+	Intel Core i7, i5, i3, P6000, P4000	PGA
Socket P	AMD Phenom, Athlon II, Sempron	PGA
Socket 441	Intel Core i7, i5, Xeon, Pentium G5000, G1000	PGA

Connector type	Processor	Package type
Socket LGA 1366/B	AMD Opteron 6000 series	LGA
G1/G2/rPGA 988A/B	AMD Opteron 4000 series	rPGA
Socket AM3	Intel Titanium 9300 series	PGA
Socket H/LGA 1156	Intel Xeon 6500/7500 series	LGA
Socket G34	Intel Sandy Bridge-DT	PGA
Socket C32	Intel Sandy Bridge B2	LGA
LGA 1248	AMD Llano	LGA
AM3+	AMD FX, Zambezi	PGA
FMI	AMD Llano Processor	PGA
LGA 1155	Intel Sandy Bridge-DT	LGA

Chipsets

The *chipset* is the set of controller chips that monitors and directs the traffic on the motherboard between the buses. It usually consists of two or more chips. Motherboards use two basic chipset designs: the *north/south bridge chipset* and the *hub chipset*.

The hub chipset, a 2008 innovation, includes a memory controller hub (equivalent to the north bridge), an I/O controller hub (equivalent to the south bridge), and a SuperIO chip.

North Bridge

The north bridge connects the system bus to the other relatively fast buses (AGP and PCIe). The north bridge typically handles communications between the CPU, RAM, and PCIe (or AGP) video cards and the south bridge.

South Bridge

The south bridge connects ISA, IDE, USB, audio, serial, the BIOS, the ISA bus, the IDE channels, and the interrupt controller. It handles all of the computer's I/O functions. The relationship between the chipsets is shown in Figure 1.12.

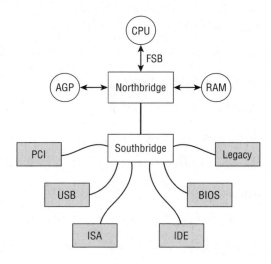

CMOS battery

The CMOS chip must have a constant source of power to keep its settings. To prevent the loss of data, motherboard manufacturers include a small battery to power the CMOS memory. On modern systems, this is a coin-style battery, about the diameter of a U.S. dime and about as thick.

Jumpers

Jumpers and dual inline package (DIP) switches are used to configure various hardware options on the motherboard. Processors use different voltages and multipliers to achieve their target voltage and frequency. You must set these parameters on the motherboard by changing the jumper or DIP switch settings. Figure 1.13 shows a jumper and two types of DIP switches. Individual jumpers are often labeled with the moniker JPx (where x is the number of the jumper). These are far less common than they used to be; many settings are now configured through the BIOS.

FIGURE 1.13 A jumper set and DIP switches

Jumper   "Rocker-type" DIP switch   "Slide-type" DIP switch

Power connections and types

A power connector allows the motherboard to be connected to the power supply. On an ATX, there is a single power connector consisting of a block of 20 holes (in two rows). On an AT, there is a block consisting of 12 pins sticking up; these pins are covered by two connectors with six holes each.

Figure 1.14 shows a versatile motherboard that has both kinds, so you can compare. The upper connector is for ATX, and the lower one is for AT.

FIGURE 1.14   Power connectors on a motherboard

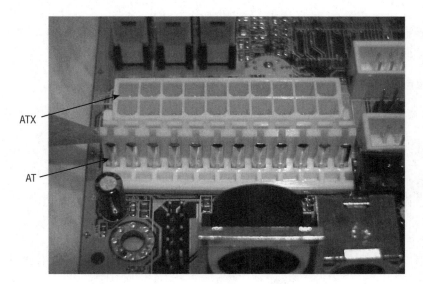

When using the AT power connector, the power cable coming from the power supply will be have two separate connectors, labeled P8 and P9. When you are attaching the two parts to the motherboard, the black wires on one should be next to black wires on the other for proper function.

The 20-pin main connector from the power supply to the motherboard is standard for all ATX power supplies. In addition to this connector, many will include an auxiliary power connector of either 4 or 6 pins to provide additional power.

In 2004, the ATX 12V 2.0 (now 2.03) standard was passed, changing the main connector from 20 pins to 24. The additional pins provide +3.3V, +5V, and +12V (the fourth pin is a ground) for use by PCIe cards. When a 24-pin connector is used, there is no need for the optional 4- or 6-pin auxiliary power connectors.

Most power supplies have a recessed, two-position slider switch, often a red one, on the rear that is exposed through the case. Selections read 110 and 220; 115 and 230; or 120 and 240. This voltage selector switch is used to select the voltage level used in the country where the computer is in service. For example, in the United States, the power grid supplies anywhere from 110 to 120VAC. However, in Europe, for instance, the voltage supplied is double, ranging from 220 to 240VAC.

Fan connections

Connectors usually used for computer fans are called Molex connectors, and there can be several types. Among them are:

- A 3-pin Molex connector that is used when connecting a fan to the motherboard or other circuit board.

- A 4-pin Molex connector, where the additional pin is used for a pulse-width modulation signal to provide variable speed control. These connectors can be plugged into 3-pin headers but will lose their fan speed control.

The 4-pin Molex connector is shown in Figure 1.15.

FIGURE 1.15 Pin Fan Connector

Front Panel connectors

There are a number of interfaces, buttons, lights, and audio jacks in the front panel of the computer that must be connected to the board for power and functionality. In this section each of these and their respective methods of connection to the motherboard are discussed.

USB

When USB ports exist on the front panel (as they almost always do these days), they must be connected to the motherboard so that the connected USB device can communicate with the computer. This is done with a 10-pin connector located on the board, as shown in Figure 1.16.

FIGURE 1.16   Front panel power connectors

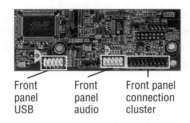

Front   Front   Front panel
panel   panel   connection
USB   audio   cluster

Audio

When audio plugs or jacks exist in the front panel, as they do in most computers now, they must be connected to the motherboard if you are using the integrated sound card. (Otherwise they may connect directly to the sound card.) An example of the audio plug on the board is shown in Figure 1.16.

Power button

The power button located in the front panel must also be connected to the motherboard to communicate on and off to the computer. This connector is located along with the remaining connectors discussed in this section, clustered in a group on the motherboard, as shown in Figure 1.16.

Power light

The power indicator light must also be provided with power and a connection to the board. It is also located in the cluster of connections shown in Figure 1.16.

Drive activity lights

The drive activity light, which indicates when a hard drive is either being read or written to, must have a connection to the motherboard both for power and to transmit the drive activity information. It is also located in the cluster of connections shown in Figure 1.16.

Reset button

The reset switch, like all the other front panel components, has a connection to the motherboard and is located in the cluster of connections shown in Figure 1.16.

Exam Essentials

Differentiate the motherboard form factors.   The ATX is the oldest and largest of the motherboard sizes still being manufactured. The micro-ATX is for smaller and cheaper systems. The smaller ITX motherboards come in three sizes: the Mini-ITX, the Nano-ITX, and the Pico-ITX.

Identify expansion slot types.   PCI slots are the standard for general-purpose cards. The PCI-X provides higher bandwidth for servers. PCIe is a newer high-speed slot based on the PCI system. MiniPCI slots are used in laptops. The Communications and Networking Riser (CNR) slot (a slot found on certain PC motherboards and used for specialized networking, audio, and telephony equipment) has been phased out with the integration of the components it served into the board. AGP slots provide connections for enhanced graphics.

Describe RAM slots.   Memory slots accept either single inline memory modules (SIMMs) or dual inline memory modules (DIMMs). DIMMs utilize connectors on both sides of the board, whereas SIMMS utilize single connectors that are mirrored on both sides. DIMM is 64-bit and SIMM is 32-bit. There is also a high-speed type of RAM called RDRAM (Rambus dynamic RAM), which comes on circuit boards called RIMMs (Rambus inline memory modules).

Locate the CPU socket on the motherboard.   The CPU socket can take on several different forms. In the past, the CPU socket was a rectangular box called a PGA socket, with many small holes to accommodate the pins on the bottom of the chip. With the release of the Pentium II, the architecture of the socket went from a rectangle to more of an expansion-slot style of interface called an SECC.

Understand the function of the chipsets.   The north bridge connects the system bus to the other relatively fast buses (AGP and PCIe). The south bridge connects ISA, IDE, and USB, audio, serial, the BIOS, the IDA bus, the IDE channels, and the interrupt controller. It handles all of the computer's I/O functions.

Make settings changes through the use of jumpers.   Jumpers and DIP switches are used to configure various hardware options on the motherboard. Processors use different voltages and multipliers to achieve their target voltage and frequency. You must set these parameters on the motherboard by changing the jumper or DIP switch settings.

Utilize fan and power connections.   A 20- or 24-pin main connector from the power supply to the motherboard is standard for all ATX power supplies. Fans connect with either 3- or 4-pin Molex connections.

Identify front connections.   While the USB and audio jacks will be connected with 10-pin connectors, the remaining front panel components will connect with much smaller plugs in a cluster in one area on the board.

1.3 Compare and contrast RAM types and features

Physically, RAM is a collection of integrated circuits that store data and program information as patterns of 1s and 0s (on and off states) in the chip. Most memory chips require constant power (also called a constant refresh) to maintain those patterns of 1s and 0s. If power is lost, all those tiny switches revert back to the off position, effectively erasing the data from memory. Some memory types, however, don't require a refresh.

In this section those RAM types and features will be discussed. The topics addressed in objective 1.3 include:

- Types
- RAM compatibility and speed

Types

There are many types of RAM. They differ in their speed, form factor, their ability to identify errors, and their bandwidth. Let's examine each type in detail.

DDR

Double Data Rate (DDR) is clock-doubled SDRAM (covered later in this section). The memory chip can perform reads and writes on both sides of any clock cycle (the up, or start, and the down, or ending), thus doubling the effective memory executions per second. So, if you're using DDR SDRAM with a 100 MHz memory bus, the memory will execute reads and writes at 200 MHz and transfer the data to the processor at 100 MHz. The advantage of DDR over regular SDRAM is increased throughput and thus increased overall system speed.

DDR2

The next generation of DDR SDRAM is DDR2 (Double Data Rate 2). This allows for two memory accesses for each rising and falling clock and effectively doubles the speed of DDR. DDR2-667 chips work with speeds of 667 MHz and PC2-5300 modules.

DDR3

The primary benefit of DDR3 over DDR2 is that it transfers data at twice the rate of DDR2 (eight times the speed of its internal memory arrays), enabling higher bandwidth or peak data rates. By performing two transfers per cycle of a quadrupled clock, a 64-bit wide DDR3 module may achieve a transfer rate of up to 64 times the memory clock speed in megabytes per second. In addition, the DDR3 standard permits chip capacities of up to 8 GB. Selected memory standards, speeds, and formats are shown in Table 1.3.

TABLE 1.3   Selected memory details

Module standard	Speed	Format
DDR500	4000 MBps	PC4000
DDR533	4266 MBps	PC4200
DDR2-667	5333 MBps	PC2-5300
DDR2-750	6000 MBps	PC2-6000
DDR2-800	6400 MBps	PC2-6400
DDR3-800	6400 MBps	PC3-6400
DDR3-1600	12800 MBps	PC3-12800

SDRAM

Synchronous DRAM (SDRAM) is synchronized to the speed of the motherboard's system bus and works at half the speed of DDR. Synchronizing the speed of the systems prevents the address bus from having to wait for the memory because of different clock speeds. A 100 MHz clock signal produces 800 Mbps, and such memory modules are referred to as PC100. PC133, which replaced PC100, uses a 133 MHz clock to produce 1,067 Mbps of throughput.

The relationship between clock speed and throughput is always roughly 1:8. Thus PC2700 modules are designed specifically for a motherboard with a speed of 333 MHz, and PC3200 modules are designed for a motherboard with a speed of 400 MHz.

SDRAM typically comes in the form of 168-pin DIMMs or 184-pin RIMMs.

SODIMM

Portable computers (notebooks and subnotebooks) require smaller sticks of RAM because of their smaller size. One of the two types is small outline DIMM (SODIMM), which can have 72, 144, or 200 pins.

Rambus

Rambus inline memory modules (RIMMs) are an extremely fast (up to 800 MHz) technology that uses, for the most part, a new methodology in design. Rambus (also known as direct Rambus) is a memory bus that transfers data at 800 MHz and is named after the company that designed it. Rambus memory modules, like DDR SDRAM, can transfer data on both the rising and falling edges of a clock cycle. That feature, combined with the 16-bit bus for efficient transfer of data, results in the ultra-high memory transfer rate (800 MHz) and high bandwidth of up to 1.6 GBps.

DIMM

DIMMs (dual inline memory modules) are double sided. DIMM has separate connectors on both sides of chip. They typically have 168 pins and are 64 bits in width. Figure 1.17 shows a DIMM.

FIGURE 1.17   Dual inline memory module (DIMM)

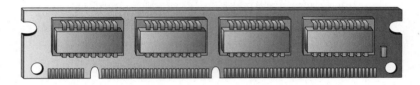

Parity vs. non-parity

RAM is supplied with no parity (8 data bits per byte) or with parity (8 data bits and 1 parity bit per byte for a total of 9 bits per byte). You can identify parity SIMMs by counting the number of chips on the stick. If there are nine, it's parity RAM. If there are eight, it's nonparity.

When do you choose parity RAM? Usually the motherboard requires either parity or nonparity RAM; a few motherboards will accept either. Nowadays parity RAM is needed only in highly critical computing tasks because advances in RAM technology have created reliable RAM that seldom makes errors.

ECC vs. non-ECC

Another type of RAM error correction is Error Correction Code (ECC). RAM with ECC can detect and correct errors. As with parity RAM, additional information needs to be stored and more processing needs to be done, making ECC RAM more expensive and a little slower than nonparity and logic parity RAM. Both ECC and parity memory work in ECC mode. However, ECC memory does not work in plain parity checking mode, meaning the extra bits cannot be individually accessed when ECC memory is used. This is a now obsolete type of parity RAM. Most RAM today is non-ECC.

RAM configurations

As we discussed earlier in this section, RAM can be either single sided or double sided. It can also use single, dual, or triple channels. In this section we'll review and discuss the use of channels in RAM.

Single channel vs. dual channel vs. triple channel

Utilizing multiple channels between the RAM and the memory controller increases the transfer speed between these two components. Single-channel RAM does not take advantage of this concept, but dual-channel memory does and creates two 64-bit data channels. Do *not* confuse this with DDR or double data rate. DDR doubles the rate by accessing the memory module twice per clock cycle.

This requires a motherboard that supports this and two or more memory modules. The modules go in separate color-coded banks, as shown in Figure 1.18.

FIGURE 1.18   Dual-channel memory slots

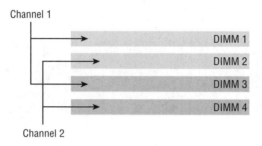

Triple-channel architecture adds a third memory module and reduces memory latency by interleaving or accessing each module sequentially with smaller bits of data rather than completely filling up one module before accessing the next one. Data is spread among the modules alternatingly with the potential to triple bandwidth as opposed to storing the data all on one module.

Single sided vs. double sided

Earlier we discussed the difference between SIMMs and DIMMs. In review, SIMMs have connectors on one side whereas DIMMs (dual inline memory modules) have connectors on both sides of the chip. DIMMs have twice the pins, meaning twice the contact with the motherboard, creating a larger interface with it and resulting in a wider data path.

RAM compatibility and speed

RAM speed used to be expressed in nanoseconds but is also sometimes expressed in MHz like with CPUs. Faster memory can be added to a PC with slower memory installed, but the system will only operate at the speed of the slowest module present.

While you can mix speeds, you cannot mix memory types. For example, you cannot use SDRAM with DDR and DDR cannot be mixed with DDR2. When looking at the name of the memory, the larger the number, the faster the speed. For example, DDR2-800 is faster than DDR2-533.

Exam Essentials

Identify the types of memory.   Types of memory include single data rate (SDRAM), double data rate (DDR), DDR2, DDR3, and Rambus (RIMM). These types differ in their data rate. Memory can also differ in packaging. There are SIMMS (single module) and DIMMs (double modules). They also can either use parity or ECC for error checking and can be single, dual, or triple channel, with multiple channels widening the path between the memory and the memory controller.

Follow RAM speed and compatibility guidelines.   Faster memory can be added to a PC with slower memory installed, but the system will only operate at the speed of the slowest module present. RAM types cannot be mixed.

1.4 Install and configure expansion cards

Expansion cards allow you to add functionality to the PC. In the section "Expansion Slots," we examined the types of expansion slots that can be found on the motherboard. In this section, we'll discuss the types of cards and the functionality they provide. We'll also talk about installing them and configuring them properly.

Older expansion cards might be plugged into an ISA slot and in that case will probably not be Plug and Play. That means you must install the card physically, install it in Device Manager, and finally install the device driver.

Newer cards will install in the PCI or PCIe slots and will probably be detected by the operating system. If the operating system already contains the driver for the device in its pre-installed driver library, the process will be done as soon as you restart the PC. If it is not present in the driver cache, you will have to install the driver that came with it. These guidelines apply to all the expansion cards discussed in this section.

Sound cards

Most computers these days come with an integrated sound card, but for more robust sound or advanced features you may need to install a sound card. Sound cards can either be internal or external. Internal cards require opening the case and installing the card in a slot. External cards plug into the USB socket.

In some cases an audio cable will be connected from the card to the CD-ROM. This is rarely required these days.

Sound Card Problems

Sound cards are traditionally one of the most problem-ridden components in a PC. They demand a lot of PC resources and are notorious for being inflexible in their configuration. The most common problems related to sound cards involve resource conflicts (IRQ, DMA, or I/O address). The problem is much less pronounced on PCI than on ISA cards.

Luckily, most sound card vendors are aware of the problems and ship very good diagnostic utilities to help resolve them. Use your PC troubleshooting skills to determine the conflict, and then reconfigure until you find an acceptable set of resources that aren't in use.

Some legacy sound cards aren't completely Plug and Play. Windows may detect that new hardware has been installed but be unable to identify the new hardware as a working sound card. To fix this problem, run the setup software that came with the sound card.

Video cards

PCs today also contain internal video cards, but as with sound cards you can achieve better video quality with more expensive video cards. This is especially true when the video card has its own dedicated memory. In earlier times most internal cards were vastly inferior to the cards you could buy, but that is much less the case today when users have learned to expect better video quality.

Newer operating systems, like Windows Vista and Windows 7, have helped raise the bar for internal cards as well in that they require a card with a minimum set of features and a minimum amount of dedicated RAM to appreciate the visual capabilities of the operating system.

Video cards can be installed in the AGP, PCI, and PCIe slots. At one point the best choice was clear, and that was the AGP slot. However, the newer PCIe slots provide more bandwidth. AGP provides a wider data path because it's parallel whereas PCIe is serial. But PCIe now goes go up to 16,000 MBps as compared to AGP, which is 2,000 MBps.

Some of the special functions you may get with a more expensive video card are 3D imaging, MPEG decoding, and TV output (discussed later in this section). The ability to use multiple monitors is also built into many cards.

Network cards

Network cards do exactly what you would think; they provide a connection for the PC to a network. In general, network interface cards (NICs) are added to a PC via an expansion slot or they are integrated into the motherboard, but they may also be added through a USB or PCMCIA slot (also known as PC card). The most common issue that prevents network connectivity is a bad or unplugged patch cable.

Network cards are made for Ethernet, fiber optic, token ring (very rarely used now), and 802.11 (wireless) connections. The Ethernet, token ring, and fiber-optic cards accept the appropriate cable, and the wireless cards have radio transmitters and antennas.

The most obvious difference in network cards is the speed of which they are capable. Most networks today operate at 100 MBps or 1 GBps. Regardless of other components, the PC will operate at the speed of the slowest component , so if the card is capable of 1 GBps but the cable is only capable of 100 MBps, the PC will transmit only at 100 MBps.

Another significant feature to be aware of is the card's ability to perform auto-sensing. This feature allows the card to sense whether the connection is capable of full duplex and to operate in that manner with no action required.

There is another type of auto-sensing, in which the card is capable of detecting what type of device is on the other end and changing the use of the wire pairs accordingly. For example, normally a PC connected to another PC requires a crossover cable, but if both ends can perform this sensing, that is not required. These types of cards are called auto-MDIX.

Serial and parallel cards

As discussed in the section "Video Cards," expansion cards and the slots they live in can be either serial or parallel. The difference is in how the bits are sent to and from the card. In standard parallel, these bits are sent eight at time using eight wires, one for each bit, whereas in serial the bits are sent one at a time down the same wire.

Serial has the following advantages over parallel:

- A serial link transmits less data per clock cycle but can achieve a higher data rate because it can be clocked considerably faster than parallel links. (Clock skew between different channels is not an issue as it is in parallel.)

- Fewer interconnecting cables occupy less space, allowing for better isolation of the channel from its surroundings.

- Crosstalk (which occurs when wires in the same cable interfere with one another) is less of an issue, because there are fewer conductors in proximity.

- It is cheaper to implement. Serial card interfaces have fewer pins and are therefore less expensive.

USB cards

Universal Serial Bus (USB) expansion cards are used to provide a USB connection (or an additional connection) to a PC that has none (pretty rare today). All motherboards today have at least two USB slots. Some of the advantages of USB include hot-plugging and the capability for up to 127 USB devices to share a single set of system resources. USB 1.1 runs at 12 Mbps, and USB 2.0 runs at 480 Mbps. Because USB is a serial interface, its width is 1 bit. USB 3.0 specifies a maximum transmission speed of up to 5 Gbps (625 MBps), which is over 10 times as fast as USB 2.0 (480 Mbps, or 60 MBps), although this speed is typically only achieved using powerful, professional-grade or developmental equipment.

These cards are made to plug into PCI, PCIe, or PCMCIA slots (Chapter 3, "Laptops," discussed laptops in more detail).

FireWire cards

FireWire expansion cards, like USB cards, provide this connection when none is present or when more are required. Most new motherboards have a built-in IEEE 1394/FireWire port, although this port can be added with a PCI expansion board. It transfers data at 400 Mbps and supports up to 63 chained devices on a single set of resources. It's hot-pluggable, like USB. Figure 1.23 shows the connections on a FireWire/USB combo card. These cards also are made to plug into PCI, PCIe, or PCMCIA slots.

Storage cards

Storage cards plug into a slot (usually PCIe) and have storage devices attached to the card. Increasingly these are solid-state drives. This is like adding an external drive except it is added by placing the card in a slot inside the box.

Other ways these cards may be connected to the PC are:

- Serial ATA
- Serial attached SCSI (generally found on servers)
- PCIe
- Fibre Channel (almost exclusively found on servers)
- USB
- Parallel ATA (IDE) interface (mostly replaced by SATA)
- (Parallel) SCSI

Modem cards

Many PCs already have built-in modems and therefore will have an RJ-11 connector on the back in which to plug a phone line. However, modems can be added with an expansion card. This arrangement makes it possible to connect to your ISP through the phone line, an increasingly rare event that you might only use in an emergency, since much faster and simpler connection methods are available. These are usually PCI or PCIe.

Wireless/cellular cards

A more likely modem connection you may use is one that connects to your mobile phone provider for wireless connectivity through the same system that your mobile phone uses. These can be either PCMCIA cards or USB devices. One of these (PCMCIA) is shown in Figure 1.19.

FIGURE 1.19   PCMCIA 3G modem

WIKIMEDIA COMMONS/WOOOKIE

TV tuner cards

TV tuner cards are designed to receive TV signals on the computer and usually contain a built-in video capture card (discussed more in the next section). The interfaces are most commonly either PCI or PCIe, but PCMCIA, ExpressCard, and USB devices also exist.

Video capture cards

Video capture is the process of converting an analog video signal to digital video. The resulting computer files create a digital video stream. This means that a video capture card takes input—such as that produced by an analog video camera—and converts it to a digital file. These cards usually come in PCI or PCIe format.

Riser cards

Although it isn't common, you may occasionally encounter a slim-line case, which is a desktop-orientation case that is shorter and thinner than a normal one—so short that normal expansion boards won't fit perpendicular to the motherboard. In such cases a riser card is installed, which sits perpendicular to the motherboard and contains expansion slots. The expansion cards can then be oriented parallel to the motherboard when installed. So it's a card that hosts other cards. Figure 1.20 shows a riser card from two angles.

Exam Essentials

Describe the installation process as it applies to any legacy expansion cards.   Older expansion cards might be plugged into an ISA slot and in that case will probably not be Plug and Play. That means you have to install the card physically, install it in Device Manager, and finally install the device driver.

Describe the installation process as it applies to Plug and Play expansion cards.   Newer cards will install in the PCI or PCIe slots and will probably be detected by the operating system. If the operating system already contains the driver for the device in its preinstalled driver library, the process will be done as soon as you restart the PC. If it is not present in the driver library, you will have to install the driver that came with it.

Differentiate each expansion card type.   Understand the function of each of the following card types:

- Sound cards
- Video cards
- Network cards
- Serial and parallel cards
- USB cards
- FireWire cards

- Storage cards
- Modem cards
- Wireless/cellular cards
- TV tuner cards
- Video capture cards

Explain the purpose of riser cards.   Riser cards are used to provide expansions slot types that are not present on the system or that exist in insufficient numbers.

FIGURE 1.20   Riser card

1.5 Install and configure storage devices and use appropriate media

Storage media hold the data being accessed, as well as the files the system needs to operate and data that needs to be saved. The various types of storage differ in terms of capacity, access time, and the physical type of media being used. This section covers the installation and configuration of various storage devices. The topics addressed in objective 1.5 include:

- Optical drives
- Combo drives and burners
- Connection types
- Hard drives
- Solid state/flash drives
- RAID types
- Floppy drive
- Tape drive
- Media capacity

Optical drives

Optical drives work by using a laser rather than magnetism to change the characteristics of the storage medium. This is true for CD-ROM drives, DVD drives, and Blu-Ray, all of which are discussed in the following sections.

CD-ROM

CD-ROM stands for Compact Disc Read-Only Memory. The CD-ROM media is used for long-term storage of data. CD-ROM media is read-only, meaning that once information is written to a CD, it can't be erased or changed. Access time for CD-ROM drives is considerably slower than for a hard drive. Standard CDs normally hold 650–700 MB of data and use the ISO 9660 standard, which allows them to be used in multiple platforms.

DVD-ROM

Because DVD-ROMs drives use slightly different technology than CD-ROM drives, they can store up to 4.7 GB of data in a single-layer configuration. This makes DVDs a better choice than CDs for distributing large software bundles. Many software packages today are so huge that they require multiple CDs to hold all the installation and reference files. A single DVD, in a double-sided, double-layered configuration, can hold as much as 17 GB (as much as 26 regular CDs).

Blu-Ray

Blu-Ray recorders have been available since 2003, and they have the ability to record more information than a standard DVD using similar optical technology. In recent years, Blu-Ray has been more synonymous with recording television and movie files than data, but the Blu-Ray specification (1.0) includes two data formats: BD-R for write and read once and BD-RE for rewritable media (more later in this section). BD-J is capable of more sophisticated bonus features than provided by standard DVD, including network access, picture-in-picture, and access to expanded local storage. With the exception of the Internet access component, these features are called "Bonus View." The addition of Internet access is called "BD Live."

 In the official specification, as noted on the Blu-ray Disc Association website (http://us.blu-raydisc.com/), the "r" is lowercase. CompTIA favors the uppercase "R."

The current capacity of a Blu-Ray is 100 GB, with 400 GB on the horizon and an aim for 1 terabyte (TB) by 2013. As a final note, there was a long-running (but finally complete) battle between Blu-Ray and HD DVD to be the format of the future, and Blu-Ray won.

Combo drives and burners

In addition to drives that can read various optical formats, there are drives that can add data to or *burn* data to these formats. Many of these drives also have the ability to read multiple formats discussed in the previous section. This section discusses some of these drive types.

CD-RW

CD-RW (Compact Disc-ReWritable) media is a rewritable optical disc. A CD-RW drive requires more sensitive laser optics. It can write data to the disc but also has the ability to erase that data and write more data to the disc. It does this by liquefying the layer where the data resides (removing the reflectivity placed there by the writing process used to create the old data) and then creating new reflectivity in the same layer upon writing again that represents the new data. Two states of reflectivity are used to represent the 0s and 1s for the data. CD-RWs cannot be read in some CD-ROM drives built prior to 1997.

DVD-RW

As you might expect, the primary advantage of DVD-RW drives over DVD-R drives is the ability to erase and rewrite to a DVD-RW disc. In these drives a layer of metal alloy on the disk is manipulated to erase and write the data, rather than burning into the disc itself, similar to the operation of CD-RW.

Dual Layer DVD-RW

A dual-layer DVD-RW disc employs a second physical layer within the disc itself. The drive with dual-layer capability accesses the second layer by shining the laser through the first semitransparent layer.

BD-R

Blu-Ray players have two data formats: BD-R for recording computer data and BD-RE for rewritable media. BD-R can only be written to one time.

BD-RE

BD-RE (Blu-Ray Disc Recordable Erasable) can be erased and written to multiple times. Disc capacities are 25 GB for single-layer discs, 50 GB for double-layer discs, 100 GB for triple-layer discs, and 128 GB for quad-layer discs.

Connection types

Drives can be installed internally or can be connected externally to the PC. There are various options to connect the drives in both cases. This section discusses those options.

External

When a PC does not have the type of drive needed and has neither the internal connection type required nor the space inside the box to install the drive internally, external drives are made that can connect to the computer using several types of external interfaces. These connection types are discussed in this section.

USB

USB connections are probably the most widely used because of their inclusion on almost all front or back panels of computers these days. In fact, most have several USB slots, and it is simple to add more with a USB hub. USB drives also have the benefit of being Plug and Play, which makes them very user friendly for setup.

FireWire

Although not as widely seen as USB or IEEE 1394, FireWire connections are also present on many computers. It transfers data at 400 Mbps and supports up to 63 chained devices on a single set of resources. It's hot-pluggable, like USB.

eSATA

eSATA provides a form of serial ATA (SATA) meant for external connectivity. SATA (discussed more completely in the section "Internal SATA, IDE, and SCSI") is used for drive connections internally on many PCs. eSATA uses a more robust connector, longer shielded cables, and stricter (but backward-compatible) electrical standards. The interface resembles that of USB and IEEE 1394 (FireWire), but the cable cannot be as long, and the cable does not supply power to the device. The advantage it has over the other technologies is speed—it is approximately three times as fast as either FireWire or USB 2.0 (although USB 3.0 is faster).

Ethernet

There are drives that you connect to across the network or through Ethernet. These drives, also sometimes referred to as Network Attached Storage (NAS) devices, may also allow for wireless access, just as a laptop is capable of both wired and wireless communication. These devices are *not* seen as an attached device to the PC but rather as another device on the network, so they appear as a drive with shared folders as if you were connecting to a server. They only need to be on the same network as the PC.

Internal SATA, IDE, and SCSI

When drives are connected internally, there are several options, and the options available on your PC will be a function of how old it is and, in the case of SCSI, whether it is a computer designed to operate as a server.

IDE drives are the most common type of hard drive found in computers. But IDE is much more than a hard drive interface; it's also a popular interface for many other drive types, including CD-ROM, DVD, and Zip drives. IDE drives are easy to install and configure, and they provide acceptable performance for most applications. Their ease of use relates to their most identifiable feature—the controller is located on the drive itself.

The design of the IDE is simple: build the controller right on the drive, and use a relatively short ribbon cable to connect the drive/controller to the IDE interface. This offers the benefits of decreasing signal loss (thus increasing reliability) and making the drive easier to install. The IDE interface can be an expansion board, or it can be built into the motherboard, as is the case on almost all systems today.

IDE generically refers to any drive that has a built-in controller.

The IDE we know today is more properly called AT IDE; two previous types of IDE (MCA IDE and XT IDE) are obsolete and incompatible with it.

There have been many revisions of the IDE standard over the years, and each one is designated with a certain AT attachment (ATA) number—ATA-1 through ATA-8. Drives that support ATA-2 and higher are generically referred to as enhanced IDE (EIDE).

With ATA-3, a technology called ATA Packet Interface (ATAPI) was introduced to help deal with IDE devices other than hard disks. ATAPI enables the BIOS to recognize an IDE CD-ROM drive, for example, or a tape backup or Zip drive.

Starting with ATA-4, a new technology was introduced called UltraDMA, supporting transfer modes of up to 33 Mbps.

ATA-5 supports UltraDMA/66, with transfer modes of up to 66 Mbps. To achieve this high rate, the drive must have a special 80-wire ribbon cable, and the motherboard or IDE controller card must support ATA-5.

ATA-6 supports UltraDMA/100, with transfer modes of up to 100 Mbps.

 If an ATA-5 or ATA-6 drive is used with a normal 40-wire cable or is used on a system that doesn't support the higher modes, it reverts to the ATA-4 performance level.

ATA-7 supports UltraDMA/133, with transfer modes of up to 150 Mbps and serial ATA.

ATA-8 made only minor revisions to ATA-7 and also supports UltraDMA/133, with transfer modes of up to 150 Mbps and serial ATA.

ATA standards and their details are shown in Table 1.4.

TABLE 1.4   ATA standards

Standard	Speed	Cable type	New feature
ATA 1	8.3 Mbps	40 wire	Multiword DMA
ATA 2	16.6 Mbps	40 wire	PIO mode
ATA 3	16.6 Mbps	40 wire	ATAPI
ATA 4	33 Mbps	40 or 80 wire	Ultra DMA
ATA 5	66 Mbps	40 or 80 wire	Ultra DMA 66
ATA 6	100 Mbps	40 or 80 wire	Ultra DMA 100
ATA 7	150 Mbps	40 or 80 wire	Ultra DMA 133
ATA 8	150 Mbps	40 or 80 wire	Hybrid drive capability

Serial ATA (SATA) drives are ATA drives that use serial transmission as opposed to parallel. They use a different cable because of this. It is not a ribbon cable but a smaller cable. The cable and its connecter are shown in Figure 1.21.

FIGURE 1.21   Serial ATA

Small Computer System Interface (SCSI) is most commonly used for hard disks and tape drives, but it can connect a wide range of other devices, including scanners and CD drives. These devices reside on a single bus, which must be terminated on either end. Eight or sixteen devices can be attached to a single bus, depending on whether the SCSI bus is wide (0–15) or narrow (0–7) bus. There also is a host bus controller, which is usually plugged into a slot in the computer or can be integrated into the motherboard.

IDE configuration and setup (Master, Slave, Cable Select)

The primary benefit of IDE is that it's nearly universally supported. Almost every motherboard has IDE connectors.

A typical motherboard has two IDE connectors, and each connector can support up to two drives on the same cable. That means you're limited to four IDE devices per system unless you add an expansion board containing another IDE interface. In contrast, with SCSI (covered in the next section) you can have up to seven drives per interface (or even more on some types of SCSI).

Performance also may suffer when IDE devices share an interface. When you're burning CDs, for example, if the hard drive you are reading from is on the same cable as the CD drive you are writing to, errors may occur. SCSI drives are much more efficient with this type of transfer.

To install an IDE drive, do the following:

Installation and Configuration

1. Set the master/slave jumper on the drive.

2. Install the drive in the drive bay.

3. Connect the power-supply cable.

4. Connect the ribbon cable to the drive and to the motherboard or IDE expansion board.

5. Configure the drive in BIOS Setup if it isn't automatically detected.

6. Partition and format the drive using the operating system.

Each IDE interface can have only one master drive on it. If there are two drives on a single cable, one of them must be the slave drive. This setting is accomplished via a jumper on the drive. Some drives have a separate setting for Single (that is, master with no slave) and Master (that is, master with a slave); others use the Master setting generically to refer to either case. The cable select setting will assume that you have the primary first on cable and the secondary second. Figure 1.22 shows a typical master/slave jumper scenario, but different drives may have different jumper positions to represent each state. Today, the need for jumper settings has decreased as many drives can auto-detect the master/slave relationship.

Most BIOS Setup programs today support Plug and Play, so they detect the new drive automatically at startup. If this doesn't work, the drive may not be installed correctly, the jumper settings may be wrong, or the BIOS Setup may have the IDE interface set to None rather than Auto. Enter BIOS Setup, and find out. Setting the IDE interface to Auto and then allowing the BIOS to detect the drive is usually all that is required.

FIGURE 1.22   Master/slave jumpers

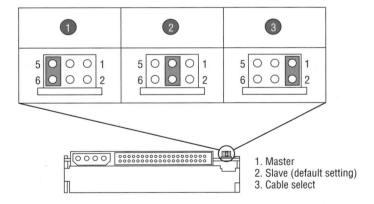

In BIOS Setup for the drive, you might have the option of selecting a DMA or programmed input/output (PIO) setting for the drive. Both are methods for improving drive performance by allowing the drive to write directly to RAM, bypassing the CPU when possible. For modern drives that support UltraDMA, neither of these settings is necessary or desirable.

When the drive is installed, you can proceed to partition and format it for the operating system you've chosen. Then, finally, you can install your operating system of choice.

For a Windows Vista or Windows 7 system, allow the Windows Setup program to partition and format the drive (when installing the operating system), or use the Disk Management utility in Windows to perform those tasks. To access Disk Management, from the Control Panel choose Administrative Tools and then choose Computer Management.

SCSI IDs (0–15)

The devices are identified by a unique SCSI ID. The SCSI ID of a device in a drive enclosure that has a backplane is set either by jumpers or by the slot in the enclosure the device is installed into, depending on the model of the enclosure. In the latter case, each slot on the enclosure's backplane delivers control signals to the drive to select a unique SCSI ID. It is important that all devices have unique IDs. The bootable hard disk should be set with an ID of 0, and the host controller should be set at 7 or 15 in the case of 16-bit SCSI (it will be the highest number possible based on the SCSI width). Each end of the chain must be terminated.

In some cases a single SCSI *target* (as they are called) may contain multiple drives within the unit. In these cases the drives are differentiated with a second number called a logical unit number (LUN).

Hot swappable drives

If a drive can be attached to the PC without shutting down the PC, then it is a hot swappable drive. Drive types that are hot swappable include USB, FireWire, SATA, and those that connect through Ethernet. You should always check the documentation to ensure that your drive supports this feature.

Hard drives

Hard drives can be differentiated in several ways. One of those ways is their mode of operations (magnetic or solid state) and the other is their speed. In this section, the speed and the operation of a magnetic drives is discussed, and the next section covers the operation of solid-state drives.

Magnetic

Before the development and use of solid-state drives, magnetic drives were—and are still as of this writing—the main type of hard drive used. The drive itself is a mechanical device that spins a number of disks or platters and uses a magnetic head to read and write data to the surface of the disks. One of the advantages of solid-state drives (discussed in the next section) is the absence of mechanical parts that can malfunction. The parts of a magnetic hard drive are shown in Figure 1.23.

The basic hard disk geometry consists of three components: the number of sectors that each track contains, the number of read/write heads in the disk assembly, and the number of cylinders in the assembly. This set of values is known as CHS (for cylinders/heads/sectors). A *cylinder* is the set of tracks of the same number on all the writeable surfaces of the assembly. It is called a cylinder because the collection of all same-number tracks on all writable surfaces of the hard disk assembly looks like a geometric cylinder when connected together vertically. Therefore, cylinder 1, for instance, on an assembly that contains three platters comprises six tracks (one on each side of each platter), each labeled track 1 on its respective surface. Figure 1.24 illustrates the key terms presented in this discussion.

FIGURE 1.23 Magnetic HD

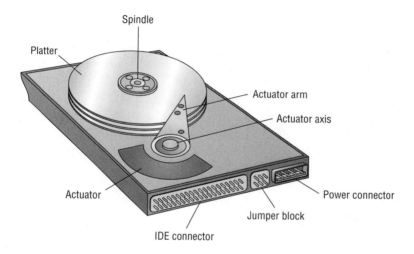

FIGURE 1.24 CHS

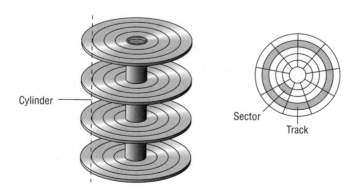

5400 rpm

The rotational speed of the disk or platter has a direct influence on how quickly the drive can locate any specific disk sector on the drive. This locational delay is called *latency* and is measured in milliseconds (ms). The faster the rotation, the smaller the delay will be. A drive operating at 5,400 rpms will experience about 5.5 ms of this delay.

7200 rpm

Drives that operate at 7,200 rpm will experience about 4.16 ms of latency. As of 2010, a typical 7,200 rpm desktop hard drive has a sustained data transfer rate up to 1,030 Mbps. This rate depends on the track location, so it will be higher for data on the outer tracks and lower toward the inner tracks.

10,000 rpm

At 10,000 rpm, the latency will decrease to about 3 ms. Data transfer rates also generally go up with a higher rotational speed but are also influenced by the density of the disk (the number of tracks and sectors present in a given area).

15,000 rpm

Drives that operate at 15,000 rpm are higher end drives and suffer only 2 ms of latency. These drives also generate more heat, requiring more cooling to the case. They also offer faster data transfer rates for the same areal density.

Solid-state/flash drives

Solid-state drives (SSDs) retain data in nonvolatile memory chips and contain no moving parts. Compared to electromechanical hard disk drives (HDDs), SSDs are typically less susceptible to physical shock, are silent, have lower access time and latency, but are more expensive per gigabyte.

Thumb drives are USB flash drives that have become extremely popular for transporting files. Figure 1.25 shows three thumb drives (also known as keychain drives) next to a pack of gum for size comparison.

As with other flash drives, you can find these in a number of different size capacities. Many models include a write-protect switch to keep you from accidentally overwriting files stored on the drive. Most include an LED to show when they're connected to the USB port. Other names for thumb drives include travel drives, flash drives, and jump drives.

Flash drives (which are solid state) have been growing in popularity for years and replacing floppy disks due to their capacity and small size. Flash technology is ideally suited for use not only with computers, but also with many other things—digital cameras, MP3 players, and so on. In this section the various forms of these drives are discussed.

FIGURE 1.25   USB flash

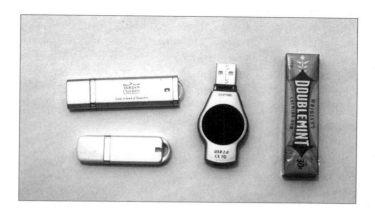

Compact flash

Compact flash (CF) cards are a widely used form of solid-state storage. There are two main subdivisions of CF cards: Type I (3.3 mm thick) and the thicker Type II (CF2) cards (5 mm thick). CF cards can be used directly in a PC card slot with a plug adapter, used as an ATA (IDE) or PCMCIA storage device with a passive adapter or with a reader, or attached to other types of ports such as USB or FireWire. A CF card is shown in Figure 1.26.

FIGURE 1.26   SD and compact flash

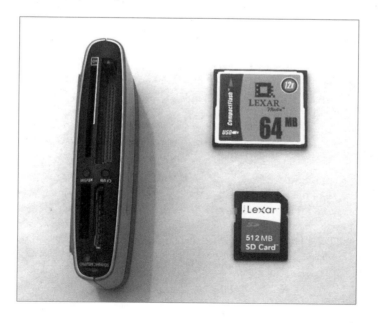

SD

Secure Digital (SD) cards are just one type of flash; there are many others. The maximum capacity of a standard SD card is 4 GB, and there are two other standards that go beyond this: SDHC can go to 32 GB and SDXC to 2 TB. Figure 1.26 shows a Compact flash card (the larger of the two) and an SD card along with an 8-in-1 card reader/writer. The reader shown connects to the USB port and then interacts with CompactFlash, CompactFlash II, Memory Stick, Memory Stick PRO, SmartMedia, xD-Picture Cards, SD, and MultiMediaCards. The SD card specification defines four physical sizes, discussed in the following sections.

Micro-SD

Micro-SD is the smallest of the three. It is 11 mm by 15 mm by 1 mm.

Mini-SD

Mini-SD is the middle child of the three SD form factors. It is 20 mm by 21.5 mm by 1.4 mm.

xD

xD-Picture Card is a flash memory card format, used mainly in older digital cameras. xD stands for Extreme Digital. xD cards are available in capacities of 16 MB up to 2 GB. Pictures are transferred from a digital camera's xD card to a PC by plugging the camera into the USB or IEEE 1394 (FireWire) cable, or by removing the card from the camera and inserting it into a card reader.

SSD

A solid-state drive is a form of flash drive that takes the place of a magnetic hard drive as the main storage device in the PC. As of 2010, most SSDs use memory that retains data even without power. Some SSDs use volatile RAM and external power or batteries to maintain the data after power is removed.

These drives access the data faster because there is no wait for the platters to spin up. Also, with no moving parts there is less to go wrong with these drives and they make no noise, as magnetic drives will do. Smart phones are an example of the growing number of devices that use solid-state storage.

RAID types

RAID stands for Redundant Array of Independent Disks. It's a way of combining the storage power of more than one hard disk for a special purpose such as increased performance or fault tolerance. RAID is more commonly done with SCSI drives, but it can be done with IDE or SATA drives. Several types of RAID are covered in the following sections. Due to the methods used to provide fault tolerance, the total amount of usable space in the array will vary, as discussed in each section.

RAID 0

RAID 0 is also known as *disk striping*. This is technically not RAID, because it doesn't provide fault tolerance. Data is written across multiple drives, so one drive can be reading or writing while the next drive's read/write head is moving. This makes for faster data access. However, if any one of the drives fails, all content is lost. In RAID 0, since there is no fault tolerance, the usable space in the drive is equal to the total space on the drive. So if the two drives in an array have 250 GB each of space, 500 GB will be the available drive space.

RAID 1

RAID 1 is also known as *disk mirroring*. This is a method of producing fault tolerance by writing all data simultaneously to two separate drives. If one drive fails, the other drive contains all the data and may also be used as a source of the data. However, disk mirroring doesn't help access speed, and the cost is double that of a single drive. Since RAID 1 repeats the data on two drives, only one half of the total drive space is available for data. So if two 250 GB drives are used in the array, 250 GB will be the available drive space.

RAID 5

RAID 5 combines the benefits of both RAID 0 and RAID 1 and is also known as *striping with parity*. It uses a parity block distributed across all the drives in the array, in addition to striping the data across them. That way, if one drive fails, the parity information can be used to recover what was on the failed drive. A minimum of three drives is required. RAID 5 uses $1/n$ (n = the number of drives in the array) for parity information (for example, one third of the space in a three-drive array), and only $1 - (1/n)$ is available for data. So if three 250 GB drives are used in the array (for a total of 750 GB), 500 GB will be the available drive space.

RAID 10

RAID 10 is also known as RAID 1+0. Striped sets are mirrored (a minimum of four drives, and the number of drives must be even). It provides fault tolerance and improved performance but increases complexity. Since this is effectively a mirrored stripe set and a stripe set gets 100 percent use of the drive without mirroring, this array will provide half of the total drive space in the array as available drive space. For example, if there are four 250 GB drives in a RAID 10 array (for a total of 1,000 GB), the available drive space will be 500 GB.

Floppy drive

Though not something you are likely to find on a newer PC, a floppy disk drive is a magnetic storage medium that uses a floppy disk made of thin plastic enclosed in a protective casing. The floppy disk itself (or floppy, as it's often called) enables the information to be transported from one computer to another easily. The downside of a floppy disk drive is its limited storage capacity. Floppy disks are limited to a maximum capacity of 2.88 MB, but the most common type of floppy that you may find in use today holds only 1.44 MB. Table 1.5 lists the various floppy disks and their capacity. For the most part, all of these are obsolete.

TABLE 1.5 Floppy disk capacities

Common designation	Number of tracks	Capacity
Double-sided, double-density	80	720 KB
Double-sided, high-density	80	1.44 MB
Double-sided, ultra-high-density	80	2.88 MB

You can specify how many floppy drives are installed and what types they are. Floppy drives aren't automatically detected. The settings needed for a floppy drive are size (3.5 inch or 5.25 inch) and density (double-density or high-density). You can also set each floppy drive to be enabled or disabled from being bootable. Almost all floppy drives today are high-density 3½ inch.

Tape drive

Another form of storage device is the tape backup. Tape backup devices can be installed internally or externally and use a magnetic tape medium instead of disks for storage. They hold much more data than most other media but are also much slower. They're primarily used for archival storage.

Tape drives can be connected with SCSI, Fibre Channel, SATA, USB, FireWire, or other interfaces.

One of the disadvantages of tape drives in the past has been the sequential manner in which data is located on the tape. That issue may become a thing of the past. In 2010 IBM introduced the Linear Tape File System (LTFS), which allows you to access files on tape in the same way as on a disk filesystem. Its impact on the choice of backup medium remains to be seen.

Media capacity

One of the common ways that storage options are compared is capacity. In the sections that follow, the capacity ranges of each option are briefly discussed.

CD

Standard CDs normally hold 650–700 MB of data and use the ISO 9660 standard, which allows them to be used in multiple platforms.

CD-RW

Like CDs, CD-RWs normally hold 650–700 MB of data.

DVD-RW

The capacity of DVD-RW depends on whether it is single or dual layer. A single-layer DVD-RW holds about 4.7 GB (the same as a DVD-R), and a dual-layer DVD-RW will hold 8.5 GB.

DVD

DVDs can have up to four layers, can be either single or double sided, and can come in about 10 different types or generations. All affect the capacity. The range of capacities available is from 4.7 GB (DVD-5 single-sided, single-layer) to 17.08 GB (DVD-18, double-sided, double-layer, which results in four layers total).

Blu-Ray

As mentioned earlier in the section "Optical drives," the current capacity of a Blu-Ray Disc is 100 GB, with 400 GB on the horizon, and an aim for 1 TB by 2013.

Tape

The current maximum capacity of a tape drive is 1.5 TB uncompressed (or 3.0TB compressed), but in 2011, Fujifilm and IBM announced that they were exploring technology that would allow storing 35 TB in an uncompressed format. Using media developed by using barium-ferrite (BaFe) particles and nanotechnologies, they managed to record 29.5 billion bits per square inch with magnetic tape. The technology is not expected to be commercially available for at least another decade.

Floppy

As mentioned earlier in the section "Floppy Drive," the maximum capacity of a floppy disk is 1.44 MB on a single-sided high-density disk and 2.88 MB for a double-sided ultra-high-density disk.

DL DVD

As described in the section on DVD capacity, a double-layer (DL) DVD's capacity is influenced by the type or generation of DVD and whether it is single or double sided. Single-sided DL (which results in a total of two layers) in DVD-10 holds up to 9.4 GB, and a double-sided DL (which results in a total of four layers) in DVD-18 holds up to 17.08 GB.

Exam Essentials

Identify and differentiate the optical drive options for long-term storage of data.   Those options include CD-ROM, DVD-ROM, and Blu-Ray. When the ability to erase and rewrite to the disk is required, the options include CD-RW, DVD-RW, dual-layer (DL) DVD-RW, and Blu-Ray Disc Recordable Erasable (BD-RE).

Describe the types of interfaces to connect a drive to the system. Drives can be connected externally using USB, FireWire (IEEE 1394), eSATA, and Ethernet. Internally the connection types are SATA, IDE, and SCSI.

Identify the steps to install an IDE drive. To install an IDE drive, do the following:

1. Set the master/slave jumper on the drive.
2. Install the drive in the drive bay.
3. Connect the power-supply cable.
4. Connect the ribbon cable to the drive and to the motherboard or IDE expansion board.
5. Configure the drive in BIOS Setup if it isn't automatically detected.
6. Partition and format the drive using the operating system.

Appreciate the importance of the Master/Slave settings for IDE. Each IDE interface can have only one master drive on it. If there are two drives on a single cable, one of them must be the slave drive. This setting is accomplished via a jumper on the drive.

Describe the operations of the SCSI bus. SCSI devices reside on a single bus, which must be terminated on either end. Up to 8 or 16 devices can be attached to a single bus, depending on whether the SCSI bus is wide (0–15) or narrow (0–7) bus. There also is a host bus controller, which is usually plugged into a slot in the computer or integrated into the motherboard.

Identify the advantages and disadvantage to both magnetic and solid-state drive operations. SSDs retain data in nonvolatile memory chips and contain no moving parts. Compared to electromechanical HDDs, SSDs are typically less susceptible to physical shock, are silent, have lower access time and latency, but are more expensive per gigabyte.

List the capacities of various storage systems. These range from 1.44 MB for a single-sided floppy to up to 17 GB for a double-sided DL DVD.

Identify the pros and cons of various RAID options. RAID 0 provides only performance enhancement, whereas RAID 1 and RAID 5 provide fault tolerance. RAID 10 provides both. The cost for these options is the use of multiple hard drives in various arrangements.

1.6 Differentiate among various CPU types and features and select the appropriate cooling method

The CPU is the brain of the PC and has evolved over the years both in the slots available to connect it to the PC and in its capabilities. With the addition of more processing power came the introduction of more heat in the case and the development of more advanced cooling methods. This section covers these issues as well. The topics addressed in objective 1.6 include:

- Socket types
- Characteristics
- Cooling

Socket types

Sockets are the interface with which CPUs are plugged into the motherboard. These sockets have evolved over the years along with the changes in CPU architecture and design. There are three form factors for CPU chips: pin grid array (PGA), single-edge contact cartridge (SECC), and Land Grid Array (LGA). The PGA style is a flat square or rectangular ceramic chip with an array of pins in the bottom. The actual CPU is a silicon wafer embedded inside that ceramic chip. The SECC style is a circuit board with the silicon wafer mounted on it. The circuit board is then surrounded by a plastic cartridge for protection; the circuit board sticks out of the cartridge along one edge. This edge fits into a slot in the motherboard.

The market leader in the manufacture of chips is Intel Corporation, with Advanced Micro Devices (AMD) gaining market share in the home PC market. In this section, various socket types you may encounter are discussed.

Intel: LGA 775, 1155, 1156, 1366

Table 1.2 earlier in this chapter listed the various Intel CPU slots and sockets you may find in a motherboard and explained which CPUs will fit into them.

AMD: 940, AM2, AM2+, AM3, AM3+, FM1, F

Table 1.2 also listed the various AMD CPU slots and sockets you may find in a motherboard and explained which CPUs will fit into them. These later-generation AMD sockets were launched as the successor to Socket AM2+. On February 9, 2009, AMD3 was released alongside the initial grouping of Phenom II processors designed for it. The principal change from AM2+ to AM3 is support for DDR3 SDRAM. The AM3+ socket has been designed for the AMD FX series Zambezi processors based on the Bulldozer architecture.

Characteristics

CPUs can be compared and contrasted on the basis of a number of characteristics. These characteristics ultimately define the ability of the CPU to perform its main role of processing as well as its ability to provide more advanced features to the PC. These characteristics are discussed in this section.

Speeds

When discussing CPU speed it is important to understand that there are two values that affect the overall speed of the CPU's interaction with the PC.

External speed (clock speed)   The *clock speed*, or *external speed*, is the speed at which the motherboard communicates with the CPU. It's determined by the motherboard, and its cadence is set by a quartz crystal (the system crystal) that generates regular electrical pulses.

Internal speed   The *internal speed* is the maximum speed at which the CPU can perform its internal operations. This may be the same as the motherboard's speed (the external speed), but it's more likely to be a multiple of it. For example, a CPU may have an internal speed of 1.3 GHz but an external speed of 133 MHz. That means for every tick of the system crystal's clock, the CPU has 10 internal ticks of its own clock.

Cores

CPUs can have a single-core, dual-core, quad-core, and even dual-quad core (eight CPUs totals). When multiple cores exist they operate as individual processors, so the more the better. The largest boost in performance will likely be noticed in improved response-time while running CPU-intensive processes, like virus scans, ripping/burning media (requiring file conversion), or file searching.

The addition of more cores does not have a linear effect on performance. The potential impact of multiple cores also depends on the amount of cache or memory present to serve the CPU. When a computer is designed for the processor, this will have been taken into consideration, but when adding a multicore processor to a PC, it is an issue to consider. Cache or memory is discussed in the next section.

Dual Processors

Dual-core processors, available from Intel as well as AMD, essentially combine two processors into one chip. Instead of adding two processors to a machine (making it a multiprocessor system), you have one chip splitting operations and essentially performing as if it's two processors in order to get better performance. The Centrino processor, for example, was released in 2003 and combines Wi-Fi capability with a multicore processor. A *multicore* architecture simply has multiple completely separate processor dies in the same package, whether its dual core, triple core, or quad core. The operating system and applications see multiple processors in the same way that they see multiple processors in separate sockets. Both dual-core and quad-core processors are common cases for the multicore technology. Most multicore processors from Intel come in even numbers, whereas AMD's Phenom series can contain odd numbers (such as the triple-core processor).

Cache size/type

A *cache* is an area of extremely fast memory used to store data that is waiting to enter or exit the CPU. The *Level 1 cache*, also known as the *L1* or *front-side cache*, holds data that is waiting to enter the CPU. On modern systems, the L1 cache is built into the CPU. The *Level 2 cache*, also known as the *L2* or *back-side cache*, holds data that is exiting the CPU and is waiting to return to RAM. On modern systems, the L2 cache is in the same packaging as the CPU but on a separate chip. On older systems, the L2 cache was on a separate circuit board installed in the motherboard and was sometimes called *cache on a stick* (COAST).

On some CPUs, the L2 cache operates at the same speed as the CPU; on others, the cache speed is only half the CPU speed. Chips with full-speed L2 caches have better performance. Some newer systems also have an *L3 cache*, which is external to the CPU. It sits between the CPU and RAM to optimize data transfer between them.

Hyperthreading

One of the improvements offered since the Pentium 4 is *hyperthreading* technology. This feature enables the computer to multitask more efficiently between CPU-demanding applications. An advantage of hyperthreading is improved support for multithreaded code, allowing multiple threads to run simultaneously and thus improving reaction and response time.

Virtualization support

When using virtualization technology (discussed in the "BIOS configurations" section earlier, under "Virtualization support"), a fuller realization of its benefits can be achieved when the processor supports this concept.

The benefit derived from this support is to allow the virtualization product (also called a hypervisor) to use hardware-assisted virtualization. This allows the hypervisor to dynamically allocate CPU to the VMs as required. Both AMD and Intel offer CPUs that support hardware virtualization.

Architecture (32-bit vs. 64-bit)

CPUs can either be 32-bit or 64-bit. This value describes what is called the *word size* of the processor. Sixty-four bits offer two important benefits. Data can be processed in larger chunks, which also means with greater precision. Moreover, the system can point to or address a larger number of locations in physical memory. A key consideration is the operating system. If the operating system is not 64-bit, you cannot take advantage of the 64-bit processor.

Integrated GPU

A graphics processing unit (GPU) is a specialized circuit designed to rapidly manipulate and alter memory to accelerate the building of images in a frame buffer intended for output to a display. It improves the graphic abilities of the PC when this feature is present in the CPU.

Some visual features provided by operating systems such as Windows Vista and Windows 7 are unavailable unless the CPU has dedicated graphics memory or a GPU. For example, the Aero view in Vista and Windows 7 requires a card capable of DirectX, which is a technology that requires the DirectCompute API, which in turn requires a GPU.

Cooling

CPUs produce heat, and the more powerful the CPU the more heat it produces. Heat is an enemy to the PC in general as it causes problems such as random reboots. Methods of cooling the CPU and in turn the overall interior of the case have evolved with the increasing need to remove this heat. Options that are used are covered in this section.

In methods of cooling, technology that transfers heat away from components uses thermoelectric cooling and components that perform this function are called Peltier components. Heat sinks, cooling fans, and cooling fins are Peltier components. Liquid cooling, on the other hand, cools not by transferring heat away from components but by circulating a cool liquid around them.

Heat sink

The cooling can be either active or passive. A *passive heat sink* is a block of heat-conductive material that sits close to the CPU and wicks away the heat into the air. An *active heat sink* contains a fan that pulls the hot air away from the CPU. The heat sink sits atop the CPU, in many cases obscuring it from view entirely.

Fans

Active heat sinks have a fan that sits atop the heat sink. It pulls the heat out of the heat sink and away from it. Then the case fan shunts the heat out the back or side of the case.

Thermal paste

Most *passive heat sinks* are attached to the CPU using a glue-like thermal compound (called thermal glue, thermal compound, or thermal paste). This makes the connection between the heat sink and the CPU more seamless and direct. Thermal compound can be used on active heat sinks too, but generally it isn't because of the possibility that the fan may stop working and need to be replaced. Thermal compound improves thermal transfer by eliminating tiny air pockets between the heat sink and CPU (or other device like a north bridge or video chipset). Thermal compound provides both improved thermal transfer and adds bonding for heat sinks when there are no mounting holes to clamp the heat sink to the device to be cooled.

Liquid-based

Liquid-cooled cases are available that use circulating water rather than fans to keep components cool. These cases are typically more expensive than standard ones and may be more difficult for a technician untrained in this technology to work on, but they result in an almost completely silent system.

Issues with liquid-cooled machines can include problems with hoses or fittings, the pump, or the coolant. A failure of the pump can keep the liquid from flowing and cause the system to overheat. A liquid-cooled system should also be checked every so often for leaks or corrosion on the hoses and fittings, and the reservoir should be examined to make sure it is full and does not contain contaminants. Liquid cooling is more expensive, less noisy, and more efficient than Peltier components.

Exam Essentials

Identify the CPU socket types you may encounter.   These include but are not limited to Intel LGA, 775, 1155, 1156, and 1366, as well as AMD 940, AM2, AM2+, AM3, AM3+, FM1, and F. Table 1.2 lists the various Intel and AMD CPU slots and sockets you may find in a motherboard and explains which CPUs will fit into them.

Define the characteristic of CPUs.   CPUs can differ based on speed, number of cores, cache size and type, hyperthreading support, virtualization support, architecture (32-bit vs. 64-bit), and integrated GPU support.

Understand the various options available to reduce CPU heat.   These options include heat sinks, fans, thermal paste, and liquid cooling.

1.7 Compare and contrast various connection interfaces and explain their purpose

When using various modes of connection to the PC, you should understand the characteristics of those connections. This includes those types found inside the case as well the ones that appear on the back or front panel as well as those that are provided as a result of adding an expansion card into a slot that includes a new connector type on the back panel. The topics addressed in objective 1.7 are:

- Physical connections
- Speeds, distances, and frequencies of wireless device connections

Physical connections

Many different types of cables and connectors have been developed over the years to connect devices to the PC. Some have been around almost as long as the PC, whereas many others have made their appearance only in the last few years. In this section the physical characteristics of each of these connection methods will be discussed, along with the operational characteristics, such as the speed and maximum cable length.

USB 1.1 vs. 2.0 vs. 3.0 speed and distance characteristics

USB is an expansion bus type that is used almost exclusively for external devices. All motherboards today have at least two USB ports. Some of the advantages of USB include hot-plugging and the capability for up to 127 USB devices to share a single set of system resources. A USB port requires only one interrupt request (IRQ) for all USB devices that are connected to it, regardless of the type or number of devices. USB 1.1 runs at 12 Mbps, and USB 2.0 runs at 480 Mbps.

USB 3.0 has transmission speeds of up to 5 Gbps, significantly reduces the time required for data transmission, reduces power consumption, and is backwards compatible with USB 2.0. Because USB is a serial interface, its width is 1 bit. It is useful to note, however, that a USB 2.0 device will perform at 2.0 speeds even when connected to a 3.0 port.

By utilizing USB hubs in conjunction with the USB ports available on the local machine, you can connect up to 127 of these devices to the computer. You can daisy-chain up to four external USB hubs to a USB port. *Daisy chaining* means that hubs are attached to each other in a line. A USB hub will not function if it is more than five hubs away from the root port.

Connector types: A, B, mini, micro

USB connectors come in two types and two form factors or sizes. The type A connector is what is found on USB hubs, on host controllers (cards that are plugged in slots to provide USB connections) and on the front and back panels of computers. Type B is the type of USB connector found on the end of the cable that plugs into the devices.

The connectors also come in a mini version and a micro version. The micro version is used on mobile devices, such as mobile phones, GPS units, PDAs, and digital cameras, whereas the mini is found in applications described in the previous paragraph. The choice between a standard A and B and a mini A and B will be dictated by what is present on the device. The cables used cannot exceed 5 meters in length. Figure 1.27 shows from left to right, a standard Type A, A mini Type A, a standard Type B, and a mini Type B.

FIGURE 1.27   USB connectors

FireWire 400 vs. FireWire 800 speed and distance characteristics

Some newer motherboards have a built-in IEEE 1394/FireWire socket, although this socket in the past was more commonly provided on a PCI expansion board. It transfers data at 400 Mbps and supports up to 63 chained devices on a single set of resources. It's hot-pluggable, like USB. Figure 1.28 shows the connections on a FireWire card.

FIGURE 1.28   Connections on a FireWire card

FireWire 400 (IEEE 1394) is the original standard that operates up to 400 Mbps with maximum cable length of 4.5 meters.

FireWire 800 (IEEE 1394b) uses a different encoding scheme that allows it to go up to 800 Mbps. It also can use a cable up to 10 meters.

SATA1 vs. SATA2 vs. SATA3, eSATA, IDE speeds

Connections for storage devices can be either SATA or IDE. IDE was the only option early on, and then SATA came on the scene. Serial ATA (SATA) came out as a standard and was first adopted in desktops and then laptops. Whereas ATA had always been an interface that sends 16 bits at a time, SATA sends only one bit at a time. The benefit is that the cable used can be much smaller, and faster cycling can actually increase performance. SATA uses a seven-wire cable that can be up to one meter in length. eSATA cables can be up to two meters.

The speeds of all five options are shown in Table 1.6.

TABLE 1.6   SATA and IDE speeds

Standard	Transfer speed
IDE	133.5 MBps
SATA 1.0	150 MBps
SATA 2.0	300 MBps
SATA 3.0	600 MBps
eSATA	300 MBps

Other connector types

A computer's peripheral ports are the physical connectors found outside the computer. Cables of various types are designed to plug into these ports and create a connection between the PC and the external devices that may be attached to it. A successful IT technician should have an in-depth knowledge of ports and cables.

Because the peripheral components need to be upgraded frequently, either to keep pace with technological change or to replace broken devices, a well-rounded familiarity with the ports and their associated cabling is required.

Unless a peripheral device connects directly to the motherboard, it must use a port. Ports can be distinguished from one another by three factors:

- Bits of data simultaneously conveyed
- Data transmission speed
- Type of connector

Serial

A serial cable (and port) uses only one wire to carry data in each direction; all the rest are wires for signaling and traffic control.

Common bit rates include 1,200, 2,400, 4,800, 9,600, 14,400, 19,200, 38,400, 57,600, and 115,200 bits per second. The connector used for serial is a D-shaped connector with a metal ring around a set of pins. These are named for the number of pins/holes used: DB-25, DB-9, HD-15 (also known as DB-15), and so on. DB-25, DB-15, and DB-9 are shown in Figure 1.29.

FIGURE 1.29   DB-25, DB-15, and DB-9

Parallel

A parallel cable uses eight wires to carry bits of data in each direction, plus extra wires for signaling and traffic control. The most common port of this type before the conversion of most printers to USB was the parallel printer port.

It sends data 8 bits at a time (in parallel) and uses a cable with a male DB-25 connector at the computer and a 36-pin Centronics male connector at the printer. A DB-25 connector was shown in Figure 1.29 and a Centronics is shown in Figure 1.30. Its main drawback is its cable length. Older-style Centronics parallel cables can sometimes be up to 15 feet long, although 9–12 feet is more common. Depending on the mode of operation it can provide up to 2.5 MBps of bandwidth. IEEE-1284, a newer bidirectional standard, can go up to 30 feet.

FIGURE 1.30   Centronics

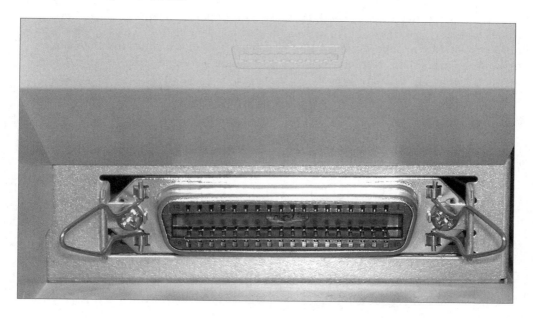

VGA

This is the traditional connector for the display of a computer and it is shaped like a D. It has three rows of five pins each, for a total of 15 pins. This is also often called the HD-15 (also known as DB-15) connector. A VGA cable carries analog signals. The cable length utilized will affect the resolution achieved: 1024×768 would operate more effectively with 30 feet or under of cable length. As the need for resolution increases, the allowable maximum cable length decreases. A VGA port is shown in Figure 1.31.

FIGURE 1.31   VGA port

HDMI

High-Definition Multimedia Interface (HDMI) connectors are used to connect compatible digital items (DVD players and conference room projectors, for example). The Type A connector has 19 pins and is backward compatible with DVI. Type B connectors have 29 pins and aren't backward compatible with DVI, but they support greater resolutions. Type C connectors are a smaller version of Type A for portable devices. Type D is an even smaller micro version that resembles a micro USB connector. Type E is planned for use in automotive applications. HDMI theoretical cable length limit is 16 feet (5 meters). Types A and C are shown in Figure 1.32 and Type B in Figure 1.33.

FIGURE 1.32   HDMI types A and C

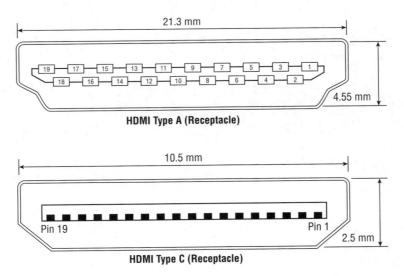

DVI

There are several types of Digital Video Interface (DVI) pin configurations, but all connectors are D-shaped. The wiring differs based on whether the connector is single-linked or dual-linked (extra pins are used for the dual link). DVI differs from everything else in that it includes both digital and analog signals at the same time, which makes it popular for LCD and plasma TVs. Figure 1.34 shows the types of DVI connectors. Maximum cable length is 16 feet (5 meters).

FIGURE 1.33 HDMI Type B

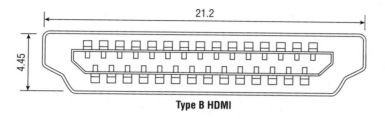

Type B HDMI

FIGURE 1.34 DVI connectors

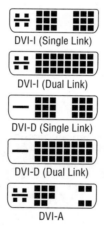

DVI-I (Single Link)

DVI-I (Dual Link)

DVI-D (Single Link)

DVI-D (Dual Link)

DVI-A

Audio

Audio connectors (sound) can be analog or digital. The most common connectors are called a mini TRS connector. There are usually two of these, one for headphones (or speakers) and the other for a microphone (or line in). A 3.5 mm plug is shown in Figure 1.35.

RJ-45

A registered jack (RJ) is a plastic plug with small metal tabs, like a telephone cord plug. Numbering is used in the naming: RJ-11 has two metal tabs, and RJ-14 has four. RJ-45 has eight tabs and is used for Ethernet 10 BaseT/100 BaseT networking. The maximum cable length is 100 meters but can vary slightly based on the category of cabling used. RJ-11 (left) and RJ-45 (right) connectors are shown in Figure 1.36.

FIGURE 1.35 TRS connector

FIGURE 1.36 RJ-11 and RJ-45

RJ-11

An RJ-11, as described earlier and shown in Figure 1.36, is a standard connector for a telephone line and is used to connect a computer modem to a phone line. It looks much like an RJ-45 but is noticeably smaller.

Analog vs. digital transmission

Audio and video can be delivered either in analog or digital form. For video this means that there are two connector types you may find on the PC for connecting the display (or monitor). Both types are discussed next.

VGA vs. HDMI

VGA connections and cables are analog in nature and we've pretty much said all there is to say about this connector type. HDMI (High-Definition Multimedia Interface) is an interface for transmitting encrypted uncompressed digital data. When these connections are available they are preferable to using the VGA connector, but they require the use of an HDMI cable between the computer and the display. DVI also has a cable that can be used with VGA—DVI-A. This is becoming a common cable when CRTs are being used with newer computers.

Speeds, distances, and frequencies of wireless device connections

Wireless connections, once considered a luxury, are now becoming a standard expected by users. There are several forms of wireless communication that serve very different purposes. These connection types differ in their speed, the distance at which they can operate, and the frequencies they use. In this section, three common types of wireless communication and their applications are discussed.

Bluetooth

Bluetooth is a type of wireless that creates what is called a personal area network (PAN). Bluetooth is a radio frequency technology that can connect a device to a computer at a range of about 35 feet. It operates in the 2.4 GHz band, which is the same band as 802.11b/g. Version 2.0 offers 3 Mbps (with actual throughput of 2.1 Mbps).

IR

Infrared technology requires direct line of sight and has been used for printers in the past. It can operate at a distance of 5 meters and can offer up to 4 Mbps. It is being replaced with Bluetooth over time.

RF

Radio frequency (RF) describes any of the technologies, like Bluetooth, that use radio waves. This also includes 802.11 WLAN technologies. These operate in two frequencies: 802.11b/g in the 2.4 GHz range, and 802.11a in the 5.0 GHz range. 802.11n can operate in both. The 802.11a maximum indoor range is 35 meters, or 115 feet, and maximum outdoor range is 120 meters, or 390 feet. The 802.11b maximum indoor range is 35 meters, or 115 feet, and the maximum outdoor range is 140 meters, or 460 feet. The 802.11g maximum indoor range is 38 meters, or 125 feet, and the maximum outdoor range is 140 meters, or 460 feet. The 802.11n maximum indoor range is 70 meters, or 380 feet, and the maximum outdoor range is 250 meters, or 820 feet. The data rates are up to 11 Mbps for 802.11b, 54 Mbps for 802.11g and 802.11a, and up to 600 Mbps for 802.11n (using 40 MHz channels in ideal conditions). These connections are used for networking.

Exam Essentials

Identify the characteristics of connector types found on most PCs.   These include but are not limited to USB, SATA, eSATA, FireWire, serial, parallel, VGA, HDMI, DVI, audio, RJ-45, and RJ-11.

Describe the difference in the operation of VGA and HDMI transmission.   VGA connections and cables are analog in nature whereas HDMI is an interface for transmitting digital data.

List the speed, distance, and frequency of wireless connections.   For device connections, Bluetooth offers up to 2.1 Mbps at about 35 feet, and infrared transmits at 4 Mbps at 5 meters. For networking, 802.11b operates at 11 Mbps, 802.11g at 54 Mbps, and 802.11n at up to 600 Mbps. The 802.11a maximum indoor range is 100 meters, or 300 feet, and maximum outdoor range is 350 meters, or 1,200 feet. The 802.11b maximum indoor range is 150 meters, or 492 feet, and the maximum outdoor range is 500 meters, or 1,640 feet. The 802.11g maximum indoor range is 150 meters, or 492 feet, and the maximum outdoor range is 500 meters, or 1,640 feet.

1.8 Install an appropriate power supply based on a given scenario

The power supply provides a number of connectors for various devices as well a plug for the motherboard itself. It is important to understand these connector types and to appreciate the power drawn by various devices. Knowledge of the power needs of the devices can allow the technician to choose a power supply that provides the total power needs of the PC. The topics addressed in objective 1.7 include:

- Connector types and their voltages
- Specifications
- Dual voltage options

Connector types and their voltages

When selecting a power supply, two issues become important. You need to supply the total wattage required by all the devices and the motherboard of the PC, and you must ensure that it has the connector types required by your devices. In this section, the voltage requirements of various connector types are discussed.

To determine the wattage a device draws, multiply voltage by current. For example, if a device uses 5 amps of +3.3 V and 0.7 amps of +12 V, a total of 25 watts is consumed. Do this calculation for every device installed. Most devices have labels that state their power requirements.

SATA

The SATA power connector is 15 pins, with 3 pins designated for 3.3 V, 5 V, and 12 V, with each pin carrying 1.5 amps. This results in a total draw of 4.95 watts + 7.5 watts + 18 watts, or about 30 watts.

Molex

A Molex connector is used to provide power to drives of various types. It has four pins, two of which have power, one 12 V and the other 5 V. These are standard for IDE (PATA) or older SCSI drives. The total power demands are from 5 to 15 watts for IDE and 10 to 40 watts for SCSI.

4/8-pin 12 V

With the introduction of the Pentium 4, the motherboard required more power. Supplemental power connections were provided to the motherboard in 4-, 6- (discussed later in this section), or 8-pin formats. These were in addition to the 20-pin connector (discussed later in this section) that was already provided.

There is a 4-pin square mini version of the ATX connector, which supplies 2 pins with 12 V, and an 8-pin version (two rows) that has four 12 V leads. These connect to other items, like the processor, or other components, like a network card that may need power that exceeds what can be provided with the ATX connection to the board.

PCIe 6/8-pin

PCIe slots also draw more power and require power in addition to the main 20-pin connector (discussed next). These additional connectors can be 6 pins and may also contain an additional 2-pin connector on the side for cases where the connection required is 8-pin.

20-pin

The main ATX connector, referenced earlier, is a 20-pin connector. The four pins carrying power are 3.3 V, 3.3 V, 5 V, and 5 V. This allows the motherboard to pull about 20 to 30 watts.

24-pin

The 24-pin ATX connector is simply the 20-pin connector discussed earlier along with the extra 4-pin connector on the side. This provides the 4 pins carrying power as discussed earlier plus an additional 4 pins with 5 V standby, 12 V, 12 V, and 3.3 V.

Floppy

The floppy power connector (an endangered species for sure) is called a Berg connector. It has four wires, two of which carry power: 5 V and 12 V. A floppy drive draws about 5 watts of power.

Specifications

When purchasing the power supply, you must take into account issues such as wattage, number of connectors, physical size or form factor, and plug types. This section addresses these considerations.

Wattage

When the wattage needs of each device and of the motherboard and CPU are totaled, you will know the wattage that the power supply must provide. A power supply has a rated output capacity in watts, and when you fill a system with power-hungry devices, you must make sure that maximum capacity isn't exceeded. Otherwise, problems with power can occur, creating lockups or spontaneous reboots. Most power supplies provide between 250 and 1200 watts. It's always a good idea to have more than the minimum required for the devices that are present so that additional devices can be added in the future.

Size

The physical dimension of the power supply must also be considered. The slot where the power supply goes in the PC will be the limiting factor. The Thin Form has been optimized for small and low-profile micro-ATX and FlexATX system layouts. The long, narrow profile of this power supply fits easily into low-profile systems.

Number of connectors

The power supply can come with any combination of the power connector types discussed earlier in this section. A quick inventory of the connectors that you need will assist you in ensuring that the power supply you purchase has the connectors required.

ATX

If the motherboard is an ATX (the larger motherboard) the power needs of the system will probably be higher than that of a micro-ATX. In that case, ensure that the supply is designed for an ATX system and can provide the higher requirements.

Micro-ATX

Micro-ATX boards are smaller and designed to operate with power supplies of a lower wattage rating. As you add more USB devices or put the board in a larger case with more internal devices, a larger power supply may become necessary.

Dual-voltage options

Most power supplies have the ability to accept input of either 110 or 220 volts. Some expensive power supplies can autosense and need not be set manually, but most have to be set manually, and you want to set the switch to the correct voltage setting or you could cause damage.

Exam Essentials

Identify common power connector types and their voltages.   These include but are not limited to SATA, Molex, 4- to 8-pin 12 V, PCIe 6- to 8-pin, 20-pin, 24-pin, and floppy connectors.

Understand the specifications of power supplies.   Differentiate power supplies by wattage, size, number of connectors, and design (ATX or mini-ATX).

Describe a dual-wattage power supply.   This is a supply that can be set to accept either 110 or 220 volts.

1.9 Evaluate and select appropriate components for a custom configuration, to meet customer specifications or needs

In many cases an off-the-shelf computer does not fill the needs of a customer. In these cases a unit must be custom built to accommodate their specific needs. This section describes some common custom configurations and options to meet specific needs. The topics addressed in objective 1.9 include:

- Graphic/CAD/CAM design workstation
- Audio/video editing workstation
- Virtualization workstation
- Gaming PC
- Home theater PC

- Standard thick client
- Thin client
- Home server PC

Graphic/CAD/CAM design workstation

Computers used for graphic design, computer-aided design (CAD) applications, and computer-aided manufacturing (CAM) require much more horsepower than the standard PC. Specifically, they require multiple or more powerful processors, more robust video cards, and significantly more memory. In this section, these needs are discussed.

Powerful processor

The resource-intensive applications used with graphics, CAD, and CAM require high-end processors. For example, to run a 64-bit version of Autodesk® AutoCAD® software, requirements are an AMD Athlon 64 with SSE2 technology, AMD Opteron processor with SSE2 technology, Intel Xeon processor with Intel EM64T support and SSE2 technology, or Intel Pentium 4 with Intel EM64T support and SSE2 technology.

Streaming Single Instruction, Multiple Data Extensions 2 (SSE2) technology is the latest version of a technology that provides additional instructions to the CPU that allows it to perform a single instruction on multiple pieces of data. Moreover, to do 3D modeling (which is very graphic intensive), an Intel 4 processor or AMD Athlon 3 GHz or greater is required. If a dual-core Intel or AMD dual-core processor is used, then it can be 2 GHz.

Keep in mind these are only the minimums. For good performance, these minimums should be exceeded.

High-end video

As you can imagine, the video demands of graphics such as 3D are much higher than those of common office applications. Continuing with our example of AutoCAD 2012, this requires a 1,280×1,024 true-color video display adapter with 128 MB of its own memory or greater and Pixel Shader 3.0 or greater, and it should be a Microsoft Direct3D-capable workstation-class graphics card. Note that the graphics card *itself* should have a minimum of 128 MB of RAM for its operations.

Maximum RAM

There can never be enough RAM, and in the case of CAD/CAM and graphics, the minimum (using the same example) is 2 GB of RAM. When the minimum to run the software is 2 GB, you need much more than that for good performance.

Audio/Video editing workstation

As we go over the requirements of these specialty solutions, you may notice a recurring theme: RAM, CPU, and graphics. It's no different with an audio or video editing machine.

These are the components that are saddled with the workload and will be the ones that require boosting above what would be used on a standard workstation.

With audio and video editing, however, additional components can make the workstation more productive to the user. In this section those items are discussed as well.

Specialized audio and video card

Many video and audio editing software packages come with a special capture card that works in concert with the accompanying software to provide ease of use. For example, it might be an internal PCI card that captures video from any analog or DV source. You can also output video to a VCR or an analog or DV camcorder from this card. They still require (you guessed it) a high-end audio and video card as well and plenty of memory and a processor that may not have quite the requirements of CAD/CAM but still should be 2.4 GHz or higher.

Large, fast hard drive

Your hard drive should be at least 7,200 RPM. You will also want at least two drives if not three. When doing audio, use one for the OS and programs and a second drive for audio files. When doing video, consider a third used exclusively for video files.

Even better, consider a RAID setup. Many motherboards include a serial ATA RAID controller built in. Use RAID 0 to enhance performance (see the section "RAID Types").

Dual monitors

Especially when doing video editing, a second monitor is well worth the money and the desk real estate. You may need to read or refer to something on one screen while using the other for the editing software. The material could be tutorials or source material.

It also may be that you move your tools (for example, Photoshop tools) over to one screen so they don't clutter the image you are working on.

Virtualization workstation

A virtualization workstation is also called a virtualization host. The virtual machines that reside on this operating system are called guest operating systems. The host operating system and the guest must all share the total amount of RAM and CPU that the host machine possesses. In this section these issues are discussed.

Maximum RAM and CPU cores

The amount of RAM that is required depends on the number of virtual machines that you anticipate operating at the same time, not how many exist on the desktop. Total the memory requirements of each VM that will be open at the same time, in addition to the requirements of the host operating system. That should be the minimum. Then add more for overhead to ensure performance.

The memory issue is not something you can fudge. If there is not enough memory, the VM will not start and you will be notified with an error message that there is insufficient memory.

With regard to CPU, it should be dual, if not quad core, and multiple CPUs would be even better.

Gaming PC

Gaming PCs may place the highest demands on the system of any specialty PC discussed here, because the machines are in competition with other machines. The skill of the player is certainly a big factor in success, but at some point the user with the more powerful PC is going to be able to raise the level of the game through hardware.

Powerful processor

When it comes to the processor, the question becomes "How much do you want to spend?" Just as a comparison (prices change daily!), for over $600 you can get the Intel core i7-3930K. (There is also the i7-3960X for $1,000). Also keep in mind that multiple processors will always improve the gaming experience.

High-end video/specialized GPU

When playing a game, it is critical that the action you are seeing (and reacting to) is rendered to the screen as quickly as possible. With gaming machines, dual GPU cards are often used. The higher-end cards also require water cooling of GPUs. In fact, the faster cards all need water cooling (covered later in this section).

Better sound card

When you're considering the features of a sound card, you want those features to be performed in hardware. Anytime these functions are performed in software, it simply means the main CPU is going to get the workload. Things to consider are:

- Using the PCI Express slot (better bandwidth) is better than using the PCI slot.
- Make sure the card has its own on-board memory (less work for the main CPU).

High-end cooling

With all the heat being generated by the CPU(s) and GPU(s), fans may not be sufficient to remove the heat. Water-cooling systems will cool the system better and will be quieter as well. Cooling kits circulate water through the case in tubes that enter and exit the box to a unit where the water is cooled again (think of the cooling system in your car). A cooling system is shown in Figure 1.37.

FIGURE 1.37   Cooling system

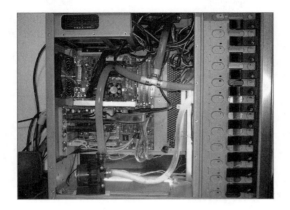

WIKIMEDIA COMMONS/SENATER CACHE

Home Theater PC

A home theater PC (HTPC) is a convergence device. It uses software to bring together video, photo, music playback, television content, and even video recording to a single computer interface. Many operating systems today include this software. To take advantage of its capabilities, however, additional components need to be in place. This section discusses some of the components that will enhance the experience.

Surround sound audio

Surround sound speaker systems can add to the experience of the home theater PC. A numbering system has been developed that indicates the number and type of speakers present. The common setups are 2.1, 4.1, 5.1, 6.1, and 7.1. The number on the left is the total number of speakers and the number on the right is the number of subwoofers (bass).

Don't forget you will need places to plug these speakers into the system. So a new card with additional plugs may be called for, or a new-generation external sound processor that can plug into the USB slot may be the solution.

HDMI output

In some cases you want to direct the content from your PC to a more suitable viewing device such as your big screen TV. That is best accomplished with an HDMI plug from the PC to the TV. If the PC does not have multiple outlets for video, you may need to get a graphics card that provides these outlets. If you do that, make sure the card has an HDMI plug. If you are lucky there will be one of these plugs present on the PC. An HDMI plug is shown in Figure 1.38.

FIGURE 1.38   HDMI plug

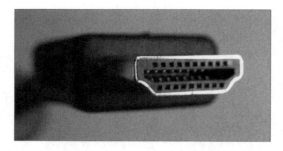

WIKIMEDIA COMMONS/ALEXEY GORAL

HTPC compact form factor

An HTPC that appears in the small form factor is one that is smaller in size and shape when compared to a regular PC while still providing the capabilities required. In some cases they are cubical in shape, and in other cases they resemble a DVR or mini audio receiver. Other changes to the layout include placing all ports in the front. An example is shown in Figure 1.39.

FIGURE 1.39   Compact form factor

WIKIMEDIA COMMONS/RICO SHEN

TV tuner

If you want to receive TV signals on the HTPC, you will need a TV tuner card. These can be installed internally in a slot or they can be external units connected with the USB port. They also can be analog, digital, or both (although broadcast analog TV has been discontinued in the United States since 2009). If recording the TV content is required, the card must also be a video capture card.

In cases where it is desired to watch one stream of content while recording another stream, a card that has two tuners in it must be used. These are called combo tuners.

Standard thick client

When discussing thin and thick clients, you should understand that a thick client is a PC that has all the capabilities of a standard PC. It runs all applications locally from its own hard drive. A thin client (discussed in the next section) is one that has minimal capabilities and runs the applications (and perhaps even the operating system itself) from a remote server.

Desktop applications

A thick client has the applications installed locally and will need to have sufficient resources to support the applications. Applications state these requirements in the documentation. With a thick client, since all application support will come from the local machine, these requirements must be met to use the software.

Meets recommended requirements for running Windows

A standard thick client will need to provide all the hardware requirements of the installed operating system. This is because unlike the thin client (discussed in the next section) none of the processing will be offloaded to a server. It all must be supplied by the thick client. Requirements for various operating systems are covered in Chapter 6, "Operating Systems."

Thin client

A thin client is a PC with minimal resources. Such a system is only responsible for receiving the processed output of an operating system and application running on a server and rendering the output in the screen.

The latest example of this is a computer running the Windows Thin PC (WinTPC) operating system, which is designed to run on older hardware.

Basic applications

Some applications are created to function in a client–server architecture. When these are used in a thin client, the client side of the application operates on the thin client but requires minimal system resources. The server side of the application performs all the processing, and the client side simply renders the output to the display and transmits keystrokes to the server.

Meets minimum requirements for running Windows

Even thin client operating systems have minimum requirements. Follow the documented requirements to ensure good performance. In many cases older computers that are of no use as thick clients are suitable candidates to be thin clients.

Home Server PC

Many homes and small offices have a network of computers to rival a small enterprise. In these cases, sometimes it makes sense to centralize the location of resources for both ease of use and security of information. There are even home server operating systems made, but that is not required to make a PC a home server. In this section some common roles of a home server are discussed.

Media streaming

The home server can act as a streaming media server to other computers in the home network if the operating system provides this capability. An example of such an operating system is Windows Home Server. Once the streaming feature is enabled, other systems can use their Windows Media Players to connect to any shared content and stream that content to the other PC. One of the benefits of this is centralized storage of the content and reduced duplication of the content on other machines in the network. This type of server should have plenty of disk space and memory.

File sharing

For the same reasons that centralized storage of media content reduces content duplication in the network, so can file sharing from a home server. Another great benefit of this is a central location to perform regular backups of the files so that this does not need to be done on all the other machines in the network. This server should have plenty of disk space.

Print sharing

Centralized control of printing can also be done with a home server. The machine can be the print server for all home printers. When done this way, printer permissions can be used to control who does what to the printers as well as whose print jobs get priority in a crunch. Print servers needs extra memory.

Gigabit NIC

When a machine is acting as the home server for all of these functions, the network card will be busy. For that reason it is probably a good idea to ensure that it is a gigabit NIC, which allows it to operate 10 times faster than the standard 100 MB NIC. Make sure that the cabling supports 1 GB, or you will be wasting your time and money.

RAID array

To speed the access to data or to provide fault tolerance to any data stored on the home server, consider using multiple hard drives and implementing a RAID 0, RAID 1, or RAID 5 hard disk system. See the section "RAID Types."

Exam Essentials

Describe the specific requirements of specialty workstations.   These include but are not limited to graphic, CAD, CAM, audio/video editing, virtualization, gaming, home theater, and home server systems.

Identify the difference between a thick and a thin client.   A thick client runs the operating system and applications from the local hard drive, whereas a thin client runs these components from a remote server.

1.10 Given a scenario, evaluate types and features of display devices

The possibilities for displaying the content from a PC used to consist of two options, cathode ray tube (CRT) technology found in television sets or the liquid crystal display (LCD) technology found on all laptop, notebook, and palmtop computers. That is no longer the case. Now this output can be directed to a number of different devices employing several technologies. In this section those options are discussed. The topics addressed in objective 1.9 include:

- Types
- Refresh rates
- Resolution
- Native resolution
- Brightness/lumens
- Analog vs. digital
- Privacy/antiglare filters
- Multiple displays

Types

Today, users need to redirect the content from the PC to other devices besides the regular monitor. Even within the monitor category, various technologies are employed to present content to a user from a computer device. In this section, devices to which computer content may be directed are discussed, along with competing technologies for rendering the content.

CRT

Now disappearing from the scene as quickly as the floppy drive, the cathode ray tube (CRT) is the original monitor type widely used since the 1970s.

In a CRT an electron gun shoots electrons toward the back of the monitor screen (see Figure 1.40). The back of the screen is coated with chemicals (called phosphors) that glow when electrons strike them. This beam of electrons scans the monitor from left to right and top to bottom to create the image.

FIGURE 1.40   CRT

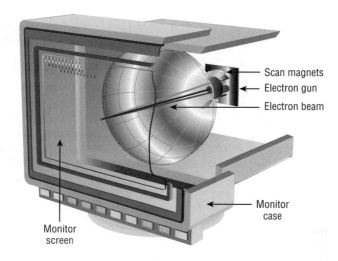

An image formed this way is called a raster. Rasterizing an image consists of determining the color and brightness of each pixel in a rectangular array and transmitting that information to the output device in a linear sequence, scanning left to right and top to bottom.

CRTs require more space than their LCD, LED, or plasma counterparts, and CRTs must be disposed of carefully because they contain heavy metals.

LCD

Liquid crystal displays (LCDs) have almost completely replaced CRTs as the default display type for both laptops and desktops. Two major types of liquid crystal displays (LCDs) are used today: active matrix screens and passive matrix screens. Their main differences lie in the quality of the image. Both types use some kind of lighting behind the LCD panel to make the screen easier to view. One or more small fluorescent tubes are used to backlight the screen.

Passive matrix   A passive matrix screen uses a row of transistors across the top of the screen and a column of them down the side. It sends pulses to each pixel at the intersection of each row and column combination, telling it what to display. Passive matrix displays are becoming obsolete because they're less bright and have poorer refresh rates and image quality than active matrix displays. However, they use less power than active matrix displays do.

Active matrix   An active matrix screen uses a separate transistor for each individual pixel in the display, resulting in higher refresh rates and brighter display quality. These screens use more power, however, because of the increased number of transistors that must be powered. Almost all notebook PCs today use active matrix. A variant called thin-film transistor (TFT) uses multiple transistors per pixel, resulting in even better display quality.

LED

LED-based monitors are still LCDs (they still use liquid crystals to express images onscreen), but they use a different type of backlight than what is normally used. Several types of backlights are used with LED. The most common for computers is white LEDs (WLED). Using a special diffuser, the light is spread to cover the entire screen.

A more expensive type is RGB LED. Instead of using white LEDs on one edge of the screen, with RGB LCD layers, like the previous technology, RGB LEDs are aligned all over the panel matrix.

Each LED is capable of red-, green-, or blue-colored light. This gives the display more accurate color than WLEDs.

Finally there is WLED on a flat array, covering the entire screen (like an RGB LED using only white LEDs). Currently, it's only used in LED-backlit HDTVs. As you've seen, however, computer output can be directed to the HDTV screen.

Plasma

Plasma displays utilize small cells containing ionized gases, similar to what is used in fluorescent lamps. They have the advantage of high-quality picture, wider viewing angles, and less motion blur—but they have the disadvantage of screen burn-in and high energy requirements.

They have mainly been used for TV displays but now can be purchased simply as display monitors that accept output from a variety of devices, including PCs.

Projector

In the business world it is frequently necessary to share the desktop with others in a meeting. This is easily accomplished by directing the output of the PC to a projector. The projector can be plugged into the same connector as the monitor, and in most cases both can be used at the same time. Some projectors require an HDMI connector.

OLED

Organic light-emitting diode technology uses a layer of organic compound with emissive electroluminescent qualities to emit light in response to an electric current. This organic layer resides between two electrodes. Although it uses no backlight, it results in a higher contrast ratio than an LCD in low-light conditions.

This technology is currently very expensive, and the materials used have a limited lifespan. As of this writing, this LED technology was very expensive, with 17-inch models running close to $5,000.

Refresh rates

A monitor's refresh rate specifies how many times in one second the scanning beam of electrons redraws the screen. The phosphors stay bright for only a fraction of a second, so they must constantly be hit with electrons to stay lit. Given in draws per second, or hertz (Hz), the refresh rate affects how much energy is being put into keeping the screen lit. Most people notice a flicker in the display at refresh rates of 75 Hz or lower because the phosphors begin to decay to black before they're revived; increasing the refresh rate can help reduce eyestrain by reducing the flickering. CRTs experienced a refresh flicker that was often visible to the naked eye. This is no longer a problem with newer LCD monitors.

Resolution

The resolution of a monitor is the number of horizontal and vertical pixels that are displayed. Most monitors allow for two or more resolutions, and you can pick the one to use in the desktop settings of the operating system. On a CRT the vertical hold (V-hold) setting can be tweaked to make the image appear properly in the monitor.

Display resolutions include the following:

VGA   Video graphics array is a 320×200 resolution and uses analog technology.

XGA   Extended graphics array has been around since 1990. It's a 1,024×768 resolution that offers fixed-function hardware acceleration for 2D tasks.

SXGA+   Super extended graphics array is a 1,400× 1,050 resolution commonly used on 14- or 15-inch laptops. It's typically considered the maximum resolution that video projectors will work with.

UXGA   Ultra extended graphics array is a 1,600×1,200 resolution and is the next step in the monitor-resolution evolution.

WUXGA   Widescreen ultra-extended graphics array is a resolution of 1,920×1,200 with a 16:10 screen aspect ratio. It's also a standard for use with television sets, at a slightly different ratio.

Native resolution

The native resolution of a display refers to its single fixed resolution. An LCD display cannot change resolution to match the signal being displayed as a CRT monitor can, meaning that optimal display quality can be reached only when the signal input matches the native resolution. Most LCD monitors are able to inform the PC of their native resolution.

Brightness/lumens

Contrast ratio is a measurement of the brightness of the LCD panels. A general rule of thumb is the greater the contrast ratio, the brighter the display can be, and thus a rating of 3,000:1 is preferred over 800:1.

You can adjust the brightness by using the controls that are usually found on the front of the monitor, but keep in mind that these adjustments will be less refined than if you use a calibration program. Standard symbols are used to represent brightness; the location and operation of these controls varies from monitor to monitor. Use the documentation that came with your monitor.

Analog vs. digital

As described in the section "VGA vs. HDMI," VGA connections and cables are analog in nature, and HDMI and DVI are interfaces for transmitting encrypted uncompressed digital data.

CRT monitors require the signal information in analog. In those cases the video adaptor converts digital data into analog. DVI and HDMI maintain the information in digital format through the process with no need for conversion. Some DVI connectors will support both analog and digital.

Privacy/antiglare filters

Privacy and antiglare filters fit over the front of a display screen and either reduce the glare on the screen or, in the case of privacy filters, make it difficult if not impossible to read the monitor unless you are squarely in front of it, which helps to reduce eavesdropping or shoulder surfing. In situations where high-security information will be displayed on the desktop, a privacy filter may be called for. When the workstation is facing sunlight, an antiglare filter may be beneficial.

Multiple displays

Most PCs allow you to use multiple monitors as long as there is a display card installed for each. Although this can be useful for running a window for each monitor, one of the most common uses is the Presenter View in Microsoft PowerPoint. When chosen, this allows a different view of the slideshow to be shown on the main monitor (typically a projector) than what is shown on the secondary monitor (such as presenter notes, the next slide that is set to appear, and so forth). Multiple displays can present the same desktop on both displays (mirroring) or can be set up as a large single desktop, which is called extending the desktop. Multiple displays are beneficial in any cases where many windows or documents need to open at the same time, especially if copying and pasting may be called for between the windows.

Exam Essentials

Identify the common technologies used on devices that display computer output.   These include but are not limited to CRT, LCD, LED, plasma, and OLED displays. Projectors are included as well.

Describe the settings and characteristics of various display types.   Understand refresh rate, resolution, native resolution, and brightness.

Describe the differences between analog and digital display.   CRT monitors require the signal information in analog. In those cases the video adapter converts digital data into analog. DVI and HDMI maintain the information in digital format through the process with no need for conversion.

1.11 Identify connector types and associated cables

A wide variety of connector types and cables are used to hook together the parts and pieces of a PC system. Many have already been covered, and in this section, those that have been covered are briefly reviewed and others are discussed for the first time. The topics addressed in objective 1.11 include:

- Display connector types
- Display cable types
- Device connectors and various connector pin-outs
- Device cable types

Display connector types

Connecting the monitor to the PC can be accomplished with many different connector types. In this section, for those types that have been covered earlier, a reference to the section discussing them will be provided.

DVI-D

DVI connectors can come in several forms. You may remember that DVI can sometimes do analog and digital at the same time. DVI-D (D stands for digital) connectors supply digital signals only. These can also come in a single- or dual-link format. A dual-link format allows provision for a second data link.

DVI-I

A DVI-I connector (I stands for integrated) has pins that can provide analog and digital. These can also come in a single- or dual-link format.

DVI-A

A DVI-A connector (A stands for analog) has pins that can provide analog and digital. This type comes in a single-link format only. The various types of DVI plugs discussed in this section are shown in Figure 1.41.

FIGURE 1.41   DVI connectors

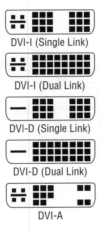

DisplayPort

DisplayPort is a digital interface standard produced by the Video Electronics Standards Association (VESA), used for audio and video. The interface is primarily used to connect a video source to a display device such as a computer monitor or television set. It resembles a USB connector (see Figure 1.42).

RCA

RCA plugs are sometimes used for audio and video in the same way that mini TRS connectors are (see the "Audio" section of "Other connector types"). They are nearly the same size but look quite different. A set of these connectors is shown in Figure 1.43.

HD-15 (i.e. DE-15 or DB-15)

The DB-15 plug is the standard VGA plug that has been around since the earliest displays. It was discussed in the section "Serial" in "Other connector types." An example is shown in Figure 1.44.

FIGURE 1.42   DisplayPort

WIKIMEDIA COMMONS/BELKIN

FIGURE 1.43   RCA plugs

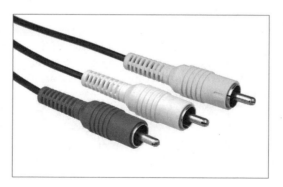

WIKIMEDIA COMMONS/EVAN-AMOS

FIGURE 1.44   DB-15

WIKIMEDIA COMMONS/EVAN-AMOS

BNC

Bayonet Neill–Concelman (BNC) connecters are sometimes used in the place of RCA connecters for video electronics, so you may encounter these connectors, especially when video equipment connects to a PC. In many cases you may be required to purchase an adapter to convert this to another form of connection, as it is rare to find one on the PC. Figure 1.45 shows a male and female BNC connector.

FIGURE 1.45   BNC

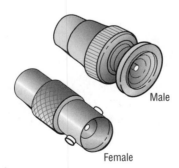

Male

Female

miniHDMI

The miniHDMI is a small form factor version of HDMI. It is intended for portable devices such as a camcorder. Cables that are made to connect a portable device to a PC will have a miniHDMI connector on one end and a standard HDMI (type A) connector on the other. A miniHDMI connector (type C) was shown in Figure 1.32.

RJ-45

A DVI or VGA to RJ-45 converter kit allows you to extend the length of the cable from source to monitor to 100 m (the normal limit in twisted pair cabling). Each end is plugged into a converter box and then an unshielded twisted pair (UTP) cable connects the two converter boxes.

miniDIN-6

MiniDIN connectors come with a number of different pin arrangements and are used in various applications. A 6-pin version, miniDIN-6, is used to connect to some projectors and speaker systems. When connecting those devices to the PC, you may encounter this plug. As with the BNC connector, you may require a converter to a connection type that exists on the PC, such as USB. A 6-pin miniDIN is shown in Figure 1.46.

FIGURE 1.46   6-pin miniDIN

Display cable types

Cables must match the connector. In this section a quick survey of the cables that go with the various connectors is provided.

HDMI

HDMI cables are rated by the resolution they can provide. Category 2 (also called high speed) provides better resolution than Category 1. These also differ in acceptable length. Category 1 is best at 5 meters whereas Category 2 can be up to 15 meters.

DVI

When purchasing DVI cables, you should make note of the connector type that exists on the PC. The cable connector must be the same type as the PC. Review the section "Display connector types."

VGA

VGA cables are quite common and come in lengths up to 50 feet. They have a HD-15 (or DB-15a) female connector on one end and a DB-15 male connector on the other.

Component

Component video is a video signal that has been split into two or more component channels. It is transmitted or stored as three separate signals. There will typically be three color-coded plugs on the cable that connect to the same color plug on the PC or the video device.

Composite

Composite video combines the signal into one line-level signal, so there is one plug on the connector, usually an RCA plug.

S-video

Separate video (S-video) is an analog video transmission scheme, in which video information is encoded on two channels. This separation results in a higher-quality video than composite video (one channel), but not as high as component video, in which it is encoded on three channels. S-video cables use a 4-pin version of the miniDIN, much like the miniDIN-6.

RGB

RGB cables are used with component video. There are three plugs in the cable, one for each of the channels that it uses. See the section "Component."

Coaxial

When BNC cables are used, the cable type will be coaxial. See the BNC section in "Display connector types."

Ethernet

When making use of a DVI or VGA to RJ-45 converter kit, the cable that is used to connect the two converter boxes will be Ethernet UTP or STP. See the section RJ-45 in "Display connector types."

Device connectors and various connector pin-outs

As with display connectors, there are a wide variety of connector types for the other devices in the PC. This includes internal devices as well as peripherals. In this section, the most common connectors are discussed along with the pin-outs. In many cases the number of pins and their arrangement is the only way to differentiate two connecter types with common form factors. In cases where the connector has been discussed earlier, a reference is provided to the section where the connector was discussed.

SATA

Internal SATA storage devices have a 7-pin data connection and a 15-pin power connection. Those connections sit next to one another on the SATA device, as shown in Figure 1.47.

FIGURE 1.47 SATA connections

WIKIMEDIA COMMONS/BAS BLOEMSAAT

eSATA

External SATA devices use receptacles rarely found in PCs as of this writing. An 8-pin eSATA connector is shown next to an internal SATA connector in Figure 1.48.

FIGURE 1.48 eSATA connections

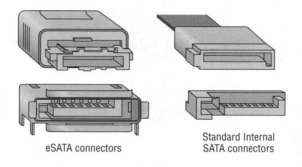

eSATA connectors

Standard Internal
SATA connectors

PATA

Parallel ATA (PATA) uses either 40-pin or 80-pin connectors located on a ribbon cable inside the box. The 80-pin version appeared with the advent of Ultra-DMA. There are three on the cable: one that connects to the motherboard, and two for devices. Figure 1.49 shows a pair of PATA connectors on the motherboard.

IDE

IDE is discussed in the section "Internal SATA, IDE, and SCSI."

EIDE

Enhanced IDE (EIDE) is the enhanced version of IDE technology, and it supports faster access to the hard disks. It uses the same connector as IDE (PATA).

FIGURE 1.49   PATA connectors

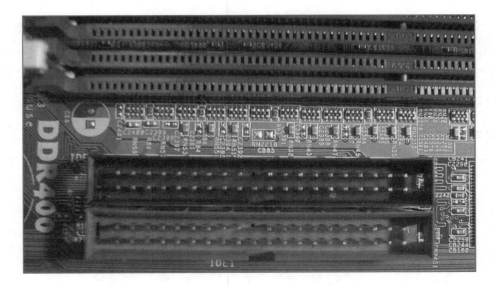

WIKIMEDIA COMMONS/ME-

Floppy

Though rarely seen anymore, the floppy drive connects to the motherboard with a ribbon cable like IDE drives (a separate cable). The connector looks much like the IDE connectors except that there are 34 pins instead of 40 (or 80), making it slightly smaller. When present, they are usually right next to IDE connecters in the motherboard. The pin-out of the 34-pin connecter is shown in Figure 1.50.

FIGURE 1.50   34-pin floppy cable

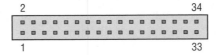

USB

USB connectors are discussed in the section "Front panel connectors."

IEEE 1394

IEEE 1394 (FireWire) is discussed in the section "FireWire cards," and the connectors on the PC are shown in Figure 1.28.

SCSI

Small Computer System Interface (SCSI) is discussed in the section "Internal SATA, IDE, and SCSI." There have been many SCSI connectors used. Some SCSI interfaces use a connector similar to the 36-pin connector used by Centronics for the parallel interface on printers. This 50-pin micro ribbon connector became popularly known as Centronics SCSI, or CN-50. Most parallel SCSI disk drives now utilize an 80-pin single connector attachment (SCA) connector or a 68-pin connector. In Figure 1.51 the top SCSI drive has an 80-pin connector and the bottom SCSI drive has a 68-pin connector.

FIGURE 1.51   SCSI connectors

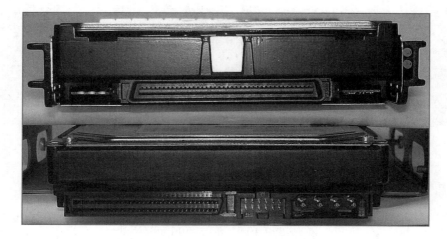

WIKIMEDIA COMMONS/ALI@GWC.ORG.UK

PS/2

Though rarely used anymore, some PCs may still have a PS-2 connector for the mouse and the keyboard. These have been replaced for the most part with USB mice and keyboards. The PS-2 connecters are shown in Figure 1.52.

Parallel

Parallel connecters transmit data 8 bits at a time. PATA connectors are parallel. Another connector type that operates in this fashion is printer cables (although many printers are switching to USB). A parallel printer connector (DB-25) is shown in Figure 1.53.

Serial

Serial connectors transmit one bit at a time. The two most common serial connectors found on the PC are the DB-15 and the DB-9. The DB-15 has 15 pins like the VGA connector, but the 15 pins are arranged in two rows rather than three. The DB-9 (shown in Figure 1.54) is used to connect legacy serial devices such as external modems. A DB-15 was shown in Figure 1.44.

FIGURE 1.52   PS/2

FIGURE 1.53   Printer connector

FIGURE 1.54   DB-9

Audio

TRS audio connectors were discussed in the section "Audio" and shown in Figure 1.35. RCA connectors were covered in the section "RCA" and shown in Figure 1.43.

RJ-45

RJ-45 connectors were discussed in the section "RJ-45" and the connector was shown in Figure 1.36, next to an RJ-11 port.

Device cable types

Cables must match the connector. In this section, a quick survey of the cables that go with the various connectors is provided.

SATA

Internal SATA storage devices have 7-pin data cables and a 15-pin power cable. SATA data cable is shown in Figure 1.55.

eSATA

eSATA cables may be either flat or round and can only be 2 meters in length. An eSATA connector was shown in Figure 1.48.

IDE

IDE cables are ribbon cables with the three plugs as described in the section on IDE. A ribbon cable is shown in Figure 1.56.

EIDE

EIDE devices use the same cable as IDE, shown in Figure 1.56.

Floppy

Floppy drives use a ribbon cable that looks the same as the cable for IDE in Figure 1.56. It has 34 pins, however, making it slightly narrower in width.

FIGURE 1.55   SATA data cable

FIGURE 1.56   Ribbon cable

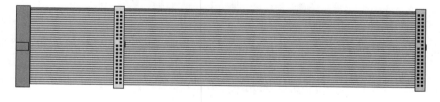

WIKIMEDIA COMMONS/WEREON

USB

USB cables are discussed in the section "USB 1.1 vs. 2.0 vs. 3.0 speed and distance characteristics" and the micro and mini versions are displayed in Figure 1.27.

IEEE 1394

IEEE 1394 (FireWire) is discussed in the section "FireWire 400 vs. FireWire 800 speed and distance characteristics." The cables look very much like USB cables.

SCSI

SCSI cables are ribbon cables when they are inside the case but are round cables for external SCSI. The ribbons look much like those of IDE and floppy drives, with the difference being there are many more connectors on the cable. The external cables are round and are limited to a length determined by the type of SCSI in use. They range from 1.5 to 25 meters in length.

68 pin vs. 50 pin vs. 25 pin

When buying SCSI cables, it important to recognize the three most common types of connecters. They come in 68-pin (HD-68), 50- pin (DB-50), and 25-pin (DB-25) designs. Make sure you know what you need for the drives you are using.

Parallel

The maximum length of the parallel printer cable is 15 feet. The cable is round with a Centronics connector on one end and a male DB-25 on the other end. The Centronics connector plugs into the print device and the DB-25 into the PC.

Serial

Serial cables are used to connect a legacy serial device such as a modem to the DB-9 serial connector that is present on most PCs. It can be no longer than 15 feet (see Figure 1.57).

FIGURE 1.57   DB-9 serial cable

WIKIMEDIA COMMONS/MOBIUS

Ethernet

Ethernet cables are used for networking and to connect converter boxes together to lengthen the allowable cable run for a DVI or VGA connection. They use twisted pair cabling that cannot exceed 100 meters in length. Figure 1.58 shows two of the four pairs contained in a twisted pair cable.

FIGURE 1.58 Twisted pair cabling

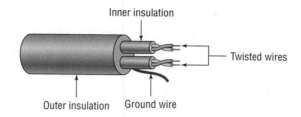

Phone

Phone cabling is used to connect a modem to a PC. It uses an RJ-11 connector but uses a flatter cable. The RJ-11 connector is also noticeably smaller than the RJ-45.

Exam Essentials

Identify display connectors, their associated cables, and the maximum cable lengths. This includes but is not limited to DVI in all variants, DisplayPort, RCA, HD-15 (or DB-15), BNC, miniHDMI, RJ-45, and miniDIN-6.

Identify other device connectors, their associated cables, and the maximum cable lengths. This includes but is not limited to SATA, eSATA, PATA, floppy, USB, IEEE 1394, SCSI, PS/2, parallel, serial, audio, and RJ-45,

1.12 Install and configure various peripheral devices

Installing devices is much easier today than it was at one time. In most cases the device is detected and set up for you by the operating system as soon as you plug it in. In this section, any deviations from that are discussed along with any special issues related to a particular device type.

Input devices

Input devices allow you to communicate with the PC either by clicking on an item or typing on the keyboard. This category also includes devices that allow you to import information into the system in other ways. In this section, the installation of each device is discussed.

Mouse

Mice are typically USB devices these days and require you only to plug them in; in moments they are functional. In some rare cases (especially for a mouse with special capabilities), you may need to install a driver for the mouse. These types typically have a CD you can access that will install those drivers for you.

Keyboard

Keyboards can be treated the same as mice. Follow the guidelines in the section on mice.

Touch screen

Touch-screen monitors allow you to interact with the screen instead of using the mouse. These monitors may require installing a driver to function. Use the CD that comes with the device to install the driver. Touch screens also require calibration. Most vendors include calibration software with the installation disc.

Scanner

Scanners are used to convert paper documents or photographs to digital files so they can be stored on a PC and transmitted as files across the network. The installation process is much like a print device. Because so many of these now are USB, plugging them in will install the driver. In cases where that does not work (usually when it is a very new model and the operating system is older), use the installation disc to install the driver.

Barcode reader

Barcode readers read and input codes used to identify products. They are used in warehouses and at retail checkouts. Once you plug the device into either the serial or the USB connector, you need to install the software that comes with the reader. Use the installation disc that comes with the reader.

KVM

A keyboard, video, and mouse (KVM) device allows you to plug multiple PCs (usually servers) into the device and to switch easily back and forth from system to system using the same mouse, monitor, and keyboard. The KVM is actually a switch that all of the systems plug into. There is usually no software to install. Just turn off all the systems, plug them all into the switch, and turn them back on; then you can switch from one to another using the same keyboard, monitor, and mouse device connected to the KVM switch.

Microphone

Microphones are very simple to install. Typically all you do is plug them into the mini TRS connector. There are usually two of these: one for headphones (or speakers) and the other for a microphone (or line in). In some systems you may be prompted to specify the mic or line in when you plug in a headset. A 3.5 mm plug is shown in Figure 1.35 in the section "Audio."

Biometric devices

Biometric devices allow for inputting information used to authenticate or identify a user to the system. That input may be a retina scan or a fingerprint, for example. Use the installation disc that comes with the device. In most cases you should install the software before you plug in the device (usually USB). During the installation process of the software, at some point you will be told to connect the device. Follow the instructions.

Game pads

You may begin to notice a pattern. Game pads are also usually USB and install in the same way as biometric devices and barcode readers. Install the software and connect the device when instructed. One additional thing you may need to do with the game pad is to calibrate it. Once it's installed, locate the device in Control Panel in the correct section (usually Game Controllers), open the properties of the device, and click the option Calibrate. Follow the instructions. This will make it operate correctly. Some game pads require a DB-15 serial port, as shown in Figure 1.59.

Joysticks

Joysticks use the same guidelines and instructions as game pads.

Digitizer

Digitizers are pad-like devices that allow you to write and draw on the pad and input that to a digital file. Treat the installation of these devices in the same way as the other devices in this section. Install the software first and connect the digitizer when instructed to do so.

FIGURE 1.59   DB-15 game port

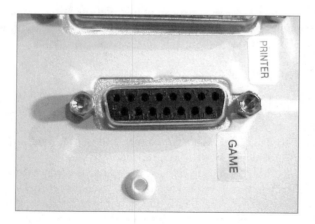

Multimedia devices

Connecting multimedia devices to the PC is less of an installation process and more of a case of just locating the correct place to plug them in. In this section we'll talk about connecting these devices and, where appropriate, installing the software.

Digital cameras

Digital cameras usually connect to the PC with a USB cable. In many cases, the operating system comes with software that may detect the camera and assist you in accessing the pictures and moving them to the computer. In other instances, you may want to install software that came with the camera. Doing so will often allow you to take fuller advantage of the features the camera offers. SD cards can be used to transfer images from the camera if a cable is not available.

Microphone

Follow the instructions in the earlier section "Input devices." In some cases, the connector on the microphone may not be one that is present on the PC. You may be able to purchase a converter to match the input on the PC.

Webcam

First install the software that came with the webcam (sound familiar?) and then connect the webcam to the USB port when instructed. If the webcam has been out for some time and the operating system is new, it may be possible to just plug in the camera and let the operating system set it up.

Camcorder

Treat camcorders like cameras for the purpose of installation. If the camcorder is an older analog model, you will need to install a signal digitizer. If you have a TV tuner card present, it can perform the conversion.

MIDI-enabled devices

Musical Instrument Digital Interface (MIDI) is an industry specification for encoding, storing, synchronizing, and transmitting musical performance information, basically allowing you to digitally record a musical instrument.

The MIDI controller (usually a keyboard) connects to the PC using MIDI cables, which use a 5-pin DIN connector. Since most computers don't have these, you may need to buy a MIDI-to-USB converter cable. Some specialized sound cards come with a MIDI port.

To use the controller, you install the software and then connect the MIDI device. The software will install the driver for the device. Once that is taken care of, install the recording software of choice. If the installation of the device went correctly, the recording software should recognize the MIDI controller and allow you to record from it.

Output devices

Output devices allow you to print, listen to, or view information from the PC. The installation of these devices is remarkably like that of input devices.

Printers

Printers and their installation are covered in Chapter 4, "Printers."

Speakers

Installing speakers is more a matter of connecting them properly than installing them. Usually one of the speakers will connect to a power source and the other will connect to the powered speaker. Once they are connected to a power source, connect the speaker cable to the proper plug in the PC. These plugs will be marked with icons that indicate which is for a microphone and which is for speakers.

Display devices

Before connecting or disconnecting a monitor, ensure that the power to both the PC and the monitor is off. Then, connect a VGA (DB-15) cable from the monitor to the PC's video card, and connect the monitor's power cord to an AC outlet. If a better connection is available (DVI, for example), use it.

Although these devices are slowly being replaced by LED and LCD displays, you should know how to handle older CRT devices. Other than the power supply, one of the most dangerous components to try to repair is the CRT monitor. To avoid the extremely hazardous environment contained inside the monitor—it can retain a high-voltage charge for hours after it has been turned off—take it to a certified monitor technician or television repair shop. The repair shop or certified technician will know the proper procedures to discharge the monitor, which involves attaching a resistor to the flyback transformer's charging capacitor to release the high-voltage electrical charge that builds up during use. They will also be able to determine whether the monitor can be repaired or needs to be replaced. Remember, the monitor works in its own extremely protective environment (the monitor case) and may not respond well to your desire to try to open it. The CRT is a large vacuum tube. Be extremely careful when handling it—if you break the glass, the CRT will implode, which can send glass in any direction. In most cases it is not cost effective to repair one of these monitors.

If you have to open a monitor, you must first discharge the high-voltage charge on it using a high-voltage probe. This probe has a large needle, a gauge that indicates volts, and a wire with an alligator clip. Attach the alligator clip to a ground (usually the round pin on the power cord). Slip the probe needle under the high-voltage cup on the monitor. You'll see the gauge spike to around 15,000 volts and slowly reduce to zero. When it reaches zero, you may remove the high-voltage probe and service the high-voltage components of the monitor.

Exam Essentials

Describe the basic steps to install peripheral devices.   In most cases you should install the software that came with the device and at the proper time during that installation follow the instructions to plug in the peripheral. In some rare cases, you may need to manually install the driver.

Describe the danger involved in handling CRT monitors.   Other than the power supply, one of the most dangerous components to try to repair is the CRT monitor. In most cases, it is not cost effective to repair one of these monitors.

Review Questions

1. List at least three items that can be configured through the BIOS setup program.

2. What is purpose of the POST test when the PC starts up?

3. What value is used to define the relationship between the bus speed and CPU speed?

4. The _____ is the set of controller chips that monitors and directs the traffic on the motherboard between the buses.

5. What is the name of the connector used to supply power to fans?

6. What is the purpose of the parity bit in memory?

7. What is the common name used for expansion cards that follow the IEEE 1394 standard?

8. What is the capacity of a CD-ROM?

9. True/False: Four devices can be placed in an IDE ribbon cable.

10. What type of cable is used for a floppy drive?

Chapter

2

Networking

COMPTIA A+ EXAM OBJECTIVES COVERED IN THIS CHAPTER:

✓ **2.1 Identify types of network cables and connectors.**

- Fiber
    - Connectors: SC, ST and LC
- Twisted Pair
    - Connectors: RJ-11, RJ-45
    - Wiring Standards: T568A, T568B
- Coaxial
    - Connectors: BNC, F-connector

✓ **2.2 Categorize characteristics of connectors and cabling.**

- Fiber
    - Types (single-mode vs. multi-mode)
    - Speed and transmission limitations
- Twisted Pair
    - Types: STP, UTP, CAT3, CAT5, CAT5e, CAT6, plenum, PVC
    - Speed and transmission limitations
- Coaxial
    - Types: RG-6, RG-59
    - Speed and transmission limitations

✓ **2.3 Explain properties and characteristics of TCP/IP.**

- IP class
    - Class A
    - Class B
    - Class C

- IPv4 vs. IPv6
- Public vs. private vs. APIPA
- Static vs. dynamic
- Client-side DNS
- DHCP
- Subnet mask
- Gateway

✓ **2.4 Explain common TCP and UDP ports, protocols, and their purpose.**

- Ports
  - 21—FTP
  - 23—TELNET
  - 25—SMTP
  - 53—DNS
  - 80—HTTP
  - 110—POP3
  - 143—IMAP
  - 443—HTTPS
  - 3389—RDP
- Protocols
  - DHCP
  - DNS
  - LDAP
  - SNMP
  - SMB
  - SSH
  - SFTP
- TCP vs. UDP

✓ **2.5 Compare and contrast wireless network standards and encryption types.**

- Standards
  - 802.11 a/b/g/n
    - Speeds, distances, and frequencies
  - Encryption types
    - WEP, WPA, WAP2, TKIP, AES

✓ **2.6 Install, configure, and deploy a SOHO wireless/wired router using appropriate settings.**

- MAC filtering
- Channels (1–11)
- Port forwarding, port triggering
- SSID broadcast (on/off)
- Wireless encryption
- Firewall
- DHCP (on/off)
- DMZ
- NAT
- WPS
- Basic QoS

✓ **2.7 Compare and contrast Internet connection types and features.**

- Cable
- DSL
- Dial-up
- Fiber
- Satellite
- ISDN
- Cellular (mobile hotspot)
- Line of sight wireless internet service
- WiMAX

✓ **2.8 Identify various types of networks.**

- LAN
- WAN
- PAN
- MAN
- Topologies
  - Mesh
  - Ring
  - Bus
  - Star
  - Hybrid

✓ **2.9 Compare and contrast network devices and their functions and features.**

- Hub
- Switch
- Router
- Access point
- Bridge
- Modem
- NAS
- Firewall
- VoIP phones
- Internet appliance

✓ **2.10 Given a scenario, use appropriate networking tools.**

- Crimper
- Multimeter
- Toner probe
- Cable tester
- Loopback plug
- Punchdown tool

CompTIA offers a number of other exams and certifications on networking (Network+, Server+, and so on), but to become A+ certified, you must have good knowledge of basic networking skills. Not only do you need to know the basics of cabling and connectors, but you also need to know how to configure a Small Office Home Office (SOHO) network and use some basic tools. There are 10 objectives for this domain, and it constitutes 27 percent of the exam.

2.1 Identify types of network cables and connectors

You're expected to know the basic concepts of networking as well as the different types of cabling that can be used. For the latter, you should be able to identify connectors and cables from figures even if those figures are crude line art (think shadows) appearing in pop-up boxes.

There are three specific types of network cables, and the connectors associated with each, that you must know for this exam: fiber, twisted pair, and coaxial. Fiber is the most expensive of the three and can run the longest distance. A number of types of connectors can work with fiber, but three you must know are SC, ST, and LC.

Twisted pair is commonly used in office settings to connect workstations to hubs or switches. It comes in two varieties: unshielded (UTP) and shielded (STP). The two types of connectors commonly used are RJ-11 (four wires and popular with telephones), and RJ-45 (eight wires and used with xBaseT networks—100BaseT, 1000BaseT, and so forth). Two common wiring standards are T568A and T568B.

Coaxial cabling is not as popular as it once was, but it's still used with cable television and some legacy networks. The two most regularly used connectors are F-connectors (television cabling) and BNC (10Base2, and so on).

Fiber

Fiber-optic cabling is the most expensive type of those discussed for this exam. Although it's an excellent medium, it's often not used because of the cost of implementing it. It has a glass core within a rubber outer coating and uses beams of light rather than electrical signals to relay data (see Figure 2.1). Because light doesn't diminish over distance the way electrical signals do, this cabling can run for distances measured in kilometers with transmission speeds from 100 Mbps up to 1 Gbps or higher.

FIGURE 2.1   Fiber-optic cable

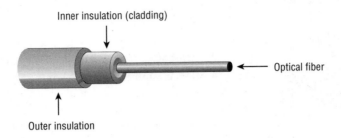

Inner insulation (cladding)

Optical fiber

Outer insulation

Connectors: SC, ST, and LC

Often, fiber is used to connect runs to wiring closets where they break out into UTP or other cabling types, or as other types of backbones. Fiber-optic cable can use either ST, SC, or LC connectors. ST is a barrel-shaped connector, whereas SC is squared and easier to connect in small spaces. The LC connector looks similar to SC but adds a flange on the top (much like an RJ-45 connector) to keep it securely connected. Figure 2.2 shows the fiber connectors.

FIGURE 2.2   Fiber connectors   ST, SC, and LC

ST   SC   LC

In addition to these listed in the A+ objectives, other connectors are used with fiber. FC connectors may also be used but are not as common. MT-RJ is a popular connector for two fibers in a small form factor.

Twisted Pair

There are two primary types of twisted-pair cabling (with categories beneath each that are addressed in the following section, "2.2 Categorize characteristics of connectors and cabling"): shielded twisted pair (STP) and unshielded twisted pair (UTP). In both cases, the cabling is made up of pairs of wires twisted around each other, as shown in Figure 2.3.

FIGURE 2.3   Twisted-pair cable

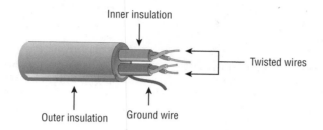

UTP offers no shielding (hence the name) and is the network cabling type most prone to outside interference. The interference can be from a fluorescent light ballast, electrical motor, or other such source (known as *electromagnetic interference* [EMI]) or from wires being too close together and signals jumping across them (known as *crosstalk*). STP adds a foil shield around the twisted wires to protect against EMI.

Connectors: RJ-11, RJ-45

STP cable uses IBM data connector (IDC) or universal data connector (UDC) ends and connects to token ring networks. While you need to know STP for the exam, you are not required to have any knowledge of the connectors associated with it. You must, however, know that most UTP cable uses RJ-45 connectors, which look like telephone connectors (RJ-11) but have eight wires instead of four. Figure 2.4 shows both RJ-45 (left) and RJ-11 (right) connectors.

FIGURE 2.4   RJ-11 and RJ-45 connectors

WIKIMEDIA COMMONS/ANDREWA

Wiring standards: T568A, T568B

Two wiring standards are commonly used with twisted-pair cabling: T568A and T568B (sometimes referred to simply as 568A and 568B). These are telecommunications standards from TIA and EIA that specify the pin arrangements for the RJ-45 connectors on UTP or STP cables. The number 568 refers to the order in which the wires within the Category 5 cable are terminated and attached to the connector. The signal is identical for both.

T568A was the first standard, released in 1991. Ten years later, in 2001, T568B was released. Figure 2.5 shows the pin number assignments for the 568A and 568B standards. Pin numbers are read left to right, with the connector tab facing down. Notice that the pin-outs stay the same, and the only difference is in the color coding of the wiring.

 Mixing cables can cause communication problems on the network. Before installing a network or adding a new component to it, make sure the cable being used is in the correct wiring standard.

FIGURE 2.5   Pin assignments for T568A and T568B

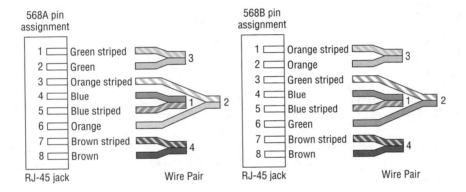

Coaxial

Coaxial cable, or *coax*, is one of the oldest media used in networks. Coax is built around a center conductor or core that is used to carry data from point to point. The center conductor has an insulator wrapped around it, a shield over the insulator, and a nonconductive sheath around the shielding. This construction, depicted in Figure 2.6, allows the conducting core to be relatively free from outside interference. The shielding also prevents the conducting core from emanating signals externally from the cable.

 Before you read any further, accept the fact that the odds are incredibly slim that you will ever need to know about coax for a new installation in the real world (with the possible exception of RG-6, which is used from the wall to a cable modem). If you do come across it, it will be in an existing installation and one of the first things you'll recommend is that it be changed. That said, you do need to know about coax for this exam.

FIGURE 2.6   Coaxial cable construction

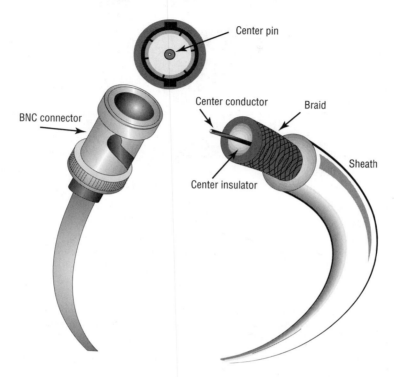

Connectors: BNC, F-connector

Connections to a coax occur through a wide variety of connectors, often referred to as *plumbing*. These connectors provide a modular design that allows for easy expansion. The three primary connections used in this case are the T-connector, the inline connector, and the terminating connector (also known as a *terminating resistor* or *terminator*). Figure 2.7 shows some of these common connectors in a coaxial cable–based network.

In addition to these, there are *F-connectors* (commonly called *F-type connectors*). These are screw-on connectors used to attach coaxial cable (including RG-59 and RG-6) to devices. They have a nut on the connection that provides something to grip as the connection is tightened by hand (or, if necessary, pliers to aid with disconnecting). F-connectors are most commonly associated with connecting Internet modems to cable or satellite Internet service provider (ISP) equipment. However, F-Type connectors are also used to connect to some proprietary peripherals.

FIGURE 2.7   Common BNC connectors

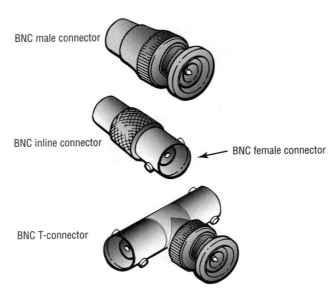

BNC male connector

BNC inline connector

BNC female connector

BNC T-connector

Coax supports both baseband and broadband signaling. *Baseband* signaling means that a single channel is carried through the coax, and *broadband* refers to multiple channels on the coax. Figure 2.8 illustrates this difference. Baseband signaling is similar in concept to a speaker wire. The speaker wire in your stereo connects one channel from the amplifier to the speaker. Broadband is similar to the cable TV connection in your home. The cable from the cable company carries hundreds of channels. Your TV set uses a tuner to select the channel you choose to watch.

In a coax network, some type of device must terminate all the coax ends. Figure 2.9 shows this termination process in more detail. Coax is present in many older networks and tends to provide reliable service once it's installed. However, if a terminator, NIC, T-connector, or inline connector malfunctions or becomes disconnected, the entire segment of wire in that network will malfunction and network services will cease operation. Coax tends also to become brittle over time, and it can fail when handled. In addition, coax is expensive per foot when compared to UTP cable. These are the primary reasons that coax is falling from favor as a primary network medium.

Coax has two primary vulnerabilities from a security perspective. The most common is the addition of a T-connector attached to a network *sniffer*. This sniffer would have unrestricted access to the signaling on the cable. The second and less common method involves a connection called a *vampire tap*. A vampire tap is a type of connection that hooks directly into a coax by piercing the outer sheath and attaching a small wire to the center conductor or core. This type of attachment allows a tap to occur almost anywhere in the network. Taps can be hard to find because they can be anywhere in the cable. Figure 2.10 shows the two common methods of tapping a coax cable. The T-connector is a standard connector that can be used any place there is a connector on the cable. An inductive pickup or RF collar can be placed around a coaxial cable to capture any stray RF that isn't blocked by the coax's shield.

FIGURE 2.8   Baseband versus broadband signaling

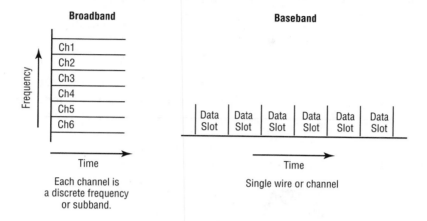

Broadband versus Baseband

FIGURE 2.9   Network termination in a coax network

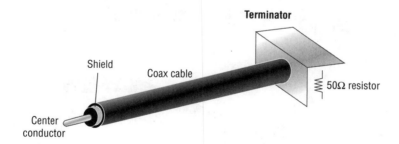

Table 2.1 lists the cabling types discussed and various attributes of each.

TABLE 2.1   Cable types

Characteristic	Fiber-optic	Unshielded twisted pair	Coaxial
Cost	Expensive	Least expensive	Rarely used
Flexibility	Fair	Most flexible	Fair

TABLE 2.1 Cable types *(continued)*

Characteristic	Fiber-optic	Unshielded twisted pair	Coaxial
Ease of Installation	Difficult	Very easy	Moderate
Interference	Not susceptible	Susceptible	Not as susceptible as UTP
Connectors	ST/SC/LC	RJ-45	BNC for Ethernet F-connector for cable modem

FIGURE 2.10 A vampire tap and a T-connector on a coax

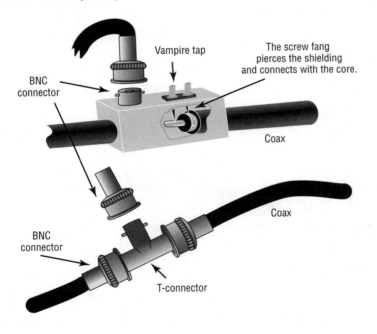

Exam Essentials

Know the network cable types. UTP is the cheapest type of cable to implement, but it's also the weakest. STP is more expensive, but it isn't subject to EMI. Fiber-optic cabling is the most expensive and most difficult to implement, but it offers the greatest combination of speed and distance. Coaxial typically exists in legacy installations with the exception of cable modems.

Know the cable connectors.   Fiber connections include ST, SC, and LC connectors. Twisted pair cabling uses RJ-45 connectors and can differ in pin-outs based on whether the wiring standard used is T568A (old) or T568B (newer). Coaxial cabling uses either BNC or F-connectors.

2.2 Categorize characteristics of connectors and cabling

The previous section introduced cabling and the connectors used with each type. This objective builds on that and reexamines each of the three major types (fiber, twisted pair, and coaxial) and looks at some of the characteristics of each with an emphasis on speed and transmission limitations.

Fiber cabling comes in two major types: single-mode and multi-mode. The speed of fiber makes it a wonderful choice for network implementations, but the cost still remains prohibitive in many situations. Twisted-pair cabling, which is available unshielded (UTP) or shielded (STP), comes in a number of types—known as categories (CAT3, CAT5, and so forth). As a general rule, the higher the category of twisted-pair cabling, the greater the speed possible. Coaxial cabling comes in a number of types, with RG-6 and RG-59 being the two to know for the exam.

Fiber

Because fiber-based media use light transmissions instead of electronic pulses, such problems as EMI, crosstalk, and attenuation become nonissues. Fiber gets around the limitations on almost everything else except cost and is well suited for transferring data, video, and voice transmissions. Since anyone trying to access data signals on a fiber-optic cable must physically tap into the medium, it is the most secure of all cable media.

Types (single-mode vs. multi-mode)

Two types of fiber-optic cable are available: single-mode and multi-mode. As the name implies, single-mode uses a single direct beam of light, thus allowing for greater distances and increased transfer speeds. With multi-mode, a lot of light beams travel through the cable, bouncing off the cable walls; this weakens the signal, reducing the length that the data signal can travel.

The most common types of fiber-optic cable include the following:

- 8.3 micron core/125 micron cladding single mode
- 50 micron core/125 micron cladding multimode
- 62.5 micron core/125 micron cladding multimode

Speed and transmission limitations

Table 2.2 lists the speed and transmission limitations for the most common fiber-optic implementations.

TABLE 2.2   Fiber speeds and limitations

Characteristic	100BaseFX	1000BaseSX	1000BaseLX	10GBaseER
Speed	100 Mbps	1000 Mbps	1000 Mbps	10,000 Mbps
Distance (multimode)	412 meters	220 to 550 meters	550 meters	(not used)
Distance (single mode)	10,000 meters	(not used)	5 km	40 km

Twisted Pair

Twisted-pair cabling is most often used in 100BaseT/1000BaseT networks.

Types

There are different grades, which are given as categories, and as you may guess, the higher the grade, the more expensive the cabling, and the higher the data rate it can support. You do not need to know all of the categories for the exam, but the ones you do need to know are described in the following sections.

STP

Shielded twisted pair (STP) differs from unshielded twisted pair (UTP) only in the presence of the shielding, which resembles aluminum foil directly beneath the outer insulation. The shielding adds to the cost of the cable and a rule of thumb based on current prices is that STP is twice as expensive as UTP for the same length of cable.

UTP

Unshielded twisted pair (UTP) is the most popular twisted-pair cabling in use.

CAT3

Transmits data at speeds up to 10 Mbps with a possible bandwidth of 16 MHz. It contains four twisted pairs of wires with three twists per foot. This is the lowest-level cabling you can safely use in a network. For many years, it was the standard used, but since cabling today considers 100 Mbps to be a minimum, CAT3 has been pushed to legacy installations.

CAT5

Transmits data at speeds up to 100 Mbps and was used with Fast Ethernet (operating at 100 Mbps) with a transmission range of 100 meters. It contains four twisted pairs of copper wire to give the most protection. Although it had its share of popularity (it's used primarily for 10/100 Ethernet networking), it is now an outdated standard. Newer implementations use the 5e standard.

CAT5e

Transmits data at speeds up to 1 Gbps (1000 Mbps). Category 5e cabling can be used up to 100 meters, depending on the implementation and standard used and provides a minimum of 100 MHz of bandwidth. It also contains four twisted pairs of copper wire, but they're physically separated and contain more twists per foot than Category 5 to provide maximum interference protection.

CAT6

Transmits data at speed up to 10 Gbps, has a minimum of 250 MHz of bandwidth, and specifies cable lengths up to 100 meters (using CAT6a). It contains four twisted pairs of copper wire and is used in 10GBaseT networks. Category 6 cable typically is made up of four twisted pairs of copper wire, but its capabilities far exceed those of other cable types. Category 6 twisted pair uses a *longitudinal separator*, which separates each of the four pairs of wires from each other and reduces the amount of crosstalk possible.

PVC

The outer insulation that covers most network cables—that part you touch when you handle the cable—is a plastic known as PVC (an acronym for polyvinyl chloride). While very inexpensive and easy to work with, PVC gives off a poisonous gas when burned. In places where this may be a problem, plenum cable must be run.

Plenum

Plenum cable is a specific type of cable that is rated for use in plenum spaces. Plenum spaces are those in a building used for heating and air-conditioning systems. Most cable cannot be used in the plenum because of the danger of fire (or the fumes the cables give off as they burn). Plenum cable is fire-rated and meets the necessary standards, which makes it okay to use in these locations. It replaces PVC with a Teflon-like material.

Speed and transmission limitations

Table 2.3 lists the speed and transmission limitations for the most common twisted-pair implementations.

TABLE 2.3   Twisted-pair speeds and limitations

Characteristic	CAT3	CAT5	CAT5e	CAT6
Speed	16 Mpbs	100 Mbps	1000 Mbps	10/100/1000 Mbps and 10 Gbps
Limitation	Ineffective for higher-speed networks; often found in older 10Base networks	Transmission range of 100 meters	Transmission range of 100 meters	Transmission range of 100 meters

Coaxial

Several types of coax exist and usually each has a very specific use. The exam expects you to know two types.

Types

RG-6

Often used for cable TV and cable modems. RG-6 can run longer distances than RG-59 and support digital signals.

RG-59

Used to generate low-power video connections. The RG-59 cable cannot be used over long distances because of its high-frequency power losses. In such cases, RG-6 cables are used instead.

Not specifically listed in the objectives, but something you should know is that RG-58 is the type traditionally used in Thin Ethernet networks (10Base2). Thick coax (10Base5) utilized RG-8, was used primarily for backbone cable, and could be run through plenum spaces since it offered significant resistance to EMI and crosstalk and could run in lengths up to 500 meters. Thick coax offered speeds up to 10Mbps—too slow for today's network environments.

 There are two types of RG-58 used in legacy Thin Ethernet implementations. RG-58/U has a solid core, whereas RG-58A/U has a stranded wire core.

Speed and transmission limitations

Table 2.4 lists the speed and transmission limitations for the most common coax implementations.

TABLE 2.4   Coax speeds and limitations

Characteristic	RG-6	RG-59
Speed	(not used in networking)	(not used in networking)
Limitation	Cannot be used over long distances (supports digital signals)	Cannot be used over long distances (supports only analog)

Exam Essentials

Know the types available for each media.   The two types of fiber available are single-mode and multi-mode. The types of twisted pair you need to know are all UTP related: CAT3, CAT5, CAT5e, and CAT6. Coax cabling includes RG-6 (TV and cable modems) and RG-59 (video).

Know the speeds of CAT cabling.   CAT3 transmits data at speeds up to 10 Mbps. CAT5 transmits data at speeds up to 100 Mbps. CAT5e transmits data at speeds up to 1000 Mbps (1 Gbps). CAT6 transmits data at speed up to 10 Gbps.

2.3 Explain properties and characteristics of TCP/IP

The protocol of the Internet is TCP/IP, and because of this it has become the de facto protocol of most networks as well. Far from the only networking protocol available, TCP/IP meets the needs of most organizations and is becoming more and more the one protocol suite that administrators must understand in order to do their jobs.

A *host* is any machine or interface that participates in a TCP/IP network—whether as a client or a server. Every interface on a TCP/IP network that must be issued an IP address is considered a host. Those addresses (which, if it is IPv4 in use, fall into three classes—A, B, and C) can be manually entered or provided dynamically to the host by a Dynamic Host Configuration Protocol (DHCP) server. The other values needed, besides the IP address, are the subnet mask (identifying the scope of the network on which the host resides) and the default gateway (the router interfacing with the outside world). Since memorizing complex numerical addresses can be difficult to do, Domain Name Service (DNS) is used to translate hostnames into IP addresses as needed.

IP Class

IPv4 addresses (IPv6 is discussed later) are 32-bit binary numbers. Because numbers of such magnitude are difficult to work with, they're divided into four octets (8 bits) and converted to decimal. Thus, 01010101 becomes 85. This is important because the limits on the size of the decimal number are due to the reality that they're representations of binary numbers. The range must be from 0 (00000000) to 255 (11111111) per octet, making the lowest possible IP address 0.0.0.0 and the highest 255.255.255.255. Many IP addresses aren't available because they're reserved for diagnostic purposes, private addressing, or some other function.

Three classes of IP addresses are available for assignment to hosts; they're identified by the first octet. Table 2.5 shows the class and the range the first octet must fall into to be within that class.

TABLE 2.5   IP address classes

Class	Range
A	1–126
B	128–191
C	192–223

There are actually five classes that exist. Class D (multicast) and Class E (experimental) are not assigned to hosts.

Class A

If you're given a Class A address, then you're assigned a number such as 125. With a few exceptions, this means you can use any number between 0 and 255 in the second field, any number between 0 and 255 in the third field, and any number between 0 and 255 in the fourth field. This gives you a total number of hosts that you can have on your network in excess of 16 million. The default subnet mask is 255.0.0.0.

Class B

If you're given a Class B address, then you're assigned a number such as 152.119. With a few exceptions, this means you can use any number between 0 and 255 in the third field and any number between 0 and 255 in the fourth field. This gives you a total number of hosts that you can have on your network in excess of 65,000. The default subnet mask is 255.255.0.0.

Class C

If you're given a Class C address, then you're assigned a number such as 205.19.15. You can use any number between 1 and 254 in the fourth field, for a total of 254 possible hosts (0 and 255 are reserved). The default subnet mask is 255.255.255.0.

The class, therefore, makes a tremendous difference in the number of hosts your network can have. In most cases, the odds of having all hosts at one location are small. Assuming you have a Class B address, will there be 65,000 hosts in one room, or will they be in several locations? Most often, it's the latter.

IPv4 vs. IPv6

IPv4 uses a 32-bit addressing scheme that provides for over 4 billion unique addresses. Unfortunately, there are a lot of IP-enabled devices added to the Internet each and every day—not to mention, not all of the addresses that can be created are used by public networks (many are reserved, in classes D and above, and are unavailable for public use). This reduces the number of addresses that can be allocated as public Internet addresses.

IPv6 offers a number of improvements, the most notable of which is its ability to handle growth in public networks. IPv6 uses a 128-bit addressing scheme, allowing a huge number of possible addresses: 340,282,366,920,938,463,463,374,607,431,768,211,456. Table 2.6 compares IPv4 to IPv6.

 In IPv6 addresses, repeating zeros can be left out so that colons next to each other in the address indicate one or more sets of zeros for that section.

TABLE 2.6   IPv4 vs. IPv6

Feature	IPv4	IPv6
Loopback address	127.0.0.1	0:0:0:0:0:0:0:1 (::1)
Private ranges	10.0.0.0 172.16.0.0 192.168.0.0	FEC0::
Autoconfigured addresses	169.254.0.0	FE80::

Public vs. Private vs. APIPA

Within each of the three major classes of IP addresses, there is a range set aside for *private addresses*. These are addresses that do not communicate directly with the Internet (often using a proxy server, or network address translation to do so), and so each host's address need be unique only within the realm of that network. Table 2.7 lists the private address ranges for Class A, B, and C addresses.

TABLE 2.7   Private address ranges

Class	Range
A	10.0.0.0 to 10.255.255.255
B	172.16.0.0 to 172.31.255.255
C	192.168.0.0 to 192.168.255.255

Automatic Private IP Addressing (APIPA) is a TCP/IP feature Microsoft added to their operating systems. If a DHCP server cannot be found and the clients are configured to obtain IP addresses automatically, the clients automatically assign themselves an IP address, some-what randomly, in the 169.254.x.x range with a subnet mask of 255.255.0.0. This allows them to communicate with other hosts that have similarly configured themselves, but they are unable to connect to the Internet. If a computer is using an APIPA address, it will have trouble communicating with other clients if those clients do not use APIPA addresses.

Static vs. dynamic

The two methods of entering address information for a host are static and dynamic. Static means that you manually enter the information for the host and it does not change. Dynamic means that DHCP is used for the host to lease information from.

Client-side DNS

As stated earlier, every computer, interface, or device on a TCP/IP network is issued a unique identifier known as an *IP address* that resembles 192.168.12.123. Because of the Internet, TCP/IP is the most commonly used networking protocol today. You can easily see that it's difficult for most users to memorize these numbers, so hostnames are used in their place. *Hostnames* are alphanumeric values assigned to a host; any host may have more than one hostname.

For example, the host 192.168.12.123 may be known to all users as Gemini, or it may be known to the sales department as Gemini and to the marketing department as Apollo9. All that is needed is a means by which the alphanumeric name can be translated into its IP address. There are a number of methods of doing so, but for this exam, you need to know only one: DNS. On a large network, you can add a server to be referenced by all hosts for the name resolution. The server runs DNS and resolves fully qualified domain names (FQDNs) from www.entrepreneurshipcamp.com into their IP address. Multiple DNS servers can serve an area and provide fault tolerance for one another. In all cases, the DNS servers divide their area into zones; every zone has a primary server and any number of secondary servers. DNS, like hosts files, works with any operating system and any version.

 FQDNs identify the host and information about it.

DHCP

Dynamic Host Configuration Protocol (DHCP) falls into a different category. Whereas DNS resolves names to IP addresses, DHCP issues IP configuration data.

Rather than an administrator having to configure a unique IP address for every host added on a network (and *default gateway* and *subnet mask*), they can use a DHCP server to issue these values. That server is given a number of addresses in a range that it can supply to clients.

For example, the server may be given the IP range (or *scope*) 192.168.12.1 to 192.168.12.200. When a client boots, it sends out a request for the server to issue it an address (and any other configuration data) from that scope. The server takes one of the numbers it has available and leases it to the client for a length of time. If the client is still using the configuration data when 50 percent of the lease has expired, it requests a renewal of the lease from the server; under normal operating conditions, the request is granted. When the client is no longer using the address, the address goes back in the scope and can be issued to another client.

DHCP is built on the older Bootstrap Protocol (BOOTP) that was used to allow diskless workstations to boot and connect to a server that provided them with an operating system and applications. The client uses broadcasts to request the data and thus—normally—can't communicate with DHCP servers beyond their own subnet (broadcasts don't route). A DHCP Relay Agent, however, can be employed to allow DHCP broadcasts to go from one network to another.

The primary purpose of DHCP is to lease IP addresses to hosts. The client contacts the DHCP server and requests an address, and the DHCP server issues one to the client to use for a period of time. This lease can continue to be renewed as long as the client needs it and the server is configured to keep renewing it. When it gives the IP address, it also often includes the additional configuration information as well: DNS server, router information, and so on.

Subnet mask

Subnetting your network is the process of taking the total number of hosts available to you and dividing it into smaller networks. When you configure TCP/IP on a host, you typically need only give three values: a unique IP address, a default gateway (router) address, and a subnet mask. The default subnet mask for each class of network is shown in Table 2.8.

Purists may argue that you don't need a default gateway. Technically this is true if your network is small and you don't communicate beyond it. For all practical purposes, though, most networks need a default gateway.

TABLE 2.8   Default subnet values

Class	Default subnet mask
A	255.0.0.0
B	255.255.0.0
C	255.255.255.0

When you use the default subnet mask, you're allowing for all hosts to be at one site and not subdividing your network. Any deviation from the default signifies that you're dividing the network into multiple subnetworks.

Gateway

A *gateway* can have two meanings. In TCP/IP, a gateway is the address of the machine to send data to that is not intended for a host on this network (in other words, a default gateway). A gateway is also a physical device operating between the Transport and Application layers of the OSI model that can send data between dissimilar systems. The best example of the latter is a mail gateway—it doesn't matter which two networks are communicating; the gateway allows them to exchange e-mail.

A gateway, as it is tested on the exam, is the server (router) that allows traffic beyond the internal network. Hosts are configured with the address of a gateway (called the default gateway), and if they need to correspond with a host outside the internal network, the data is sent to the gateway to facilitate this. When you configure TCP/IP on a host, one of the fields that should be provided is a gateway field, which specifies where data not intended for this network is sent in order to be able to communicate with the rest of the world.

Exam Essentials

Know the IP classes.   Class A addresses range from 0 to 126, Class B from 128 to 191, and Class C from 192 to 223. Within each class, there are private address ranges. Class A's private range is from 10.0.0.0 to 10.255.255.255, Class B is from 172.16.0.0 to 172.31.255.255, and Class C is from 192.168.0.0 to 192.168.255.255.

Understand what APIPA is.   Automatic Private IP Addressing (APIPA) is a TCP/IP feature for clients that cannot find a DHCP server but are configured to get their address from there. The clients automatically assign themselves an IP address, somewhat randomly, in the 169.254.$x.x$ range with a subnet mask of 255.255.0.0.

2.4 Explain common TCP and UDP ports, protocols, and their purpose

Communication across a TCP/IP-based network takes place using various protocols, such as FTP to transfer files, HTTP to view web pages, and POP3 or IMAP to work with email. Each of these protocols has a default port associated with it, and CompTIA expects you to be familiar with them for this exam.

Both TCP and UDP use port numbers to listen for and respond to requests for communication using various protocols. There are seven protocols and nine ports that you must know for this exam, as well as the differences between TCP and UDP.

Ports

TCP and UDP both use port numbers to listen for and respond to requests for communications. RFC 1060 defines *common ports* for a number of services routinely found in use, and these all have low numbers—up to 1,024. You can, however, reconfigure your service to use another port number (preferably much higher) if you're concerned about security and you don't want your site to be available to anonymous traffic.

21—FTP   The File Transfer Protocol (FTP) is both a TCP/IP protocol and software that permits the transferring of files between computer systems. Because FTP has been implemented on numerous types of computer systems, files can be transferred between disparate systems (for example, a personal computer and a minicomputer). It uses ports 20 and 21 by default. It can be configured to allow or deny access to specific IP addresses and can be configured to work with exceptions. While the protocol can be run within most browsers, a number of FTP applications are available, with FileZilla (`http://filezilla-project.org/`) being one of the most popular.

23—Telnet   Telnet is a protocol that functions at the application layer of the OSI model, providing terminal-emulation capabilities. Telnet runs on port 23, but has lost favor to SSH due to the fact that Telnet sends data—including passwords—in plain-text format.

25—SMTP   Simple Mail Transfer Protocol (SMTP) is a protocol for sending email between SMTP servers. Clients typically use either IMAP or POP to access it. SMTP uses port 25 by default.

53—DNS   As mentioned earlier, DNS is the Domain Name Service, and it is used to translate hostnames into IP addresses.

80—HTTP   Hypertext Transfer Protocol (HTTP) is the protocol used for communication between a web server and a web browser. It uses port 80 by default.

110—POP3   The Post Office Protocol (POP) is a protocol for receiving email from an SMTP server. The alternative to POP (which runs on port 110), is IMAP.

143—IMAP   Internet Message Access Protocol (IMAP) is a protocol with a store-and-forward capability. It can also allow messages to be stored on an email server instead of downloaded to the client. The current version of the protocol is 4 (IMAP4), and the counterpart to it is Post Office Protocol (POP). IMAP runs on port 143.

443—HTTPS   Hypertext Transfer Protocol over Secure Sockets Layer (HTTPS) is a protocol used to make a secure connection. It uses port 443 by default.

3389—RDP   The Remote Desktop Protocol (RDP) is used in a Windows environment to make remote desktop communications possible.

Just associating each protocol with a port doesn't do much good. You should also know what the protocol is used for. The following sections look at each of the ports in the table and explain a bit about them.

Protocols

There are seven protocols that CompTIA lists for this objective. Among them are DHCP and DNS, which were covered fully in the discussion of objective 2.3. The others are:

LDAP   Lightweight Directory Access Protocol (LDAP) is a protocol that provides a mechanism to access and query directory services systems. These directory services systems are most likely to be Microsoft's Active Directory but could also be Novell Directory Services (NDS). Although LDAP supports command-line queries executed directly against the directory database, most LDAP interactions are via utilities such as an authentication program (network logon) or locating a resource in the directory through a search utility.

SNMP   Simple Network Management Protocol (SNMP) is a protocol that facilitates network management functionality. It is not, in itself, a network management system (NMS), simply the protocol that makes NMS possible.

SMB   Server Message Blocks (SMBs) are used to share access to resources. While the newest versions of SMB (versions 2.1 and 2.2) are proprietary to Microsoft, compatible versions are available in Linux operating systems, allowing them to still share the printers, files, and other resources that have been made available across the network.

SSH   The Secure Shell (SSH) application replaces Telnet and provides the same functionality while increasing security. SSH runs on port 22 and encrypts the transmitted data, including the password.

SFTP   The *SSH File Transfer Protocol* (SFTP) replaces FTP with client and server communication across a secure channel.

TCP vs. UDP

Operating at the transport layer of the TCP/IP stack are two key protocols: *Transmission Control Protocol* (TCP) and *User Datagram Protocol* (UDP). The biggest difference between these two is that one is connection based (TCP) and the other works in the absence of a dedicated connection (UDP). Both are needed and serve key roles.

If you are sending credit card information to a website, you need a dedicated connection between your host and the server, so TCP handles that task. An example of UDP is DHCP. When a client sends a request for any DHCP server listening to give it an address, it is not requiring a dedicated communication.

Exam Essentials

Know the default ports.   There are nine protocols you need to know the default ports for: FTP (20/21), TELNET (23), SMTP (25), DNS (53), HTTP (80), POP3 (110), IMAP (143), HTTPS (443), and RDP (3389).

Know what the protocols do.   In addition to the nine protocols for which ports are given, know as well DHCP, LDAP, SNMP, SMB, SSH, and SFTP.

2.5 Compare and contrast wireless network standards and encryption types

More and more, networks are using wireless as the medium of choice. It is much easier to implement, reconfigure, upgrade, and use them than wired networks. Unfortunately, there can be downsides, with security being one of the largest.

The 802.11 standard applies to wireless networking, and there have been many versions/types of it released; the main ones are a, b, g, and n. Encryption has gone from very weak (WEP) to much stronger with increments along the way, including WPA, WAP2, and implementation of TKIP and AES.

Standards

The IEEE 802.11*x* family of protocols provides for wireless communications using radio frequency transmissions. The frequencies in use for 802.11 standards are the 2.4 GHz and the 5 GHz frequency spectrums. Several standards and bandwidths have been defined for use in wireless environments, and they aren't extremely compatible with each other:

802.11a   The *802.11a* standard provides wireless LAN bandwidth of up to 54Mbps in the 5GHz frequency spectrum. The 802.11a standard also uses orthogonal frequency division multiplexing (OFDM) for encoding rather than FHSS or DSSS.

802.11b The *802.11b* standard provides for bandwidths of up to 11 Mbps (with fallback rates of 5.5, 2, and 1 Mbps) in the 2.4G Hz frequency spectrum. This standard is also called *WiFi* or *802.11 high rate*. The 802.11b standard uses only DSSS for data encoding.

802.11g The *802.11g* standard provides for bandwidths of 20 Mbps+ in the 2.4 GHz frequency spectrum. This offers a maximum rate of 54 Mbps and is backward compatible with 802.11b.

802.11n The newest of the wireless standards you need to know for the exam is *802.11n*. The goal of the 802.11n standard is to significantly increase throughput in both the 2.4 GHz and the 5 GHz frequency range. The baseline goal of the standard was to reach speeds of 100 Mbps, but given the right conditions, it is estimated that the 802.11n speeds might be able to reach 600 Mbps. In practical operation, 802.11n speeds will be much slower.

Three technologies are used to communicate in the 802.11 standard:

Direct-Sequence Spread Spectrum (DSSS) DSSS accomplishes communication by adding the data that is to be transmitted to a higher-speed transmission. The higher-speed transmission contains redundant information to ensure data accuracy. Each packet can then be reconstructed in the event of a disruption.

Frequency-Hopping Spread Spectrum (FHSS) FHSS accomplishes communication by hopping the transmission over a range of predefined frequencies. The changing or hopping is synchronized between both ends and appears to be a single transmission channel to both ends.

Orthogonal Frequency Division Multiplexing (OFDM) OFDM accomplishes communication by breaking the data into subsignals and transmitting them simultaneously. These transmissions occur on different frequencies or subbands.

The mathematics and theories of these transmission technologies are beyond the scope of this book and far beyond the scope of this exam.

Speeds, distances, and frequencies

Table 2.9 compares the speed, distance, and frequency of each of the 802.11 standards.

TABLE 2.9 Comparison of 802.11 standards

Standard	Speed	Distance (indoors)	Frequency
802.11a	Up to 54 Mbps	Up to 115 feet	5 GHz
802.11b	Up to 11 Mbps	Up to 115 feet	2.4 GHz
802.11g	Up to 54 Mbps	Up to 125 feet	2.4 GHz
802.11n	Up to 600 Mbps	Up to 380 feet	2.4 GHz/5 GHz

Encryption Types

There are a number of wireless encryption "types" you need to know for the A+ exam. These are WEP, WPA, WPA2, TKIP, and AES.

WEP, WPA, WPA2, TKIP, AES

Let's take a closer look at each:

WEP   *Wired Equivalent Privacy* (WEP) is a standard that was created as a first stab at security for wireless devices. WEP encrypted data to provide data security and has always been under scrutiny for not being as secure as initially intended. WEP is vulnerable due to weaknesses in the way the encryption algorithms are employed. These weaknesses allow the algorithm to potentially be cracked in as few as five minutes using available PC software. This makes WEP one of the most vulnerable protocols available for security.

WPA   The *Wi-Fi Protected Access* (WPA) and *Wi-Fi Protected Access 2* (WPA2) technologies were designed to address the core problems with WEP. These technologies implement the 802.11i standard. The difference between WPA and WPA2 is that the former implements most—but not all—of 802.11i in order to be able to communicate with older wireless cards (which might still need an update through their firmware in order to be compliant) while WPA2 implements the full standard and is not compatible with older cards.

WPA2   WPA2 implements the full 802.11i standard for security and is not compatible with older wireless cards.

TKIP   WPA was able to increase security by using a *Temporal Key Integrity Protocol (TKIP)* to scramble encryption keys using a hashing algorithm. The keys are issued an integrity check to verify they have not been modified or tampered with during transit. While a good solution, it was far from perfect. Corporate security today favors WPA2 since it replaces TKIP with CCMP (Counter Mode with Cipher Block Chaining Message Authentication Code Protocol).

AES   CCMP uses 128-bit Advanced Encryption Security (*AES*) with a 48-bit initialization vector, making it much more difficult to crack and minimizing the risk of a replay attack.

Never assume that a wireless connection is secure. The emissions from a wireless portal may be detectable through walls and for several blocks from the portal. Interception is easy to accomplish, given that RF is the medium used for communication. Newer wireless devices offer data security, and you should use it. You can set newer WAPs and wireless routers to non-broadcast in addition to configuring WEP at a higher encryption level. Given the choice, you should choose to use WPA2, WPA, or WEP at its highest encryption level in that order.

Exam Essentials

Understand wired and wireless connectivity. Networks work the same whether there is a physical wire between the hosts or that wire has been replaced by a wireless signal. The same order of operations and steps are carried out regardless of the medium employed.

Know the capabilities and limitations of the 802.11x network standards. The current standards for wireless protocols are 802.11, 802.11a, 802.11b, 802.11g, and 802.11n.

Know the vulnerabilities of wireless networks. The primary method of gaining information about a wireless network is a site survey. Site surveys can be accomplished with a PC and an 802.11 card. Wireless networks are subject to the same attacks as wired networks.

2.6 Install, configure, and deploy a SOHO wireless/wired router using appropriate settings

Small office and home office (SOHO) networks can be created very easily today and relatively inexpensively. You can choose to do so with wires, or wireless. While there isn't a hard and fast rule on what the limit is for a SOHO network, the term is generally used for networks of ten or fewer workstations.

One of the biggest differences between SOHO networks and larger local area networks (LANs) is the way they connect to the outside world. While a LAN would never connect in today's world through a dial-up connection, it is not impossible to still stumble across such a configuration in a SOHO network.

This section will look at the connection types and possibilities that exist for small networks, as well as some of the basics of network configuration.

MAC filtering

One way to increase security is to implement *MAC filtering*. Every network card has a unique 48-bit address assigned to it—half of which identifies the vendor of the card, and the other half of which acts like a serial number. When MAC filtering is implemented, you identify each host by this number and determine specifically which addresses are allowed access to the network. While a great security tool, bear in mind that it is identifying the NIC card and not the person sitting at that machine, so it cannot ever be the only form of authentication employed.

An example of a MAC address is: 00-21-6A-2C-89-3C.

Channels (1–11)

Wireless routers can be set to use different channels, which are numbered 1 through 11 (1, 6, and 11 are those commonly used in the U.S.). Each channel represents a different frequency. You can change the channel to avoid interference—either from another network nearby or devices also using that frequency.

The channel change is made only on the router, as each client should automatically detect and change to the new channel.

SSID broadcast (on/off)

Many networks will regularly broadcast their name (known as an *SSID broadcast*) to announce their presence. For security reasons, you should change the SSID from its default value (if one is preconfigured) and disable broadcasts where possible. Disabling the broadcasts prevents snooping eyes from seeing that the network is there but does not affect operations in any other way—clients simply need to specify the name of the network without having the assistance of seeing it.

Wireless encryption

Domain 2.5, which preceded this one, is focused solely on wireless encryption. Information is not repeated here to avoid needless repetition, but you are advised to read it there.

Firewalls and Port Forwarding/Triggering

A firewall can be hardware- and/or software-based. At its simplest, firewall configuration is accomplished by configuring ports and rules. A *port* is an interface that is used to connect to a device and identified by number. Throughout this book, many well-known ports have been discussed by their number (SMTP on port 25, for example).

When you use a service, the default port is implied, but you can always change the *port assignment* if you want to increase security. For example, when you attempt to connect to a website, you'll use port 80 by default. (A socket is the combination of the IP address and the port number. If you were accessing a website at 192.168.0.100, the combination of these two elements would give you a socket; the full address and socket description would then be 192.168.0.100:80.)

The assignment can be changed so that a server offers the web service at a port other than the default, such as 8080. If that is done, the service can be accessed by the client by specifying the socket: `http://192.168.0.100:8080`.

Port forwarding (also known as port mapping) is the act of mapping one port to another. This is essentially the same as what NAT does, and it allows external users to access the private LAN. This is useful when you want to allow only some external users (partners, for example) to be able to access the network resources remotely. These ports can be left open all the time or turned on only when needed. If the latter is the case, this is known as *port trigger-ing*. With triggering, an inbound attempt at connection triggers the opening of an outbound port and communication is now possible. Obviously, the trigger is activated only after all authentication measures have been successfully met.

Another aspect of firewall configuration is the establishment of rules. The *rules* are criteria given for what is allowed to pass through or connect to the network. These rules are typically accept- or deny-based (but can be configured to include exceptions). For example, you may choose to deny all connections except those specifically allowed—much better than the alternative of allowing all except those specifically denied, which creates a security nightmare.

Rules can typically be created based on the following:

- Direction, which can be inbound or outbound
- Protocol source, which can be either TCP (connection-based) or UDP (connectionless)
- Address source
- Port
- Destination address
- Destination port

If you want to limit all of any one criterion—for example, all destination ports—most firewalls allow you to use the value any for this purpose.

DHCP (on/off)

DHCP has been discussed a few times already in this chapter. It serves a useful purpose of issuing IP addresses and other network-related configuration values to clients to allow them to operate on the network. The router can perform this function on a SOHO network and simplify the administrator's life.

From a security standpoint, however, having the router do this can present a serious concern. Since the values can be issued to any wireless device that comes within range, it is possible that a rogue machine could be issued these values and then be allowed on the network. In the interest of security, we recommend that the DHCP feature be turned off on the router and IP addresses (along with other networking values) manually entered for the clients.

DMZ

The networking equivalent of a security zone is a network security zone. They perform the same function. If you divide a network into smaller sections, each zone can have its own security considerations and measures—just like a physical security zone. This arrangement allows layers of security to be built around sensitive information. The division of the network is accomplished by implementing virtual LANs (VLANs) and/or instituting demilitarized zones (DMZs).

A *demilitarized zone (DMZ)* is an area where you can place a public server for access by people you might not trust otherwise. By isolating a server in a DMZ, you can hide or remove access to other areas of your network. You can still access the server using your network, but others aren't able to access further network resources. This can be accomplished using firewalls to isolate your network.

When establishing a DMZ, you assume that the person accessing the resource isn't necessarily someone you would trust with other information. By keeping the rest of the network from being visible to external users, this lowers the threat of intrusion in the internal network.

 Any time you want to separate public information from private information, a DMZ is an acceptable option.

The easiest way to create a DMZ is to use a firewall that can transmit in three directions:

- To the internal network
- To the external world (Internet)
- To the public information you're sharing (the DMZ)

From there, you can decide what traffic goes where; for example, HTTP traffic would be sent to the DMZ, and email would go to the internal network.

NAT

Network Address Translation (NAT) creates a unique opportunity to assist in the security of a network. Originally, NAT extended the number of usable Internet addresses. Now it allows an organization to present a single address to the Internet for all computer connections. The NAT server provides IP addresses to the hosts or systems in the network and tracks inbound and outbound traffic.

A company that uses NAT presents a single connection to the network. This connection may be through a router or a NAT server. The only information that an intruder will be able to get is that the connection has a single address.

NAT effectively hides your network from the world, making it much harder to determine what systems exist on the other side of the router. The NAT server effectively operates as a firewall for the network. Most new routers support NAT; it provides a simple, inexpensive firewall for small networks.

 It's important to understand that NAT acts as a proxy between the local area network (which can be using private IP addresses) and the Internet. Not only can NAT save IP addresses, but it can also act as a firewall.

Most NAT implementations assign internal hosts private IP address numbers and use public addresses only for the NAT to translate to and communicate with the outside world. The private address ranges, all of which addresses are nonroutable, are as follows:

10.0.0.0–10.255.255.255

172.16.0.0–172.31.255.255

192.168.0.0–192.168.255.255

> In addition to NAT, Port Address Translation (PAT) is possible. Whereas NAT can use multiple public IP addresses, PAT uses a single one and shares the port with the network. Because it is using only a single port, PAT is much more limited and typically used only on small and home-based networks. Microsoft's Internet Connection Sharing is an example of a PAT implementation.

WPS

Wi-Fi Protected Setup (WPS) simplifies the security configuration of small home networks by implementing WPA2 encryption and allowing new devices to join the network by pressing a button on the router instead of having to enter a complicated passphrase. When a new device (called an enrollee) needs to join, you simply press the button on the access point and the registrar enrolls the device. The access point itself can be the registrar (common), or it can pass the information on to a server that does the actual enrollment (not common).

Basic QoS

Quality of Service (QoS) describes the strategies used to manage the flow of network traffic. A network administrator can use QoS to manage the amount of bandwidth provided to applications that are latency sensitive (those that don't function well with lags—voice and video, for example).

One way QoS accomplishes this is by prioritizing latency-sensitive applications over latency-insensitive ones and then doing priority queuing. Traffic is placed in order based on its importance on delivery time. All data is given access, but the more important and latency-sensitive data is given higher priority.

Exam Essentials

Know the difference between port forwarding and port triggering.   Port forwarding is the act of mapping one port to another (essentially the same as what NAT does). Port triggering involves turning on ports only when they are needed.

Understand MAC filtering.   When MAC filtering is implemented, you identify each host by this number and determine specifically which addresses are allowed access the network.

2.7 Compare and contrast Internet connection types and features

There are a number of ways that your network can connect to the Internet. This can range from the slow dial-up connection that is only established when you need it to a high-speed fiber connection. This section looks at many of the options available, and all that you need to know for this objective on the A+ exam.

When discussing ways to connect to the Internet, most of the discussion is on broadband network techniques. It is imperative that you understand the various types of networks, including broadband. The sections that follow will focus on the key issues associated with connecting to the Internet.

Cable

Two of the most popular methods of connecting to the Internet today are using DSL or a cable. Instead of the service coming from a telephone company as with DSL, cable service is provided by the cable provider and a *cable modem* is used. While speeds vary based on the number of users the cable company is servicing, as a general rule cable-based broadband service is faster than DSL.

DSL

Digital Subscriber Line (DSL) uses existing phone lines with a DSL modem and a network card. A standard RJ-45 connector is used to connect the network card to the DSL modem, and a phone cord with RJ-11 connectors is used to connect the DSL modem to the phone jack. Multiple types of DSL exist; the most popular are *high bit-rate DSL* (HDSL), *symmetric DSL* (SDSL), *very high bit-rate DSL* (VHDSL), *rate-adaptive DSL* (RADSL), and *asymmetric DSL* (ADSL). The latter provides slower upload than download speed and is the most common for home use. While speeds may vary depending on the quality of the connection and the equipment used, Table 2.10 shows the most common upload and download speeds for the various flavors of DSL.

TABLE 2.10   DSL speeds

Type	Upload	Download
ADSL	1 Mbps	8 Mbps
ADSL2	1.3 Mbps	12 Mbps
ADSL2+	1.3 Mbps	24 Mbps

TABLE 2.10   DSL speeds *(continued)*

Type	Upload	Download
SDSL	4.5 Mbps	4.5 Mbps
VDSL	3 Mbps	55 Mbps

Dial-up

Whereas broadband holds great promise for high-speed connections, there are many people (quite a few in rural areas) who cannot take advantage of this. Thankfully, one of the first methods of remote access, dial-up networking, is still in existence. With dial-up, you add a modem to your computer and connect to an Internet service provider (ISP) over the existing phone lines, also known as the *Plain Old Telephone System* (POTS). With a good connection, you can transmit and receive at 56 Kbps.

Fiber

Fiber-optic cabling provides excellent speed and bandwidth but is expensive. Not only are the cables that you use costly, but the light-emitting/receiving hardware costs also make this an expensive undertaking. Because of the cost involved, fiber is often an option for businesses only when it comes to broadband access.

Fiber to the Home (FTTH) is an attempt some communities are undertaking to offer high-speed connectivity to residential dwellings as well. One similar implementation, Verizon's FiOS runs single-mode optical fiber to homes and includes phone and television service along with Internet access.

Satellite

Whereas the other broadband technologies discussed require the use of physical wiring, with satellite broadband the service provider sends a microwave signal from dish to orbiting satellite and back. One satellite can service many receivers and so this is commonly known as *point-to-multipoint* technology. As a general rule, satellite connections are slower than the other broadband technologies you need to know for the exam.

With satellite, download speed is much faster than upload speed.

ISDN

Integrated Services Digital Network (ISDN) is a WAN technology that performs link management and signaling by virtue of packet switching. The original idea behind it was to let existing phone lines carry digital communications by using multiplexing to support multiple channels.

Cellular (mobile hotspot)

BlackBerries have made cellular networking popular, though they are not the only devices capable of using networking; for example, a cellular modem can also be quickly added to a laptop. Cellular networks use a central access point (a cell tower) in a mesh network design. The two competing standards are the *Global System for Mobile Communications* (GSM) and the *Code Division Multiple Access* (CDMA).

> Most cellular phone companies now have specialized wireless routers that are used to create mobile hotspots. These cards act as standalone routers to the Internet using the cellular phone network.

Line of sight wireless internet service

Line-of-sight wireless, as the name implies, requires you to have a direct line of vision between your location and the Internet service provider (ISP). Because this uninterrupted path must be maintained, distances are quite short and this method is not widely used.

WiMAX

Often used synonymously with satellite, Worldwide Interoperability for Microwave Access (WiMAX) uses microwave dishes to provide 4G service for Internet access.

Exam Essentials

Know the differences between Internet connection types.   Many technologies can be used to obtain Internet access. DSL and cable are two of the most popular for SOHO networks and require modems. DSL service is provided by the telephone provider in the area and cable service is provided by the area cable television provider.

Understand ISDN's purpose.   The original idea behind it was to let existing phone lines carry digital communications by using multiplexing to support multiple channels.

2.8 Identify various types of networks

LANs and WANs differ in size and scope. You should know the terminology used for networking as well as the major topologies that are available.

Networks consist of servers and clients. A *server* is a dedicated machine offering services such as file and print sharing. A *client* is any individual workstation accessing the network. A *workstation* is a client machine that accesses services elsewhere (normally from a server). The size of the network on which these servers and clients operate can range significantly.

LAN

A *local area network* (LAN) is a network that is geographically confined within a small space—a room, a building, and so on. Because it's confined and does not have to span a great distance, it can normally offer higher speeds.

With Ethernet, you can often use the network type to compute the required length and speed of your cabling. For example, 100BaseT tells you three things:

100   The speed of the network, 100 Mbps.

Base   The technology used (either baseband or broadband).

T   Twisted-pair cabling. In the case of 10BaseT, it's generally UTP.

When you configure a network, one of the first places to turn your attention is the routers and access points—they are the hardware components on which network access can rely. Because these devices must always be able to be found, we suggest that you not use DHCP to issue them addresses but that you configure their addresses statically.

To increase security, devices should be behind a firewall and you should always change the administrative username and password that comes preconfigured with these devices to ones that adhere to stringent password policies (mixture of upper- and lowercase alphabet, numbers, and special characters), and you should keep the firmware updated.

With wireless access points, you should change the SSID from its default value (if one is preconfigured) and disable broadcasts. MAC filtering can be used on a wireless network, for example, to prevent certain clients from accessing the Internet. You can choose to deny service to a set list of MAC addresses (and allow all others) or allow service only to a set of MAC addresses (and deny all others).

WAN

A *wide area network* (WAN) is a collection of two or more LANs, typically connected by routers, and dedicated leased lines (not to mention complicated implementations). The geographic limitation is removed, but WAN speeds are traditionally less than LAN speeds.

PAN

A *personal area network* (PAN) is a LAN created by personal devices. Often, personal devices include networking capabilities and can communicate directly with one another. Wireless technologies have introduced a new term: *wireless personal area network* (WPAN). WPAN refers to the technologies involved in connecting devices in very close proximity to exchange data or resources. An example is connecting a laptop with a PDA to synchronize an address book. Because of their small size and the nature of the data exchange, WPAN devices lend themselves well to ad hoc wireless networking. Ad hoc wireless networks are those that have devices connect to each other directly, not through a wireless access point.

MAN

Occasionally, a WAN will be referenced as a *metropolitan area network* (MAN) when it is confined to a certain geographic area, such as a university campus or city. No formal guidelines dictate the differences between a MAN and a WAN; technically, a MAN *is* a WAN. Perhaps for this reason, the term *MAN* is used less frequently than *WAN*. If any distinction exists, it's that a MAN is smaller than a WAN. A MAN is almost always bigger than a LAN and usually is smaller than or equal to a WAN. MANs utilize an Internet service provider (ISP) or telecommunications (telco) provider.

Topologies

A *topology* is the network's physical and logical layout. The *physical topology* is the actual layout of the computer cables and other network devices, and the *logical topology* is the way the network appears to the devices that use it.

The Network+ exam from CompTIA focuses on topologies and types of networks in more detail than A+ does. If the brief descriptions here are confusing, then we recommend a Network+ book such as the *CompTIA Network+ N10-005 Authorized Exam Cram* (Que, 2012) is recommended.

Mesh

The *mesh topology* incorporates a network design in which each computer on the network connects to every other, creating a point-to-point connection between every device on the network. The purpose of the mesh design is to provide a high level of redundancy. If one network cable fails, the data always has an alternative path to get to its destination—each node can act as a relay. The wiring for a mesh network can be complicated. Furthermore, the cabling costs associated with the mesh topology can be high, and troubleshooting a failed cable can be tricky. Because of this, the mesh topology is not the first choice for many wired networks, but it is more popular with servers and routers.

Ring

The *ring topology* is actually a logical ring, meaning that the data travels in a circular fashion from one computer to another on the network. It is not a physical ring topology. Note that a hub or switch is not needed in this installation. In a true ring topology, if a single computer or section of cable fails, the signal is interrupted. The entire network becomes inaccessible. Network disruption can also occur when computers are added to or removed from the network, making it an impractical network design in environments where the network changes often.

Bus

A *bus topology* uses a trunk or backbone to connect all the computers on the network. Systems connect to this backbone using T connectors or taps (known as vampire taps, if you must pierce the wire). To avoid signal reflection, a physical bus topology requires that each end of the physical bus be terminated, with one end also being grounded. Note that a hub or switch is not needed in this installation.

Star

In the *star topology*, the most widely used topology today, all computers and other network devices connect to a central device called a hub or switch. Each connected device requires a single cable to be connected to the hub, creating a point-to-point connection between the device and the hub. Using a separate cable to connect to the hub allows the network to be expanded without disruption. A break in any single cable does not cause the entire network to fail.

Hybrid

A variation on a true mesh topology is the hybrid mesh. It creates a redundant point-to-point network connection between only specific network devices (such as the servers). The hybrid mesh is most often seen in WAN implementations but can be used in any network.

Exam Essentials

Know the various types of networks.   A network is a collection of computers that can interact with one another and share files and resources. The network may be peer-to-peer or client/server-based. LANs are confined to local, whereas WANs expand that limit.

Know the various topologies.   The four major topology types are ring, bus, star, and mesh. The star topology is the most used today, whereas the mesh is the most difficult to implement. A fifth type, hybrid, is a less-than-full implementation of mesh.

2.9 Compare and contrast network devices and their functions and features

To make a network, you need a number of devices. The most common of those devices are tested on the A+ exam and discussed in this section.

Networks are built using a number of devices. Know those that are covered in this section to be able to answer questions on their functions and features when presented with them on the A+ exam.

Hub

Hubs are used in networks that use twisted-pair cabling to connect devices and they can be used to join segments into larger networks. Hubs direct data packets to all devices connected to the hub, regardless of whether the data package is destined for the device. This makes them inefficient by nature and can create a performance bottleneck on busy networks. In its most basic form, a hub does nothing except provide a pathway for the electrical signals to travel along. Such a device is called a *passive* hub. Far more common nowadays is an *active* hub, which, as well as providing a path for the data signals, regenerates the signal before it forwards it to all the connected devices. In addition, an active hub can buffer data before forwarding it. However, a hub does not perform any processing on the data it forwards, nor does it perform any error checking.

Switch

Like hubs, *switches* are the connectivity points of an Ethernet network. Devices connect to switches via twisted-pair cabling, one cable for each device. The difference between hubs and switches is in how the devices deal with the data they receive. Whereas a hub forwards the data it receives to all the ports on the device, a switch forwards it to only the port that connects to the destination device. It does this by learning the MAC address of the devices attached to it and then by matching the destination MAC address in the data it receives.

Router

A *router* is used to connect LANs together; you can even use a router to connect dissimilar topologies that use the same protocol, because physical specifications don't apply. A router can be a dedicated hardware device or a computer system with more than one network interface and the appropriate routing software. All modern network operating systems include the functionality to act as a router.

Access point

Access points (APs) are transmitter and receiver (transceiver) devices used to create a wireless LAN (WLAN). APs typically are a separate network device with a built-in antenna, transmitter, and adapter. APs use the wireless infrastructure network mode to provide a connection point between WLANs and a wired Ethernet LAN. APs also typically have several ports, giving you a way to expand the network to support additional clients.

Depending on the size of the network, one or more APs might be required. Additional APs are used to allow access to more wireless clients and to expand the range of the wireless network. Each AP is limited by a transmission range—the distance a client can be from an AP and still obtain a usable signal. The actual distance depends on the wireless standard being used and the obstructions and environmental conditions between the client and the AP.

Bridge

Bridges are used to divide larger networks into smaller sections. Bridges accomplish this by sitting between two physical network segments and managing the flow of data between the two. By looking at the MAC address of the devices connected to each segment, bridges can elect to forward the data (if they believe that the destination address is on another interface) or block it from crossing (if they can verify that it is on the interface from which it came).

Modem

A *modem*, short for modulator/demodulator, is a device that converts the digital signals generated by a computer into analog signals that can travel over conventional phone lines. The modem at the receiving end converts the signal back into a format that the computer can understand. Modems can be used as a means to connect to an ISP or as a mechanism for dialing up a LAN. Modems can be internal add-in expansion cards or integrated with the motherboard, external devices that connect to a system's serial or USB port, PCMCIA cards designed for use in laptops, or proprietary devices designed for use on other devices, such as portables and handhelds.

NAS

A *Network Attached Storage* (NAS) unit can be used to provide storage space for the network—either for files currently in use by the users or for backups. Not only does it operate as a file server but it also typically includes redundancy features in the form of RAID to recover the data in the event of a failure.

Firewall

A firewall is a server that sits between the internal network and the rest of the world and filters what goes between the two. While the filter can be done on programs, most are done on ports since applications and protocols use ports that are recognized. Open ports are those that allow traffic, whereas closed ports are those that block traffic. The firewall can be software- or hardware-based, and most incorporate both. The firewall may incorporate a proxy, a gateway, and a filter.

VoIP phones

Voice over IP (VoIP) is also known as IP telephony and Internet telephony. It's the routing of voice traffic over the Internet (it could be across any smaller IP-based network, but generally it's the Internet).

Internet appliance

Internet appliances are home-based network solutions intended to provide Internet access. The difference between this type and other devices (such as a router) is that their main purpose—and often sole purpose—is just to provide access to something on the Internet (allowing mail service, for example). Although still around, these have fallen from favor in recent years.

Exam Essentials

Know the two types of hubs.   Hubs can be passive or active. If the hub does nothing except provide a pathway for the electrical signals to travel along, it is passive. It if regenerates the signal, it is considered active.

Be able to recognize a firewall.   A firewall is a server that sits between the internal network and the rest of the world and filters what goes between the two.

2.10 Given a scenario, use appropriate networking tools

To create a network and solve problems with it, you need a toolbox full of tools. While some of the tools you use will be in the form of software, many others are hardware, and those are the ones this objective focuses on.

No networking administrators worth their pay would try to troubleshoot a problem without a set of tools. The tools that should be readily on hand include a crimper for fixing connectors, a multimeter for checking signals, a toner probe to find breaks in a cable, a cable tester, a loopback plug, and a punchdown tool.

Crimper

Wire *crimpers* look like pliers but are used to attach media connectors to the ends of cables. For instance, you use one type of wire crimper to attach RJ-45 connectors on unshielded twisted-pair (UTP) cable. You use a different type of wire crimper to attach Bayonet Neill-Councelman (BNCs) to coaxial cabling.

Multimeter

A *multimeter* combines a number of tools into one. There can be slight variations, but a multimeter always includes a voltmeter, an ohmmeter, and an ammeter (and is sometimes called VOM as an acronym). With one basic multimeter, you can measure voltage, current, and resistance (some will even measure temperature).

A multimeter has a display, terminals, probes, and a dial to select various measurement ranges. A digital multimeter has a numeric digital display, and an analog has a dial display. Inside a multimeter, the terminals are connected to different resistors, depending on the range selected.

Toner probe

A *toner probe* has two parts—the tone generator (called the toner), and the tone locator (called the probe). The toner sends the tone, and at the other end of the cable, the probe receives the toner's signal. This tool makes it easier to find the beginning and end of a cable. The purpose of the toner probe is to generate a signal that is transmitted on the wire you are attempting to locate. At the other end, you press the probe against individual wires. When it makes contact with the wire that has the signal on it, the locator emits an audible signal or tone.

   A toner probe can be used to find breaks in a cable.

Cable tester

Cable testers (sometimes called *media testers*) are used to verify that the cable you are using is good. Commonly used with network cabling, you can perform many of the same tests with a multimeter. Any tool that facilitates the testing of a cable can be deemed a cable tester, but a specific tool called a media tester allows administrators to test a segment of cable, looking for shorts, improperly attached connectors, or other cable faults. All media testers have a way of telling you whether the cable is working correctly and where the problem in the cable might be.

Loopback plug

Also called wrap plugs, *loopback plugs* take the signal going out and essentially echo it back. This allows you to test ports to make certain they're working correctly.

> To simply test an implementation of TCP/IP on a host, you can always use the loopback address of 127.0.0.1. This is often used with ping (discussed in Chapter 6, "Operating Systems").

Punchdown tool

Punchdown tools are used to attach twisted-pair network cable to connectors within a patch panel. Specifically, they connect twisted-pair wires to the insulation displacement connector (IDC).

Exam Essentials

Know the tools for working with networks.   A good administrator's toolbox will include wire crimpers, a multimeter, a toner probe, cable tester, loopback plugs, and a punchdown tool.

Know the two parts of a toner probe.   A toner probe has two parts—the tone generator (called the toner), and the tone locator (called the probe).

Review Questions

1. What is the default port for DNS?

2. What is the speed possible with CAT6 cabling?

3. How many bits are in an IPv4 address? How many are in an IPv6 address?

4. What is the maximum speed possible with 802.11n?

5. When _____ is implemented, you identify each host by this number and determine specifically which addresses are allowed access the network.

6. What type of encryption does WPA use?

7. In what type of network design does each computer on the network connect to every other?

8. Which type of server translates hostnames to IP addresses?

9. What is the default subnet mask value for a host with a Class B address?

10. What type of high-speed Internet connection uses existing phone lines with a modem and a network card?

Chapter

3

Laptops

COMPTIA A+ 220-801 EXAM OBJECTIVES COVERED IN THIS CHAPTER:

✓ **3.1 Install and configure laptop hardware and components.**

- Expansion options
  - ExpressCard/34
  - ExpressCard/54
  - PCMCIA
  - SODIMM
  - Flash
- Hardware/device replacement
  - Keyboard
  - Hard Drive (2.5 vs. 3.5)
  - Memory
  - Optical drive
  - Wireless card
  - Mini-PCIe
  - Screen
  - DC jack
  - Battery
  - Touchpad
  - Plastics
  - Speaker
  - System board
  - CPU

✓ **3.2 Compare and contrast the components within the display of a laptop.**

- Types
  - LCD
  - LED
  - OLED
  - Plasma
- Wi-Fi antenna connector/placement
- Inverter and its function
- Backlight

✓ **3.3 Compare and contrast laptop features.**

- Special function keys
  - Dual displays
  - Wireless (on/off)
  - Volume settings
  - Screen brightness
  - Bluetooth (on/off)
  - Keyboard backlight
- Docking station vs. port replicator
- Physical laptop lock and cable lock

In this chapter, we will focus on the exam topics related to laptops. We will follow the structure of the CompTIA A+ 220-801 exam blueprint, Objective 3, and we will explore the three subobjectives that the prospective exam taker will need to master before taking the exam.

3.1 Install and configure laptop hardware and components

Whether you choose to call them laptops, notebooks, tablets, or something different is mostly a matter of semantics. In this section some of the basic components of laptops and their installation (when possible and called for) are discussed. In many cases, the components are the same as in a desktop computer, and they were discussed already. We'll focus now on those that are different. The topics addressed in objective 3.1 include:

- Expansion options
- Hardware/device replacement

Expansion options

A portable computer must provide all the functionality of a desktop counterpart yet be able to withstand travel, run in the absence of AC power, and be much smaller and more compact. When you get right down to it, there is not a great deal of difference between laptop and desktop computers, with the exception that laptops are more difficult to disassemble and form factors on items such as motherboards, memory, and hard drives become important. In this section the options available to expand the functionality of a laptop are discussed (and in some cases simply reviewed), and the type of memory packages used in laptops is covered.

ExpressCard/34

The ExpressCard standard is an alternative to the use of PC Cards (PCMCIA cards, covered later in this section). ExpressCards are inserted into a slot that will accept either of two form factors. Neither card type is installed or configured as such; they are simply plugged into the slot if present on the laptop.

The ExpressCard/34 is 34 mm wide with a connector that runs the full width of the card. The cards are 75 mm long (10.6 mm shorter than CardBus, discussed in the section "PCMCIA" later in this section) and 5 mm thick. In some cases the functionality provided by the card requires the thickness of the card to be more than 5 mm, such as when it must provide a port or an antenna. ExpressCard slots may be either 34 or 54 mm wide. The 54 mm slot (covered in the next section) will accept either card whereas the 34 mm slot will only accept a 34 mm card.

ExpressCard/54

By using a guide at the rear of the slot the 54 mm slot will accept both card form factors. Adapters are made for connecting an ExpressCard/34 card to a CardBus (but not 16-bit PC Card) slot.

Both the 34 and 54 mm versions of these cards are used in the same way PC Cards are—that is, to provide functionality that does not presently exist on the laptop. They could be used to add an 802.11 wireless connection or access to a mobile phone network, for example. Figure 3.1 shows both types of ExpressCards and a PC Card for comparison.

FIGURE 3.1   Laptop expansion cards

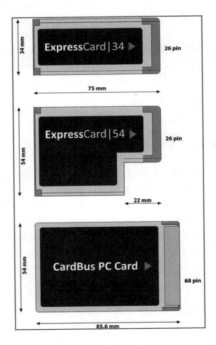

PCMCIA

PCMCIA cards (named for the Personal Computer Memory Card International Association) are the expansion cards for notebook PCs. Technicians often use the more popular term PC Card rather than PCMCIA card. Like ExpressCards, PCMCIA cards are neither installed or configured as such; they are simply plugged into the slot if present on the laptop. Some notebook PCs have a PCMCIA bay that can accept one Type III device or two Type I or Type II devices:

Type I Up to 3.3 mm thick. Used mostly for memory. These are rarely used in today's systems, since new laptops have other means of increasing memory, such as SoDIMMs.

Type II The most common type. Up to 5.5 mm thick. Used for devices that would typically be expansion boards in a desktop PC, such as network interface cards.

Type III Up to 10.5 mm thick. Used for drives. Not common.

 A Type IV PCMCIA card was developed by Toshiba but never standardized. These cards are 16 mm thick.

In addition to these types based on thickness, there are other types based on technology.

CardBus devices are backward compatible with older PCMCIA slots. Even newer is the Peripheral Component Interconnect Express (PCIe) bus—a serial bus addition that uses low-voltage differential signaling (LVDS), allowing you to attach several devices at the same time (using serial communication instead of the parallel communication standard with most PC buses).

SoDIMM

For space reasons memory modules that are used in desktops cannot be used in laptops. Laptop memory comes in smaller form factors known as small outline DIMMs (SoDIMMs). Figure 3.2 shows the form factor for 144-pin and 72-pin SoDIMMS compared to memory modules used in desktops. Notice that they basically look the same but the memory module sizes are different. The most common sizes are 512 MB and 1 GB. They are also available in 4 GB and 8 GB sizes. The speeds of these modules range from 677 MHz to 1,333 MHz. They can have can have 72, 144, or 200 pins.

Another option is the MicroDIMM, which has either 172 pins (DDR) or 214 pins (DDR2). These modules are slightly shorter than the SoDIMM and slightly wider. They do not use the same slots. Keep in mind that many manufacturers have proprietary memory, which means it does not conform to a standard and that you will have to buy the memory from them. Consult the documentation in all cases.

To install laptop memory:

1. Turn off the computer.

2. Disconnect the computer and any peripherals from their power sources, and remove any installed batteries.

FIGURE 3.2   SoDIMMS, SIMMs, and DIMMs

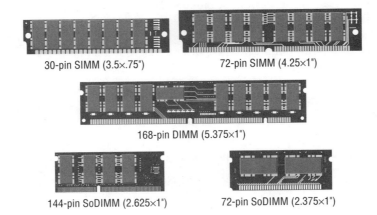

30-pin SIMM (3.5×.75")   72-pin SIMM (4.25×1")

168-pin DIMM (5.375×1")

144-pin SoDIMM (2.625×1")   72-pin SoDIMM (2.375×1")

3. Remove the screws holding the memory door in place.

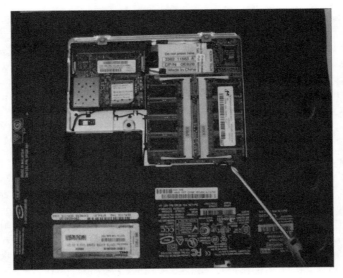

4. Use your fingers to gently separate the plastic tabs holding the memory module in place. The module should pop up so you can grab it.

5. Align the notch in the new memory module to the one in the connector.

6. Insert the new memory module into the socket at a 45-degree angle. Once full contact is made, press the module down. It should click into place.

7. Replace the memory door and fasten the screws.

Once the memory is installed there really is no configuration, but you should check System Tools ➤ System Information to ensure that the memory has been recognized by the system at reboot.

Flash

Flash memory is a type of solid-state storage (covered in Chapter 1, "PC Hardware") that is beginning to be considered as an option for not only additional storage in a laptop but as a replacement for the hard drive. The advantages are reduced heat, lower power consumption, less noise, and better reliability since you have no moving parts. The disadvantage is higher cost and less capacity. The Lenova IdeaPad (called the Yoga) released in 2012 will cost about $1,200 with Solid State drives (SSDs) up to 256 GB. A similar model by the same manufacturer with a 500 GB hard drive will be only $700.

Hardware/device replacement

Replacing hardware and devices in a laptop can be a challenge because of the size limitations. The best way to determine the proper disassembly method is to consult the documentation from the manufacturer.

Some models of notebook PCs require a special T-8 Torx screwdriver. Most PC toolkits come with a T-8 bit for a screwdriver with interchangeable bits, but you may find that the T-8 screws are countersunk in deep holes so that you can't fit the screwdriver into them. In such cases, you need to buy a separate T-8 screwdriver, available at most hardware stores or auto parts stores.

 Many laptop manufacturers will consider a warranty void if an unauthorized person opens a laptop case and attempts to repair a laptop.

Prepare a clean, well-lit, flat work surface, assemble your tools and manuals, and ensure that you have the correct parts. Shut down the PC, unplug it, and detach any external devices such as an external keyboard, mouse, or monitor. In this section, with these general guidelines for opening the laptop in mind, we'll look at replacing various components of a laptop. Always ensure that you have grounded yourself before working with computer components of any kind. Use an antistatic wristband and attach it to the case.

Keyboard

When replacing the keyboard, one of the main things you want to keep in mind is to *not* damage the data cable connector to the system board. With the laptop fully powered off and unplugged from the wall, remove the battery.

Examine the screws on the back of the laptop. Hopefully icons indicating which screws are attached to the keyboard will be available. If not, look up the model online and determine which of the screws are attached to the keyboard.

Remove the screws with a T-8 or Phillips-head screwdriver. With the laptop turned back over, open it up. If the keyboard is tucked under any plastic pieces, determine if those pieces need to have screws removed to get them out of the way; if so, remove the screws and the plastic pieces. In some cases there may just be clamps that are easily removed.

With any plastic covers out of the way, remove any screws at the top and remove the keyboard itself from top to bottom. There should be a thin, but wide, data cable to the system board at the bottom. (This is the piece to be careful with!)

Take a pick and lift the plastic connectors that hold this data cable in place. Remove the data cable. Take the new keyboard and slip the data cable back in between the plastic connectors on the system board. Ensure it's all the way in.

Put the plastic connector back into place, and make sure it's holding the data cable in. Position the keyboard into place, and refasten the keyboard in place at the top, replacing any screws that were there before.

Replace any plastic pieces that were covering the keyboard, turn the laptop over, and replace all of the keyboard screws. When you replace the battery and turn it on, check the functionality. If the keyboard doesn't work, the main component to check is the data connecter.

Hard Drive (2.5″ vs. 3.5″)

The 2.5″ hard drives are smaller (which makes them attractive for a laptop where space is at a minimum) but in comparison to 3.5″ hard drives, they have less capacity and cache and they operate at a lower speed. Whereas 3.5″ drives often can store up to 3 TB of data and have as much as 64 MB of cache, 2.5″ drives usually store only 1 TB of data and use up to 16 MB of cache.

Moreover, whereas 2.5″ drives operate from 5,400 to 7,200 RPM, 3.5″ drives can operate from 7,200 to 10,000 RPM. However, 2.5″ drives use about half the power (again, good for a laptop) of a 3.5″ drive (2.5 W rather than 5 W).

To change the drive, turn the laptop upside down and look for a removable panel or a hard drive release mechanism. Laptop drives are usually accessible from the bottom or side of the chassis. Release the drive by flicking a lock/unlock button and/or removing a screw that holds the drive in place.

You may be required to remove the drive from a caddy or detach mounting rails from its sides. Attach the rails or caddy to the new drive using the same screws and washers. If required, remove the connector attached to the old drive's signal pins and attach it to the new drive. Make sure it's right side up and do not force it. Damaging the signal pins may render the drive useless.

Reverse your steps to place the drive (and caddy if present) into the case. Replace the screws and start up the laptop. The system should recognize the drive. If you or the customer created a bootable backup disc or a complete image disc (before the drive failed, by the way), place it in the optical drive and follow the instructions for restoring the data. You may have to update a driver or two, but you should otherwise be ready to go.

Memory

There should be a panel used for access to the memory modules. If the panels are not marked (many are not), refer to your laptop instruction manuals to locate the panel on the bottom.

Remove any screws holding the panel in place, remove the panel from the laptop, and set it aside. If removing an existing memory module, remove them by undoing the module clamps, gently lifting the edge of the module to a 45-degree angle, and then pulling the module out of the slot.

Align the notch of the new module with that of the memory slot, and gently insert the module into the slot at a 45-degree angle. With all pins in the slot, gently rotate the module down flat until the clamps lock the module into place.

Replace the memory access panel, replace any screws, and power up the system. When the computer is powered back up, it may be necessary to go into the computer BIOS to let the system properly detect the new RAM that has been installed in the computer. Please refer to the user manual for the computer system for any additional information.

Optical drive

Replacing an optical drive is usually easier than it is to replace a hard drive or memory. Remove the screw that secures the optical drive to the bottom of the notebook. Grasp the edge of the optical drive bezel and slide the optical drive out of the base enclosure. Insert the new optical drive into the base enclosure until the connector is seated and replace the screw that secures the optical drive to the bottom of the notebook.

Wireless card

Both 802.11 and Bluetooth wireless cards that are built in can be replaced if they go bad. Sometimes they reside near the memory, so open the same panel that holds the memory. In other cases (such as a Dell Inspiron), you have to remove the memory, keyboard, optical drive, and hand rest to get to it. The Bluetooth card may be located in the same place, or it may be located at the edge of the laptop with its own small panel to remove. Consult your documentation.

Once you've found either type of wireless card, disconnect the two antenna contacts from the card. Do *not* pull by the wire; pull by the connector itself. Remove any screws from the wireless card and gently pull out the card from the slot. Insert the replacement card into the slot at a 45-degree angle, replace the screws, and reconnect the antenna to the adapter. Replace the parts you were required to remove to get to the card, reversing your steps carefully.

Mini-PCIe

Since many of the wireless cards are mini-PCIe, replacing any other card in this format will follow the same procedure, with the exception of removing and the reconnecting the antenna cables. The location of the card can be found in the documentation. Make sure that the new card is firmly inserted into the slot after removing the old card.

Screen

The screen is one of the more involved parts to replace, which is why many people throw a laptop away when damage to the screen occurs. Replacement can be done, but you have to remove a lot of parts to get at this replacement. Start by removing the battery, and then hold the power on for a bit to drain the power out of the capacitors.

Remove all of the screws on the back of the unit, and then turn the laptop over. Remove the speaker bezel, and you will see six wires coming from the old screen to the laptop. Remove the keyboard (see the instructions in the section "Keyboard"). Under the keyboard locate where these six wires connect, and disconnect them. Make note of what went where so you can replace them correctly when you reconnect the new monitor.

Remove the screws that are holding the old screen to the hinges of the laptop. Position the new screen in place and screw it into the hinges. Reroute the six wires coming from the new screen through any holes or spaces that lead them to their connection points. These are usually for the video cable, mic jacks, and wireless antenna. Reconnect the keyboard and reinstall it. Replace all parts that were required to get at the keyboard and replace all screws on the back of the unit.

These are general guidelines for this replacement, and you should always check the documentation for any departures from this general approach.

DC jack

Replacing a bad DC jack usually requires soldering. If this is not a skill you possess, just replace the motherboard. If you want to attempt it, remove all of the parts to get to the motherboard. In some cases the old DC jack can still be used; it just needs to have the old solder removed and replaced. If that is not the case, remove the old DC jack by unsolder-ing it from the connector. Then put the new jack in place and solder it to the connectors. Replace all of the parts and pieces you removed to get to the board. In general, a bad DC jack usually means a new board.

Battery

Replacing the battery in a laptop is simply a matter of removing the battery storage bay, removing the old battery from the bay, inserting the new battery into the bay and replacing the bay. Determining the battery type for the replacement will probably take longer than the replacement procedure. In fact many users carry extra batteries for situations where they know they will need to use the laptop for longer than the battery life (such as a long plane trip) and change the battery as needed.

Touchpad

This is another repair where many parts must be removed just to get to the piece to be replaced. Remove all the covers from the back of the system first. This may include those for the hard drive, RAM, and wireless card compartments. Remove the RAM, hard drive, and wireless card. Take the screw holding the CD-ROM in place and remove it as well.

Turn the laptop back over, open the lid, and remove any plastic pieces in the way of the keyboard. Remove the keyboard (see the section "Keyboard"). Disconnect the video and antenna cables from the motherboard (see the section "Screen"). Remove the Phillips-head screws from the LCD hinges, and then remove the LCD.

Disconnect the touchpad cable from the motherboard. Separate the upper casing assembly from the bottom casing and set it aside. Remove the touchpad from the upper casing assem-bly. Install the new touchpad by reversing the previous steps.

Plastics

In the course of explaining some of the replacement procedures in this section, several times we have mentioned plastic pieces that either hold something in place or cover something. These pieces may be held in place by screws or they may use snaps. In either case it is easy to damage these parts (especially the snaps) in the disassembly or assembly process. If this occurs, consult the documentation for the laptop. Even these pieces will have part numbers and can be ordered. It's easier to just take great care not to damage them in the first place. The best way to keep damage to these pieces from happening is to *never* force a piece in place. If you meet resistance, back out and try to determine what the obstruction is.

Speaker

To replace speakers, first follow the earlier instructions to remove the hard drive, the battery pack, and all of the screws holding the body together. Lift the screen up and separate it from the body (see the section "Screen"). Do *not* remove the wires connecting the screen to the motherboard.

Separate the two pieces of plastic body frame to view the inside of the laptop. Locate the speakers, using the documentation if necessary. Unscrew the speakers and note where they connect to the motherboard. Disconnect the old speakers and connect the new ones to the same location as where the old speakers were removed. Replace all of the parts in the reverse order you removed them.

System board

Replacing the system board requires the removal of all parts discussed to this point, since they all are either in the way of or connected to the motherboard. Once that is done, open the processor access door if there is one on the machine. If the processor is removable, and one did not come with the new motherboard, remove it and set it aside in a safe place.

Disconnect any remaining wires that are connected to the motherboard. Unplug any cards, such as the video card, that are not built directly into the motherboard. Locate the mounting screws for the motherboard and unscrew them. Remove the old motherboard, mount the new unit, and reassemble the parts in reverse order.

CPU

If the CPU is not built into the motherboard, it can be replaced. If it is built in, then you will be replacing the motherboard as well. If you are upgrading the processor and not simply replacing it, make sure your BIOS will support the new processor. It may be that you need to flash the BIOS to support the new CPU. You can determine this at either the website of the CPU maker or of the laptop. This is very important!

Follow the earlier instructions to remove the case, keyboard, and display. This will allow you to separate the two parts of the case. Remove the graphic card, and note where it plugs back in. Remove the heat sink from the top of the CPU by removing the screws holding it in place.

Remove the single screw holding the CPU in place and pull it out. Place the new CPU in place and replace the screw. (In some cases it is not a screw but a locking bar.) Place some thermal grease between the CPU and the heat sink. Replace the heat sink and its screws. Reverse your steps to reattach all the other parts and pieces.

In some cases, you may encounter a laptop that allows you to get at this from the bottom without removing the keyboard and display. This is why it is best to follow the specific directions in the documentation to save unnecessary component removal.

Exam Essentials

Describe the options available to expand the functionality of a laptop.   Understand the differences between ExpressCards (both 34 and 54 pin) and PCMCIA cards. Describe the memory options for a laptop (SoDIMMs) and the relative advantages and disadvantages of solid-state drives.

List the steps to install or replace laptop components.   This includes but is not limited to keyboards, hard drives, memory, optical drives, wireless cards, mini-PCIe cards, screens, DC jacks, batteries, touchpads, speakers, system boards, and CPUs.

3.2 Compare and contrast the components within the display of a laptop

The display of a laptop contains more components than you may expect. In this section these components will be discussed, and in some cases competing technologies are covered. The topics addressed in objective 3.2 include:

- Types
- Wi-Fi antenna connector/placement
- Inverter and its function
- Backlight

Types

Laptop displays can use several technologies. These were covered in Chapter 1 (all of these can also be used in a desktop as well). This section contains a quick review of these display types and their characteristics as they apply to laptops.

LCD

Two major types of liquid crystal displays (LCDs) are used today: active matrix screens and passive matrix screens. Their main differences lie in the quality of the image. Both types use some kind of lighting behind the LCD panel to make the screen easier to view. For more information on both active and passive LCD displays, see the section "Given a scenario, evaluate types and features of display devices" in Chapter 1.

LED

LED-based monitors are still LCDs (they still use liquid crystals to express images onscreen), but they use a different type of backlight than what is normally used. Several types of backlights are used with LED, including white LED (WLED), RGB LED, and WLED on a flat array. For more information on all three LED display types, see the section "Given a scenario, evaluate types and features of display devices" in Chapter 1.

OLED

An OLED (organic light-emitting diode) is another type of LED technology. It uses an emissive electroluminescent layer of organic compounds that emit light in response to an electric current. For more information, see the section "Given a scenario, evaluate types and features of display devices" in Chapter 1.

An interesting characteristic of these displays is their flexibility and transparency. This means they can roll up for storage (like a mat) and you can see through the display to objects behind the display. These displays are now available but quite expensive.

Plasma

Plasma displays utilize small cells containing ionized gases, similar to what is used in fluorescent lamps. They have the advantage of high-quality picture, wider viewing angles, and less motion blur, but have the disadvantage of screen burn-in and high energy requirements.

Because of the high energy requirements, using plasma for laptops is a challenge; however, laptop makers are working to reduce the power consumption of plasma to bring this technology to wider use.

Wi-Fi antenna connector/placement

The wireless antenna is located in the display. You may recall that when replacing a laptop screen you encountered a number of wires coming from the screen to the laptop body. One of these is the cable that connects the wireless antenna (located in the display) with the wireless card located in the body of the laptop.

The antennas that are in the display usually work quite well. In any specific situation you may improve your signal by moving the laptop around. This changes the polarization of the antenna and may cause it to line up better to the incoming signal.

Inverter and its function

An inverter is a component that takes DC power and converts it to a form that can be used by the LCD screen. It is implemented as a circuit board that is located behind the LCD display. If problems with flickering display or dimness occur, the inverter is a prime suspect.

If the inverter needs to be replaced, you should be aware that it may contain stored energy, so it may need to be discharged to be safe.

Backlight

LCD screens do not produce light. The light comes from a source behind the screen called the backlight. It is a small fluorescent lamp about 8 inches long and as big around as a pencil behind or to the side of the display. The light is spread across the screen. In most cases it is a cold cathode fluorescent lamp.

Exam Essentials

Differentiate the types of displays available in laptops.   Two major types of LCDs are used today: active matrix screens and passive matrix screens. LED-based monitors are still LCDs, but they use a different type of backlight than what is normally used. An OLED is another type of LED technology. It uses an emissive electroluminescent layer of organic compounds that emit light in response to an electric current. Because of the high energy requirements, using plasma for laptops is a challenge.

Describe the location and operational characteristics of the wireless antenna in a laptop.   The wireless antenna is located in the display. Moving the laptop changes the polarity of the antenna and may result in a better signal.

Identify the location and function of the inverter.   An inverter is a component that takes DC power and converts it to a form that can be used by the LCD screen. It is implemented as a circuit board behind the LCD display.

Locate and describe the backlight.   The backlight is a small fluorescent lamp about 8 inches long and as big around as a pencil behind or to the side of the display.

3.3 Compare and contrast laptop features

Due to the nature of its physical implementation, laptops have some features not found in desktops and some issues that need to be handled differently than with desktops. In this section some of these features and issues are discussed along with the use of some special function keys. The topics addressed in objective 3.3 include:

- Special function keys
- Docking station vs. port replicator
- Physical laptop lock and cable lock

Special function keys

Special function keys exist in both desktops and laptops, but in laptops function keys exist that may not be present in desktops. In the lower left-hand corner of the keyboard is a key with blue text on it that says Fn. When this key is held, other keys with a similar blue marking (such as F1, F2, and so on) will perform a different function than their normal function. This section describes some of the most common uses of these keys, although manufacturers sometimes implement these keys differently, so you should consult the documentation.

Dual displays

When additional displays are connected to the laptop (for example, a projector or second monitor), holding down the Fn key and pressing the appropriate Function key (located on the top row of the keyboard) will move the active screen from display to display (or display to projector) and then to a setting where all monitors have the same output. Normally, the F key that you press has an image of a monitor on it. This is valuable when making a presentation or when you would like to direct the image to the projector and/or the laptop screen. It is also worth noting that some laptop keyboards have the F1 key on the top line marked with an icon of a laptop display and another screen. If this is the case, this key is used to toggle between dual-monitor settings rather than the Fn and F8 key.

Wireless (on/off)

There is also a function key that will turn the wireless off and on. Consult the documentation to determine which key does this. Many laptops now have an antenna icon just above the blue text on F2 (or maybe another key in the top line). In that case, you do not have to hold the Fn key to use it. If wireless does not work (especially if the system is telling you to turn the wireless on), check this setting. It is very easy to hit this key and disable the wireless!

Volume settings

On the top row where the keys labeled F1–F12 are located, there are usually a couple of keys (usually F8 and F9) that have icons on them that look like speakers. These keys can be used to raise and lower the volume of the sound. If the icon is blue, you have to hold down the Fn key. Otherwise, you do not need to use the Fn key to activate them. (As a matter of fact, if you hold down the Fn key and use the F8 key you may be changing the location of the display output, as described in the section on dual display). If these keys are not present, consult the documentation for the key to use in conjunction with Fn to lower and raise the volume. Most laptops also include a mute button marked as such.

Screen brightness

On the top row where the keys labeled F1–F12 are located, there are usually a couple of keys (usually F4 and F5) that have icons on them that look like suns with arrow pointing up and down, respectively. They could also be located on the lower right on the keyboard.

These keys can be used to increase and decrease the brightness of the display. As with the volume settings described in the previous section, you do not need to use the Fn key to activate them. If these keys are not present, consult the documentation for the key to use in conjunction with Fn to increase and decrease the brightness.

Bluetooth (on/off)

In most cases the same key that turns 802.11 wireless off and on also does the same for Bluetooth. See the section "Wireless (on/off)."

Keyboard backlight

Some keyboards come with backlighting. These models will usually allow you to turn the backlighting on and off by using the Fn key in combination with another key, such as the Z key on some models. Consult the documentation to determine which key combination will perform this function.

Docking station vs. port replicator

Some notebook PCs have optional accessories called docking stations or port replicators. They let you quickly connect/disconnect with external peripherals and may also provide extra ports that the notebook PC doesn't normally have.

A docking station essentially allows a laptop computer to be converted to a desktop computer. When plugged into a docking station, the laptop has access to things it doesn't have as a standalone—the network, a workgroup printer, and so on. The cheapest form of docking station (if it can be called that) is a port replicator. Typically, you slide a laptop into the port replicator, and the laptop can then use a full-sized monitor, keyboard (versus the standard 84 keys on a laptop), mouse, and so on. Extended, or enhanced, replicators add other ports not found on the laptop, such as PC slots, sound, and more. The most common division between port replicators and docking stations is that port replicators duplicate the ports the laptop already has to outside devices and a docking station expands the laptop to include other ports and devices that the laptop does not natively have.

Laptops can support Plug and Play at three levels, depending on how dynamically they're able to adapt to changes:

Cold docking   The laptop must be turned off and back on for the change to be recognized.

Warm docking   The laptop must be put in and out of suspended mode for the change to be recognized.

Hot docking   The change can be made and is recognized while running normal operations.

Each docking station works a little differently, but there is usually a button you can press to undock the notebook from the unit. There may also be a manual release lever in case you need to undock when the button is unresponsive.

Because different hardware is available in docked versus undocked configurations, you may want to set up hardware profiles in Windows (not available in Windows Vista and Windows 7) to account for the differences.

Physical laptop lock and cable lock

Laptops are easily stolen. Therefore they come with a lock slot to which a cable lock can be attached. The lock slot is shown in Figure 3.3, and the connected lock (sometimes called a Kensington lock) is shown in Figure 3.4.

FIGURE 3.3   Lock slot

FIGURE 3.4   Connected lock

Exam Essentials

Describe the purpose of special function keys.   In the lower left-hand corner of the keyboard is a key with blue text on it that says Fn. When this key is held, other keys with a similar blue marking (such as F1–F12) will perform a different function than their normal function.

Differentiate docking stations and port replicators.   A docking station essentially allows a laptop computer to be converted to a desktop computer. Extended, or enhanced, replicators add other ports not found on the laptop, such as PC slots, sound, and more. The most common division between port replicators and docking stations is whether the peripheral provides network access and expands the laptop's capabilities.

Describe approaches to the physical security of a laptop.   Laptops come with a lock slot to which a cable lock can be attached. Also there is a lock on some models for the lid of the laptop.

Review Questions

1. What is the name of the laptop expansion port that is replacing PCMCIA?

2. What are the two form factors of ExpressCard?

3. What form factor of PCMCIA is used for memory?

4. The PCMCIA (PC Card) standard has been updated to a new standard called _____.

5. What type of memory is used in laptops?

6. What are the advantages of solid-state drives in laptops?

7. What special tool is typically required to work on laptops?

8. What is the easiest part to damage when changing a laptop keyboard?

9. True/False: Laptops use 3.5″ drives, which have lower capacity, lower cache, and lower velocity compared to 2.5″ drives.

10. Where is the wireless antenna located in a laptop?

Chapter

4

Printers

COMPTIA A+ 220-801 EXAM OBJECTIVES COVERED IN THIS CHAPTER:

✓ **4.1 Explain the differences between the various printer types and summarize the associated imaging process.**

- Laser
    - Imaging drum, fuser assembly, transfer belt, transfer roller, pickup rollers, separate pads, duplexing assembly
    - Imaging process: processing, charging, exposing, developing, transferring, fusing, and cleaning
- Inkjet
    - Ink cartridge, print head, roller, feeder, duplexing assembly, carriage, and belt
    - Calibration
- Thermal
    - Feed assembly, heating element
    - Special thermal paper
- Impact
    - Print head, ribbon, tractor feed
    - Impact paper

✓ **4.2 Given a scenario, install, and configure printers.**

- Use appropriate printer devices for a given operating system
- Print device sharing
    - Wired
        - USB
        - Parallel
        - Serial
        - Ethernet

- Wireless
    - Bluetooth
    - 802.11x
    - Infrared (IR)
- Printer hardware print server
- Printer sharing
    - Sharing local/networked printer via Operating System settings

✓ **4.3   Given a scenario, perform printer maintenance.**

- Laser
    - Replacing toner, applying maintenance kit, calibration, cleaning
- Thermal
    - Replace paper, clean heating element, remove debris
- Impact
    - Replace ribbon, replace print head, replace paper

This domain covers a lot of ground but is very focused. In the 600-series of A+ certifications, printers and scanners were considered so important that they constituted a domain on each of the two exams. With the 700-series of A+ certifications, the domains were absorbed into hardware and lost their standalone status. With this iteration (the 800-series), the topic of printers now has a domain all to itself once more, and it amounts to 11 percent of the total weighting on the 801 exam.

4.1 Explain the differences between the various printer types and summarize the associated imaging process

This objective tests your knowledge of four types of printers: laser, inkjet (sometimes called ink dispersion), thermal, and impact. Make certain you understand the imaging process associated with each of these printer types and—in particular—can name the steps in the laser imaging process. The A+ certification exams have traditionally focused heavily on laser printers, but you can expect to also see questions about other printer types.

Printers may be differentiated from one another in several ways, including the following:

Impact vs. Nonimpact Impact printers physically strike an inked ribbon and therefore can print multipart forms; nonimpact printers deliver ink onto the page without striking it. Dot matrix is impact; all the other printers you need to know for the exam are nonimpact.

Continuous Feed vs. Sheet Fed Continuous-feed paper feeds through the printer using a system of sprockets and tractors. Sheet-fed printers accept plain paper in a paper tray. Dot matrix is continuous feed; everything else is sheet fed.

Line vs. Page Line printers print one line at a time; page printers compose the entire page in memory and then place it all on the paper at once. Dot matrix and inkjet are line printers; laser is a page printer.

Laser

Laser printers are referred to as *page printers* because they receive their print job instructions one page at a time. They're sheet-fed, nonimpact printers. Another name for a laser printer is an *electrophotographic* (EP) printer.

LED printers are much like laser printers except they use light-emitting diodes (LEDs) instead of lasers. Their process is similar to that of laser printers.

An electrophotographic (laser) printer consists of the following major components:

Printer Controller A large circuit board that acts as the motherboard for the printer. It contains the processor and RAM to convert data coming in from the computer into a picture of a page to be printed.

Imaging Drum The toner cartridge and drum are typically packaged together as a consumable product that contains the toner. Toner is a powdery mixture of plastic resin and iron oxide. The plastic allows it to be melted and fused to the paper, and the iron oxide allows it to be moved around via positive or negative charge. Toner comes in a cartridge, like the one shown in Figure 4.1.

FIGURE 4.1 An EP toner cartridge

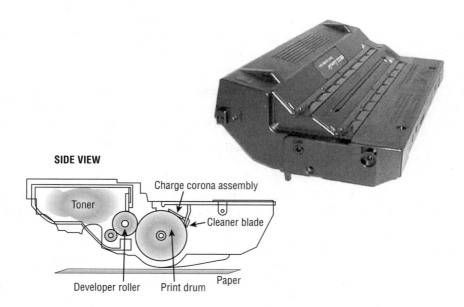

The drum is light sensitive; it can be written to with the laser scanning assembly. The toner cartridge in Figure 4.1 contains the print drum, so every time you change the toner cartridge, you get a new drum. In some laser printers, the drum is a separate part that lasts longer, so you don't have to change it every time you change the toner.

 There are quite a few images included with this discussion. You need not memorize the images for the exam; they are included to help make concepts that may seem difficult more easily explainable.

Primary Corona (Charge Corona)   Applies a uniform negative charge (around −600V) to the drum at the beginning of the printing cycle.

Laser Scanning Assembly   Uses a laser beam to neutralize the strong negative charge on the drum in certain areas, so toner will stick to the drum in those areas. The laser scanning assembly uses a set of rotating and fixed mirrors to direct the beam, as shown in Figure 4.2.

FIGURE 4.2   The EP laser scanning assembly (side view and simplified top view)

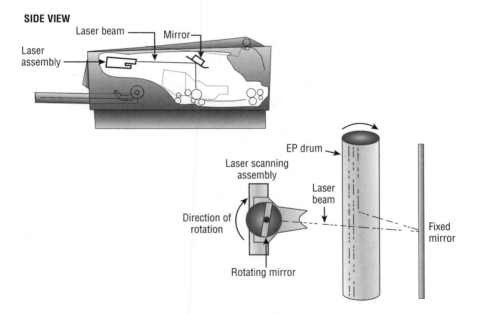

Paper Transport Assembly   Moves the paper through the printer. The paper transport assembly consists of a motor and several rubberized rollers. These rollers are operated by an electronic stepper motor. See Figure 4.3 for an example.

FIGURE 4.3   Paper transport rollers

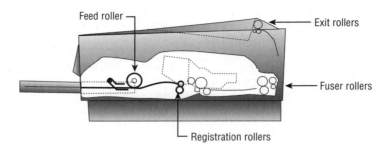

Feed roller

Exit rollers

Fuser rollers

Registration rollers

Transfer Corona   Applies a uniform positive charge (about +600V) to the paper. When the paper rotates past the drum, the toner jumps off the drum and onto the paper. Then the paper passes through a static eliminator that removes the positive charge from it (see Figure 4.4). Some printers use a transfer corona wire; others use a transfer corona roller.

FIGURE 4.4   The transfer corona assembly

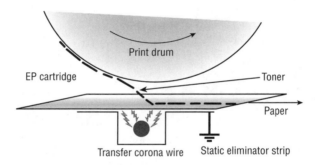

Print drum

EP cartridge

Toner

Paper

Transfer corona wire   Static eliminator strip

High-Voltage Power Supply (HVPS)   Delivers the high voltages needed to make the printing process happen. It converts ordinary 120V household AC current into high-DC voltages used to energize the primary and transfer corona wires (discussed later).

DC Power Supply   Delivers lower voltages to components in the printer that need much lower voltages than the corona wires do (such as circuit boards, memory, and motors).

Fusing Assembly   Melts the plastic resin in the toner so that it adheres to the paper. The fusing assembly contains a halogen heating lamp, a fusing roller made of Teflon-coated aluminum, and a rubberized pressure roller. The lamp heats the fusing roller, and as the paper passes between the two rollers, the pressure roller pushes the paper against the hot fusing roller, melting the toner into the paper (see Figure 4.5).

FIGURE 4.5   The fusing assembly

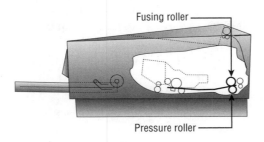

Fusing roller

Pressure roller

Imaging process

The laser (EP) print process consists of six steps. Here are the steps in the order you'll see them on the exam:

Step 1: Cleaning   In the first part of the laser print process, a rubber blade inside the EP cartridge scrapes any toner left on the drum into a used-toner receptacle inside the EP cartridge, and a fluorescent lamp discharges any remaining charge on the photosensitive drum (remember that the drum, being photosensitive, loses its charge when exposed to light). See Figure 4.6.

FIGURE 4.6   The cleaning step of the EP process

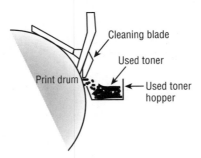

Cleaning blade

Used toner

Print drum

Used toner
hopper

The EP cartridge is constantly cleaning the drum. It may take more than one rotation of the photosensitive drum to make an image on the paper. The cleaning step keeps the drum fresh for each use. If you didn't clean the drum, you would see ghosts of previous pages printed along with your image.

The actual amount of toner removed in the cleaning process is quite small. The cartridge will run out of toner before the used toner receptacle fills up.

Step 2: Conditioning   In the *conditioning* step (Figure 4.7), a special wire (called a *primary corona* or *charge corona*) within the EP toner cartridge (above the photosensitive drum) gets a high voltage from the HVPS. It uses this high voltage to apply a strong, uniform negative charge (around −600VDC) to the surface of the photosensitive drum.

FIGURE 4.7   The conditioning step of the EP process

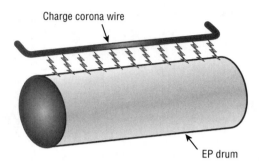

Step 3: Writing   In the *writing* step of the EP process, the laser is turned on and scans the drum from side to side, flashing on and off according to the bits of information the printer controller sends it as it communicates the individual bits of the image. In each area where the laser touches the photosensitive drum, the drum's charge is severely reduced from −600VDC to a slight negative charge (around −100VDC). As the drum rotates, a pattern of exposed areas is formed, representing the image to be printed. Figure 4.8 shows this process.

FIGURE 4.8   The writing step of the EP process

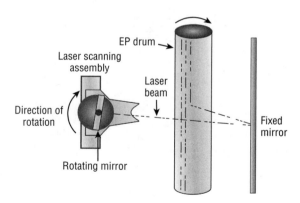

At this point, the controller sends a signal to the pickup roller to feed a piece of paper into the printer, where it stops at the registration rollers.

Step 4: Developing   Now that the surface of the drum holds an electrical representation of the image being printed, its discrete electrical charges need to be converted into something that can be transferred to a piece of paper. The EP process's *developing* step accomplishes this (Figure 4.9). In this step, toner is transferred to the areas that were exposed in the writing step.

FIGURE 4.9   The developing step of the EP process

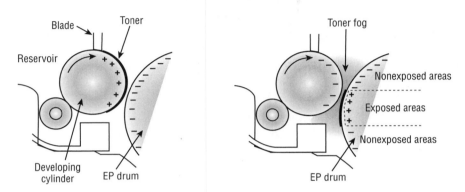

A metallic *developing roller* or *cylinder* inside an EP cartridge acquires a –600VDC charge (called a *bias voltage*) from the HVPS. The toner sticks to this roller because there is a magnet located inside the roller and because of the electrostatic charges between the toner and the developing roller. While the developing roller rotates toward the photosensitive drum, the toner acquires the charge of the roller (–600VDC). When the toner comes between the developing roller and the photosensitive drum, the toner is attracted to the areas that have been exposed by the laser (because these areas have a lesser charge, of –100VDC). The toner also is repelled from the unexposed areas (because they're at the same –600VDC charge, and like charges repel). This toner transfer creates a fog of toner between the EP drum and the developing roller.

The photosensitive drum now has toner stuck to it where the laser has written. The photosensitive drum continues to rotate until the developed image is ready to be transferred to paper in the next step.

Step 5: Transferring   At this point in the EP process, the developed image is rotating into position. The controller notifies the registration rollers that the paper should be fed through. The registration rollers move the paper underneath the photosensitive drum, and the process of transferring the image can begin, with the *transferring* step.

The controller sends a signal to the corona wire or corona roller (depending on which one the printer has) and tells it to turn on. The corona wire/roller then acquires a strong *positive* charge (+600VDC) and applies that charge to the paper. The paper, thus charged, pulls the toner from the photosensitive drum at the line of contact between the roller and the paper, because the paper and toner have opposite charges. Once the registration rollers move the paper past the corona wire, the static-eliminator strip removes all charge from that line of the paper. Figure 4.10 details this step. If the strip didn't bleed this charge away, the paper would attract itself to the toner cartridge and cause a paper jam.

FIGURE 4.10   The transferring step of the EP process

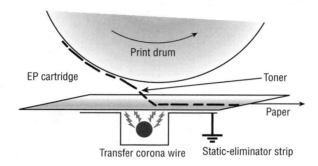

The toner is now held in place by weak electrostatic charges and gravity. It won't stay there, however, unless it's made permanent, which is the reason for the fusing step.

Step 6: Fusing   In the final step, the *fusing* step, the toner image is made permanent. The registration rollers push the paper toward the fuser rollers. Once the fuser grabs the paper, the registration rollers push for only a short time more. The fuser is now in control of moving the paper.

As the paper passes through the fuser, the fuser roller melts the polyester resin of the toner, and the rubberized pressure roller presses it permanently into the paper (Figure 4.11). The paper continues on through the fuser and eventually exits the printer.

FIGURE 4.11   The fusing step of the EP process

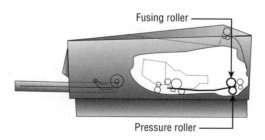

Once the paper completely exits the fuser, it trips a sensor that tells the printer to finish the EP process with the cleaning step. At this point, the printer can print another page, and the EP process can begin again.

Putting It All Together

Figure 4.12 summarizes all the EP process printing steps. First, the printer uses a rubber scraper to clean the photosensitive drum. Then the printer places a uniform, negative, –600VDC charge on the photosensitive drum by means of a charge corona. The laser paints an image onto the photosensitive drum, discharging the image areas to a much lower voltage (–100VDC). The developing roller in the toner cartridge has charged (–600VDC) toner stuck to it. As it rolls the toner toward the photosensitive drum, the toner is attracted to (and sticks to) the areas of the photosensitive drum that the laser has discharged. The image is then transferred from the drum to the paper at its line of contact by means of the corona wire (or corona roller) with a +600VDC charge. The static-eliminator strip removes the high, positive charge from the paper, and the paper, now holding the image, moves on. The paper then enters the fuser, where the fuser roller and the pressure roller make the image permanent. The paper exits the printer, and the printer starts printing the next page or returns to its ready state.

FIGURE 4.12   The EP print process

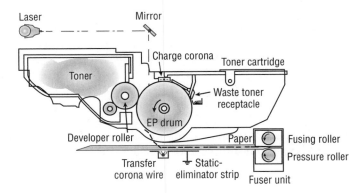

 A color laser is much like a regular laser printer except that multiple passes over the page are made, one for each ink color. Consequently, the printing speed is rather low.

 An optional component that can be added to printers (usually laser, but also inkjet) is a duplexer. This can be an optional assembly added to the printer, or built into it, but the sole purpose of *duplexing* is to turn the printed sheet over so it can be run back through the printer and allow printing on both sides.

Inkjet

Inkjet printers are one of the most popular types in use today. This type of printer sprays ink on the page to print text or graphics. It's a nonimpact, sheet-fed printer.

Figure 4.13 shows an ink cartridge. Some cartridges, like this one, contain the print head for that color of ink; you get a new print head each time you replace the cartridge. On other printer models, the ink cartridge is just an ink reservoir, and the heads don't need replacing.

FIGURE 4.13   A typical ink cartridge

There are two kinds of inkjet printers: *thermal* and *piezoelectric*. These terms refer to the way the ink is sprayed onto the paper. A thermal inkjet printer heats the ink to about 400° F, creating vapor bubbles that force the ink out of the cartridge. Thermal inkjets are also sometimes called *bubble jets*. A piezoelectric printer does the same thing but with electricity instead of heat.

Inkjet printers are popular because they can print in color and are inexpensive. However, their speed isn't quite as good as that of a laser printer and the per-page cost of ink can be higher than for a laser printer. Therefore, most businesses prefer laser printers for their main printing needs, perhaps keeping one or two inkjet printers around for situations requiring color printing.

Calibration

On an inkjet printer, calibration is more commonly known as head alignment. The printer will automatically try to align ink cartridges each time they are replaced (or installed). If you want to make sure they are in the right place, most printers allow you to print an alignment page from the maintenance menu.

If characters are not properly formed or are appearing as straight lines along the margin (usually the left), you can use the maintenance menu settings to align the ink cartridges.

Thermal

Thermal printers can be found in many older fax machines (most newer ones use either inkjet or laser printing) that print on a waxy paper that comes on a roll; the paper turns black when heat passes over it. These are also found on many handheld package tracking and point-of-sale (POS) devices such as credit card terminals. Thermal printers work by using a print head the width of the paper. When it needs to print, the print head heats and cools spots on the print head. The paper below the heated print head turns black in those spots. As the paper moves through the printer, the pattern of blackened spots forms an image on the page of what is being printed.

Another type of thermal printer uses a heat-sensitive ribbon instead of heat-sensitive paper. A thermal print head melts wax-based ink from the ribbon onto the paper. These are called thermal transfer or thermal wax-transfer printers.

Thermal direct printers typically have long lives because they have few moving parts. However, the paper is somewhat expensive, doesn't last long, and produces poorer-quality images than most of the other printing technologies.

There are some deviations of thermal printing that exist. They're all high-end color graphics printers designed for specialty professional usage. Four popular ones are:

Thermal Wax Transfer   A color nonimpact printer that uses a solid wax. A heater melts the wax and then sprays it onto the page, somewhat like an inkjet. The quality is very high, but so is the price.

Dye Sublimation   Another color nonimpact line printer. This one converts a solid ink into a gas that is then applied to the paper. Color is applied in a continuous tone, rather than individual dots, and the colors are applied one at a time. The ink comes on film rolls. The paper is very expensive, as is the ink. Print speeds are very low. The quality is extremely high.

Feed Assembly   Feed assemblies, commonly called feeders, are available to allow you to feed in the media you are printing on (paper, cards, etc.). Some feeders allow you to switch between multiple feeds, which is helpful if you need to alternate printing on different types of stock.

Heating Element   The heating element for a thermal printer is what generates the heat and does the actual printing. It is often the most expensive component of the printer.

Special thermal paper

To print with a thermal printer, you need to use heat-sensitive paper designed for the thermal printer as opposed to paper for any other type of printer. Rolls of thermal paper are available in a variety of sizes and colors.

Impact

A dot-matrix printer is an impact printer; it prints by physically striking an inked ribbon, much like a typewriter. It's an impact, continuous-feed printer.

The print head on a dot-matrix printer consists of a block of metal pins that extend and retract. These pins are triggered to extend in patterns that form letters and numbers as the print head moves across the paper. Early models, known as near letter quality (NLQ), printed using only nine pins. Later models used 24 pins and produced much better letter-quality (LQ) output.

The main advantage of dot matrix is its impact (physical striking of the paper). Because it strikes the paper, you can use it to print on multipart forms. Nonimpact printers can't do that. Dot-matrix printers aren't commonly found in most offices these days because of their disadvantages, including noise, slow speed, and poor print quality.

 Dot-matrix printers are still found in many warehouses, and other businesses, where multipart forms are used or where continuous feed is required.

Key elements of an impact printer are discussed in the sections which follow.

Printhead   The pins in the printhead are wrapped with coils of wire to create a solenoid and are held in the rest position by a combination of a small magnet and a spring. To trigger a particular pin, the printer controller sends a signal to the printhead, which energizes the wires around the appropriate print wire. This turns the print wire into an electromagnet, which repels the print pin, forcing it against the ink ribbon and making a dot on the paper.

Ribbon   The ribbon is like that on an old typewriter. Most impact printers have an option to adjust how close the printhead rests from the ribbon. So if your printing is too light, you may be able to adjust the print head closer to the ribbon. If it's too dark or you get smeared printing, you may be able to move the print head back.

Tractor Feed   The tractor feed unit feeds in the continuous feed paper. This paper has holes running down both edges.

Impact paper

An impact printer uses continuous feed paper fed to it by the tractor feed unit.

Exam Essentials

Know the common types of printers.   Know and understand the types of printers, such as impact printers, inkjet printers, and laser printers (page printers), as well as their interfaces and print media.

Understand the process of printing for each type of printer.   Each type of printer puts images or text on paper. Understand the process that each type of printer uses to accomplish this task.

Know the specific components of each type of printer.   Each type of printer uses similar components to print. Know the different components that make up each type of printer, and their jobs.

Understand the print process of a laser printer.   You'll most likely be asked questions about certain processes of a laser printer. Know and understand the different steps that make up the print process of a laser printer.

4.2 Given a scenario, install and configure printers

Printers are one of the most common elements in any computing environment, from home to office. The range they cover is phenomenal—everything from a free printer included by a vendor with the purchase of a PC up to a monolith in a large office churning out hundreds of pages a minute. Regardless of where a printer falls in that spectrum, they are all the same in that they must be installed and properly configured in order to be of use.

In addition to the physical body of the printer, components and consumables are associated with it. Components include the following:

Memory   As a general rule, the more memory a laser printer has, the better. The memory is used to hold the print jobs in the printer queue; the more users, and the larger the print jobs, the more memory you'll want. Dot-matrix and inkjet printers contain very little memory, the former using only a buffer to hold a few characters.

Drivers   These are the software components of the printer—allowing the device to communicate with the operating system. It's important to always have the correct and most current drivers, for the greatest efficiency. The printer drivers vary based on the operating system being used on the client computer, and if a printer is attached to more than one operating system, you have to make sure you have the appropriate driver for each operating system in use.

Firmware   Although drivers can be updated, firmware rarely is. Firmware is installed on the printer and can be thought of as the operating system for that device.

Consumables for printers are those items you must change as you use the printer—the variable items that get consumed and must be replenished. These include toner (or ink, depending on the type of printer you're using) and paper. Be sure to always order and use the correct grade of consumables that are recommended for your machine. For example, don't use inkjet media in a laser printer or you will run the risk of the laser printer's fuser melting it.

Use appropriate printer drivers for a given operating system

Besides understanding the printer's operation, for the exam you need to understand how these devices talk to a computer. The *driver* software controls how the printer processes the print job. When you install a printer driver for the printer you are using, it allows the computer to print to that printer correctly (assuming you have the correct interface configured between the computer and printer).

An *interface* is the collection of hardware and software that allows the device to communicate with a computer. Each printer, for example, has at least one interface, but some printers have several, in order to make them more flexible in a multiplatform environment. If a printer has several interfaces, it can usually switch between them on the fly so that several computers can print at the same time.

Print device sharing

Printer sharing covers the hardware technologies involved in getting the information to and from the computer. There are several types, which can be broken into two broad categories: wired and wireless.

Wired

The wired forms of connection this exam test on are USB, parallel, serial, and Ethernet. Each is addressed in the sections that follow.

USB

The most popular type of printer interface as this book is being written is the USB. It's the most popular interface for just about every peripheral. The benefit for printers is that it has a higher transfer rate than either serial or parallel and it automatically recognizes new devices. USB is also fully Plug and Play, and it allows several printers to be connected at once without adding ports or using up additional system resources.

Parallel

Until recently, the parallel port on a PC was the overwhelming favorite interface for connecting printers, to the point where the parallel port has become synonymous with *printer port*. It sends data 8 bits at a time (in parallel) and uses a cable with a male DB-25 connector at the computer and a 36-bin Centronics male connector at the printer. Its main drawback is its cable length, which must be less than 10 feet.

Serial

This is the traditional RS-232 serial port found on most PCs. The original printer interface on the earliest computers, it has fallen out of favor and is seldom used anymore for printing because it's so slow.

Ethernet

Most large-environment printers (primarily laser and LED printers) have a special interface that allows them to be hooked directly to a network. These printers have a network interface card (NIC) and ROM-based software that let them communicate with networks, servers, and workstations.

Wireless

The wireless forms of connection this exam test on are Bluetooth, 802.11x, and Infrared (IR). Each is addressed in the sections that follow.

Bluetooth

Bluetooth is an infrared technology that can connect a printer to a computer at a short range; its absolute maximum range is 100 meters (330 feet), and most devices are specified to work within 10 meters (33 feet). When printing with a Bluetooth-enabled device (like a PDA or mobile phone) and a Bluetooth-enabled printer, all you need to do is get within range of the device (that is, move closer), select the print driver from the device, and choose Print. The information is transmitted wirelessly through the air using radio waves and is received by the device.

802.11x

A network-enabled printer that has a wireless adapter can participate in a wireless Ethernet (IEEE 802.11b, a, g, or n) network, just as it would as a wired network client.

Infrared (IR)

With the explosion of personal digital assistants (PDAs), the need grew for printing under the constraints they provide. The biggest hurdle faced by PDA owners who need to print is the lack of any kind of universal interface. Most interfaces are too big and bulky to be used on handheld computers such as PDAs. The solution was to incorporate the standardized technology used on some remote controls: infrared transmissions. *Infrared transmissions* are simply wireless transmissions that use radiation in the infrared range of the electromagnetic spectrum. Many laser printers (and some computers) come with infrared transmitter/receivers (transceivers) so that they can communicate with the infrared ports on many handhelds. This allows the user of a PDA, handheld, or laptop to print to that printer by pointing the device at the printer and initiating the print process.

As far as configuring the interface is concerned, very little needs to be done. The infrared interfaces are enabled by default on most computers, handhelds, and printers equipped with them. The only additional item that must be configured is the print driver on the PDA, handheld, or computer. The driver must be the correct one for the printer to which you are printing.

Printer hardware print server

A print server is a popular option for adding a printer to the network and not adding a host computer. To be a print server, the network interface card (NIC) in the printer differs from a NIC in a computer in that it has a processor on it to perform the management of the NIC interface and it is made by the same manufacturer as the printer.

To qualify as a print server, when someone on the network prints, the print job goes directly to the printer and not through any third-party device. This tends to make printing to that printer faster and more efficient—that NIC is dedicated to receiving print jobs and sending printer status to clients.

Firmware Updates

Printers resemble computers in many ways. Like a computer, they can have their own motherboard, memory, and CPU. They also have firmware—that is, software permanently stored on a chip. If you're using an old computer with a new operating system, an update may be available for the printer's or scanner's firmware. You can find out that information at the printer or scanner manufacturer's website and download the update from there along with a utility program for performing the update.

Printer sharing

All Windows-based operating systems (which are the ones you must know for this certification) allow you to share a local printer or connect over the network to one that has been shared. To connect to a printer in Windows 7, choose Start ➢ Devices And Printers and it will show the currently recognized printers (see Figure 4.14) and allow you to add new ones.

FIGURE 4.14   Printers in Windows 7

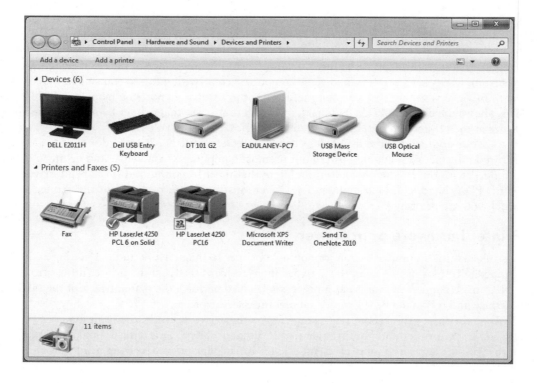

The image of a check box on the first instance of the HP 4250 shows that the printer is the current default, and the image of two people on the second instance of the HP 4250 means that it is shared. Clicking Add A Printer (at the top of the dialog box) starts the wizard shown in Figure 4.15.

FIGURE 4.15   Adding a printer in Windows 7

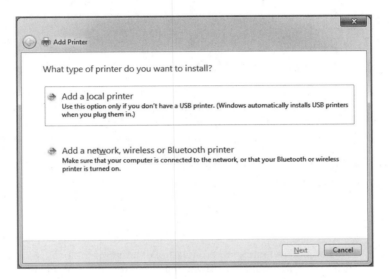

Sharing local/networked printer via Operating System settings

To share a local/networked printer via the Windows operating systems that you need to know for the exam, right-click on the icon for the printer (beneath Devices And Printers or Printers And Faxes, depending on your operating system) and choose either Sharing (Windows XP) or Printer Properties. If you choose Printer Properties, next click the Sharing tab.

Select Share This Printer, and provide a name that the printer will be known by on the network. This is the name that will appear when adding a new network printer on a client, and it can also be referenced by the entire qualified name using the syntax \\host\share_name.

Exam Essentials

Be familiar with the possible interfaces that can be used for printing.   The types generally fall into two categories: wired (USB, parallel, serial, Ethernet) and wireless (Bluetooth, 802.11*x*, and Infrared).

Know how to install printers. The manufacturer is the best source of information about installing printers. You should, however, know about the wizards available in Windows as well.

Know to keep firmware up-to-date. Firmware updates can be found at the manufacturer's website and installed according to the instructions accompanying them.

4.3 Given a scenario, perform printer maintenance

Most printing problems today are due to either improper configuration or actual physical problems that arise from poor maintenance of the printer. As far as configuration goes, the Windows architecture is such that when a client wants to print to a network printer, a check is first done to see if the client has the latest printer driver. If it doesn't—as judged by the print server—the new driver is sent from the server to the client, and then the print job is accepted. This is an enormous help to the administrator, for when a new driver comes out, all the administrator must do is install it on the server, and the distribution to the clients becomes automatic.

This objective tests your knowledge of some of the basic operations of printers. The emphasis, however, is on detecting and solving problems with them. If you truly want to show your expertise with printers, CompTIA offers another certification, PDI+, which is meant for that purpose.

To keep your printers working efficiently and extend their life as much as possible, you should start by creating a log of scheduled maintenance as outlined by the vendor's guidelines and then make certain this maintenance log is adhered to. For many printers, the scheduled maintenance includes installing maintenance kits. Maintenance kits typically include a fuser, transfer roller, pick-up rollers (for the trays), separation rollers, and feed rollers.

After installing the maintenance kit, you need to reset the maintenance counter as explained in the vendor's documentation.

Pay a great deal of attention to the ambient surroundings of the printers as well. High temperature, high humidity, and high levels of dust and debris can negatively affect the life of the printer and the quality of print jobs. Always make certain you use recommended supplies. It may be cheaper to buy off-brand supplies that aren't intended for your equipment, but you're taking a gamble with shortening the life of your printer and decreasing the quality of your output.

Some generic preventive maintenance includes the following:

- Never reuse paper that has been through the printer once. Although it may look blank, you're repeating the charging and fusing process on a piece of paper that most likely has *something* already on it.

- Change the toner when needed. You should recycle; most toner manufacturers participate in a recycling program of some type. The toner cartridge should never be exposed to light for longer than a few minutes; it usually comes sealed in a black plastic light-resistant bag.

- Clean any toner that accidentally spills into the printer with a dry, lint-free cloth. Bear in mind that spilled toner in the paper path should clear after you run a few blank pages through. If toner gets on your clothes, wipe them with a dry cloth and wash them with cold water (hot water works like the fusing process to set them into the material).

- Clean any paper shreds, dust, or dander that gets deposited in the printer. Pressurized air is the most effective method of removal.

- Keep the drum in good working order. If it develops lines, replace it.

- Install the maintenance kit when needed and reset the page count. The maintenance kit (sometimes called a fuser kit), typically includes a fusing assembly, rollers, and separation pads. A printer display similar to "Perform Printer Maintenance" indicates the printer has reached its maintenance interval and a maintenance kit needs to be installed.

- Don't be afraid to cycle the power on an unresponsive printer. Turning it off, leaving it off for one minute to clear, then turning it back on can solve a great many problems.

While the above list is a good rule of thumb, for this objective CompTIA wants you to be familiar with maintenance for three types of printers: laser, thermal, and impact. The following sections will look at each of those.

Laser

Just as laser printers are the most complicated of the types (and offer the most capabilities), they also have the most things that can go awry. A thermal fuse is included to keep the system from overheating, and if it becomes faulty, it can prevent the printer from printing. Many high-capacity laser printers also include an ozone filter to prevent the corona's ozone output from reaching too high a level. On these printers, the filter should be changed as a part of regular maintenance.

Other common problems and solutions are as follows:

Paper Jams   While paper jams can be caused by numerous problems, two common ones are the paper not feeding correctly and moisture. To correct improper feeds, make sure you set the alignment guides for the paper you are using and verify the paper is feeding in straight. Keep paper from getting any moisture before feeding into the printer, as moisture often causes pages to stick together and bind. Paper jams can also be caused by using paper that is not approved for the printer—particularly thick cardstock.

One employee routinely had problems with a printer each time he went to print on high-quality paper—a problem experienced by no one else. Upon close examination, it turned out that each time he chose to print to the expensive paper, he counted the number of sheets he loaded into the printer—counting that involved licking his finger and then touching each page. A simple directive to stop doing this solved the problem.

Regardless of the cause of a paper jam, you need to always fully clear the printer of any traces of paper (torn or whole) before attempting to print again.

Error Codes   Many laser printers include LCD displays for interaction with the printer. When error codes appear, refer to the manufacturer's manuals or website for information on how to interpret the codes and solve the problem causing them.

Out of Memory Error   While PCs now may need a minimum of 1 GB of RAM to run at a minimal level, it is not uncommon to find printers that still have only 4 MB or 8 MB of memory. If you are routinely running out of memory on a printer, add more memory if possible, and replace the printer when it is no longer possible to do so.

Lines and Smearing   Lines and smearing can be caused by the toner cartridge or the fuser. Try replacing the toner first (and cleaning any that may have spilled). If this does not fix the problem, replace the fuser.

Blank Pages Print   Verify that there is toner in the cartridge. If it's an old cartridge, you can often shake it slightly to free up toner once before replacing. If it's a new cartridge, make sure the sealing tape has been removed from the cartridge prior to placing it in the printer.

Be very careful when doing this operation. Someone who has asthma or who is sensitive to microfine particles could be adversely affected by the toner.

Dark Spots Print   The most likely culprit is too much toner. Run blank pages through the printer to clean it.

Garbled Pages Print   Make sure you're using the right printer driver in your application.

Ghosted Images Print   Ghosting—repeating text or images on the page—is usually caused by a bad cartridge. There can be damage to the drum or charging roller and, if so, replacing the cartridge will help with the problem.

No Connectivity   If a network printer is not able to receive jobs, it can be an issue with the IP address that it has (or, more correctly, does not have). Often the printer will need to be manually assigned an IP address to make sure that it has the same one each time. Read the manufacturer's documentation for assigning an IP address to the printer and walk through the steps to do so.

Never overlook the obvious. Connectivity problems also occur when the printer is turned off.

Print-Quality Problems   See if your printer has the ability to turn Resolution Enhancement Technology (RET) on and off. This is what allows the printer to use partial-sized dots for images that are rounded. If it's turned off, turn it back on. If there are small marks or defects in the exact same spot on every page printed, the most likely culprit is a scratch on the drum.

Replacing Toner   Toner represents the consumable within the laser printer. Toner cartridges are used by laser printers to store toner. Use toner that is recommended for your printer. Using bad supplies could ruin your printer and void your warranty. Remove the toner before moving or shipping a printer to avoid spills.

Applying a Maintenance Kit   Maintenance kits are marketed by the manufacturer. Each kit varies in contents based on the printer in question but typically consists of a fuser, transfer roller and the feed/separation rollers. A counter on the laser printer often identifies when the maintenance kit is needed and you can reset the counter after applying the new kit.

Calibration   With laser printers, and inkjets as well, there is often a need to calibrate. Calibration is the process by which the result produced matches what was created: all hardware, including monitor, scanner, and printer match on color, margins, and so forth.

The calibration process is different for each manufacturer, but is usually similar to the following:

1. During installation of the software, you are asked (by the installation wizard) if you want to calibrate now (and you say Yes).

2. The printer prints out multiple sets of numbered lines. Each set of lines represents an alignment instance and you are asked which set looks the best.

3. You enter the set number and click OK. In some cases, the alignment ends here. In other cases, the alignment page is reprinted to verify that the settings are correct and you are given a chance to change.

4. You exit the alignment routine.

Cleaning   It is important to keep the printer and the area around it clean. Each time you replace the toner or perform any maintenance, be sure to clean the debris.

Thermal

The amount of maintenance required on a thermal printer pales in comparison to laser since there are no moving parts to speak of. The following sections look at the key items to be aware related to thermal printers as you study for the exam.

Replace Paper   Replace the thermal paper as it is needed; be sure to keep the feed area clean of paper slivers and other debris.

Clean Heating Element   Before even looking at a heating element, always unplug the printer and make certain it is cool. Thermal printer cleaning cards, cleaning pens, and kits are available and recommended for cleaning.

Remove Debris   Keep the printer free of dust and debris. Any particulates that get into the printer can interfere with the paper feeding properly or affect the print quality. Use compressed air or computer vacuum to remove any debris.

Impact

A dot-matrix print head reaches high temperatures, and care must be taken to avoid a user or technician touching it and getting burned. Most dot-matrix printers include a temperature sensor to tell if the print head is getting too hot. The sensor interrupts printing to let the print head cool down and then allows printing to start again. If this sensor becomes faulty, it can cause the printer to print a few lines, stop for a while, print more, stop, and so on. The following sections look at the key items to be aware related to impact printers as you study for the exam.

Replace Ribbon   A common culprit with poor printing is the ribbon. A tight ribbon, or one that isn't advancing properly, will cause smudges or overly light printout. To solve this problem, replace the ribbon.

Replace Print Head   The print head should never be lubricated, but you can clean off debris with a cotton swab and denatured alcohol. Print pins missing from the print head will cause incomplete images or characters or white lines running through the text. This can be remedied by replacing the print head.

If the print head isn't at fault, make certain its close enough to the platen to make the right image. The print head can be moved closer and farther from the platen depending on the thickness of the paper and other considerations.

Replace Paper   Preventive maintenance includes not only keeping the print head dry and clean, but also vacuuming paper shreds from inside the machine. This should be done more often if needed, but always when you replace the paper.

Exam Essentials

Know how to interact with printers.   Know that the Properties page for each, available from Windows, allows you to interact with them, but many printers also include advanced utilities that go beyond basic interaction.

Know the common printing problems listed.   Understand the most common problems that occur in an environment.

Know the importance of running scheduled maintenance.   Scheduled maintenance can prolong the life of your equipment and help ensure that your output continues to live up to the quality you expect.

Understand the importance of a suitable environment.   If you want your equipment to last as long as possible and deliver quality, you should pay attention to the environment in which you place it.

Review Questions

1. What are two examples of wired printers?

2. What advantage does an impact printer have over other printer technologies?

3. What is the purpose of the primary corona in the laser printing process?

4. List the six steps in the laser printing process in the correct order.

5. If there is loose toner on the printer after a laser print, which part is defective?

6. What are some advantages of USB as a printer interface as opposed to parallel?

7. What do you need to do if there are stripes on an inkjet printout?

8. True or false: A laser printer that prints a completely blank page may be suffering from a nonfunctioning fuser.

9. Why should you not use media designed for an inkjet printer in a laser printer?

10. What is the most common cause of small marks or defects in the same spot on every page of a laser printer's printout?

Chapter

5

Operational Procedures

COMPTIA A+ 220-801 EXAM OBJECTIVES COVERED IN THIS CHAPTER:

✓ **5.1 Given a scenario, use appropriate safety procedures.**

- ESD straps
- ESD mats
- Self-grounding
- Equipment grounding
- Personal safety
  - Disconnects power before repairing PC
  - Remove jewelry
  - Lifting techniques
  - Weight limitations
  - Electrical fire safety
  - CRT safety—proper disposal
  - Cable management
- Compliance with local government regulations

✓ **5.2 Explain environmental impacts and the purpose of environmental controls.**

- MSDS documentation for handling and disposal
- Temperature, humidity level awareness and proper ventilation
- Power surges, brownouts, blackouts
  - Battery backup
  - Surge suppressor

- Protection from airborne particles
  - Enclosures
  - Air filters
- Dust and debris
  - Compressed air
  - Vacuums
- Component handling and protection
  - Antistatic bags
- Compliance to local government regulations

✓ **5.3 Given a scenario, demonstrate proper communication and professionalism.**

- Use proper language—avoid jargon, acronyms, slang when applicable
- Maintain a positive attitude
- Listen and do not interrupt the customer
- Be culturally sensitive
- Be on time (if late contact the customer)
- Avoid distractions
  - Personal calls
  - Talking to co-workers while interacting with customers
  - Personal interruptions
- Dealing with difficult customer or situation
  - Avoid arguing with customers and/or being defensive
  - Do not minimize customer's problems
  - Avoid being judgmental
  - Clarify customer statements (ask open ended questions to narrow the scope of the problem, restate the issue, or question to verify understanding)

- Set and meet expectations/timeline and communicate status with the customer
  - Offer different repair/replacement options if applicable
  - Provide proper documentation on the services provided
  - Follow up with customer/user at a later date to verify satisfaction
- Deal appropriately with customers confidential materials
  - Located on computer, desktop, printer, etc.

✓ **5.4 Explain the fundamentals of dealing with prohibited content/activity.**

- First response
  - Identify
  - Report through proper channels
  - Data/device preservation
- Use of documentation/documentation changes
- Chain of custody
  - Tracking of evidence/documenting process

If you looked back over the history of the A+ certification, you would be hard-pressed to find any domain or topics that have changed as much as this one. This time around, for example, the can of worms of dealing with prohibited content is added in. Much of what is here is common sense, but don't dismiss the chapter based on that. Since these topics are worth 11 percent of the weighting, doing well on this portion of the exam can increase your chances of acing the 220-801 exam.

5.1 Given a scenario, use appropriate safety procedures

This objective deals with potential hazards, both to you and to the computer system. It focuses on protecting humans from harm due to electricity and on protecting computer components from harm due to electrostatic discharge (ESD).

ESD is one of the most dangerous risks associated with working with computers. Not only does ESD have the potential to damage components of the computer, but it can also injure you. Not understanding the proper way to avoid it could cause you great harm.

The ESD that we are speaking about here does not have the capability to kill you since it doesn't have the amperage. What does represent a threat, though, is using a wrist strap of your own design that does not have the resistor protection built into it and then accidentally touching something with high voltage while wearing the wrist strap. Without the resistor in place, the high voltage would be grounded through you!

Electrostatic discharge (ESD) is the technical term for what happens whenever two objects of dissimilar charge come in contact—think of rubbing your feet on a carpet and then touching a light switch. The two objects exchange electrons in order to equalize the electrostatic charge between them. If the device receiving the charge happens to be an electronic component, there is a good chance it can be damaged.

The likelihood that a component will be damaged increases with the growing use of complementary metallic oxide semiconductor (CMOS) chips, because these chips contain a thin metal oxide layer that is hypersensitive to ESD. The previous generation's transistor–transistor logic (TTL) chips are more robust than the newer CMOS chips because they don't contain this metal oxide layer. Most of today's integrated circuits (ICs) are CMOS chips, so ESD is more of a concern lately.

The lowest static voltage transfer that you can feel is around 3,000 volts (it doesn't electrocute you because there is extremely little current). A static transfer that you can *see* is at least 10,000 volts! Just by sitting in a chair, you can generate around 100 volts of static electricity. Walking around wearing synthetic materials can generate around 1,000 volts. You can easily generate around 20,000 volts simply by dragging your smooth-soled shoes across a carpet in the winter. (Actually, it doesn't have to be winter to run this danger; it can occur in any room with very low humidity. It's just that heated rooms in wintertime generally have very low humidity.)

It would make sense that these thousands of volts would damage computer components. However, a component can be damaged with as little as 80 volts. That means if your body has a small charge built up in it, you could damage a component without even realizing it.

ESD straps

There are measures you can implement to help contain the effects of ESD. The easiest one to implement is the *antistatic wrist strap*, also referred to as an *ESD strap*. You attach one end of the ESD strap to an earth ground (typically the ground pin on an extension cord) and wrap the other end around your wrist. This strap grounds your body and keeps it at a zero charge. Figure 5.1 shows the proper way to attach an antistatic strap.

FIGURE 5.1   Proper ESD strap connection

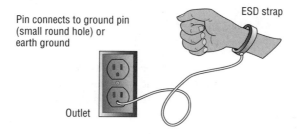

Pin connects to ground pin (small round hole) or earth ground

ESD strap

Outlet

If you do not have a grounded outlet available, you can achieve partial benefit simply by attaching the strap to the metal frame of the PC case. Doing so keeps the charge equalized between your body and the case so that there is no electrostatic discharge when you touch components inside the case.

WARNING   An ESD strap is a specially designed device to bleed electrical charges away *safely*. It uses a 1 megaohm resistor to bleed the charge away slowly. A simple wire wrapped around your wrist will not work correctly and could electrocute you!

WARNING   Do not wear the antistatic wrist strap when there is the potential to encounter a high-voltage capacitor, such as when working on the inside of a monitor or power supply. The strap could channel that voltage through your body.

ESD mats

It is possible to damage a device simply by laying it on a bench top. For this reason, you should have an *ESD mat* (also known as an *antistatic mat*) in addition to an ESD strap. This mat drains excess charge away from any item coming in contact with it (see Figure 5.2). ESD mats are also sold as mouse/keyboard pads to prevent ESD charges from interfering with the operation of the computer.

You can also purchase ESD floor mats for technicians to stand on while performing computer maintenance. These include a grounding cord, usually 6 to 10 feet in length.

FIGURE 5.2   Proper use of an ESD mat

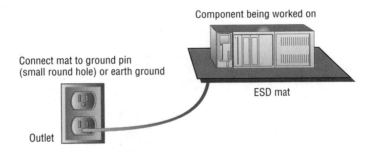

Vendors have methods of protecting components in transit from manufacture to installation. They press the pins of ICs into antistatic foam to keep all the pins at the same potential, and circuit boards are shipped in antistatic bags, discussed later. However, keep in mind that unlike antistatic mats, antistatic bags do not drain the charges away—they should never be used in place of antistatic mats.

Self-grounding

Grounding is the electrical term for providing a path for an electrical charge to follow to return to earth. This term was mentioned earlier as it relates to ESD straps and mats but it is the element of those that saves you from harm in the event of an electrical discharge—the charge passes to ground. The easiest way to ground yourself is to use a grounding strap.

Equipment grounding

Just as you can ground yourself by using a grounding strap, you can ground equipment. This is most often accomplished by using a mat or a connection directly to a ground.

Personal safety

There is nothing on a computer, a server, a router, and so on that cannot be replaced or repaired. The same, however, is not true for you. It is imperative that you protect yourself from harm and follow safety procedures when working with computers.

Disconnect power before repairing PC

You should never attempt to remove a case, open a case, or work on any element that is carrying electricity without first disconnecting it. If removing power on the device you are working on is more complicated than just unplugging it (requiring circuit breakers to be thrown, fuses to be removed, and so forth), then use a voltmeter to make sure the current is off at the device before proceeding.

Remove jewelry

Gold and other metals are great conductors of electrical current. The last thing you want while working on a problem is for the gold chain around your neck to fall against a capacitor. Take it off. While not all jewelry is metallic, all jewelry is a snagging hazard.

Lifting techniques

An easy way to get hurt is by moving equipment in an unsafe or improper way. Here are some safe lifting techniques to always keep in mind:

- Lift with your legs, not your back. When you have to pick something up, bend at the knees, not at the waist. You want to maintain the natural curve of the back and spine when lifting.
- Be careful to not twist when lifting. Keep the weight on your centerline.
- Keep objects as close to your body as possible and at waist level.
- Where possible, push instead of pull.

The goal in lifting should be to reduce the strain on lower back muscles as much as possible, since muscles in the lower back aren't nearly as strong as those in the legs or other parts of the body. Some people use a back belt or brace to help maintain the proper position while lifting.

Weight limitations

Closely related to lifting and moving equipment is the topic of weight limitations. If you believe the load is too much for you to carry, don't try to pick it up. Get help!

When possible, use a cart and always be aware of the environment. While you may be able to carry 80 pounds on a level surface without trouble, that number will lessen if there are stairs, uneven floors, or narrow doorways. Map out the path you are going to take before you begin lifting and moving items.

Electrical fire safety

Repairing a computer is not often the cause of an electrical fire. However, you should know how to extinguish such a fire properly. Three major classes of fire extinguishers are available, one for each type of flammable substance: A for wood and paper fires, B for flammable liquids, and C for electrical fires. The most popular type of fire extinguisher today is the multipurpose, or ABC-rated, extinguisher. It contains a dry chemical powder that smothers the fire and cools it at the same time. For electrical fires (which may be related to a shorted-out wire in a power supply), make sure the fire extinguisher will work for class C fires. If you don't have an extinguisher that is specifically rated for electrical fires (type C), you can use an ABC-rated extinguisher.

CRT safety—proper disposal

Two computer devices have the potential to carry high voltages: the monitor and the power supply. The power supply converts AC current into DC current, and the capacitor associated with it holds 120 volts for quite a while.

The monitor uses a lot of power as it directs electrons on the screen via a strong magnet. The electrons and magnet require a considerable amount of voltage in order to be able to do their task. Like power supplies, monitors have the ability to hold their charge a long time after the power has been disconnected.

You should never open a power supply or a monitor for the reasons discussed here. The risk of electrocution with these two devices is significant.

If you question the presence of electricity, or the voltage of it, use a voltmeter. Figure 5.3 shows a simple voltmeter capable of working with both AC and DC currents.

Many states have laws that govern the disposal of monitors since they are often classified as hazardous. CRT monitors contain high amounts of lead and other harmful materials such as arsenic, beryllium, cadmium, chromium, mercury, nickel, and zinc. To dispose of a monitor, contact a computer recycling firm and let them get rid of the monitor for you.

Cable management

It can be time-consuming to tie cables up, run them in channels, and snake them through walls, but it is time well spent when it keeps one person from harm. It is all too easy to get tangled in a cable or trip over one that is run across the floor. Exposed cables should be routed properly and covered using cable troughs and pass-throughs to reduce the likelihood of tripping as well as damage to the cables themselves.

Take the extra time to manage cables, and it will increase your safety as well as that of others who work in that environment.

FIGURE 5.3 A simple voltmeter

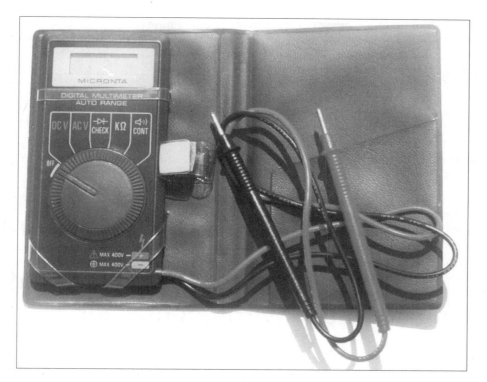

Compliance with local government regulations

It is your responsibility, as an administrator and a professional, to know—or learn—of the regulations that exist for dealing with safety. You should know them from the local level to the federal level and be familiar with the reporting procedures for incidents that you are faced with.

If employees are injured, for example, you may need to contact the Occupational Safety and Health Administration (OSHA). On their website (www.osha.gov), you can find links to information on issues of compliance, laws and regulation, and enforcement.

When it comes to disposal, a list of state laws can be found here:

http://www.electronicsrecycling.org/public/ContentPage.aspx?pageid=14

The Environmental Protection Agency (EPA) offers basic information here:

http://www.epa.gov/osw/conserve/materials/ecycling/index.htm

Exam Essentials

Understand ESD.   Electrostatic discharge occurs when two objects of unequal electrical potential meet. One object transfers some charge to the other one, just as water flows into an area that has a lower water level.

Understand the antistatic wrist strap.   The antistatic wrist strap is also referred to as an ESD strap. To use the ESD strap, you attach one end to an earth ground (typically the ground pin on an extension cord) and wrap the other end around your wrist. This strap grounds your body and keeps it at a zero charge, preventing discharges from damaging the components of a PC.

Know the fire extinguisher types.   Class C is the type of fire extinguisher needed for electrical fires.

Know that you may need to report incidents.   When incidents happen, you must always document them and every attempt should be made to do so both fully and truthfully. Depending upon the type of incident, you may also need to report it to other authorities, such as OSHA.

5.2 Explain environmental impacts and the purpose of environmental controls

This objective deals with potential environmental hazards and is truly a continuation of 5.1. Whereas the focus there was on protecting humans from harm due to electricity, this one focuses on heat and other hazards.

Environmental harms can come from many sources. Not only are temperature and humidity elements that must be controlled, but administrators need to also carefully monitor power, air, and particulates that can harm humans and computers. Not understanding environmental impact and controls can cause great harm.

MSDS documentation for handling and disposal

It is important that you know the potential safety hazards that exist when working with computer elements and how to address them. It is imperative that you understand such issues as *material safety data sheets (MSDSs)* and know how to reference them when needed. Any type of chemical, equipment, or supply that has the potential to harm the environment or people has to have an MSDS associated with it. These are traditionally created by the manufacturer, and you can obtain them from the manufacturer or from the Environmental Protection Agency at www.epa.gov.

These sheets are not intended for consumer use but are aimed at emergency workers and employees who are exposed to the risks of the particular product. Among the information they include are such things as boiling point, melting point, flash point, and potential health risks. They also cover storage and disposal recommendations, and the procedures to follow in the case of a spill or leak.

Temperature, humidity level awareness, and proper ventilation

Three items closely related to an environmentally friendly computing environment are temperature, humidity, and ventilation. We will look at the most important elements with all three.

Temperature   Heat and computers don't mix well. Many computer systems require both temperature and humidity control for reliable service. The larger servers, communications equipment, and drive arrays generate considerable amounts of heat; this is especially true of mainframe and older minicomputers. An environmental system for this type of equipment is a significant expense beyond the actual computer system costs. Fortunately, newer systems operate in a wider temperature range. Most new systems are designed to operate in an office environment.

If the computer systems you're responsible for require special environmental considerations, you'll need to establish cooling and humidity control. Ideally, systems are located in the middle of the building, and they're ducted separately from the rest of the heating, ventilation, and air conditioning (HVAC) system. It's a common practice for modern buildings to use a zone-based air conditioning environment, which allows the environmental plant to be turned off when the building isn't occupied. A computer room will typically require full-time environmental control.

Humidity Level   Another preventive measure you can take is to maintain the relative humidity at around 50 percent. Be careful not to increase the humidity too far—to the point where moisture starts to condense on the equipment! It is a balancing act keeping humidity at the right level since low humidity causes ESD and high humidity causes moisture condensation. Both extremes are bad but have completely different effects.

Also, use antistatic spray, which is available commercially, to reduce static buildup on clothing and carpets. In a pinch, a solution of diluted fabric softener sprayed on these items will do the same thing.

At the very least, you can be mindful of the dangers of ESD and take steps to reduce its effects. Beyond that, you should educate yourself about those effects so you know when ESD is becoming a major problem.

Ventilation   Rounding out temperature and humidity is ventilation. It is important that air—clean air—circulate around computer equipment to keep it cool and functioning properly. Server rooms require much more attention to ventilation than office spaces but are the subject of other exams (Server+, for example) and not test fodder for A+.

What is test fodder is the topic of ventilation within the computer itself—an inadequate flow of internal air within a computer is a common cause of overheating. To prevent this, know that all slot covers should remain in place and be replaced if a card is removed from the system. Know as well that internal fans should be periodically cleaned to ensure proper air flow. A missing slot cover or malfunctioning fan can lead to that inadequate flow of internal air.

Power surges, brownouts, blackouts

There are a number of power-related threats that can harm computers. Among them are the following:

Blackout   A complete failure of the power supplied.

Brownout   A drop in voltage lasting more than a few minutes.

Sag   A very short-term voltage drop.

Spike   The opposite of a sag, this is a short (typically under 1 second) increase in voltage that can do irreparable damage to equipment.

Surge   A long spike (sometimes lasting many seconds). Though they are typically a less intense increase in power, they can also damage equipment.

The two solutions to know for the power issues on the exam are battery backups and surge suppressors.

Battery backup

A battery backup, or *uninterruptible power supply (UPS)*, keeps the system up and running when the normal power is removed (blackout, brownout, etc.). Even in installations that use generators to keep the systems running, battery backups are usually still used so they can keep the machines running while the generators come up to speed.

Most UPS units come with software that can be used to configure the actions to take when the battery backup is active. The software, for example, can be configured to shut the connected devices down when the battery begins to get low.

Surge suppressor

A surge suppressor keeps a spike from passing through it and on to the equipment that could be damaged. *Tripping* occurs when the breaker on a device such as a power supply, surge protector, or UPS turns off the device because it received a spike. If the device is a UPS, when the tripping happens, the components plugged in to the UPS should go to battery instead of pulling power through the line. Under most circumstances, the breaker is reset and operations continue as normal. Figure 5.4 shows a surge-protector power strip, with the trip button to reset at the top.

FIGURE 5.4   The reset button on the top of a surge-protector power strip

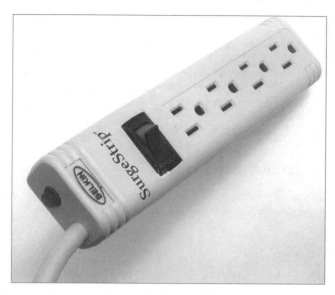

Nuisance tripping is the phrase used if tripping occurs often and isn't a result of a serious condition. If this continues, you should isolate the cause and correct it, even if it means replacing the device that continues to trip.

Surge suppressors (also known as *surge protectors)*, either standalone or built into the UPS, can help reduce the number of nuisance trips. If your UPS doesn't have a surge protector, you should add one to the outlet before the UPS in order to keep the UPS from being damaged if it receives a strong surge. Figure 5.5 shows an example of a simple surge protector for a home computer.

FIGURE 5.5   A simple surge protector

All units are rated by Underwriters Laboratories (UL) for performance. One thing you should never do is plug a UPS or computer equipment into a ground fault circuit interrupter (GFCI) receptacle. These receptacles are intended for use in wet areas, and they trip very easily.

WARNING   Don't confuse a GFCI receptacle with an isolated ground receptacle. Isolated ground receptacles are identifiable by orange outlets and should be used for computer equipment to avoid their picking up a surge passed to the ground by any other device.

Protection from airborne particles

Computers don't do well with airborne particles. To protect them from such, you can use *enclosures* for your sensitive equipment and *air filters* to condition the air.

Enclosures

Enclosures can be considered the first line of defense against particulates. Enclosures are available that can filter the air, keep air out, etc. Make certain that the enclosure you turn to for a solution still offers the necessary ventilation needed to prevent overheating.

Air filters

Most enclosures incorporate an air filter to clean the air before allowing it to enter. An analogy to think of is the air filter on a car which keeps dirt, dust, bugs, and other things from the intake. When working with air filters, make certain they are kept clean and are changed per the manufacturer's requirements.

Dust and debris

One of the most harmful atmospheric hazards to a computer is dust. Dust, dirt, hair, and other airborne contaminants can get pulled into computers and build up inside. Because computer fans work by pulling air through the computer (usually sucking it in through the case and then pushing it out the power supply), it's easy for these items to enter and then become stuck. Every item in the computer builds up heat, and these particles are no exception. As they build up, they hinder the fan's ability to perform its function, and the components get hotter than they would otherwise. Figure 5.6 shows the inside of a system in use for only six months in an area with carpeting and other dusty surroundings.

The heat that builds up can lead to *chip creep* and other conditions. Heating the pins too much causes expansion and keeps them seated tighter, but heating them too far and then cooling them repeatedly (at shutdown) causes the chips to gradually creep out of the sockets.

FIGURE 5.6 Dust builds up inside the system.

Compressed air

You can remove dust and debris from inside computers with *compressed air* blown in short bursts. The short bursts are useful in preventing the dust from flying too far out and entering another machine, as well as in preventing the can from releasing the air in liquid form. Compressed air cans should be held 2–3 inches from the system and always used upright so the content is released as a gas. If the can becomes cold to the touch, discontinue using it until it heats back to room temperature.

It's possible to use an air compressor instead of compressed-air cans when you need a lot of air. If you take this approach, make sure you keep the pounds per square inch (PSI) at or below 40, and include measures on the air compressor to remove moisture.

Vacuums

Dust can build up not just within the computer but also in crevices on the outside. Figure 5.7 shows USB ports on the back of a system that have become a haven for small dust particles. These ports need to be blown out with compressed air, or cleaned with an electronic *vacuum*, before being used, or degradation with the device connected to them could occur.

FIGURE 5.7   Dust collects in unused ports as well.

Handling and Protecting Components

When handling components, take appropriate measures to make certain you do not inflict harm by so doing. Common sense is usually a good rule of thumb.

Antistatic bags

Antistatic bags protect sensitive electronic devices from stray static charges. The bags are designed so that static charges collect on the outside of the bags rather than on the electronic components. You can obtain these bags from several sources. The most direct way to acquire antistatic bags is to go to an electronics supply store and purchase them in bulk. Most supply stores have several sizes available. Perhaps the easiest way to obtain them, however, is to hold onto the ones that come your way. That is, when you purchase any new component, it usually comes in an antistatic bag. Once you have installed the component, keep the bag. It may take you a while to gather a sizable collection of bags if you take this approach, but eventually you will have a fairly large assortment.

Always put the component in an antistatic bag and not on the bag. The outside of the bag is a common location for ESD to collect.

Complying with Regulations

As careful as you try to be, there is always the possibility for accidents to occur. Accidents can be environment-related (for example, a flash flood no one could predict suddenly overtakes the server room and shorts out the wiring) or caused by humans (someone mixes the wrong cleaning chemicals together to try and make their own concoction). Regardless of the cause or circumstances, one thing is written in stone: You must fully and truthfully document the problem.

While that documentation must be seen by internal parties (managers, human resources, etc.), it may also need to be seen by external parties. The latter depends on the type of industry that you are in and the type of incident that occurred. For example, if a large amount of battery acid is spilled in the ground, you should contact the Environmental Protection Agency (see reporting procedures at www.epa.gov).

Exam Essentials

Know what an MSDS is.   An MSDS is a material safety data sheet containing instructions for handling an item. It can be acquired from the manufacturer or from the EPA.

Know that you may need to report incidents.   When incidents happen, you must always document them and every attempt should be made to do so both fully and truthfully. Depending on the type of incident, you may also need to report it to other authorities, such as the EPA.

Know what components are not suitable for a landfill.   Batteries, CRTs, and circuit boards are all examples of items that should not be thrown away normally because of the elements used in them. Batteries contain metals such as lead and nickel, circuit boards contain lead solder, and CRTs contain phosphors.

Know the safety procedures to follow when working with computers.   Be careful when moving computers or working around any electrical components. Know that liquids and computers don't mix, and keep the systems as clean and dust-free as possible to ensure optimal operation.

5.3 Given a scenario, demonstrate proper communication and professionalism

It's possible that you chose computers as your vocation instead of public speaking because you want to interact with people on a one-on-one basis. As unlikely as that possibility may be, it still exists.

Some have marveled at the fact that CompTIA includes questions about customer service on the A+ exam. A better wonder, however, is that there are those in the business who need to know these items and don't. Possessing a great deal of technology skill does not immediately endow one with great people skills. A bit more on appropriate behavior as it relates to the IT field follows.

Use proper language—avoid jargon, acronyms, slang when applicable

Avoid using jargon, abbreviations, slang, and acronyms. Every field has its own language that can make those from outside the field feel lost. Put yourself in the position of someone not in the field, and explain what is going on using words they can relate to.

Be honest and fair with the customer, and try to establish a personal rapport. Tell them what the problem is, what you believe is the cause, and what can be done in the future to prevent it from reoccurring.

Alert your supervisor if there is a communication barrier with the customer (for example, the customer is deaf or does not speak the same language as you do). This is particularly important if the barrier will affect the problem resolution or the amount of time it will take.

If you're providing phone support, do the following:

- Always answer the telephone in a professional manner, announcing the name of the company and yourself.

- Make a concentrated effort to ascertain the customer's technical level, and communicate at that level, not above or below it.

Maintain a positive attitude

Maintain a positive attitude. Your approach to the problem, and the customer, can be mirrored back.

Listen and do not interrupt the customer

Good communication includes listening to what the user, manager, or developer is telling you and making certain that you understand completely what they are trying to say. Just because a user or customer doesn't understand the terminology, syntax, or concepts that you do doesn't mean they don't have a real problem that needs addressing. You must, therefore, be skilled not only at listening, but also at translating. Professional conduct encompasses politeness, guidance, punctuality, and accountability. Always treat the customer with the same respect and empathy you would expect if the situation were reversed. Likewise, guide the customer through the problem and the explanation. Tell them what has caused the problem they're currently experiencing and offer the best solution to prevent it from reoccurring.

Listen intently to what your customer is saying. Make it obvious to them that you're listening and respecting what they're telling you. If you have a problem understanding them, go to whatever lengths you need to in order to remedy the situation. Look for verbal and nonverbal cues that can help you isolate the problem.

Be culturally sensitive

It is important as well to be culturally sensitive—not everyone enjoys the same humor.

Be on time (if late contact the customer)

Punctuality is important and should be a part of your planning process before you ever arrive at the site. If you tell the customer you'll be there at 10:30, you need to make every attempt to be there at that time. If you arrive late, you have given them false hope that the problem would be solved by a set time. That false hope can lead to anger when you arrive late and appear to not be taking their problem as seriously as they are. Punctuality continues to be important throughout the service call and doesn't end with your arrival. If you need to leave to get parts, tell the customer when you'll be back, and then be there at that time. If for some reason you can't return at the expected time, alert the customer and inform them of your new return time.

In conjunction with time and punctuality, if a user asks how much longer the server will be down, and you respond that it will up in 5 minutes, only to have it remain down for 5 more hours, you're creating resentment and possibly anger. When estimating downtime, always allow for more time than you think you'll need, just in case other problems occur. If you greatly underestimate the time, always inform the affected parties and give them a new time estimate. Here's an analogy that will put it in perspective: if you take your car to get the oil changed, and the counter clerk tells you it will be "about 15 minutes," the last thing you want is to be sitting there 4 hours later.

Avoid distractions

It is important that you avoid distractions while working on a customer's or user's problem. Those distractions can come in the form of personal calls, talking to co-workers, or personal interruptions.

If you arrive on site to troubleshoot a problem and there are distractions there of the customer's making (children present, TV on, etc.), you should politely ask the customer to remove the distractions if possible. If the area you will be working in is cluttered with personal items (mementos from the state fair, stuffed animals, etc.), ask the customer to relocate the items as needed, or ask them if it is okay to do so before you relocate the items.

Personal calls

Taking personal calls while working with a customer can make the customer feel as if their problem is being minimized. Spend time solving the problem and interacting with the customer, and then attend to the personal calls when you leave.

If you are anticipating an important call that cannot be avoided, let the customer know beforehand so they will understand that this interruption is coming.

Talking to co-workers while interacting with customers

Just as taking personal calls can seem to minimize the importance of interacting with the customer, so too can talking to co-workers. The customer needs to be the focus of your attention until their problems have been addressed and then you can attend to other matters.

If you must contact someone else while troubleshooting, always ask the customer's permission.

Personal interruptions

The broad category of personal interruptions includes anything that takes you away from focusing on the customer and is not job related. Spend your time dealing with the customer first and solving their problems before attending to personal issues.

Dealing with difficult customer or situation

Handle complaints as professionally as possible. Accept responsibility for errors that may have occurred on your part, and never try to pass the blame. Remember, the goal is to keep them as a customer, not to win an argument.

Avoid arguing with customers and/or being defensive

Avoid arguing with a customer, because doing so serves no purpose; resolve their anger with as little conflict as possible.

Do not minimize customer's problems

Just as personal calls and interruptions can make it seem as if you are not taking the customer seriously enough, so too can dismissing their problems as less important than they believe they are. It is important to put yourself in their shoes and see the issue from their perspective. What may seem trivial to you may be a vital issue for them.

Avoid being judgmental

It is important to not minimize their problem or appear as if you are being judgmental.

Clarify customer statements (ask open ended questions to narrow the scope of the problem, restate the issue, or question to verify understanding)

The most important skill you can have is the ability to listen. You have to rely on the customer to tell you the problem and describe it accurately. They can't do that if you're second-guessing them or jumping to conclusions before the whole story is told. Ask questions that are broad and open-ended at first and then narrow them down to help isolate the problem. This is particularly necessary when you are trying to solve the problem remotely.

It's your job to help guide the user's description of the problem. Here are some examples:

- Is the printer plugged in?
- Is it online?
- Are any lights flashing on it?

Restate the issue to the customer to make sure you are correctly understanding what they are telling you (for example, "there is only one green light lit, correct?"). Ask questions, as needed, that verify your understanding of the problem. The questions you ask should help guide you toward isolating the problem and identifying possible solutions.

Set and meet expectations/timeline and communicate status with the customer

Customer satisfaction goes a long way toward generating repeat business. If you can *meet* the customer's expectations, you'll almost assuredly hear from them again when another problem arises. If you can *exceed* the customer's expectations, you can almost guarantee that they will call you the next time a problem arises.

Customer satisfaction is important in all communication media—whether you're on-site, providing phone support, or communicating through email or other correspondence.

Share the customer's sense of urgency. What may seem like a small problem to you can appear to the customer as if the whole world is collapsing around them.

Offer different repair/replacement options if applicable

If there are multiple solutions to the problem the customer is encountering, offer options to them. Those options often include repairing what they already have or replacing it. If the repair could leave to a reoccurrence of the situation but the replacement will not, then that should be explained to them clearly.

The ramifications of each choice should be clearly explained along with costs (estimates, if necessary) so they can make the decision they deem in their best interest.

If you are unable to resolve the issue, explain to the customer what to do and make sure to follow up properly to forward the issue to appropriate personnel.

Provide proper documentation on the services provided

Document the services you provided so there is no misunderstanding on the part of the customer. Supply them with the documentation and keep a copy handy to refer back to should any questions arise. Explain clearly the cause of the problem and how to avoid it in the future.

It is important enough that the documentation be complete that if you do not refer to it for quite some time (years), you will still be able to understand and explain what was done.

Follow up with customer/user at a later date to verify satisfaction

When you finish a job, notify the user that you're done. Make every attempt to find the user and inform them of the resolution. If it's difficult to find them, leave a note for them to find when they return, explaining the resolution. You should also leave a means by which they can contact you, should they have a question about the resolution or a related problem. In most cases, the number you leave should be that of your business during working hours and your pager, where applicable, after hours.

If you do not hear back from the customer, follow up with them at a later date to verify that the problem is resolved and they are satisfied with the outcome. One of the best ways to keep customers is to let them know that you care about their success and satisfaction.

Deal appropriately with customers confidential materials

The goal of *confidentiality* is to prevent or minimize unauthorized access to files and folders and disclosure of data and information. In many instances, laws and regulations require specific information confidentiality. For example, Social Security records, payroll and employee records, medical records, and corporate information are high-value assets. This information could create liability issues or embarrassment if it fell into the wrong hands. Over the last few years, there have been several cases in which bank account and credit card numbers were published on the Internet. The costs of these types of breaches of confidentiality far exceed the actual losses from the misuse of this information.

Confidentiality entails ensuring that data expected to remain private is seen only by those who should see it. Confidentiality is implemented through authentication and access controls.

Just as confidentiality issues are addressed early in the design phase of a project, you—as a computer professional—are expected to uphold a high level of confidentiality. Should a user approach you with a sensitive issue—telling you their password, asking for assistance obtaining access to medical forms, and so on—it's your obligation as a part of your job to make certain that information passes no further.

Located on computer, desktop, printer, etc.

Technicians may come into contact with confidential information in the course of performing their job duties. That information could come in the form of data stored on a computer, information on a desktop, data (in any form) on a printer, and many other locations. When the possibility exists, ask users to remove such confidential information or close the application that displays it (saving their work before they close).

If the area where you will be working is cluttered with personal information (printed customer lists, etc.), ask the customer to relocate the items if possible. No confidential information should ever be disclosed to outside parties.

Exam Essentials

Use good communication skills.   Listen to the customer. Let them tell you what they understand the problem to be, and then interpret the problem and see if you can get them to agree to what you're hearing them say. Treat the customer, whether an end user or a colleague, with respect, and take their issues and problems seriously.

Deal appropriately with confidential data.   You—as a computer professional—are expected to uphold a high level of confidentiality. No confidential information should ever be disclosed to outside parties.

5.4 Explain the fundamentals of dealing with prohibited content/activity

Working in the IT profession, it is entirely plausible that you will encounter a situation where you find proof of a user, or a number of users, engaging in activities that are prohibited. Those activities can include any number of things, and the prohibition may range from a company policy (you cannot use social media during working hours) all the way up to a federal law (you cannot traffic in child pornography). You have an obligation to respond appropriately and accordingly.

Regardless of whether or not you agree with a prohibition, when you encounter instances wherein activities are in violation of it, you must respond in a professional and legal manner.

First response

There are three crucial components to the first response: identifying the problem, reporting it through the proper channels, and preserving the data.

Identify

A part of identifying the problem involves identifying what policy or law prohibits such an action. Prohibited content generally falls within the following categories (this list should not be considered to represent everything prohibited, as many companies have other policies):

- Exploiting people (in any way: sexually, violently, and so on)
- Promoting harassment of any person or group
- Containing or promoting anything illegal or unauthorized
- Promoting racism, hatred, bigotry, or physical harm
- Containing adult content involving nudity or sexual acts
- Violating privacy rights, copyrights, contract rights, or defamation rights
- Viruses or malware of any sort
- Impersonation
- Soliciting information from anyone under 18
- Involving pyramid schemes, junk mail, chain letters, spamming, or the like

Report through proper channels

Once you have identified prohibited content or activity, you must report it through the proper channels. If the violation is one only of company policy, then usually the company's human resources department is the proper channel. If the violation is of a law, then often you must contact legal authorities—notifying the appropriate internal resources as well.

If the violation is of a federal law and you only tell an internal resource (HR manager, for example), it does not absolve you of the responsibility if that person does not continue to report it up the appropriate chain.

Law enforcement personnel are governed by the rules of evidence, and their response to an incident will be largely out of your control. You need to carefully consider involving law enforcement before you begin. There is no such thing as dropping charges. Once they begin, law enforcement professionals are required to pursue an investigation.

Data/device preservation

You have as well an obligation to preserve the content found until it is turned over to the appropriate authority. Doing so may require commandeering anything from a flash drive up to a network server. Until someone in a position of authority relieves you of the responsibility, you must preserve the data or device in the state in which you discovered it. If you are ever unsure of how to proceed, you should immediately contact your supervisor.

Because knowing what to do when something is discovered is something that may not come naturally, it is a good idea to include the procedures you'll generally follow in an *incident response plan (IRP)*. The IRP outlines what steps are needed and who is responsible for deciding how to handle a situation.

Your policies should clearly outline who needs to be informed in the company, what they need to be told, and how to respond to the situation.

Use of documentation/documentation changes

During the entire process, you should document the steps you take to identify, detect, and report the problem. This information is valuable and will often be used should the problem escalate to a court of law. Many helpdesk software systems provide detailed methods you can use to record procedures and steps.

Chain of custody

An important concept to keep in mind when working with incidents is the *chain of custody*.

Tracking of evidence/documenting process

When you begin to collect evidence, you must keep track of that evidence at all times and show who has it, who has seen it, and where it has been. The evidence must always be within your custody, or you're open to dispute about whether it has been tampered with.

Exam Essentials

Report prohibited content and activities. You have an obligation to report prohibited activities and content to the appropriate authorities when you uncover them. You must ascertain which authority is prohibiting the actions and notify them.

Document and preserve the evidence. It is imperative that the evidence be documented and preserved until turned over to the appropriate authority. In some cases, this can include commandeering a removable drive, a computer, or even a server. Failure to do so can leave you facing fines and other punishments.

Review Questions

1. From which government agency can you find material safety data sheets?

2. What is the tangible and environmentally unfriendly part of laser printers?

3. True or false: An ESD strap should connect to the ground of an electrical outlet.

4. What is the danger to humans when disassembling and working on a monitor?

5. What type of fire extinguisher is appropriate for electrical fires?

6. While troubleshooting a customer's LAN, you determine the server must be rebooted. This will affect over a dozen current users. What should you do?

7. A customer complains that he cannot print to the workgroup laser printer. What should be the first question you ask?

8. A customer states that they may need to reach you quickly for troubleshooting a mission-critical application and asks for your mobile number. What should you do?

9. When you begin to collect evidence, you must keep track of that evidence at all times and show who has it, who has seen it, and where it has been. What is this process known as?

10. True or false: Once law enforcement is invited into a potential prohibited content case, there is no such thing as dropping charges.

CompTIA A+ 220-802

PART II

Chapter

6

Operating Systems

COMPTIA A+ 220-802 EXAM OBJECTIVES COVERED IN THIS CHAPTER:

✓ **1.1 Compare and contrast the features and requirements of various Microsoft Operating Systems.**

- Windows XP Home, Windows XP Professional, Windows XP Media Center, Windows XP 64-bit Professional

- Windows Vista Home Basic, Windows Vista Home Premium, Windows Vista Business, Windows Vista Ultimate, Windows Vista Enterprise

- Windows 7 Starter, Windows 7 Home Premium, Windows 7 Professional, Windows 7 Ultimate, Windows 7 Enterprise

- Features:

  - 32-bit vs. 64 bit

  - Aero, gadgets, user account control, bit-locker, shadow copy, system restore, ready boost, sidebar, compatibility mode, XP mode, easy transfer, administrative tools, defender, Windows firewall, security center, event viewer, file structure and paths, category view vs. classic view

  - Upgrade paths – differences between in place upgrades, compatibility tools, Windows upgrade OS advisor

✓ **1.2 Given a scenario, install, and configure the operating system using the most appropriate method.**

- Boot methods

  - USB

  - CD-ROM

  - DVD

  - PXE

- Types of installations

  - Creating image

  - Unattended installation

- Upgrade
- Clean install
- Repair installation
- Multiboot
- Remote network installation
- Image deployment
- Partitioning
  - Dynamic
  - Basic
  - Primary
  - Extended
  - Logical
- File system types/formatting
  - FAT
  - FAT32
  - NTFS
  - CDFS
  - Quick format vs. full format
- Load alternate third party drivers when necessary
- Workgroup vs. Domain setup
- Time/date/region/language settings
- Driver installation, software and windows updates
- Factory recovery partition

✓ **1.3 Given a scenario, use appropriate command line tools.**

- Networking
  - PING
  - TRACERT
  - NETSTAT
  - IPCONFIG
  - NET

- NSLOOKUP
- NBTSTAT
- OS
  - TASKKILL
  - BOOTREC
  - SHUTDOWN
  - TASKLIST
  - MD
  - RD
  - CD
  - DEL
  - FDISK
  - FORMAT
  - COPY
  - XCOPY
  - ROBOCOPY
  - DISKPART
  - SFC
  - CHKDSK
  - [command name] /?
- Recovery console
  - Fixboot
  - Fixmbr

✓ **1.4 Given a scenario, use appropriate operating system features and tools.**

- Administrative
  - Computer management
  - Device manager
  - Users and groups
  - Local security policy

- Performance monitor
- Services
- System configuration
- Task scheduler
- Component services
- Data sources
- Print management
- Windows memory diagnostics
- Windows firewall
- Advanced security
- MSCONFIG
  - General
  - Boot
  - Services
  - Startup
  - Tools
- Task Manager
  - Applications
  - Processes
  - Performance
  - Networking
  - Users
- Disk management
  - Drive status
  - Mounting
  - Extending partitions
  - Splitting partitions
  - Assigning drive letters
  - Adding devices
  - Adding arrays

- Other
    - User State Migration tool (USMT), File and Settings Transfer Wizard, Windows Easy Transfer
- Run line utilities
    - MSCONFIG
    - REGEDIT
    - CMD
    - SERVICES.MSC
    - MMC
    - MSTSC
    - NOTEPAD
    - EXPLORER
    - MSINFO32
    - DXDIAG

✓ **1.5 Given a scenario, use Control Panel utilities.**

- Common to all Microsoft Operating Systems
    - Internet options
        - Connections
        - Security
        - General
        - Privacy
        - Programs
        - Advanced
    - Display
        - Resolution
    - User accounts
    - Folder options
        - Sharing
        - View hidden files
        - Hide extensions
        - Layout

- System
  - Performance (virtual memory)
  - Hardware profiles
  - Remote settings
  - System protection
- Security center
- Windows firewall
- Power options
  - Hibernate
  - Power plans
  - Sleep/suspend
  - Standby
- Unique to Windows XP
  - Add/remove programs
  - Network connections
  - Printers and faxes
  - Automatic updates
  - Network setup wizard
- Unique to Vista
  - Tablet PC settings
  - Pen and input devices
  - Offline files
  - Problem reports and solutions
  - Printers
- Unique to Windows 7
  - HomeGroup
  - Action center
  - Remote applications and desktop applications
  - Troubleshooting

✓ **1.6 Setup and configure Windows networking on a client/desktop.**

- HomeGroup, file/print sharing
- WorkGroup vs. domain setup
- Network shares/mapping drives
- Establish networking connections
  - VPN
  - Dialups
  - Wireless
  - Wired
  - WWAN (Cellular)
- Proxy settings
- Remote desktop
- Home vs. Work vs. Public network settings
- Firewall settings
  - Exceptions
  - Configuration
  - Enabling/disabling Windows firewall
- Configuring an alternative IP address in Windows
  - IP addressing
  - Subnet mask
  - DNS
  - Gateway
- Network card properties
  - Half duplex/full duplex/auto
  - Speed
  - Wake-on-LAN
  - PoE
  - QoS

✓ **1.7 Perform preventive maintenance procedures using appropriate tools.**

- Best practices
    - Scheduled backups
    - Scheduled check disks
    - Scheduled defragmentation
    - Windows updates
    - Patch management
    - Driver/firmware updates
    - Antivirus updates
- Tools
    - Backup
    - System restore
    - Check disk
    - Recovery image
    - Defrag

✓ **1.8 Explain the differences among basic OS security settings.**

- Users and groups
    - Administrator
    - Power user
    - Guest
    - Standard user
- NTFS vs. Share permissions
    - Allow vs. deny
    - Moving vs. copying folders and files
    - File attributes
- Shared files and folders
    - Administrative shares vs. local shares
    - Permission propagation
    - Inheritance

- System files and folders
- User authentication
  - Single sign-on

✓ **1.9 Explain the basics of client-side virtualization.**

- Purpose of virtual machines
- Resource requirements
- Emulator requirements
- Security requirements
- Network requirements
- Hypervisor

The previous chapters mostly focused on the hardware and physical elements of the computing environment. We looked at the hardware that makes up a personal computer's and laptop's physical components, as well as networking, printers, and operational procedures. That completes the coverage of the topics on the 220-801 exam, and this chapter marks a departure from that.

In this chapter, the focus is on operating systems (OSs). To be specific, the focus is on Microsoft Windows operating systems, which you must know well for the 220-802 certification exam.

1.1 Compare and contrast the features and requirements of various Microsoft Operating Systems

While there are many operating systems available, this exam asks that you know the intricacies of only three that run on the desktop, and all three are versions of Microsoft Windows: Windows XP, Windows Vista, and Windows 7.

This section contains numerous tables due to the nature of the information that it covers. It is imperative that you be familiar with Windows XP, Windows Vista, and Windows 7. Make certain you understand the features available in each of these versions of Windows as well as the editions that were made available for each of them.

Windows XP Home, Windows XP Professional, Windows XP Media Center, Windows XP 64-bit Professional

Windows XP was released in a number of editions. The four you are required to know for the exam are Windows XP Home, Windows XP Professional, Windows XP Media Center, and Windows XP 64-bit Professional. The latter was the only one of the lot released as a 64-bit edition; it can work with a maximum of two physical CPUs and 128 GB of maximum RAM. All three of the remaining editions are limited to 4 GB of RAM, and Windows XP Home is limited to one processor (Professional and Media Center are limited to two).

The OS precedes most of the features CompTIA lists beneath this objective. It does not support or offer the following: Aero, gadgets, User Account Control, BitLocker, ReadyBoost, Sidebar, Compatibility Mode, or XP Mode (though it can run Virtual PC 2007). It does support Shadow Copy (with 64-bit) and System Restore (with all editions). It does not have Easy Transfer, but it has an earlier tool that serves the same purpose (File and Settings Transfer Wizard). Windows Defender, though not included originally with the operating system, can be downloaded and installed.

Windows Firewall and the Security Center are included with all editions, as is Event Viewer. A description of each of these utilities and features appears later in this chapter.

Windows Vista Home Basic, Windows Vista Home Premium, Windows Vista Business, Windows Vista Ultimate, Windows Vista Enterprise

Windows Vista was intended to be the successor to Windows XP, but it failed to find the traction in the market that was expected. A number of editions were released, but the five you need to know for the exam are Windows Vista Home Basic, Windows Vista Home Premium, Windows Vista Business, Windows Vista Ultimate, and Windows Vista Enterprise. The first four were released through retail channels, while Enterprise is available only to large organizations licensing it from Microsoft. While not an exact match, what was called "Professional" with XP became "Business" with Vista, and what was called "Media Center" became "Ultimate."

All five editions are available in either 32-bit or 64-bit versions and 4 GB of RAM is the most supported for any 32-bit version. For the 64-bit versions, Windows Vista Home Basic supports 8 GB of RAM, whereas Windows Vista Home Premium supports 16 GB and all others support 128 GB. Both Home Basic and Home Premium support only a single CPU; the others support up to two CPUs.

Table 6.1 shows the features CompTIA lists for this objective and the editions of Windows Vista with which they work.

TABLE 6.1   Windows Vista features

Feature	Windows Vista Home Basic	Windows Vista Home Premium	Windows Vista Business	Windows Vista Ultimate	Windows Vista Enterprise
Aero	No	Yes	Yes	Yes	Yes
Gadgets	Yes	Yes	Yes	Yes	Yes
User Account Control (UAC)	Yes	Yes	Yes	Yes	Yes

TABLE 6.1 Windows Vista features *(continued)*

Feature	Windows Vista Home Basic	Windows Vista Home Premium	Windows Vista Business	Windows Vista Ultimate	Windows Vista Enterprise
BitLocker	No	No	No	Yes	Yes
Shadow Copy	No	No	Yes	Yes	Yes
System Restore	Yes	Yes	Yes	Yes	Yes
ReadyBoost	Yes	Yes	Yes	Yes	Yes
Sidebar	Yes	Yes	Yes	Yes	Yes
Compatibility Mode	Yes	Yes	Yes	Yes	Yes
XP Mode	Can run Virtual PC 2007	Can run Virtual PC 2007	Can run Virtual PC 2007	Can run Virtual PC 2007	Can run Virtual PC 2007
Easy Transfer	Yes	Yes	Yes	Yes	Yes
Windows Defender	Yes	Yes	Yes	Yes	Yes
Windows Firewall	Yes	Yes	Yes	Yes	Yes
Security Center	Yes	Yes	Yes	Yes	Yes
Event Viewer	Yes	Yes	Yes	Yes	Yes

Windows 7 Starter, Windows 7 Home Premium, Windows 7 Professional, Windows 7 Ultimate, Windows 7 Enterprise

Windows 7 was released by Microsoft with the intention of replacing both Windows Vista and Windows XP in the market. A number of editions were released, but the five you need to know for the exam are Windows 7 Starter, Windows 7 Home Premium, Windows 7 Professional, Windows 7 Ultimate, and Windows 7 Enterprise. Neither Starter nor Enterprise was released through retail channels. Starter is marketed to OEMs for inclusion on netbooks, whereas Enterprise is available only to large organizations licensing it from Microsoft. Note that Microsoft went back to the "Professional" title that existed with XP (dropping "Business") and stayed with "Ultimate" (over "Media Center").

Starter is available only in a 32-bit version and supports a single processor with a maximum of 2 GB of RAM. The remaining four editions are available in either 32- or 64-bit versions, and 4 GB of RAM is the most supported for any 32-bit version. For the 64-bit versions, Windows 7 Home Premium supports 16 GB of RAM, whereas all others support 192 GB. Home Premium supports only a single CPU, and the others support up to two CPUs.

Table 6.2 shows the features CompTIA lists for this objective and the editions of Windows 7 with which they work.

TABLE 6.2   Windows 7 features

Feature	Windows 7 Starter	Windows 7 Home Premium	Windows 7 Professional	Windows 7 Ultimate	Windows 7 Enterprise
Aero	No	Yes	Yes	Yes	Yes
Gadgets	Yes	Yes	Yes	Yes	Yes
User Account Control (UAC)	Yes	Yes	Yes	Yes	Yes
BitLocker	No	No	No	Yes	Yes
Shadow Copy	No	No	Yes	Yes	Yes
System Restore	Yes	Yes	Yes	Yes	Yes
ReadyBoost	Yes	Yes	Yes	Yes	Yes
Sidebar	No	No	No	No	No
Compatibility Mode	Yes	Yes	Yes	Yes	Yes
XP Mode	No	No	Yes	Yes	Yes
Easy Transfer	Yes	Yes	Yes	Yes	Yes
Windows Defender	Yes	Yes	Yes	Yes	Yes
Windows Firewall	Yes	Yes	Yes	Yes	Yes
Security Center	Called Action Center	Called Action Center	Called Action Center	Called Action Center	Called Action Center
Event Viewer	Yes	Yes	Yes	Yes	Yes

Features

There are a number of features that separate one operating system—and even one edition of an operating system—from another. These features range from utilities that may or may not be present, up to whether the operating system is 32-bit or 64-bit. The sections that follow examine these features.

32-bit vs. 64-bit

The primary difference between 32-bit and 64-bit is the amount of data the processor (CPU) is able to process effectively. To run a 64-bit version of the operating system, you must have a 64-bit processor. To find out whether you are running the 32-bit or 64-bit version of Windows, you can look at the information shown on the System applet in the Control Panel in any of the Windows versions you need to know for this exam.

Aero, gadgets, user account control, bit-locker, shadow copy, system restore, ready boost, sidebar, compatibility mode, XP mode, easy transfer, administrative tools, defender, Windows firewall, security center, event viewer, file structure and paths, category view vs. classic view

There are a number of operating system features listed for this objective, the majority of which appeared in Tables 6.1 and 6.2 but without much elaboration. Table 6.3 describes each of the features.

> In most of the operating systems you need to know for this exam, there are two ways of viewing the Control Panel and applets—Classic and Category view. CompTIA prefers the Classic view, and for the sake of consistency as well as exam preparation, that is what we used for all discussion in this chapter.

TABLE 6.3   Windows 7 features

Feature	Significance
Aero	The Aero interface offers a glass design that includes translucent windows. It was new with Windows Vista.
Gadgets	These are mini programs, introduced with Windows Vista, that can be placed on the desktop (Windows 7) or on the Sidebar (Windows Vista), allowing them to run quickly and letting you personalize the PC (clock, weather, etc.). Windows 7 renamed these Windows Desktop Gadgets (right-click on the desktop, and click Gadgets in the context menu; then double-click on the one you want to add). In 2011, Microsoft announced they are no longer supporting development or uploading of new gadgets.

Feature	Significance
Sidebar	Windows Vista had an area known as the Sidebar designed for gadgets that could be placed on the desktop. Windows 7 did away with the Sidebar and the gadgets are now placed directly on the desktop. Interestingly enough, though, sidebar.exe is the program that runs if any gadgets are installed.
User Account Control (UAC)	The UAC is intended to prevent unintentional or unauthorized changes to the computer by either prompting for permission to continue or requiring the administrator password before continuing. Changes to this from Windows Vista allow you to control how strict UAC intercedes.
BitLocker	What CompTIA calls "bit-locker" allows you to use drive encryption to protect files—including those needed for startup and logon. This is available only with more complete editions of Windows 7 and Windows Vista. For removable drives, BitLocker To Go provides the same encryption technology to help prevent unauthorized access to the files stored on them.
Shadow Copy	The Volume Shadow Copy Service creates copies that you can recover from should a file be accidentally deleted or overwritten. Windows 7 adds to what Vista included by adding an interface for configuring storage used by volume shadow copies. The properties dialog box for a file contains a Previous Versions tab that can be used to return to another edition of the file.
ReadyBoost	This feature allows you to use free space on a removable drive to speed up a system by caching content and is used when you are running low on available memory. In Windows 7, it can work with a USB drive, flash memory, SD card, or CompactFlash. Up to eight devices can employ ReadyBoost in Windows 7 (each needing a minimum of 256 MB of free space). ReadyBoost is configured from the ReadyBoost tab of the properties dialog box for the removable media device.
Compatibility Mode	Program Compatibility is included with Windows 7 to configure programs to believe they are running with an older version of Windows: choose Start ➤ Control Panel ➤ Programs, and then click Run Programs Made For Previous Versions Of Windows.
XP Mode	Included with Windows 7 Professional, Enterprise, and Ultimate is the ability to run applications in Windows XP Mode (XPM). This is a virtual client (emulating Windows XP Professional with Service Pack 3), which requires that you also download and install Windows Virtual PC to use. This can be downloaded from the Windows Virtual PC site at www.microsoft.com/windows/virtual-pc/. You should have 2 GB RAM and 15 GB hard drive space for each virtual Windows instance.

TABLE 6.3   Windows 7 features *(continued)*

Feature	Significance
Easy Transfer	Can be used to migrate a few accounts from one OS to another (for a large number of accounts, Microsoft recommends using the User State Migration Tool [USMT]).
	When transferring to Windows 7, you can download a version of Windows Easy Transfer in either 32-bit or 64-bit versions for Windows Vista or Windows XP from www.microsoft.com/downloads.
Windows Defender	Windows 7 includes Windows Defender anti-spyware program. This was also included with Windows Vista and can be downloaded for Windows XP.
Windows Firewall	Windows 7, as well as Windows Vista and XP, incorporates Windows Firewall which can be used to stop incoming and outgoing traffic. There are only three basic settings: On, Off, and Block All Incoming Connections.
Security Center	Rolled into the Action Center in Windows 7, this interface shows the status of, and allows you to configure, the firewall, Windows Update, virus protection, spyware and unwanted software protection, Internet security settings, UAC, and network access protection.

Four items are not shown in Table 6.3 because they are large enough to warrant more discussion than the table allows: System Restore, Administrative Tools, Event Viewer, and File Structure/Paths. Administrative Tools is a sizable portion of objective 1.4 and is not covered here to avoid needless repetition. The others are covered next.

System Restore

System Restore appears in all three versions of Windows. It allows you to restore the system to a previous point in time. This feature is accessed from Start ➢ All Programs ➢ Accessories ➢ System Tools ➢ System Restore and can be used to roll back as well as create a restore point.

In Windows XP, you can also choose to create a restore point manually from here. In Windows 7 and Vista, you can only restore a restore point from here; to create a restore point, you should access the System Protection tab of the System Properties dialog box.

Event Viewer

Windows employs comprehensive error and informational logging routines. Every program and process theoretically could have its own logging utility, but Microsoft has come up with a rather slick utility, Event Viewer, which, through log files, tracks all events on a particular Windows computer. Normally, though, you must be an administrator or a member of the Administrators group to have access to Event Viewer.

The process for starting Event Viewer differs based on the operating system you are running, but always log in as an administrator (or equivalent). With Windows 7, choose Start ➢ Control Panel ➢ Administrative Tools ➢ Event Viewer; on earlier systems choose Start ➢ Programs ➢ Administrative Tools ➢ Event Viewer (or you can always right-click on the Computer desktop icon and choose Manage ➢ Event Viewer). In the resulting window (shown in Figure 6.1), you can view the System, Application, and Security log files. If you are running Windows 7, you will also see log files available for Setup and Forwarded Events.

FIGURE 6.1   The opening interface of Event Viewer

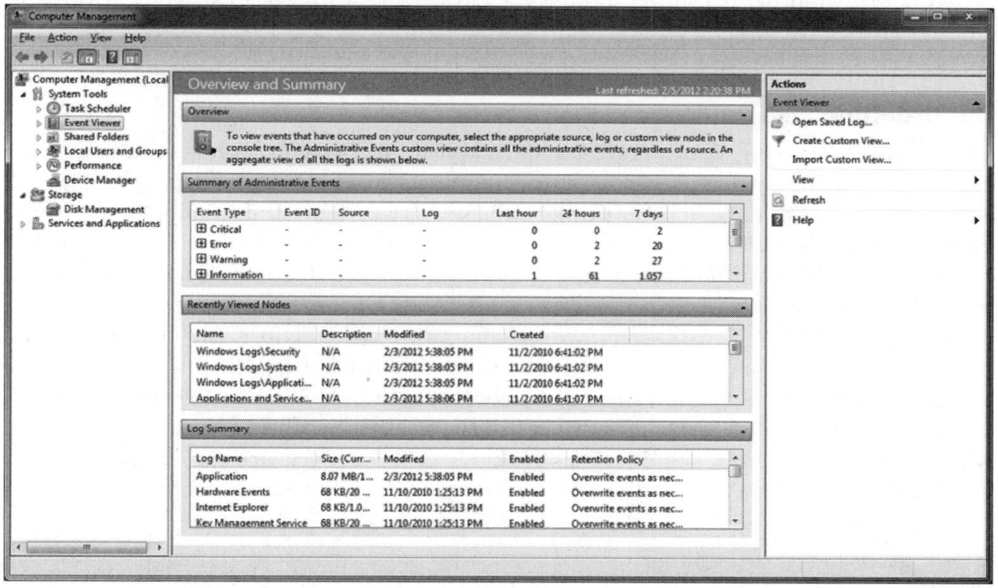

- The System log file displays alerts that pertain to the general operation of Windows.
- The Application log file logs application errors.
- The Security log file logs security events such as login successes and failures.

These log files can give a general indication of a Windows computer's health.

One situation that does occur with Event Viewer is that the log files get full. Although this isn't really a problem, it can make viewing log files confusing because there are so many entries. Even though each event is time- and date-stamped, you should clear Event Viewer every so often. To do this, open Event Viewer, and in Windows 7, right-click on the log, choose Properties, and click the Clear Log button; in earlier OSs, choose Clear All Events from the Log menu. Doing so erases all events in the current log file, allowing you to see new events more easily when they occur. You can set maximum log size by right-clicking on the log and choosing Properties. By default, when a log fills to its maximum size, old entries are deleted in first in, first out (FIFO) order.

You can save the log files before erasing them. The saved files can be burned to a CD or DVD for future reference. Often, you are required to save the files to CD or DVD if you are working in a company that adheres to strict regulatory standards.

In addition to just erasing logs, you can configure three different settings for what you want to occur when the file does reach its maximum size. The first option is "Overwrite events as needed (oldest events first)" and this replaces the older events with the new entries. The second option is "Archive the log when full, do not overwrite events," and this will create another log file as soon as the current one runs out of space. The third option, "Do not overwrite events (Clear logs manually)," will not record any additional events once the file is full.

File Structures and Paths

In the Windows environment, users are required to authenticate in some way (even if it is just as Guest) before gaining access to a user account. The operating system then uses a user profile to deliver the computer settings (theme, screen saver, and so on) that are configured for them. It is important to realize that the user account (which authenticates the user) and the user profile (which holds their settings) are two separate things—one is needed before the other.

Part of the user profile involves allowing each user to have a set of files that are specific to them. The same set of folders is automatically created for each user. While the address bar for a user often simply shows the location as edulaney, in reality the folder being viewed is beneath *%systemdrive%*\Users\ (usually C:\Users\) in Windows 7 and Vista and beneath *%systemdrive%*\Documents and Settings\ (usually C:\Documents and Settings\) in Windows XP.

When settings need to apply to everyone who uses the machine, they can be placed in All Users instead of being copied beneath each user's folder set.

Whereas user files are placed in folders specific to them, system files are those used by the operating system and are used by all users. In all the operating systems you need to know for the exam, these files are beneath *%systemroot%* and many, such as System32, appear in the default path. A number of files reside in this directory, with most residing in subdirectories.

The variable *systemroot* (referenced as *%systemroot%*) is usually set to C:\Windows in the operating systems this exam focuses on. Because it is a variable, it can be changed to other values as well.

Temporary files are written to a system on an almost nonstop basis. The purpose behind these files is to hold any information that is needed for only a short time. In addition to temporary files used for print queues, you have cache from Internet sites and many other programs. You can manually pick files to delete, but one of the simplest solutions is to choose Properties for a drive and then click the General tab. A command button for the Disk Cleanup utility will appear, which you can use to delete most common temporary files, including the following:

- Downloaded program files
- Temporary Internet files
- Offline web pages
- Office setup files
- Recycle Bin contents
- Setup log files
- Temporary files
- Web client and publisher temporary files
- Temporary offline files
- Offline files
- Catalog files for the Content Indexer

The `Program Files` directory, beneath *%systemdrive%* (usually `C:\`), holds the files needed for each of the installed applications on a machine. Windows Vista also added a `Program Data` directory, which is hidden by default. It contains the settings needed for applications and works similar to how the `Local Settings` folder did in previous operating systems.

Upgrade paths—differences between in place upgrades, compatibility tools, Windows upgrade OS advisor

One Windows operating system can often be upgraded to another, if compatible. With the case of Windows 7, it is even possible to upgrade from one edition of the operating system to another. When you are faced with a scenario in which you cannot upgrade, you can always do a clean installation.

There's one more thing to consider when evaluating installation methods. Some methods only work if you're performing a clean installation and not an upgrade. Table 6.4 lists the minimum and recommended hardware specifications for Windows XP. Note that in addition to these minimums, the hardware must be compatible with Windows. Additional hardware may be required if certain features are installed (for example, a NIC is required for networking support).

TABLE 6.4 Windows XP minimum and recommended hardware

Hardware	XP Professional Requirement	XP Professional Recommendation
Processor	233 MHz Pentium/ Celeron or AMD K6/ Athlon/Duron	300 MHz or higher Intel-compatible processor
Memory	64 MB	128 MB
Free Hard Disk Space	1.5 GB	1.5 GB
Floppy Disk	Not required	Not required
CD-ROM or DVD	Required	Required
Video	SuperVGA or better	SuperVGA or better
Mouse	Required	Required
Keyboard	Required	Required
Sound Board and speakers/head phones	Required	Required

Table 6.5 lists the minimum system requirements for the various versions of Windows Vista.

TABLE 6.5 Windows Vista minimum hardware

Hardware	Minimum supported for all versions	Home Basic recommendation	Home Premium/ Business/ Ultimate recommendation
Processor	800 MHz	1 GHz 32-bit (x86) or 64-bit (x64) processor	1 GHz 32-bit (x86) or 64-bit (x64) processor
Memory	512 MB	512 MB	1 GB
Free Hard Disk Space	15 GB free on a 20 GB drive	15 GB free on a 20 GB drive	15 GB free on a 40 GB drive
CD-ROM or DVD	CD-ROM	DVD-ROM	DVD-ROM

Hardware	Minimum supported for all versions	Home Basic recommendation	Home Premium/ Business/ Ultimate recommendation
Video	SVGA	Support for DirectX 9 graphics and 32 MB graphics memory	Support for DirectX 9 with WDDM Driver, 128 MB of graphics memory; Pixel Shader 2.0 in hardware; 32 bits per pixel
Mouse	Required (but not listed as a requirement)	Required (but not listed as a requirement)	Required (but not listed as a requirement)
Keyboard	Required (but not listed as a requirement)	Required (but not listed as a requirement)	Required (but not listed as a requirement)
Internet Access	Not listed as a requirement	Required	Required

Table 6.6 lists the minimum system requirements for the various versions of Windows 7. It should be noted that Windows XP Mode requires an additional 1 GB of RAM and 15 GB of hard drive space.

TABLE 6.6 Windows 7 minimum hardware

Hardware	Minimum supported for all versions
Processor	1 GHz
Memory	1 GB for 32-bit; 2 GB for 64-bit
Free Hard Disk Space	16 GB free for 32-bit; 20 GB free for 64-bit
CD-ROM or DVD	DVD-ROM
Video	DirectX 9 with WDDM 1.0 (or higher) driver
Mouse	Required (but not listed as a requirement)
Keyboard	Required (but not listed as a requirement)
Internet Access	Not listed as a requirement

Certain features in Windows 7 have further hardware requirements that are listed at

`http://windows.microsoft.com/en-US/windows7/products/system-requirements`

The easiest way to see if your current hardware can run Windows 7 is to download and run the Windows 7 Upgrade Advisor available at

`http://windows.microsoft.com/en-us/windows/downloads/upgrade-advisor`

You can also always check hardware in the Windows 7 Compatibility Center at

`www.microsoft.com/windows/compatibility/windows-7/en-us/default.aspx`

If there is one thing to be learned from Tables 6.4 through 6.6, it is that Microsoft is nothing if not optimistic. For your own sanity, though, we strongly suggest that you always take the minimum requirements with a grain of salt. They are minimums. Even the recommended requirements should be considered minimums. Bottom line: Make sure you have a good margin between your system's performance and the minimum requirements listed. Always run Windows on more hardware rather than less!

Upgrading to Windows 7

If you want to do an upgrade instead of a clean installation, review the upgrade options in Table 6.7 (it is worth pointing out again that a "No" does not mean you can't buy the upgrade version of Windows 7, but rather that you can't keep your files, programs, and settings).

TABLE 6.7   Windows 7 upgrade options

Existing operating system	Windows 7 Home Premium 32-bit	Windows 7 Home Premium 64-bit	Windows 7 Professional 32-bit	Windows 7 Professional 64-bit	Windows 7 Ultimate 32-bit	Windows 7 Ultimate 64-bit
Windows XP	No	No	No	No	No	No
Windows Vista Starter 32-bit	No	No	No	No	No	No
Windows Vista Starter 64-bit	No	No	No	No	No	No

Existing operating system	Windows 7 Home Premium 32-bit	Windows 7 Home Premium 64-bit	Windows 7 Professional 32-bit	Windows 7 Professional 64-bit	Windows 7 Ultimate 32-bit	Windows 7 Ultimate 64-bit
Windows Vista Home Basic 32-bit	Yes	No	No	No	Yes	No
Windows Vista Home Basic 64-bit	No	Yes	No	No	No	Yes
Windows Vista Home Premium 32-bit	Yes	No	No	No	Yes	No
Windows Vista Home Premium 64-bit	No	Yes	No	No	No	Yes
Windows Vista Business 32-bit	No	No	Yes	No	Yes	No
Windows Vista Business 64-bit	No	No	No	Yes	No	Yes
Windows Vista Ultimate 32-bit	No	No	No	No	Yes	No
Windows Vista Ultimate 64-bit	No	No	No	No	No	Yes

The Enterprise versions play by different rules since they are licensed direct from Microsoft. In the case of Windows 7, both Windows Vista Business and Windows Vista Enterprise can be upgraded to Windows 7 Enterprise.

Those operating systems not listed in Table 6.7 do not include any upgrade options to Windows 7 and cannot be done with upgrade packages (you must buy the full version of Windows 7). An easy way to remember upgrade options for the exam is that you must have at least Windows Vista in order to be able to upgrade to Windows 7. In the real world, the Windows Vista machine should be running Service Pack 1 at a minimum, and you can always take an earlier OS and upgrade it to Vista SP1 and then upgrade to Windows 7.

As of this writing, Service Pack 1 is the latest available for Windows 7, Service Pack 2 is the latest available for Windows Vista, and Service Pack 3 is the latest available for Windows XP. You can find the latest at

http://windows.microsoft.com/en-US/windows/downloads/service-packs

In the past, all Service Packs used to be cumulative—meaning you needed only load the last one. Starting with XP SP3, however, all Windows Service Packs released have been incremental, meaning that you must install the previous ones before you can install the new one.

Microsoft created the Windows 7 Upgrade Advisor to help with the upgrade to this operating system. You can download the advisor from windows.microsoft.com/upgradeadvisor. It will scan your hardware, devices, and installed programs for any known compatibility issues. Once it is finished, it will give you advice on how to resolve the issues found and recommendations on what to do before you upgrade. The reports are divided into three categories: System Requirements, Devices, and Programs.

After all incompatibilities have been addressed, the upgrade can be started from an installation disc or from a download (preferably to a USB drive). If the setup routine does not begin immediately on boot, look for the setup.exe file and run it. When the Install Windows page appears, click Install now.

You'll be asked if you want to get any updates (recommended) and to agree to the license agreement. After you've done so, choose Upgrade for the installation type and follow the steps to walk through the remainder of the installation. We highly recommend that after the installation is complete, you run Windows Update to get the latest drivers.

New to Windows 7 is the ability at any time to upgrade from one edition of the operating system to a higher one (for example, from Home Premium to Professional) using the Windows Anytime Upgrade utility in the System And Security section of the Control Panel (it can also be accessed by clicking the Start button and choosing All Programs; scroll down the list and choose Windows Anytime Upgrade).

Upgrading to Windows Vista

With Windows Vista you can upgrade to various versions based on the operating system that you are coming from. Table 6.8 lists the upgrade paths for each Windows Vista version based on the operating system you are coming from. Those listed as No must be clean installations.

TABLE 6.8   Windows Vista upgrade options

Existing operating system	Vista Home Basic	Vista Home Premium	Vista Business	Vista Ultimate
Windows XP Home	Yes	Yes	Yes	Yes
Windows XP Professional	No	No	Yes	Yes
Windows XP Professional x64	No	No	No	No
Windows XP Media Center (2002 Edition)	No	No	No	No
Windows XP Media Center (2004 and 2005 Edition)	No	Yes	No	Yes
Windows XP Tablet PC	No	No	Yes	Yes
Windows Vista Home Basic	N/A	Yes	No	Yes
Windows Vista Home Premium	No	N/A	No	Yes
Windows Vista Business	No	No	N/A	Yes
Windows Vista Ultimate	No	No	No	N/A

 For the exam, recognize that no version of Windows older than Windows XP can be upgraded to Windows Vista.

Note that Windows Vista Enterprise does not appear in the table as it is typically done as a clean install. The only "upgrade" possibility with it is that it can be installed over Windows Vista Business. Note as well that where N/A appears in the table, it is always possible to do a repair installation or clean installation but not a true upgrade.

A clean installation is one that keeps no previous settings and copies over or removes the old operating system. An upgrade installation is one that keeps previous settings (usually related to accounts and configuration) from the older operating system. A repair installation involves keeping the same operating system and performing a reinstall of system files.

The Windows Vista Upgrade Advisor from Microsoft can be useful in the upgrade process. It will check your system, verify that it can run Windows Vista, and give you a report of any identified compatibility issues.

To begin the upgrade, insert the DVD, and the Setup program should automatically begin (if it doesn't, run setup.exe from the root folder) and a menu appears. From the menu, choose Install Now and then select Upgrade when the Which Type Of Installation Do You Want? screen appears. Answer the prompts to walk through the upgrade.

If you need CDs instead of the Windows Vista DVD, you could once obtain them from Microsoft, but they are no longer available.

Booting from the DVD is also possible but recommended only if the method just described does not work. When you boot, you will get a message upon startup that tells you Press Any Key To Boot From CD, and at this point you simply press a key (don't worry that it is a DVD and not a CD) and walk through the upgrade.

If the edition of Windows Vista you are upgrading to fully supports networking, you can download the *User State Migration Tool (USMT)* from Microsoft. It is intended to be used by administrators and requires a client computer connected to a Windows Server–based domain controller. It allows you to migrate user file settings related to applications, desktop configuration, and accounts. More information on USMT can be found at http://technet .microsoft.com/en-us/library/cc722032(WS.10).aspx.

Windows Easy Transfer is also available for transferring items to Windows Vista (Start ➢ All Programs ➢ Accessories ➢ System Tools ➢ Windows Easy Transfer). This tool is intended for the one-time transfer of user settings, as well as applications and files, to Vista, whereas USMT is meant for wide-scale migrations.

Upgrading to Windows XP

With Windows XP, you can upgrade to the Home version only from Windows 98 or Windows Me. You can upgrade to the Professional version from Windows 98, Windows Me, Windows NT Workstation 4.0, Windows 2000 Professional, or even Windows XP Home.

Upgrading to Windows XP is quite simple:

1. Insert the CD and choose Install Windows XP from the menu that appears.

2. The Setup program detects that you already have an OS installed and presents you with a menu that says Upgrade (Recommended). Click Next to begin the upgrade.

3. Setup asks you to agree to the EULA, enter the product key, and download an updated version of the Setup program (if necessary).

4. Setup copies several files over, reboots a couple of times, and continues like a standard Windows XP installation.

Once you have finished the installation, you must activate it (like a standard installation of Windows XP), but that's about it. Windows XP Setup makes most of the decisions about the upgrade for you, so only a minimal amount of interaction is necessary.

Real World Scenario

Should You Be Upgrading to Windows XP?

While you need to know installation and upgrade options involving Windows XP for the exam, in the real world you should avoid doing so. Microsoft announced many years ago that the support for Windows XP SP3 will end in 2014 (April 8, to be exact).

The "end of support" from Microsoft's standpoint means that they will not issue anything new for the product after that date. That means there will not be any security updates, hotfixes, or support from them (paid or unpaid). No administrator should be installing what will soon be an unsupported/unsecure client operating system on workstations.

Know the material in this chapter for the exam, but in the real world, recognize that Windows 7 should be the choice you consider.

This objective also includes a reference to "category view vs. classic view." This is only meaningful as it pertains to the Control Panel and is discussed in objective 1.5 rather than here.

Exam Essentials

Understand version and edition differences of Windows. For each version of Windows (Windows XP, Windows Vista, and Windows 7), know how to group the editions (Home, Professional, etc.) according to similarity and explain how one group differs from the other.

Know the system requirements of Windows. You should know the minimum system requirements for Windows 7, Windows Vista, and Windows XP.

Understand upgrading. You should know that an installation overwrites any existing files whereas an upgrade keeps the same data/application files.

1.2 Given a scenario, install and configure the operating system using the most appropriate method

The focus of this objective is on installing and configuring the Windows operating systems discussed in the previous section. Some of the topics that CompTIA lists here also appear beneath other objectives and they are only touched on here to avoid needless repetition.

Operating system installations can be lumped into two generic methods: attended or unattended. During an attended installation, you walk through the installation and answer the questions as prompted. Questions typically ask for the product key, the directory in which you want to install the OS, and relevant network settings.

As simple as attended installations may be, they're time-consuming and administrator-intensive in that they require someone to fill in a fair number of fields to move through the process. Unattended installations allow you to configure the OS with little or no human intervention. Table 6.9 shows you four common unattended installation methods and when they can be used.

TABLE 6.9   Windows unattended installation methods

Method	Clean installation	Upgrade
Unattended Install	Yes	Yes
Bootable Media	Yes	No
Sysprep	Yes	No
Remote Install	Yes	No

Boot methods

You can begin the installation or upgrade process by booting from a number of sources. There are four in particular that CompTIA wants you to be familiar with: USB, CD-ROM, DVD, and PXE.

USB

Most systems will allow you to boot from a USB device, but you must often change the BIOS settings to look for the USB first. Using a large USB drive, you can store all the necessary installation files on the one device and save the time of needing to swap media.

CD-ROM

The most commonly used for an attended installation is the CD-ROM/DVD boot (they are identical). Since Windows 7 only comes on DVD, though, CD-ROM applies to older operating systems and not this one.

DVD

A DVD boot is the most common method of starting an installation.

PXE

Booting the computer from the network without using a local device creates a *Preboot Execution Environment* (PXE). Once it is up, it is common to load the Windows Preinstallation Environment (WinPE) into RAM as a stub operating system and install the operating system image to the hard drive.

WinPE can be installed onto a bootable CD, USB, or network drive using the copype.cmd command. This environment can be used in conjunction with a Windows deployment from a server for unattended installations.

Types of installations

Another decision you must make is which method you are going to use to install Windows. Windows XP is still small enough that it comes on a single CD (Windows Vista added DVDs and that media is also used by Windows 7). It is possible to boot to this disc and begin the installation process. However, your system must have a system BIOS that is capable of supporting bootable media.

If you don't have a bootable CD, you must first boot the computer using some other bootable media, which then loads the disk driver so that you can access the installation program on the CD.

Creating image

Creating an image involves taking a snapshot of a model system (often called a *reference computer*) and then applying it to other systems (see the section "Image Deployment" later). A number of third-party vendors offer packages that can be used to create images, and you can use the system preparation tool, or *Sysprep*. The Sysprep utility works by making an exact image or replica of the reference computer (sometimes also called the *master computer*), to be installed on other computers. Sysprep removes the master computer's Security ID and will generate new IDs for each computer the image is used to install.

All Sysprep does is create the system image. You still need a cloning utility to copy the image to other computers.

Perhaps the biggest caveat to using Sysprep is that because you are making an exact image of an installed computer (including drivers and settings), all of the computers that you will be installing the image on need to be identical (or very close) to the configuration of the master computer. Otherwise, you could have to go through and fix driver problems on every installed computer. Sysprep images can be installed across a network or copied to a CD for local installation. Sysprep cannot be used to upgrade a system; plan on all data on the system (if there is any) being lost after a format.

 Similar to Sysprep, ImageX is the preferred command line utility for imaging Windows 7. More information on it can be found at: http://technet.microsoft.com/en-us/library/cc722145(v=ws.10).

There are several third-party vendors that provide similar services, and you'll often hear the process referred to as *disk imaging* or *drive imaging*. The process works the same way as Sysprep, except that the third-party utility makes the image as well. Then the image file is transferred to the computer without an OS. You boot the new system with the imaging software and start the image download. The new system's disk drive is made into an exact sector-by-sector copy of the original system.

Imaging has major upsides. The biggest one is speed. In larger networks with multiple new computers, you can configure tens to hundreds of computers by using imaging in just hours, rather than the days it would take to individually install the OS, applications, and drivers.

Unattended installation

Answering the myriad of questions posed by Windows Setup doesn't qualify as exciting work for most people. Fortunately, there is a way to answer the questions automatically: through an unattended installation. In this type of installation, an *answer file* is supplied with all of the correct parameters (time zone, regional settings, administrator user name, and so on), so no one needs to be there to tell the computer what to choose or to hit Next 500 times.

Unattended installations are great because they can be used to upgrade operating systems. The first step is to create an answer file. Generally speaking, you'll want to run a test installation using that answer file first before deploying it on a large scale, because you'll probably need to make some tweaks to it. After you create your answer file, place it on a network share that will be accessible from the target computer. (Most people put it in the same place as the Windows installation files for convenience.)

Boot the computer that you want to install on using a boot disk or CD, and establish the network connection. Once you start the setup process, everything should run automatically.

Upgrade

An upgrade involves moving from one operating system to another and keeping as many of the settings as possible. An example of an upgrade would be changing the operating system on a laptop computer from Windows Vista to Windows 7 and keeping the user accounts that existed.

It is also possible to upgrade from one edition of an operating system to another—for example, from Windows 7 Professional to Windows 7 Ultimate. This is known as an *Anytime Upgrade*.

Clean install

With a clean installation, you overwrite the operating system that existed on a machine and place a new one there. An example of a clean installation would be changing the operating system on a laptop from Windows XP to Windows 7. The user accounts and other settings that existed with Windows XP would be removed in the process and need to be re-created under Windows 7.

Repair installation

A repair installation overwrites system files with a copy of new ones from the same operating system version and edition. For example, a laptop running Windows 7 is hanging on boot and the cause is traced to a corrupted system file. A repair installation can replace that corrupted file with a new one (from the DVD or other source) without changing the operating system or settings (for configuration, accounts, and so on).

Multiboot

Multiple operating systems can exist on the same machine in one of two popular formats: in a multiboot configuration or in virtual machines. With a multiboot configuration, when you boot the machine, you choose which operating system you want to load of those that are installed. You could, for example, boot into Windows XP, reboot and bring up Windows Vista, reboot and bring up Windows 7, and test a software application you've created in each OS. It is possible, in this scenario, to have multiple editions of the same OS installed (Professional, Ultimate, and so forth) and choose which to boot into in order to test your application. The key to this configuration, however, is that you can only have one operating system running at a time.

An alternative to multiboot that has become more popular in recent years is to run virtual machines. You could boot into Windows 7, for example, and run a virtual machine of Windows XP and one of Windows Vista and test your application in the three environments that are all running at the same time.

Remote network installation

Older Windows Server operating systems have a feature called Remote Installation Service (RIS), which allows you to perform several network installations at one time. Beginning with Windows Server 2003 SP2, RIS was replaced by Windows Deployment Service (WDS). This utility offers the same functionality as RIS.

A *network installation* is handy when you have many installs to do and installing by CD is too much work. In a network installation, the installation CD is copied to a shared location on the network. Then individual workstations boot and access the network share. The workstations can boot either through a boot disk or through a built-in network boot device known as a *Preboot Execution Environment (PXE) ROM*. Boot ROMs essentially download a small file that contains an OS and network drivers and has enough information to boot the computer in a limited fashion. At the very least, it can boot the computer so it can access the network share and begin the installation.

Image deployment

System images created with Sysprep and other tools can be deployed for installation on hosts across the network. The Windows Automated Installation Kit (AIK) can be useful for this purpose (`http://technet.microsoft.com/library/dd349348.aspx`).

Partitioning

For a hard disk to be able to hold files and programs, it has to be partitioned and formatted. Partitioning is the process of creating logical divisions on a hard drive. A hard drive can have one or more partitions. Formatting is the process of creating and configuring a file allocation table (FAT) and creating the root directory. Several filesystem types are supported by the various versions of Windows, such as FAT16, FAT32, and NTFS (partitions are explored later in the discussion of disk management under objective 1.4).

The partition that the operating system boots from must be designated as *active*. Only one partition on a disk may be marked active. Each hard disk can be divided into a total of four partitions, either four primary partitions or three primary and one extended partition. Some of the other possibilities are examined in the following sections.

Dynamic

Partitions can be made dynamic, which—as the name implies—have the ability to be configured and reconfigured on the fly. The big benefit they offer is that they can increase in size (without reformatting) and can span multiple physical disks. Dynamic partitions can be simple, spanned, or striped.

Dynamic partitions that are simple are similar to primary partitions and logical drives (which exist on basic partitions, discussed next). This is often the route you choose when you have only one dynamic disk and want the ability to change allocated space as needed.

Spanned means that you want space from a number of disks (up to 32) to appear as a single logical volume to the user(s). A minimum of two disks must be used, and no fault tolerance is provided by this option.

Striped is similar to spanned in that multiple disks are used, but the big difference is that data is written (in fixed sized stripes) across the disk set in order to increase I/O performance. Although read operations are faster, a concern is that if one disk fails, none of the data is retrievable (like spanned, there is no fault tolerance).

Basic

With basic storage, Windows drives can be partitioned with *primary* or *logical* partitions. Basic partitions are a fixed size and are always on a single physical disk. This is the simplest storage solution and has been the traditional method of storing data for many years.

You can change the size of primary and logical drives by *extending* them into additional space on the same disk. You can create up to four partitions on a basic disk: either four primary or three primary and one extended.

Primary

A primary partition contains the boot files for an operating system. In older days, the operating system had to also be on that partition, but with the Windows versions you need to know for this exam, the OS files can be elsewhere as long at the boot files are in that primary partition.

Primary partitions cannot be further subdivided.

Extended

Extended partitions differ from primary in that they can be divided into one or more logical drives, each of which can be assigned a drive letter.

Logical

In reality, all partitions are logical in the sense that they don't necessarily correspond to one physical disk. One disk can have several logical divisions (partitions). A logical partition is any partition that has a drive letter.

 Sometimes, you will also hear of a logical partition as one that spans multiple physical disks. For example, a network drive that you know as drive H: might actually be located on several physical disks on a server. To the user, all that is seen is one drive, or H:.

File system types/formatting

NTFS (New Technology Filesystem) is available with all the versions of Windows you need to know for the exam, but they also recognize and support FAT16 and FAT32. The file table for the NTFS is called the Master File Table (MFT).

This section lists the major filesystems that are used with Windows and the differences among them.

FAT

FAT (File Allocation Table) is an acronym for the file on a filesystem used to keep track of where files are. It's also the name given to this type of filesystem, introduced in 1981. Many OSs have built their filesystem on the design of FAT, but without its limitations. A FAT filesystem uses the *8.3 naming convention* (eight letters for the name, a period, and then a three-letter file identifier). This later became known as *FAT16* (to differentiate it from FAT32) because it used a 16-bit binary number to hold cluster-numbering information. Because of that number, the largest FAT disk partition that could be created was approximately 2 GB.

VFAT (Virtual FAT) is an extension of the FAT filesystem that was introduced with Windows 95. It augmented the 8.3 filenaming convention and allowed filenames with up to 255 characters. It created two names for each file: a long name and an 8.3-compatible name so that older programs could still access files. When VFAT was incorporated into Windows 95, it used 32-bit code for improved disk access while keeping the 16-bit naming system for backward compatibility with FAT. It also had the 2 GB disk partition limitation.

FAT32

FAT32 was introduced along with Windows 95 OEM Service Release 2. As disk sizes grew, so did the need to be able to format a partition larger than 2 GB. FAT32 was based more on VFAT than on FAT16. It allowed for 32-bit cluster addressing, which in turn provided for a maximum partition size of 2 terabytes (2048 GB). It also included smaller cluster sizes to avoid wasted space (discussed later). FAT32 support is included in current Windows versions.

NTFS

Introduced along with Windows NT (and available on Windows 7, Vista, and XP), NTFS (NT File System) is a much more advanced filesystem in almost every way than all versions of the FAT filesystem. It includes such features as individual file security and *compression*, RAID support, as well as support for extremely large file and partition sizes and disk transaction monitoring. It is the filesystem of choice for higher-performance computing.

CDFS

While not a filesystem that can be used on a hard drive, CDFS (CD-ROM File System) is the filesystem of choice for CD media and has been used with 32-bit Windows versions since Windows 95. A CD mounted with the CDFS driver appears as a collection.

Quick format vs. full format

When you're installing any Windows OS, you will be asked first to format the drive using one of these disk technologies. Choose the disk technology based on what the computer will be doing and which OS you are installing.

To format a partition, you can use the FORMAT command. FORMAT.EXE is available with all versions of Windows. You can run FORMAT from a command prompt or by right-clicking a drive in Windows Explorer and selecting Format. However, when you install Windows it performs the process of partitioning and formatting for you if a partitioned and formatted drive does not already exist. You can usually choose between a *quick format* or a *full format*. With both formats, files are removed from the partition; the difference is that a quick format does not then check for bad sectors (a time-consuming process).

Be extremely careful with the FORMAT command! When you format a drive, all data on the drive is erased.

Load alternate third party drivers when necessary

During the installation of Windows, it may be necessary to load a third-party driver that you update later. The goal during installation is to get the operating system up and running and in a state where you can interact with it. Some of the drivers included with media are not the latest from the vendor but can be used to complete the installation. Once installation is done, you can access the website of third-party vendors and download and then install the latest drivers.

Time/date/region language settings

During installation of the operating system, you are asked to choose the correct settings for the local time, date, and region. As was mentioned earlier, the goal during installation is to complete the process as quickly as possible and you may need to tweak these settings later.

Once the installation is complete, there are a number of ways to change these values, the easiest of which is to right-click on the clock in the lower-right corner of the taskbar and choose Adjust Date/Time. In the Control Panel, you can choose the Region and Language applet to configure date and time formats, as well as change language and location settings. Language Interface Packs (LIPs) are available that can be installed to modify what appears in wizards, dialog boxes, and such (see: `http://windows.microsoft.com/en-US/windows7/Install-or-change-a-display-language` for more information).

Other Concerns

This objective also lists a number of other topics that can be lumped beneath two areas: workgroup versus domain, and recovery partitions. These reappear beneath other objectives within this domain and are not discussed here since they are explored elsewhere in this chapter.

Exam Essentials

Know the difference between basic and dynamic partitions.   Basic partitions are a fixed size and are always on a single physical disk. Dynamic partitions can increase in size (without reformatting) and can span multiple physical disks.

Be familiar with the various boot methods.   You can begin the installation or upgrade process by booting from a number of sources. There are four in particular that CompTIA wants you to be familiar with: USB, CD-ROM, DVD, and PXE. The most commonly used for an attended installation is the CD-ROM/DVD boot.

1.3 Given a scenario, use appropriate command line tools

Although the exam is on the Windows operating systems, it tests many concepts that carry over from the Microsoft Disk Operating System (MS-DOS), which was discussed earlier. MS-DOS was never meant to be extremely friendly. Its roots are in CP/M, which was command line–based, and so is MS-DOS. In other words, they all use long strings of commands typed in at the computer keyboard to perform operations. Some people prefer this type of interaction with the computer, including many folks with technical backgrounds (such as yours truly). Although Windows has left the full command-line interface behind, it still contains a bit of DOS, and you get to it through the command prompt.

Although you can't tell from looking at it, the Windows command prompt is actually a Windows program that is intentionally designed to have the look and feel of a DOS command line. Because it is, despite its appearance, a Windows program, the command prompt provides all the stability and configurability you expect from Windows. You can access a command prompt by running `CMD.EXE`.

A number of diagnostic utilities are often run at the command prompt, and they can be broken into two categories: networking and operating system. Since knowledge of each is required for the exam, they are discussed next in the order given, starting with the networking command-line tools.

Networking

The networking command-line tools you are expected to know for this exam are `PING`, `TRACERT`, `NETSTAT`, `IPCONFIG`, `NET`, `NSLOOKUP`, and `NBTSTAT`.

PING

The `PING` command is one of the most useful commands in TCP/IP. It sends a series of packets to another system, which in turn sends back a response. This utility can be extremely useful for troubleshooting problems with remote hosts. Pings are also called ICMP echo requests/replies, as they use ICMP.

The `PING` command indicates whether the host can be reached and how long it took for the host to send a return packet. Across wide area network links, the time value will be much larger than across healthy LAN links.

The syntax for `PING` is **ping *hostname*** or **ping *IP address***. There are several options for the `PING` command, and you can see them all by typing **ping /?** at the command prompt. Table 6.10 lists some useful ones.

TABLE 6.10   PING options

Option	Function
-t	Persistent ping. Will ping the remote host until stopped by the client (by using Ctrl+C).
ping -4	Forces ping to use an IPv4 address.
ping -6	Forces ping to use an IPv6 address.
-n *count*	Specifies the number of echo requests to send.
-l *size*	Specifies the packet size to send.
-a	Resolves addresses to hostnames.

NOTE   Some webmasters have configured their routers to block pings in order to avoid problems such as someone trying to eat up bandwidth with a *ping of death* (sending a persistent ping with a huge buffer to overwhelm the recipient). For example, if you ping www.microsoft.com you won't get a response, even though the site is functional.

TRACERT

Tracert (trace route) is a command-line utility that enables you to verify the route to a remote host. Execute the command TRACERT *hostname*, where *hostname* is the computer name or IP address of the computer whose route you want to trace. Tracert returns the different IP addresses the packet was routed through to reach the final destination. The results also include the number of hops needed to reach the destination. If you execute the TRACERT command without any options, you see a help file that describes all the TRACERT switches.

This utility determines the intermediary steps involved in communicating with another IP host. It provides a road map of all the routing an IP packet takes to get from host A to host B.

Timing information from TRACERT can be useful for detecting a malfunctioning or overloaded router.

NETSTAT

The Netstat utility is used to check out the inbound and outbound TCP/IP connections on your machine. It can also be used to view packet statistics, such as how many packets have been sent and received and the number of errors.

There are several useful command-line options for NETSTAT, as shown in Table 6.11.

TABLE 6.11   NETSTAT options

Option	Function
-a	Displays all connections and listening ports.
-b	Displays the executable involved in creating each connection or listening port. In some cases, well-known executables host multiple independent components, and in these cases the sequence of components involved in creating the connection or listening port is displayed. In this case, the executable name is in brackets, [ ], at the bottom; at the top is the component it called; and so forth until TCP/IP was reached. Note that this option can be time consuming and will fail unless you have sufficient permissions.
-e	Displays Ethernet statistics. This may be combined with the -s option.
-f	Displays fully qualified domain names (FQDN) for foreign addresses.
-n	Displays addresses and port numbers in numerical form.
-o	Displays the owning process ID associated with each connection.
-p *proto*	Shows connections for the protocol specified by *proto*; *proto* may be any of the following: TCP, UDP, TCPv6, or UDPv6. If used with the -s option to display per-protocol statistics, proto may be any of IP, IPv6, ICMP, ICMPv6, TCP, TCPv6, UDP, or UDPv6.
-r	Displays the routing table.
-s	Displays per-protocol statistics. By default, statistics are shown for IP, IPv6, ICMP, ICMPv6, TCP, TCPv6, UDP, and UDPv6; the -p option may be used to specify a subset of the default.

IPCONFIG

With Windows-based operating systems, you can determine the network settings on the client's network interface cards, as well as any that a DHCP server has leased to your computer, by typing the following at a command prompt: **ipconfig /all**.

IPCONFIG /ALL also gives you full details on the duration of your current lease. You can verify whether a DHCP client has connectivity to a DHCP server by releasing the client's IP address and then attempting to lease an IP address. You can conduct this test by typing the following sequence of commands from the DHCP client at a command prompt:

```
ipconfig /release
ipconfig /renew
```

Ipconfig is one of the first tools to use when experiencing problems accessing resources, because it will show you whether an address has been issued to the machine. If the address displayed falls within the 169.254.*x.x* category, this means the client was unable to reach the DHCP server and has defaulted to Automatic Private IP Addressing (APIPA), which will prevent the card from communicating outside its subnet, if not altogether. Table 6.12 lists useful switches for IPCONFIG.

TABLE 6.12   IPCONFIG switches

Switch	Purpose
/ALL	Shows full configuration information
/RELEASE	Releases the IP address, if you are getting addresses from a Dynamic Host Configuration Protocol (DHCP) server
/RELEASE6	Releases the IPv6 address
/RENEW	Obtains a new IP address from a DHCP server
/RENEW6	Renews the IPv6 address
/FLUSHDNS	Flushes the domain name server (DNS) name resolver cache

In the Linux world, a utility similar to ipconfig is ifconfig.

NET

Depending on the version of Windows you are using, NET can be one of the most powerful commands at your disposal. While all Windows versions include a NET command, the capabilities of it differ based on whether it is server or workstation based and the version of the operating system.

While always command line based, this tool allows you to do almost anything you want with the operating system.

Table 6.13 shows common NET switches.

TABLE 6.13   NET switches

Switch	Purpose
NET ACCOUNTS	Set account options (password age, length, etc.)
NET COMPUTER	Add and delete computer accounts

TABLE 6.13 NET switches *(continued)*

Switch	Purpose
NET CONFIG	See network-related configuration
NET CONTINUE, NET PAUSE, NET START, NET STATISTICS, and NET STOP	Control services
NET FILE	Close open files
NET GROUP and NET LOCALGROUP	Create, delete, and change groups
NET HELP	See general help
NET HELPMSG	See specific message help
NET NAME	See the name of the current machine and user
NET PRINT	Interact with print queues and print jobs
NET SEND	Send a message to user(s)
NET SESSION	See session statistics
NET SHARE	Create a share
NET TIME	Set the time to that of another computer
NET USE	Connect to a share
NET USER	Add, delete, and see information about a user
NET VIEW	See available resources

The commands in Table 6.13 are invaluable troubleshooting aids when you cannot get the graphical interface to display properly. You can also use them when interacting with hidden ($) and administrative shares that do not appear within the graphical interface.

The NET command used with the SHARE parameter enables you to create shares from the command prompt, using this syntax:

NET SHARE *<share_name>*=*<drive_letter>*:*<path>*

To share the C:\EVAN directory as SALES, you would use the following command:

NET SHARE SALES=C:\EVAN

You can use other parameters with NET SHARE to set other options. Table 6.14 summarizes the most commonly used parameters.

TABLE 6.14   NET SHARE parameters

Parameter	Purpose
/DELETE	Stop sharing a folder
/REMARK	Add a comment for browsers
/UNLIMITED	Set the user limit to Maximum Allowed
/USERS	Set a specific user limit

The NET /? command is basically a catch-all help request. It will instruct you to use the NET command you are interested in for more information.

NSLOOKUP

Nslookup is a command-line utility that enables you to verify entries on a DNS server. You can use the NSLOOKUP command in two modes: interactive and noninteractive. In interactive mode, you start a session with the DNS server, in which you can make several requests. In noninteractive mode, you specify a command that makes a single query of the DNS server. If you want to make another query, you must type another noninteractive command.

One of the key issues regarding the use of TCP/IP is the ability to resolve a hostname to an IP address—an action usually performed by a DNS server.

NBTSTAT

Nbtstat is a command-line utility that shows NetBIOS over TCP/IP information. While not used as often as other entries in this category, it can be useful when trying to diagnose a problem with NetBIOS name resolution. The /? parameter can be used to see the available switches.

OS

The OS command-line tools you are expected to know for this exam are TASKKILL, BOOTREC, SHUTDOWN, TASKLIST, MD, RD, CD, DEL, FDISK, FORMAT, COPY, XCOPY, ROBOCOPY, DISKPART, SFC, CHKDSK, and /?. The OS command-line tools are discussed in the sections that follow.

TASKKILL Command

The TASKKILL.EXE utility is used to terminate processes. Those processes can be identified by either name or process ID number (PID) and the process can exist on the machine where the administrator is sitting (the default) or on another machine – in which case you signify the other system by using the /S switch.

The /IM name is used to specify an (image) name of a process to kill and can include the wildcard (*) characters. If the process ID number is used in place of the name, then the /PID switch is needed. The processes in question are the same which can be killed through the Task Manager. There are two signals that can be sent: the default is SIGTERM (a gentle kill, related to code 15) and the /F switch issues a SIGKILL (a terminate at all cost kill, related to code 9).

BOOTREC

The BOOTREC.EXE utility can be run in the Windows 7 or Windows Vista to interact with the Master Boot Record (MBR), boot sector, or Boot Configuration Data (BCD) store. It cannot be used with Windows XP since it uses a different boot structure.

BOOTREC.EXE can be thought of as the replacement for the FIXBOOT.EXE and FIXMBR.EXE commands from the Windows XP Recovery Console. In Windows Vista and Windows 7, the Recovery Environment replaces the Recovery Console that existed in Windows XP.

To run the tool, you must boot from the installation disc, choose the Repair Your Computer option, and enter the *Recovery Environment*. Choose Command Prompt from the System Recovery Options and then type **bootrec.exe**.

The options for BOOTREC are /FIXBOOT (to write a new boot sector), /FIXMBR (to write a new MBR), /REBUILDBCD (to rebuild the BCD store), or /SCANOS (to scan all disks for installations the Boot Manager menu is not listing).

SHUTDOWN

The SHUTDOWN.EXE utility can be used to schedule a shutdown (complete or a restart) locally or remotely. A variety of reasons can be specified and announced to users for the shutdown. Three parameters to be aware of are /S (turns the computer off), /R (restarts the computer), and /M (lets you specify a computer other than this one).

TASKLIST

The TASKLIST.EXE utility is used at the command line to see a list of all the running processes (and their process ID number), similar to what you see in the GUI by using Task Manager. By default, it shows the processes on the current machine, but the /S switch can be used to see the processes on a remote machine. /SVC will show the services hosted in each process and you can use /U if you need to run the command as another user (/P allows you to specify a password associated with that user).

MD

The MD command is used to make directories. It's a shorthand version of the MKDIR command. Table 6.15 describes its use and switches (we discuss RD and CD next).

TABLE 6.15   CD, MD, and RD use and switches

Command	Purpose
CD *[path]*	Changes to the specified directory.
CD /D *[drive:][path]*	Changes to the specified directory on the drive.
CD ..	Changes to the directory that is up one level.
CD\	Changes to the root directory of the drive.
MD *[drive:][path]*	Makes a directory in the specified path. If you don't specify a path, the directory will be created in your current directory.
RD *[drive:][path]*	Removes (deletes) specified directory.
RD /S *[drive:][path]*	Removes all directories and files in the specified directory, including the specified directory itself.
RD /Q *[drive:][path]*	Quiet mode. It won't ask whether you're sure you want to delete the specified directory when you use /S.

RD

The RD command is used to remove directories. It's a shorthand version of the RMDIR commands. Table 6.15 describes its use and switches.

CD

The CD command is used to change (or display). It's a shorthand versions of the CHDIR command. Table 6.15 describes its use and switches.

DEL

The DEL command is used to delete files and directories at the command line. Wildcards can be used with it. ERASE performs the same operations.

FDISK

The FDISK command used to be included with earlier operating systems to make disk partitioning possible. This command does not exist in Windows 7, Vista, or XP, having been replaced with DISKPART. CompTIA lists it as a command to know, and for the exam you should know that it is not included with the current versions of Windows.

FORMAT

The FORMAT command is used to wipe data off disks and prepare them for new use. Before a hard disk can be formatted, it must have partitions created on it. (Partitioning was done in the DOS days with the FDISK command, but as we just mentioned, that command does not exist in Windows 7, Vista, or XP, having been replaced with DISKPART.) The syntax for FORMAT is as follows:

FORMAT [volume] [switches]

The *volume* parameter describes the drive letter (for example, D:), mount point, or volume name. Table 6.16 lists some common FORMAT switches.

TABLE 6.16   FORMAT switches

Switch	Purpose
/FS:[filesystem]	Specifies the type of filesystem to use (FAT, FAT32, or NTFS)
/V:[label]	Specifies the new volume label
/Q	Executes a quick format

There are other options as well to specify allocation sizes, the number of sectors per track, and the number of tracks per disk size. However, we don't recommend that you use these unless you have a very specific need. The defaults are just fine.

So, if you wanted to format your D: drive as NTFS with a name of HDD2, you would type the following:

FORMAT D: /FS:NTFS /V:HDD2

    Before you format anything, be sure you have it backed up or be prepared to lose whatever is on that drive!

COPY

The COPY command does what it says: it makes a copy of a file in a second location. (To copy a file and remove it from its original location, use the MOVE command.) Here's the syntax for COPY:

COPY [filename] [destination]

It's pretty straightforward. There are several switches for COPY, but in practice they are rarely used. The three most used ones are /A, which indicates an ASCII text file; /V, which verifies that the files are written correctly after the copy; and /Y, which suppresses the prompt asking whether you're sure you want to overwrite files if they exist in the destination directory.

The COPY command cannot be used to copy directories. Use XCOPY for that function.

One useful tip is to use wildcards. For example, in DOS (or at the command prompt), the asterisk (*) is a wildcard that means *everything*. So you could type **COPY *.EXE** to copy all files that have an .EXE extension, or you could type **COPY *.*** to copy all files in your current directory.

XCOPY

If you are comfortable with the COPY command, learning XCOPY shouldn't pose too many problems. It's basically an extension of COPY with one notable exception—it's designed to copy directories as well as files. The syntax is as follows:

XCOPY [*source*] [*destination*][*switches*]

There are 26 XCOPY switches; some of the commonly used ones are listed in Table 6.17.

TABLE 6.17 XCOPY switches

Switch	Purpose
/A	Copies only files that have the Archive attribute set and does not clear the attribute. Useful for making a quick backup of files while not disrupting a normal backup routine.
/E	Copies directories and subdirectories, including empty directories.
/F	Displays full source and destination filenames when copying.
/G	Allows copying of encrypted files to a destination that does not support encryption.
/H	Copies hidden and system files as well.
/K	Copies attributes. (By default, XCOPY resets the Read-Only attribute.)
/O	Copies file ownership and ACL information (NTFS permissions).
/R	Overwrites read-only files.
/S	Copies directories and subdirectories but not empty directories.
/U	Copies only files that already exist in the destination.
/V	Verifies each new file.

Perhaps the most important switch is /O. If you use XCOPY to copy files from one location to another, the filesystem creates a new version of the file in the new location without changing the old file. In NTFS, when a new file is created it inherits permissions from its new parent directory. This could cause problems if you copy files. (Users who didn't have access to the file before might have access now.) If you want to retain the original permissions, use XCOPY /O.

ROBOCOPY

The ROBOCOPY command (Robust File Copy for Windows) is included with Windows 7 and has the big advantage of being able to accept a plethora of specifications and keep NTFS permissions intact in its operations. The /MIR switch, for example, can be used to mirror a complete directory tree.

An excellent TechNet article on how to use Robocopy can be found at http://technet .microsoft.com/en-us/magazine/ee851678.aspx.

DISKPART

The DISKPART command shows the partitions and lets you manage them on the computer's hard drives. A universal tool for working with hard drives from the command line, it allows you to convert between disk types, extend/shrink volumes, format partitions and volumes, list them, create them, and so on. A list of all the available commands can be found at: http://technet.microsoft.com/en-us/library/bb490893.aspx.

SFC

The System File Checker (SFC) is a command line–based utility that checks and verifies the versions of system files on your computer. If system files are corrupted, the SFC will replace the corrupted files with correct versions.

The syntax for the SFC command is as follows:

SFC [*switch*]

While the switches vary a bit between different versions of Windows, Table 6.18 lists the most common ones available for SFC.

TABLE 6.18   SFC switches

Switch	Purpose
/CACHESIZE=*X*	Sets the Windows File Protection cache size, in megabytes
/PURGECACHE	Purges the Windows File Protection cache and scans all protected system files immediately
/REVERT	Reverts SFC to its default operation

Switch	Purpose
/SCANFILE (Windows 7 and Vista only)	Scans a file that you specify and fixes problems if they are found
/SCANNOW	Immediately scans all protected system files
/SCANONCE	Scans all protected system files once
/SCANBOOT	Scans all protected system files every time the computer is rebooted
/VERIFYONLY	Scans protected system files and does not make any repairs or changes
/VERIFYFILE	Identifies the integrity of the file specified, and makes any repairs or changes
/OFFBOOTDIR	Does a repair of an offline boot directory
/OFFFWINDIR	Does a repair of an offline windows directory

To run the SFC, you must be logged in as an administrator or have administrative privileges. If the System File Checker discovers a corrupted system file, it will automatically overwrite the file by using a copy held in the *%systemroot%*\system32\dllcache directory. If you believe that the dllcache directory is corrupted, you can use SFC /SCANNOW, SFC /SCANONCE, SFC /SCANBOOT, or SFC /PURGECACHE to repair its contents.

 The C:\Windows\System32 directory is where many of the Windows system files reside.

If you attempt to run SFC, or many other utilities, from a standard command prompt in Windows Vista, for example, you will be told that you must be an administrator running a console session in order to continue. Rather than opening a standard command prompt, choose Start ➢ All Programs ➢ Accessories, and then right-click on Command Prompt and choose Run As Administrator. The UAC will prompt you to continue, and then you can run SFC without a problem.

CHKDSK

You can use the Windows Chkdsk utility to create and display status reports for the hard disk. Chkdsk can also correct filesystem problems (such as cross-linked files) and scan for and attempt to repair disk errors. You can manually start Chkdsk by right-clicking the problem disk and selecting Properties. This will bring up the Properties dialog box for that disk, which shows the current status of the selected disk drive.

By clicking the Tools tab at the top of the dialog box, and then clicking the Check Now button in the Error-Checking section, you can start Chkdsk.

[command name] /?

The HELP command does what it says: it gives you help. Actually, if you just type **HELP** and press Enter, your computer gives you a list of system commands you can type. Type the name of a command you want to know about after typing HELP. For example, type **HELP RD** and press Enter, and you will get information about the RD command.

You can also get the same help information by typing **/?** after the command.

The /? switch is slightly faster and provides more information than the HELP command. The HELP command only provides information for system commands (it does not include network commands). For example, if you type **help ipconfig** at a command prompt, you get no useful information (except to try /?); however, typing **ipconfig /?** provides the help file for the ipconfig command.

Recovery console

The Recovery Console is a command-line utility used for troubleshooting in Windows XP only. From it, you can format drives, stop and start services, and interact with files. The latter is extremely important because many boot/command-line utilities bring you into a position where you can interact with files stored on FAT or FAT32, but not NTFS. The Recovery Console can work with files stored on all three filesystems.

The Recovery Console isn't installed on a system by default. To install it with Windows XP, use the following steps:

As mentioned in the discussion of BOOTREC, Windows Vista and Windows 7 use a tailored version of Windows PE which is a RAM-based version of Windows. It is called Windows RE (Recovery Environment) and it replaces the Recovery console.

1. Place the Windows CD in the system.
2. From a command prompt, change to the i386 directory of the CD.
3. Type **winnt32 /cmdcons**.
4. A prompt appears, alerting you to the fact that 7 MB of hard drive space is required and asking if you want to continue. Click Yes.

Upon successful completion of the installation, the Recovery Console is added as a menu choice at the bottom of the startup menu. To access it, you must choose it from the list at startup. If more than one installation of Windows exists on the system, another boot menu will appear, asking which you want to boot into, and you must make a selection to continue.

To perform this task, you must give the administrator password. You'll then arrive at a command prompt. You can give a number of commands from this prompt, two of which are worth special attention: EXIT restarts the computer, and HELP lists the commands you can give. Table 6.19 lists the other commands available, most of which will be familiar to administrators who have worked with MS-DOS.

TABLE 6.19   Recovery Console commands

Command	Purpose
ATTRIB	Shows the current attributes of a file or folder, and lets you change them.
BATCH	Runs the commands within an ASCII text file.
CD	Used without parameters, it shows the current directory. Used with parameters, it changes to the directory specified.
CHDIR	Works the same as CD.
CHKDSK	Checks the disk for errors.
CLS	Clears the screen.
COPY	Allows you to copy a file (or files, if used with wildcards) from one location to another.
DEL	Deletes a file.
DELTREE	Recursively deletes files and directories.
DIR	Shows the contents of the current directory.
DISABLE	Allows you to stop a service/driver.
DISKPART	Shows the partitions on the drive, and lets you manage them.
ENABLE	Allows you to start a service/driver.
EXPAND	Extracts compressed files.
FIXBOOT	Writes a new boot sector.
FIXMBR	Checks and fixes (if possible) the master boot record.
FORMAT	Allows you to format a floppy or partition.
LISTSVC	Shows the services/drivers on the system.

TABLE 6.19   Recovery Console commands *(continued)*

Command	Purpose
LOGON	Lets you log on to Windows 2000.
MAP	Shows the maps currently created.
MD	Makes a new folder/directory.
MKDIR	Works the same as MD.
MORE	Shows only one screen of a text file at a time.
RD	Removes a directory or folder.
REN	Renames a file or folder.
RENAME	Works the same as REN.
RMDIR	Works the same as RD.
SYSTEMROOT	Works like CD but takes you to the system root of whichever OS installation you're logged on to.
TYPE	Displays the contents of an ASCII text file.

Fixboot

This utility is used to write a new boot sector.

Fixmbr

This utility is used to check, and fix, the master boot record (MBR).

Exam Essentials

Know the main command-line utilities.   Those discussed in this chapter include the ones CompTIA wants you to know for the exam. The commands include (in alphabetical order): /?, CD, CHKDSK, COPY, FORMAT, IPCONFIG, MD, NET, NSLOOKUP, PING, RD, SFC, TRACERT, and XCOPY.

Know the switches for specified commands.   CompTIA expects you to know the switches for the most common utilities. Make sure you look at each command and utility they have listed and the switches and parameters for each that have been listed in this section.

1.4 Given a scenario, use appropriate operating system features and tools

This objective requires you to know how to work at the command line and run common command-line utilities available with the Windows-based operating systems as well as use administrative tools. Some of the material here overlaps with other objectives, but you'll want to make certain you know each utility discussed.

Although most of the information presented about Windows utilities and administration should seem like second nature to you (on-the-job experience is expected for A+ certification), you should read these sections thoroughly to make certain you can answer any questions that may appear about them.

Administrative

Table 6.20 lists the administrative tools, and the purpose for each, that you need to know for this objective. The majority of these run in the Microsoft Management Console (MMC).

TABLE 6.20   Windows administrative tools

Tool	Purpose
Computer Management	The Computer Management Console is a power-packed interface and includes the following system tools: Device Manager, Event Viewer, Shared Folders, Performance/Performance Logs and Alerts (based on the OS you are running, you may also see Local Users and Groups, or Task Scheduler here as well). Computer Management also has the Storage area, which lets you manage removable media, defragment your hard drives, or manage partitions through the Disk Management utility. Finally, you can manage system services and applications through Computer Management as well.
Device Manager	Device Manager shows a list of all installed hardware and lets you add items, remove items, update drivers, and more.
Users and Groups	If Local Users and Groups is not visible in the left pane of MMC, choose File ➢ Add/Remove Snap-in and select Local Users And Groups from the list of possible snap-ins. You can choose to manage the local computer or another computer (requiring you to provide its address). The built-in groups for a domain are a superset of local groups.
	Local Users and Groups is not available for Windows 7 editions lower than Professional. In all other editions, you must manage user accounts using the User Accounts applet in the Control Panel, and you cannot create or manage groups. The default users created are Administrator, Guest, and the administrative account created during the install.

TABLE 6.20   Windows administrative tools *(continued)*

Tool	Purpose
Local Security Policy	The Local Security Policy (choose Start and then enter **secpol.msc**) allows you to set the default security settings for the system. This feature is not available for Windows 7 in any edition other than Windows 7 Professional, Windows 7 Ultimate, and Windows 7 Enterprise.
Performance Monitor	Performance Monitor differs a bit in versions but has the same purpose throughout: to display performance counters. While lumped under one heading, two tools are available—System Monitor and Performance Logs And Alerts. System Monitor will show the performance counters in graphical format. The Performance Logs And Alerts utility will collect the counter information and then send it to a console (such as the one in front of the admin so they can be aware of the problem) or event log.
Services	This interface is listed, and discussed, with the Run line utilities later in this objective.
System Configuration	MSCONFIG, known as the System Configuration utility, helps you troubleshoot startup problems by allowing you to selectively disable individual items that normally are executed at startup. It works in all versions of Windows, although the interface window is slightly different among versions.
Task Scheduler	Task Scheduler allows you to configure jobs to automatically run unattended. For the run frequency, you can choose any of the following options: Daily, Weekly, Monthly, One Time Only, When The Computer Starts, or When You Log On.
	You can access a job's advanced properties any time after the job has been created. To do so, double-click the icon for the job in the Scheduled Tasks screen. In the resulting dialog box, you can configure such things as the username and password associated with the job, the actual command line used to start the job (in case you need to add parameters to it), and the working directory.
	At any time, you can delete a scheduled job by deleting its icon, or you can simply disable a job by removing the check mark from the Enabled box on the Task tab of the task's properties dialog box. For jobs that are scheduled to run, a picture of a clock appears in the bottom-left corner of the icon; jobs not scheduled to run do not have that clock.
Component Services	Component Services is an MMC snap-in that allows you to administer, as well as deploy, component services and configure behavior like security (Component Services is located beneath Administrative Tools).

Tool	Purpose
Data Sources	ODBC Data Source Administrator (located beneath Administrative Tools) allows you to interact with database management systems.
Print Management	Available in Windows 7 and Windows Vista, Print Management (located beneath Administrative Tools) allows you to manage multiple printers and print servers from a single interface.
	Print Management is not available for Windows 7 in any edition lower than Windows 7 Professional. In all other editions, you must manage individual printers using the Printers applet in the Control Panel, and you are very limited in what you can manage.
Windows Memory Diagnostic (not available in Windows XP)	The Windows Memory Diagnostic Tool (located beneath Administrative Tools) can be used to check a system for memory problems. In order for the tool to work, the system must be restarted. The two options that it offers are to restart the computer now and check for problems, or wait and check for problems on the next restart.
	Upon reboot, the test will take several minutes and the display screen will show which pass number is being run and the overall status of the test (percentage complete). When the memory test concludes, the system will restart again and nothing related to it is apparent until you log in. If the test is without error, you'll see a message that no errors were found. If anything else is found, the results will be displayed.
Windows Firewall	Windows Firewall (Start ➢ Control Panel ➢ Windows Firewall) is used to block access from the network, and in Windows 7, it is divided into separate settings for private networks and public networks.
	While host-based firewalls are not as secure as other types of firewalls, this provides much better protection than previously and is turned on by default. It is also included in the Security component of the Action Center and can be tweaked significantly using the Advanced Settings.
Advanced Security	Continuing the discussion of Windows Firewall, once you click Advanced Settings, *Windows Firewall with Advanced Security* opens (not available in Windows XP).
	Here, you can configure inbound and outbound rules as well as import and export policies and monitor. Monitoring is not confined only to the firewall; you can also monitor security associations and connection security rules. In short, Windows Firewall with Advanced Security is an incredibly powerful tool that builds on what Windows Vista started. Not only can this MMC snap-in do simple configuration, but it can also configure remote computers and work with Group Policy.

MSCONFIG

The Msconfig system configuration tool features different tabs based on the Windows version you are running, but the key ones are General, Boot, Services, Startup, and Tools. In Windows XP, Boot is named Boot.ini, and this tab lets you modify the Boot.ini file and specify other boot options. On the Services tab, you can view the services installed on the system and their current status (running or stopped). You can also enable and disable services as necessary.

General

On the General tab, you can choose the startup type. There are three sets of options: Normal, Diagnostic, and Selective. A normal startup loads all drivers and services, whereas a diagnostic startup only loads the basic drivers and services. Between the two extremes is the selective startup that gives you very limited options on what to load.

Boot

The Boot tab (called Boot.ini in Windows XP), shows the boot menu and allows you to configure parameters such as the number of seconds the menu should appear before the default option is chosen and whether you want go to Safe boot or not. You can toggle on/off the displaying of drivers as they load during startup and choose to log the boot, go with basic video settings, and similar options.

Services

The Services tab shows the services configured and their current status. From here, you can enable or disable all and hide Microsoft services from the display (which greatly reduces the display in most cases).

Startup

The Startup tab shows the items scheduled to begin at startup, the command associated with them, and the location where the configuration is done (usually, but not always, in the Registry). From here, you can enable or disable all. If a particular startup item has been disabled in Windows 7 and Windows Vista, the date and time it was disabled will appear in the display.

Tools

The Tools tab contains quick access to some of the most useful diagnostic tools in Windows. You can launch such items as the Registry Editor as well as many Control Panel applets, and enable or disable UAC (User Account Control).

Task Manager

This tool lets you shut down nonresponsive applications selectively in all Windows versions. In current versions of Windows, it can do so much more: Task Manager allows you to see which processes and applications are using the most system resources, view network usage, see connected users, and so on. To display Task Manager, press Ctrl+Alt+Del and click the Task Manager button to display it (in earlier Windows versions, you needed only press Ctrl+Alt+Del). In Windows XP, whether the Security screen displays depends on whether you're using the Windows XP Welcome screen (you can change this setting on the Screen Saver tab of the computer's Display Properties). By default, in Windows 7, Vista, and XP, the Windows Security screen does not display if you press Ctrl+Alt+Del; instead, Task Manager opens right away or you are given a set of tasks, among them Start Task Manager.

You can also right-click on an empty spot in the Taskbar and choose it from the pop-up menu that appears.

 To get to the Task Manager directly in any of the Windows versions, you can press Ctrl+Shift+Esc.

Task Manager has at least five tabs: Applications, Processes, Performance, Networking, and Users. A sixth tab—Services—appears in Windows 7 and Windows Vista.

The Networking tab is only shown if your system has a network card installed (it is rare to find one that doesn't). The Users tab is displayed only if the computer you are working on is a member of a workgroup or is a standalone computer. The Users tab is unavailable on computers that are members of a network domain. Let's look at these tabs, in the order of their appearance, in more detail.

Applications

The Applications tab lets you see which tasks are open on the machine. You also see the status of each task, which can be either Running or Not Responding. If a task or application has stopped responding (that is, it's hung), you can select the task in the list and click End Task. Doing so closes the program, and you can try to open it again. Often, although certainly not always, if an application hangs you have to reboot the computer to prevent the same thing from happening again shortly after you restart the application. You can also use the Applications tab to switch to a different task or create new tasks.

Processes

The Processes tab lets you see the names of all the processes running on the machine. You also see the user account that's running the process, as well as how much CPU and RAM resources that each process is using. To end a process, select it in the list and click End Process. Be careful with this choice since ending some processes can cause Windows to shut down. If you don't know what a particular process does, you can look for it in any search engine and find a number of sites that will explain it.

You can also change the priority of a process in Task Manager's Processes display by right-clicking on the name of the process and choosing Set Priority. The six priorities, from lowest to highest, are as follows:

Low   For applications that need to complete sometime but that you don't want interfering with other applications. On a numerical scale from 0 to 31, this equates to a base priority of 4.

Below Normal For applications that don't need to drop all the way down to Low. This equates to a base priority of 6.

Normal The default priority for most applications. This equates to a base priority of 8.

Above Normal For applications that don't need to boost all the way to High. This equates to a base priority of 10.

High For applications that must complete soon, when you don't want other applications to interfere with the applications' performance. This equates to a base priority of 13.

Realtime For applications that must have the processor's attention to handle time-critical tasks. Applications can be run at this priority only by a member of the Administrators group. This equates to a base priority of 24.

If you decide to change the priority of an application, you'll be warned that changing the priority of an application may make it unstable. You can generally ignore this option when changing the priority to Low, Below Normal, Above Normal, or High, but you should heed this warning when changing applications to the Realtime priority. Realtime means that the processor gives precedence to this process over all others—over security processes, over spooling, over everything—and is sure to make the system unstable.

Task Manager changes the priority only for that instance of the running application. The next time the process is started, priorities revert back to that of the base (typically Normal).

Services (Windows 7 and Vista Only) The Services tab lists the name of each running service as well as the process ID associated with it, its description, status, and group. A button labeled Services appears on this tab, and clicking it will open the MMC console for Services, where you can configure each service. Within Task Manager, right-clicking on a service will open a context menu listing three choices: Start Service, Stop Service, and Go To Process (this takes you to the Processes tab).

Performance

The Performance tab contains a variety of information, including overall CPU usage percentage, a graphical display of CPU usage history, page-file usage in MB, and a graphical display of page-file usage. This tab also provides you with additional memory-related information such as physical and kernel memory usage, as well as the total number of handles, threads, and processes. Total, limit, and peak commit-charge information also displays. Some of the items are beyond the scope of this book, but it's good to know that you can use the Performance tab to keep track of system performance. Note that the number of processes, CPU usage percentage, and commit charge always display at the bottom of the Task Manager window, regardless of which tab you have currently selected.

On Windows 7 this pane has a button marked Resource Monitor which breaks down resource usage on a per-process basis.

Networking

The Networking tab provides you with a graphical display of the performance of your network connection. It also tells you the network adapter name, link speed, and state. If you have more than one network adapter installed in the machine, you can select the appropriate adapter to see graphical usage data for that adapter.

Users

The Users tab provides you with information about the users connected to the local machine. You'll see the username, ID, status, client name, and session type. You can right-click on any connected user to perform a variety of functions, including sending the user a message, disconnecting the user, logging off the user, and initiating a remote-control session to the user's machine.

Use Task Manager whenever the system seems bogged down by an unresponsive application.

Disk Management

In Windows, you can manage your hard drives through the Disk Management component. To access Disk Management, access the Control Panel and double-click Administrative Tools. Then double-click Computer Management. Finally, double-click Disk Management.

The Disk Management screen lets you view a host of information regarding all the drives installed in your system, including CD-ROM and DVD drives. The list of devices in the top portion of the screen shows you additional information for each partition on each drive, such as the filesystem used, status, free space, and so on. If you right-click a partition in either area, you can perform a variety of functions, such as formatting the partition and changing the name and drive letter assignment. For additional options and information, you can also access the properties of a partition by right-clicking it and selecting Properties.

The basic unit of storage is the disk. Disks are partitioned (primary, logical, extended) and then formatted for use. With the Windows operating systems this exam focuses on, you can choose to use either FAT32 or NTFS; the advantage of the latter is that it offers security and many other features that FAT32 can't handle. Both Windows 7 and Windows Vista can only be installed in NTFS, but they will recognize FAT partitions.

 If you're using FAT32 and want to change to NTFS, the convert utility will allow you to do so. For example, to change the E: drive to NTFS, the command is convert e: /FS:NTFS.

Once the disk is formatted, the next building block is the directory structure, in which you divide the partition into logical locations for storing data. Whether these storage units are called directories or folders is a matter of semantics—they tend to be called *folders* when viewed in the graphical user interface (GUI) and *directories* when viewed from the command line.

Drive status

The status of a drive can have a number of variables associated with it (System, Boot, and so on) but what really matters is whether it falls into the category of *healthy* or *unhealthy*. As the title implies, if it is healthy, it is properly working and if it is unhealthy, you need to attend to it and correct problems.

A list of status states that are possible and require action can be found at http://technet .microsoft.com/en-us/library/cc771775.aspx.

Mounting

Drives must be mounted before they can be used. Within Windows, most removable media (flash drives, CDs, and so forth) are recognized when attached and mounted. Volumes on basic disks, however, are not automatically mounted and assigned drive letters by default. To mount them, you must manually assign them drive letters or creating mount points in Disk Management.

You can also mount from the command line using either the Diskpart or the Mountvol utilities.

Extending partitions

It is possible to add more space to partitions (and logical drives) by extending them into unallocated space. This is done in Disk Management by right-clicking and choosing Extend or using the Diskpart utility.

Splitting partitions

Just as you can extend a partition, you can also reduce the size of it. While generically known as splitting the partition, the menu option in Disk Management is Shrink. By shrinking an existing partition, you are creating another with unallocated space that can then be used for other purposes. You can only shrink basic volumes that use the NTFS filesystem (and space exists) or that do not have a filesystem.

Assigning drive letters

Mounting drives and assigning drive letters are two tasks that go hand in hand. When you mount a drive, you typically assign it a drive letter in order to be able to access it. Right-clicking on a volume in Disk Management gives the option choice Change Drive Letter And Paths.

Adding drives

When removable drives are added, the Windows operating system is configured, by default, to identify them and assign a drive letter. When nonremovable drives are added, you must mount them and assign a drive letter as mentioned earlier.

Adding arrays

Arrays are added to increase fault tolerance (using RAID) or performance (striping). Disk Management allows you to create and modify arrays as needed.

Other (User State Migration tool (USMT), File and Settings Transfer Wizard, Windows Easy Transfer)

Microsoft Windows User State Migration Tool (USMT) allows you to migrate user files settings related to the applications, desktop configuration, and accounts. Version 4.0 works with Windows 7, is a part of the Windows Automated Installation Kit (AIK), and can be found at `http://technet.microsoft.com/en-us/library/dd560801(WS.10).aspx`. Version 3.0 works with Windows Vista and XP, whereas previous versions—such as 2.6—also worked with Windows 2000. You can download this tool from `http://technet.microsoft.com/en-us/library/cc722032.aspx`. If all you are doing is a simple migration from one OS to another, you do not need this tool, but it is invaluable during large deployments.

If you are only migrating a few accounts, Microsoft recommends *Windows Easy Transfer* instead of USMT. This tool works with both Windows 7 and Windows Vista. When transferring to Windows 7, for example, a version of Windows Easy Transfer can be downloaded in either 32-bit or 64-bit versions for Windows Vista or Windows XP from `www.microsoft.com/downloads`.

Windows Easy Transfer is not available for use when transferring to Windows XP and the *Files and Settings Transfer Wizard* exists for that purpose. Located at Start ➤ All Programs ➤ Accessories ➤ System Tools ➤ Files And Settings Transfer Wizard, this tool can transfer such settings as those related to the display, desktop, IE, Outlook Express, and so on.

Run line utilities

Table 6.21 lists the utilities CompTIA singles out as relevant to know for this section. All of these can be started from Start ➤ Run by entering their name and pressing Enter.

TABLE 6.21   Run line utilities

Command	Purpose
MSCONFIG	Discussed previously, the Msconfig configuration utility is useful for looking at start-related settings.

TABLE 6.21   Run line utilities *(continued)*

Command	Purpose
REGEDIT	Used to open and edit the Registry. Regedit does not have Save or Undo features (though you can import and export); once you make a change, you've made the change for better or worse, and this is not a place to play around in if you're not sure what you're doing.
	The Registry is divided into five "hives" that hold all settings. The two main hives are HKEY_USERS (which contains settings for all users) and HKEY_LOCAL_MACHINE (which contains settings for the machine itself). HKEY_CURRENT_USER is a subset of HKEY_USERS holding information only on the current user. HKEY_CURRENT_CONFIG and HKEY_CLASSES_ROOT are both subsets of HKEY_LOCAL_MACHINE for the current configuration.
CMD	Starts a command prompt window intentionally designed to have the look and feel of a DOS command line. Because it is, despite its appearance, a Windows program, the command prompt provides all the stability and configurability you expect from Windows.
SERVICES.MSC	An MMC snap-in that allows you to interact with the services running on the computer. The status of the services will typically either be started or stopped, and you can right-click and choose Start, Stop, Pause, Resume, or Restart from the context menu. Services can be started automatically or manually, or they can be disabled. If you right-click on the service and choose Properties from the context menu, you can choose the startup type as well as see the path to the executable and any dependencies.
MMC	Starts the management console, allowing you to run any snap-in (such as SERVICES.MSC).
MSTSC	Remote Desktop Connection Usage is used to configure remote desktop connections.
NOTEPAD	Starts a simple editor. You can edit a file that already exists or create a new one.
EXPLORER	Starts the Windows interface, allowing you to interact with files and folders.
MSINFO32	The System Information dialog box, this tool displays a thorough list of settings on the machine. You cannot change any values from here, but you can search, export, save, and run a number of utilities. It is primarily used during diagnostics because it is an easy way to display settings such as IRQs and DMAs.

Command	Purpose
DXDIAG	DirectX Diagnostic tool (which has the executable name dxdiag) allows you to test DirectX functionality, with a focus on display, sound, and input. When started, you can also verify that your drivers have been signed by Microsoft. DirectX is a collection of APIs related to multimedia.

Exam Essentials

Know the main administrative tools.   Know the primary graphical tools for troubleshooting Windows and working with the operating system. These include the administrative tools, Device Manager, Task Manager, and others discussed.

Know the run line utilities.   Those administrative tools, which can be started from the Run menu, are considered "run line utilities." The commands include MSCONFIG, REGEDIT, CMD, SERVICES.MSC, MMC, MSTSC, NOTEPAD, EXPLORER, MSINFO32, and DXDIAG.

1.5 Given a scenario, use Control Panel utilities

The Control Panel is often the first place to turn for configuration settings. The applets contained within allow you to customize the system and personalize it for each user.

There are a number of applets that every version of Windows has in common, but CompTIA specifically singles out eight for you to know. In addition to those eight, there are another fourteen you need to be familiar with—five that are unique to Windows XP, five that are unique to Windows Vista, and four that are unique to Windows 7.

Common to all Microsoft Operating Systems

A number of Control Panel applets have stayed the same throughout various versions of Windows. In the current version of Windows, when you first open Control Panel it displays in Category view. This view provides you with different categories to choose from, into which Control Panel programs have been organized. Once you choose a category, you can pick a task and the appropriate Control Panel program is opened for you, or you can select one of the Control Panel programs that is part of the category. However, you can change this view to Classic View, which displays all the Control Panel programs in a list, as in older versions of Windows. The specific wording of the CompTIA objective for this exam reads: "Given a scenario, use Control Panel utilities (the items are organized by 'classic view/large icons' in

Windows)." Because of this, we strongly suggest that administrators change to this view. To do so, click Switch To Classic View in the left pane; in Windows 7, select either the Small icons or Large icons options from the View by drop-down list on the right. Throughout this chapter, when we refer to accessing Control Panel programs, we will assume that you have changed the view to Classic View.

Internet options

This configuration settings for Internet Options provide a number of Internet connectivity possibilities. The tabs here include General, Security, Privacy, Content, Connections, Programs, and Advanced.

General

On the General tab, you can configure the home page that appears when the browser starts or a new tab is opened. You can also configure the history settings, search defaults, what happens by default when new tabs are opened, and the appearance of the browser (colors, languages, fonts, and accessibility).

Security

On the Security tab, you can choose both a zone and security level for the zone. The zones include Internet, Local Intranet, Trusted Sites, and Restricted Sites. The default security level for most of the zones is between High and Medium-High, but lower levels can also be selected.

Privacy

Privacy settings allow you to configure the privacy level, choose whether or not you want to provide location information, use Pop-up Blocker, and disable toolbars (and extensions) when InPrivate browsing starts.

Content

Contains Parental Controls and Content Advisor, which can both be helpful for troubleshooting purposes.

Connections

As the name implies, from this tab you can configure connections for an Internet connection, a dial-up or VPN connection, and LAN settings.

Programs

On the Programs tab, you specify which browser you want to be the default browser, what editor to use if HTML needs editing, and what programs to associate with various file types. You can also manage add-ons from here.

Advanced

On the Advanced tab, you can reset settings to their default options. You can also toggle configuration settings for very granular settings not found on other tabs.

Display

This dialog box lets you configure screensavers, colors, display options, and monitor drivers.

Resolution

The resolution settings vary based on the OS, but typically range from Low (800×600) to High (1280×800).

User accounts

This dialog box lets you create and manage user accounts, parental controls, and related settings. The default users created are Administrator, Guest, and the administrative account created during the install.

Folder options

This dialog box lets you configure the look and feel of how folders are displayed in Windows Explorer.

Sharing

Sharing can be configured on the View tab, beneath Advanced Settings. An option will appear here: Use Sharing Wizard (Recommended).

View hidden files

On the View tab, beneath Advanced Settings, you can choose the option Show Hidden Files And Folders and this will allow you to see those items. The opposite of this—the default setting—is Do Not Show Hidden Files And Folders. Radio buttons allow you to choose only one of these options.

Closely related, but a check box setting you should also clear in order to see all files, is Hide Protected Operating System Files (Recommended). When this check box is cleared, those files will also appear in the view you are seeing.

Hide extensions

On the View tab, beneath Advanced Settings, you must clear the check box Hide Extensions For Known File Types in order for the extensions to be shown with the files.

Layout

You can configure the layout on the General tab of Folder Options. From here, you can choose whether to use Windows classic folders or show the preview and filters. Browsing options allow you to choose whether each folder will open in its own folder or the same folder.

System

This utility allows you to view and configure various system elements. From within this one relatively innocuous panel, you can make a large number of configuration changes to a

Windows machine. The different versions of Windows have different options available in this panel, but they will include some of the following: General, Network Identification, Device Manager, Hardware, Hardware Profiles, User Profiles, Environment, Startup/Shutdown, Performance, System Restore, Automatic Updates, Remote, Computer Name, and Advanced.

The General tab gives you an overview of the system, such as OS version, registration information, basic hardware levels (Processor and RAM), and the Service Pack level that's installed, if any.

Performance (virtual memory)

Performance settings are configured on the Advanced tab. Clicking the Settings button allows you to change the visual effects used on the system and configure Data Execution Prevention (DEP). You can also configure virtual memory on the Advanced tab. Virtual memory is the paging file used by Windows as RAM.

Hardware profiles

Hardware profiles can be configured in Windows XP. This functionality was removed in Windows Vista and Windows 7.

Remote settings

On the Remote tab, you can choose whether or not to allow Remote Assistance to be enabled.

System protection

On the System Protection tab, you can choose to do a System Restore as well as create a manual restore point and see the date and time associated with the most recent automatic restore point.

Security center

This interface is used to manage the firewall, automatic updates, and virus protection. From here, you can manage settings for Internet options as well and see any maintenance or troubleshooting issues that you need to attend to.

 With Windows 7, the Security Center was rolled into the Action Center. You can access it by choosing Action Center in the Control Panel, or by typing **Security Center** in the Start button's search box.

Windows firewall

As the name implies, the Windows Firewall applet can be used to manage the firewall included with the operating system.

Power options

Here you can configure different power schemes to adjust power consumption dictating when devices—the display and the computer—will turn off or be put to sleep. Through the Advanced Settings, you can configure the need to enter a password to revive the devices, as well as configure wireless adapter settings, Internet options (namely JavaScript), and the system sleep policy. Common choices include Hibernate, Sleep/Suspend, and Standby.

Unique to Windows XP

You need to be aware of a number of Control Panel applets unique to Windows XP. These include Add Or Remove Programs, Network Connections, Printers and Faxes, Automatic Updates, and the Network Setup Wizard.

Add/remove programs

The Add Or Remove Programs applet (Start ➢ Control Panel ➢ Add Or Remove Programs) in Windows XP can be used to add or delete programs. It can also be used to add or delete Windows components, to set program access and defaults, and to change programs (add or remove portions of it, for example).

When first opened, the applet shows the currently installed programs. If you click Add/Remove Windows Components, it will open the Windows Components Wizard.

Network connections

The Network Connections applet (Start ➢ Control Panel ➢ Network Connections) in Windows XP can be used to add or remove network connections. It can also be used to set up a home or small office network, and to change Windows Firewall settings.

When first opened, the applet shows the currently configured connections. If you choose the option Set Up A Home Or Small Office Network, it brings up the Network Setup Wizard, which is discussed a bit later in this chapter.

Clicking on a connection will change the network tasks to those that are relevant to that type of connection, thus adding to what is currently shown; choices include Disable This Network Device, Rename This Connection, and so on. Right-click on the connection to bring up the properties and change the settings for the connection.

Printers and faxes

The Printers and Faxes applet (Start ➢ Control Panel ➢ Printers And Faxes) in Windows XP can be used to add, delete, and manage printers and faxes. When first opened, the applet shows the currently configured devices.

When you select a device, the tasks that can be done with that device will appear in the left pane. For example, clicking on an installed printer will list such options here as Pause Printing, Share This Printer, Rename This Printer, and Set Printer Properties.

Automatic updates

The Automatic Updates applet (Start ➢ Control Panel ➢ Automatic Updates) in Windows XP can be used to configure how often a check is done for new software, and what to do when new software is found. You can choose one of the following settings:

- Automatic (Recommended) automatically downloads updates and installs them. You configure the frequency; a typical setting would be to check every day at 3:00 a.m.
- Download Updates For Me, But Let Me Choose When To Install Them.
- Notify Me But Don't Automatically Download Or Install Them.
- Turn Off Automatic Updates. This option will leave the computer more vulnerable unless you install updates from the Windows Update website regularly.

Network setup wizard

The Windows Setup Wizard (`netsetup.cpl`) is available by clicking the option Set Up A Home Or Small Office Network in Network Connections, or directly from the Control Panel (Start ➢ Control Panel ➢ Network Setup Wizard).

This tool offers a great deal of flexibility and can be used to share an Internet connection, set up Windows Firewall, share files and folders, or share a printer. As you walk through it, you will provide the name of the workgroup or domain that the system will be a part of. While the networking chapters of this book spend more time on the subject, for now know that a workgroup essentially lacks a server (creating a peer-based network), whereas a domain utilizes a domain controller.

File And Printer Sharing Configuration configures Windows Firewall to either allow or disallow file and printer sharing traffic to pass. When configuring the connection method for accessing the Internet, you have three choices: This Computer Connects Directly To The Internet, This Computer Connections Through A Residential Gateway Or Another Computer, and Other. If you choose the first option, you can turn on Internet Connection Sharing (ICS) and allow this machine to service as a proxy. The network connection you configure can be wireless or wired, dial-up, or even a virtual private network (VPN).

Unique to Vista

A number of Control Panel applets are unique to Windows Vista. You need to be familiar with the Tablet PC Settings, Pen And Input Devices, Offline Files, Problem Reports And Solutions, and Printers.

Tablet PC settings

The Tablet PC Settings applet (Start ➢ Control Panel ➢ Tablet PC Settings) in Windows Vista can be used to configure the device on which the operating system is installed to function as a true tablet. You can tweak handwriting recognition, handedness (left versus right), and other tablet-relevant settings.

The Home Basic edition of Windows Vista does not support a tablet PC input panel, but all other editions of the operating system you need to know for the exam do.

Pen and input devices

The Pen And Input Devices applet (Start ➤ Control Panel ➤ Pen And Input Devices) in Windows Vista is used in conjunction with the Tablet PC Settings. It is used to configure the pen and pointer options.

The Home Basic edition of Windows Vista does not support a tablet PC or have this applet, but all other editions of the operating system you need to know for the exam do.

Offline files

Only Windows Vista Business, Windows Vista Ultimate, and Windows Vista Enterprise support offline files. Beginning with Windows 2000, the Windows-based operating systems added the capability to work with resources that are "online" (accessed through the network or other connection) and "offline" (replicated copies of the resource stored locally). The key is to keep the files in synchronization so that multiple versions of the same file stored in different locations match each other.

Windows Vista includes a Sync Center (choose Start ➤ Control Panel, and then click Network And Internet). Sync partnerships can be set up with a large number of devices, ranging from a flash drive to handheld devices. It is worth noting again that you cannot sync with network folders if you are using Windows Vista Starter, Home Basic, or Home Premium editions.

Problem reports and solutions

Building on the error reporting features offered in Windows XP, the Problem Reports And Solutions applet with Windows Vista (Start ➤ Control Panel ➤ Problem Reports And Solutions) can help solve problems on a particular machine. To configure (or disable) the feature, choose Change Settings and then Advanced Settings. Click Change Setting to open a window that allows you to make changes.

Your two major choices are to disable or enable error reporting. If you choose to disable it, you can still be notified when errors occur. Windows Vista offers the third choice of allowing each user to choose their settings. After choosing to enable error reporting, you can choose to report Windows operating system and/or program errors. By clicking the Programs button, you can configure which programs you want to report errors on. By default, all program errors from all programs are reported, but you can configure the reporting of errors on an app-by-app basis.

Printers

The Printers applet in Windows Vista (Start ➤ Control Panel ➤ Printers) provides a simple interface for adding a new printer or managing existing ones. By right-clicking on any printer shown in the interface, you can choose to make it the default printer from the options menu that appears. Clicking Add A Printer will start the Add Printer Wizard and allow you to add a network, wireless, or Bluetooth printer as well as one that is locally connected.

Unique to Windows 7

Four Control Panel applets are unique to Windows 7: HomeGroup, Action Center, RemoteApp And Desktop Connections, and Troubleshooting.

HomeGroup

The purpose behind HomeGroup (Start ➤ Control Panel ➤ HomeGroup) is to simplify home networking (the sharing of files and printers). Windows 7 Starter can only join a HomeGroup, while all other editions of Windows 7 can both join and create a HomeGroup. The location must be set to Home.

Shared files can include libraries (a big feature of Windows 7). All computers participating in the HomeGroup must be running Windows 7 and the network cannot extend outside of the small group.

Action center

What was previously known as the Security Center has been modified in Windows 7 to become the Action Center (Start ➤ Control Panel ➤ Action Center). This interface still includes security, but it has been expanded to include such maintenance issues as problem reports and backup settings.

The Security settings show the status of, and allow you to configure, the firewall, Windows Update, virus protection, spyware and unwanted software protection, Internet security settings, UAC, and network access protection. The solutions portion of Maintenance rolls in the problem reporting features from earlier versions of Windows. In Windows 7, there are four options for error reporting settings:

- Automatically Check For Solutions (Recommended)
- Automatically Check For Solutions And Send Additional Data If Needed
- Each Time A Problem Occurs, Ask Me Before Checking For Solutions
- Never Check For Solutions (Not Recommended)

You can configure the setting you want in the Action Center by choosing Problem Report Settings. The administrator may choose to set one universal setting for the machine (not the default), or allow each user to make their own setting (the default).

Remote applications and desktop applications

This applet (Start ➤ Control Panel ➤ RemoteApp And Desktop Connections) in Windows 7 is used to access remote computers and virtual machines made available over the network through port 3389.

For the exam, remember that all versions of Windows 7 support outgoing connections but only Professional, Enterprise, and Ultimate can be used for hosting. To enable a remote connection, click Start, right-click on Computer, select Properties, and then choose Remote Settings. You can then turn on Remote Assistance and/or Remote Desktop.

Remote Assistance is either on or off, whereas Remote Desktop offers three options:

- Don't Allow Connections To This Computer
- Allow Connections From Computers Running Any Version Of Remote Desktop (Less Secure)
- Allow Connections Only From Computers Running Remote Desktop With Network Level Authentication (More Secure)

Troubleshooting

This applet (Start ➢ Control Panel ➢ Troubleshooting) in Windows 7 is used to provide a simple interface to use to attack many common problems. All links preceded by a shield require administrator permissions to run and are often tied to UAC prompts before continuing. Most of the problems found will be "automatically fixed" without any prompts. For example, clicking on the link Improve Power Usage will start the Power Troubleshooter and then fix problems that it identifies. Clicking the link to get help from a friend brings up Remote Assistance, allowing someone to connect to this computer. You can also offer to be the one helping another.

Exam Essentials

Be able to name the eight common Control Panel applets.   While there are others, CompTIA specifies eight Control Panel applets that are common between all versions of Windows: Display, Folder Options, Internet Options, Power Options, Security Center, System, User Accounts, and Windows Firewall.

Know what Control Panel utilities are unique to each version of Windows.   The Control Panel applets unique to Windows XP are Add/Remove Programs, Network Connections, Printers and Faxes, Automatic Updates, and Network Setup Wizard. Those unique to Windows Vista are Tablet PC Settings, Pen And Input Devices, Offline Files, Problem Reports And Solutions, and Printers. Those unique to Windows 7 are HomeGroup, Action Center, Remote Applications And Desktop Applications, and Troubleshooting.

1.6 Setup and configure Windows networking on a client/desktop

CompTIA offers a number of exams and certifications on networking (Network+, Server+, and so on), but to become A+ certified, you must have good knowledge of basic networking skills as they relate to the Windows operating system.

It's important to know how network addressing works and the features offered in the Windows operating systems to simplify configuration. CompTIA expects you to have a broad range of knowledge in this category on some obscure features (such as PoE and QoS).

HomeGroup, file/print sharing

HomeGroup was discussed under objective 1.5 where the Control Panel applet (Start ➤ Control Panel ➤ HomeGroup) unique to Windows 7 was addressed. HomeGroup offers a simplified way to set up a home network. It allows you to share files (including libraries) and prevent changes from being made to those files by those sharing them (unless you give them permission to do so).

All computers participating in the HomeGroup must be running Windows 7 and the network can never grow beyond a limited size. While all editions of Windows 7 can join a HomeGroup, not all can create a HomeGroup.

Workgroup vs. domain setup

A peer-to-peer network—also known as a *workgroup*—consists of a number of workstations (two or more) that share resources among themselves. The resources shared are traditionally file and print access, and every computer has the capacity to act as a workstation (by accessing resources from another machine) and as a server (by offering resources to other machines). The primary distinction between workgroups and client/server networks is where security is controlled: locally on each workstation or centrally on a server. A *domain* is a centrally managed group of computers and physical proximity does not matter; the computers within a domain may all be on the same LAN or spread across a WAN.

In a domain (also known as a *client/server network*), users log on to the server by supplying a username and password. They're then authenticated for the duration of their session. Rather than requiring users to give a password for every resource they want to access (share-level), security is based on how they authenticated themselves at the beginning of their session. This is known as *user-level* security, and it's much more powerful than share-level security.

The advantage of a peer-to-peer network is that the cost is lower—you need only add cards and cables to the computers you already have if you're running an operating system that allows such modifications. With a server-based network, you must buy a server—a dedicated machine—and thus the costs are higher. It's never recommended that a peer-to-peer network be used for more than 10 workstations, because the administration and management become so significant that a server-based network makes far greater sense.

Network shares/mapping drives

Network shares can be mapped to drives to appear as if the resources are local. The NET USE command is used to establish network connections via a command prompt. For example, to connect to a shared network drive and make it your M drive, you would use the syntax **net use m:** *server**share*. Figure 6.2 shows an example of mapped drives.

NET USE can also be used to connect to a shared printer: **net use lpt1:** *printername*.

FIGURE 6.2   Mapped network drives

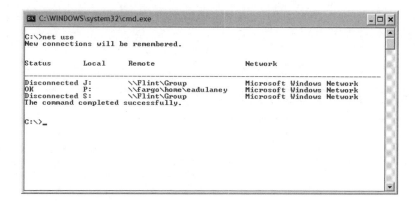

Establish networking connections

When configuring the connection method for accessing the Internet, the three choices Windows offers are This Computer Connects Directly To The Internet, This Computer Connections Through A Residential Gateway Or Another Computer, and Other. If the first option is chosen, you can turn on Internet Connection Sharing (ICS) and allow this machine to serve as a proxy. The network connection you configure can be wireless or wired, dial-up, or a VPN.

VPN

A virtual private network (VPN) is used when you want to connect from a remote location (such as home) to the company's network (authenticating the user and encrypting the data).

Dialups

Dial-up connections are used when a modem must be used to gain access. Typically, the dial-up connection is to an ISP (Internet service provider) and used in remote locations where faster forms of access are not available.

Wireless

A wireless connection uses one of the 802.11 technologies, along with encryption (discussed in Chapter 7, "Security") to connect to the network.

Wired

A wired connection uses a wire to connect the computer to the network. Typically, this is an Ethernet cable, such as 100BaseT (discussed in Chapter 2, "Networking"), which connects to a hub or switch and offers network access to the host.

WWAN (Cellular)

A Wireless Wide Area Network (WWAN) connection is one that uses cellular to connect the host to the network. A wireless service provider (such as AT&T, Sprint, or T-Mobile) will provide a card that is plugged into the host to make the cellular connection possible.

The choices will vary slightly based on the version of Windows you are using, but those commonly available are elaborated on in Table 6.22.

TABLE 6.22 Network connection options

Option	Purpose
Connect To The Internet	Use for connection to a proxy server or other device intended to provide Internet access. This includes wireless, broadband, and dial-up.
Set Up A Wireless Router Or Access Point	If the wireless device will be connected to this machine, this is the option to use.
Manually Connect To A Wireless Network	If you have a wireless network already in place and the device (such as the router) is not directly connected to this machine, then use this option.
Set Up A Wireless Ad Hoc (Computer-To-Computer) Network	This is meant for peer-to-peer resource sharing via wireless network cards and typically a temporary connection.
Set Up A Dial-Up Connection	If you live in the middle of nowhere and the only way to access a network is by using a dial-up modem, then this is the option to select.
Connect To A Workplace	If you are needing to dial into a VPN from a remote location, this is the option to use.

Regardless of which option you choose, you will need to fill out the appropriate fields for the device to be able to communicate on the network. With TCP/IP, required values are an IP address for the host, subnet mask, address for the gateway, and DNS information.

Proxy settings

Proxy settings identify the proxy server to be used to gain Internet access. The proxy server is responsible for making the Internet access possible and utilizes Network Address Translation (NAT) to translate between the public network (Internet) and the private network (on which the host sits).

Remote desktop

Remote Desktop, which is not included in the Home editions of the operating systems, allows members of the administrators group to gain access to the workstation (you can specifically allow other users as well). By default, Remote Desktop is not enabled on Windows 7 or Windows Vista, but you can enable it from Remote Settings in the Control Panel applet System And Security.

Home vs. Work vs. Public network settings

In Windows 7 and Windows Vista, when you make a new connection, you are asked to identify if it is a home network, work network, or public network. If you choose one of the first two, *network discovery* is on by default, allowing you to see other computers and other computers to see you. If you choose Public, network discovery is turned off.

Firewall settings

Windows Firewall (Start ➢ Control Panel ➢ Windows Firewall) is used to block access from the network. In Windows 7, it is divided into separate settings for private networks and public networks.

Exceptions

Exceptions are configured as variations from the rules. Windows Firewall will block incoming network connections except for the programs and services that you choose to allow through. For example, you can make an exception for Remote Assistance to allow communication from other computers when you need help (the scope of the exception can be set to allow any computer, only those on the network, or a custom list of allowed addresses you create). Exceptions can include programs as well as individual ports.

Configuration

Most of the configuration is done as network connection settings. You can configure both ICMP and Services settings. Examples of ICMP settings include allowing incoming echo requests, allowing incoming router requests, and allowing redirects. Examples of services often configured include FTP Server, Post-Office Protocol Version 3 (POP3), and Web Server (HTTP).

Enabling/disabling Windows firewall

On the General tab of Windows Firewall, it is possible to choose the radio button Off (Not Recommended). As the name implies, this turns Windows Firewall completely off. The other radio button option, On (Recommended), enables the firewall. You can also toggle the check box Don't Allow Exceptions. This option should be enabled when you're connecting to a public network in an unsecure location (such as an airport or library) and it will then ignore any exceptions that were configured.

Configuring an alternative IP address in Windows

Windows 7, Windows Vista, and Windows XP all allow the use of an alternate IP address. This is an address that is configured for the system to use in the event the first choice is not available. The first choice can be either a dynamic or static address, and the alternate is used only if the primary cannot be found or used, such as when the DHCP server is down.

The Properties dialog box for each instance of IPv4—on any of the Windows operating systems this exam focuses on—contains an Alternate Configuration tab. To make changes, you must click on it.

IP addressing

Two radio buttons appear on the Alternate Configuration tab: Automatic Private IP Address and User Configured. The default is the first, meaning that the alternate address used is one in the APIPA range (169.254.x.x). Selecting User Configured requires you to enter a static IP address to be used in the IP address field. The entry entered must be valid for your network in order for it to be usable (see Chapter 2 for more information on IP addressing).

Subnet mask

When you select the User Configured radio button on the Alternate Configuration tab, you must enter a value in the Subnet mask field. This value must correspond with the subnet values in use on your network and work with the IP address you enter in the field above (see Chapter 2 for more information on subnet addresses).

DNS

When you select the User Configured radio button on the Alternate Configuration tab, you should enter values in the fields Preferred DNS Server and Alternate DNS Server. These entries are needed in order to translate domain names into IP addresses (see Chapter 2 for more information on DNS).

Gateway

When you select the User Configured radio button on the Alternate Configuration tab, you must enter a value in the Default gateway field. This value must correspond with the subnet values and the IP address you enter in the fields above. This address identifies the router to be used to communicate outside the local network (see Chapter 2 for more information on default gateways).

Network card properties

Like other devices, network cards can be configured to optimize performance. Configuration is done through the Properties dialog box for each card.

Half duplex/full duplex/auto

Duplexing is the means by which communication takes place:

- With *full duplexing*, everyone can send and receive at the same time. The main advantage of full-duplex over half-duplex communication is performance. NICs can operate twice as fast in full-duplex mode as they do normally in half-duplex mode.

- With *half duplexing*, communications travel in both directions, but in only one direction at any given time. Think of a road where construction is being done on one lane— traffic can go in both directions but in only one direction at a time at that location.

- With *auto duplexing*, the mode is set to the lowest common denominator. If a card senses another card is manually configured to half duplex, then it also sets itself at that.

Speed

The speed allows you to configure or not whether the card should run at its highest possible setting. You often need to be compatible with the network on which the host resides. If, for example, you are connecting a workstation with a 10/100BaseT card to a legacy network, you will need to operate at 10 MBps to match the rest of the network.

Wake-on-LAN

Wake-on-LAN (WoL) is an Ethernet standard implemented via a card that allows a "sleeping" machine to awaken when it receives a wakeup signal.

PoE

If the device you are networking is in a remote location (such as a router in a ceiling or other place with no easy access to an electrical outlet), *Power over Ethernet (PoE)* is a handy technology to supply both power and an Ethernet connection. The purpose of PoE is self-evident from its name—electrical power is transmitted over twisted-pair Ethernet cable (along with data). A key advantage of PoE is that a UPS is required only in the main facility instead of at each device.

QoS

Quality of Service (QoS) implements packet scheduling to control the flow of traffic and help with network transmission speeds. No properties can be configured for the service itself.

Exam Essentials

Know what values are needed for network connectivity. Regardless of which network access method you choose, you will need to fill out the appropriate fields for the device to be able to communicate on the network. With TCP/IP, required values are an IP address for the host, subnet mask, address for the gateway, and DNS information.

Understand the purpose of HomeGroup. The HomeGroup feature was added to Windows 7 as a simplified way to set up a home network. It only works with Windows 7 and allows you to share files (including libraries) and resources.

1.7 Perform preventive maintenance procedures using appropriate tools

Taking care of your company's desktop and laptop computers can extend their life and save considerable money. Most of the actions necessary to maintain laptops fall under the category of what is reasonable, and you would undoubtedly think of them on your own.

Best practices exist to define what should be done to keep systems maintained. The first section under this objective focuses on the best practices related to preventive maintenance, and the second section explores the tools used to put many of those practices into play.

Best practices

Preventive maintenance is more than just manipulating hardware; it also encompasses running software utilities on a regular basis to keep the filesystem fit. These utilities can include scheduled backups, check disks, defragmentation, and updates.

Scheduled backups

Backups are duplicate copies of key information, ideally stored in a location other than the one where the information is currently stored. Backups include both paper and computer records. Computer records are usually backed up using a backup program, backup systems, and backup procedures.

The primary starting point for disaster recovery involves keeping current backup copies of key data files, databases, applications, and paper records available for use. Your organization must develop a solid set of procedures to manage this process and ensure that all key information is protected. A security professional can do several things in conjunction with systems administrators and business managers to protect this information. It's important to think of this problem as an issue that is larger than a single department.

The information you back up must be immediately available for use when needed. If a user loses a critical file, they won't want to wait several days while data files are sent from a remote storage facility. Several types of storage mechanisms are available for data storage:

Working Copies *Working copy* backups—sometimes referred to as *shadow copies*—are partial or full backups that are kept on the premises for immediate recovery purposes. Working copies are frequently the most recent backups that have been made.

Typically, working copies are intended for immediate use. These copies are often updated on a frequent basis.

Many filesystems used on servers include *journaling*. Journaled filesystems (JFSs) include a log file of all changes and transactions that have occurred within a set period of time (such as the last few hours). If a crash occurs, the operating system can look at the log files to see which transactions have been committed and which ones haven't. This technology works well and allows unsaved data to be written after the recovery and the system, usually, to be successfully restored to its pre-crash condition.

Onsite Storage   *Onsite storage* usually refers to a location on the site of the computer center that is used to store information locally. Onsite storage containers are available that allow computer cartridges, tapes, and other backup media to be stored in a reasonably protected environment in the building.

Onsite storage containers are designed and rated for fire, moisture, and pressure resistance. These containers aren't *fireproof* in most situations, but they're *fire-rated*: a fireproof container should be guaranteed to withstand damage regardless of the type of fire or temperatures, whereas fire ratings specify that a container can protect the contents for a specific amount of time in a given situation.

If you choose to depend entirely on onsite storage, make sure the containers you acquire can withstand the worst-case environmental catastrophes that could happen at your location. Make sure as well that those containers are in locations where you can easily find them after the disaster and access them (near exterior walls, and so on).

Offsite Storage   *Offsite storage* refers to a location away from the computer center where paper copies and backup media are kept. Offsite storage can involve something as simple as keeping a copy of backup media at a remote office, or it can be as complicated as a nuclear-hardened high-security storage facility. The storage facility should be bonded, insured, and inspected on a regular basis to ensure that all storage procedures are being followed.

Determining which storage mechanism to use should be based on the needs of the organization, the availability of storage facilities, and the budget available. Most offsite storage facilities charge based on the amount of space you require and the frequency of access you need to the stored information.

Three methods exist to back up information on most systems:

Full Backup   A *full backup* is a complete, comprehensive backup of all files on a disk or server. The full backup is current only at the time it's performed. Once a full backup is made, you have a complete archive of the system at that point in time. A system shouldn't be in use while it undergoes a full backup because some files may not get backed up. Once the system goes back into operation, the backup is no longer current. A full backup can be a time-consuming process on a large system.

Incremental Backup   An *incremental backup* is a partial backup that stores only the information that has been changed since the last full or incremental backup. If a full backup were performed on a Sunday night, an incremental backup done on Monday night would contain only the information that changed since Sunday night. Such a backup is typically considerably smaller than a full backup. This backup system requires that each incremental backup be retained until a full backup can be performed. Incremental backups are usually the fastest backups to perform on most systems, and each incremental tape is relatively small.

Differential Backup   A differential backup is similar in function to an incremental backup, but it backs up any files that have been altered since the last full backup; it makes duplicate copies of files that haven't changed since the last differential backup. If a full backup was performed on Sunday night, a differential backup performed on Monday night would capture the information that was changed on Monday. A differential backup completed on Tuesday night would record the changes in any files from Monday and any changes in files on Tuesday. As you can see, during the week each differential backup would become larger; by Friday or Saturday night, it might be nearly as large as a full backup. This means the backups in the earliest part of the weekly cycle will be very fast, and each successive one will be slower.

When these backup methods are used in conjunction with each other, the risk of loss can be greatly reduced. You should never combine an incremental backup with a differential backup. One of the major factors in determining which combination of these three methods to use is time—ideally, a full backup would be performed every day. Several commercial backup programs support these three backup methods. You must evaluate your organizational needs when choosing which tools to use to accomplish backups.

Almost every stable operating system contains a utility for creating a copy of configuration settings necessary to reach the present state after a disaster. As an administrator, you must know how to do backups and be familiar with all the options available to you.

Scheduled check disks

We recommend that in addition to backups you also regularly run Check Disk. You can so by manually running the tool, or you can configure Task Scheduler to run it on a routine basis.

To manually run it, you can start chkdsk.exe in a cmd window, or you can right-click on the drive in My Computer and choose Properties, click the Tools tab, and select Check Now.

Scheduled defragmentation

Defragmenting the disk moves the files on the disk so the data is contiguously located when possible. Both volume and file fragmentation occurs as files continue to grow through normal usage and thus defragmentation should be done on a regular basis.

Just as you can right-click on a drive in My Computer, choose Properties, and click the Tools tab to start a Check Disk routine, you can also start defragmentation from here by selecting Defragment Now. The Task Scheduler can be used to schedule the program (Defrag.exe or Dfrgntfs.exe) to regularly run.

Windows updates

Windows Updates were discussed in the Control Panel discussion of the Automatic Updates applet in Windows XP. Outside of that, you can go to the Windows Update applet (under System And Security) in Control Panel and configure the system to regularly check for and install updates.

Patch management

Windows Update can be configured in Windows 7 and Windows Vista to also look for and install updates to other Microsoft software programs installed on the machine. You should make a practice of routinely checking with vendors of other programs you use for patches they release, many of which address issues of security and functionality.

Always check the patches on test machines before applying them to production machines—they may occasionally disrupt or affect operations your company relies on.

Driver/firmware updates

Device drivers are the software stubs that allow devices to communicate with the operating system. Called *drivers* for short, they're used for interacting with printers, monitors, network cards, sound cards, and just about every type of hardware attached to the PC. One of the most common problems associated with drivers isn't having the current version—as problems are fixed, the drivers are updated, and you can often save a great deal of time by downloading the latest drivers from the vendor's site early in the troubleshooting process. The easiest way to see/change drivers in Windows is to click the Driver tab in the Properties dialog box for the device.

Any software that is built into a hardware device is called *firmware*. Firmware is typically in flash ROM and can be updated as newer versions become available. An example of firmware is the software in a laser printer that controls it and allows you to interact with it at the console (usually through a limited menu of options).

Firmware and driver updates are often released by hardware vendors. You should routinely check their sites for patches and updates that you need to download and install.

Antivirus updates

Antivirus updates (discussed in Chapter 7) should be regularly updated as well (with particular interest paid to the definition files).

Tools

Figure 6.3 shows the Tools tab for a hard drive in Windows 7. From here, you can run three of the five tools you need to know for this section: Backup, Check Disk, and Defrag. We will discuss these three first, and then turn to the remaining two—System Restore and Recovery Image.

Backup

The Backup utility allows you to create the backups discussed in the best practices section earlier.

Check disk

Check Disk is a Windows graphical utility for finding and fixing logical errors, and optionally also for checking each sector of the disk physically and relocating any readable data from damaged spots.

FIGURE 6.3 The Tools tab for a hard drive

Check Disk isn't a menu command on the Start menu. To run it, display the Properties box for a hard disk, and then select an option from there on the Tools tab. Depending on the version of Windows you are running, that option may be named Check Disk For Errors (Windows XP) or Error-Checking, Check Now (Windows 7 and Windows Vista).

Do not be confused by Chkdsk—an old MS-DOS utility used to correct logical errors in the FAT. The most common switch for the CHKDSK command is /F, which fixes the errors that it finds. Without /F, Chkdsk acts as an "information only" utility.

Defrag

Disk Defragmenter reorganizes the file storage on a disk to reduce the number of files that are stored noncontiguously. This makes file retrieval faster, because the read/write heads on the disk have to move less.

There are two versions of Disk Defragmenter: a Windows version that runs from within Windows and a command line version (DEFRAG.EXE). In addition to being on the Tools tab (shown in Figure 6.3), the Windows version is located on the System Tools submenu on the Start menu (Start ➢ All Programs ➢ Accessories ➢ System Tools ➢ Disk Defragmenter).

The available switches for the command-line version in Windows XP (DEFRAG.EXE) include:

-a	Analyze only
-f	Force defragmentation even if disk space is low
-v	Verbose output

The available switches for the command-line version in Windows 7 include:

/A	Perform analysis on the specified volumes.
/C	Perform the operation on all volumes.
/E	Perform the operation on all volumes except those specified.
/H	Run the operation at normal priority (default is low).
/M	Run the operation on each volume in parallel in the background.
/T	Track an operation already in progress on the specified volume.
/U	Print the progress of the operation on the screen.
/V	Print verbose output containing the fragmentation statistics.
/X	Perform free space consolidation on the specified volumes.

System restore

To access the System Restore tool, choose the System applet in the Control Panel and then the System Protection tab (see Figure 6.4). By clicking the System Restore button, you can revert to an earlier restore point and circumvent problems that have recently occurred with system settings or corrupted files.

From here, you can also manually create a restore point, configure what is included in a restore point, and specify how much space you are allowing to be used for saving these files (setting the space to 0% effectively disables the creation of restore points).

FIGURE 6.4   The System Restore option

Recovery image

A *recovery image*, also known as a *system image*, is an image that includes all the drives required for Windows to run as well as default system settings, programs, and files. If you replace a failed hard drive in a workstation, you can use the recovery image to replicate the initial settings (you can't choose individual items to restore), and then turn to the backups to bring the system back up to date.

Many OEM vendors include a recovery image with new systems they ship. That image may be on a recovery disc (CD or DVD) or on a partition that can be accessed after POST. Obviously, vendors prefer the partition approach since it saves shipping any physical item, but it is of no use at all in the event of a full failure of the hard drive.

Exam Essentials

Know the importance of running scheduled maintenance. Scheduled maintenance can prolong the life of your equipment and help ensure that your output continues to live up to the quality you expect.

Know how to access System Restore. To access the System Restore tool, choose the System applet in the Control Panel and then select the System Protection tab.

1.8 Explain the differences among basic OS security settings

There is an entire domain (and thus, the next chapter in this book) dedicated to security for A+. Add to that, CompTIA is heavily into security certifications with Security+ and CASP (CompTIA Advanced Security Practitioner) and you can see how important the topic is to those creating the exam. Because of that, make sure you have a good understanding of the topics covered here.

You want to make certain that your systems, and the data within them, are kept as secure as possible. The security prevents others from changing the data, destroying it, or inadvertently harming it. This can be done by assigning users the least privileges possible in the Administrator/Power Users/Users/Guest hierarchy and hardening as much of the environment as possible.

User and groups

There are a number of groups created on the operating system by default. The following sections look at the main ones of these.

Administrator

The *Administrator* account is the most powerful of all: it has the power to do everything from the smallest task all the way up to removing the operating system. Because of the great power it holds, and the fact that it is always created, many who try to do harm will target this account as the one they try to break into. To increase security, during the installation of the Windows operating systems in question, you are prompted for a name of a user who will be designated as the Administrator. The power then comes not from being truly called "Administrator" (it might now be edulaney, eadulaney, or something similar) but from being a member of the Administrators group (notice the plural for the group and singular for the user).

Since members of the *Administrators* group have such power, they can inadvertently do harm (such as accidentally deleting a file that a regular user could not). To protect against this, the practice of logging in with an Administrators account for daily interaction is strongly discouraged. Instead, we suggest that system administrators log in with a user account (lesser privileges) and change to the Administrators group account (elevated privileges) only when necessary.

Power user

Not as powerful as Administrators is the *Power Users* group in Windows XP. Membership in this group gives read/write permission to the system, allowing them to install most software but keeping them from changing key operating system files. This is a good group for those who need to test software (such as programmers) and junior administrators. While the Power Users group exists in Windows Vista and Windows 7, it is mostly there for legacy purposes and no longer has any more privileges than a standard user.

Guest

The *Guest* account is created by default (and should be disabled) and is a member of the *Guests* group. For the most part, members of Guests have the rights as Users except they can't get to log files. The best reason to make users members of the Guests group is if they are accessing the system only for a limited time.

 As part of operating system security, we usually recommend that you rename the default Administrator and Guest accounts that are created at installation.

Standard

This is the default that standard users belong to. Members of this group have read/write permission to their own profile. They cannot modify system-wide Registry settings or do much harm outside of their own account. Under the principle of least privilege, users should be made a member of the Users group only unless qualifying circumstances force them to have higher privileges.

NTFS vs. Share permissions

The New Technology File System (NTFS) was introduced with Windows NT to address security problems. Before Windows NT was released, it had become apparent to Microsoft that a new filesystem was needed to handle growing disk sizes, security concerns, and the need for more stability. NTFS was created to address those issues.

Although FAT was relatively stable if the systems that were controlling it kept running, it didn't do well when the power went out or the system crashed unexpectedly. One of the benefits of NTFS was a transaction tracking system, which made it possible for Windows NT to back out of any disk operations that were in progress when Windows NT crashed or lost power.

With NTFS, files, directories, and volumes can each have their own security. NTFS's security is flexible and built in. Not only does NTFS track security in ACLs, which can hold permissions for local users and groups, but each entry in the ACL can specify what type of access is given—such as Read, Write, Modify, or Full Control. This allows a great deal of flexibility in setting up a network. In addition, special file-encryption programs were developed to encrypt data while it was stored on the hard disk.

Microsoft strongly recommends that all network shares be established using NTFS. Several current OSs from Microsoft support both FAT32 and NTFS. It's possible to convert from FAT32 to NTFS without losing data, but you can't do the operation in reverse (you would need to reformat the drive and install the data again from a backup tape).

 If you're using FAT32 and want to change to NTFS, the convert utility will allow you to do so. For example, to change the E drive to NTFS, the command is convert e: /FS:NTFS.

Share permissions apply only when a user is accessing a file or folder through the network. Local permissions and attributes are used to protect the file when the user is local. With FAT and FAT32, you do not have the ability to assign "extended" or "extensible" permissions, and the user sitting at the console effectively is the owner of all resources on the system. As such, they can add, change, and delete any data or file that they want.

With NTFS as the filesystem, however, you are allowed to assign more comprehensive security to your computer system. NTFS permissions are able to protect you at the file level. Share permissions can be applied to the directory level only. NTFS permissions can affect users logged on locally or across the network to the system where the NTFS permissions are applied. Share permissions are in effect only when the user connects to the resource via the network.

Allow vs. deny

Within NTFS, permissions for objects fall into one of three categories: allow, not allow, and deny. When viewing the permissions for a file or folder, you can check the box for Allow, which effectively allows that group that action. You can also uncheck the box for Allow, which does not allow that group that action. Alternatively, you can check the box Deny, which prevents that group from using that action. There is a difference between not allowing (a cleared check box) and Deny (which specifically prohibits), and you tend not to see Deny used often. Deny, when used, trumps other permissions.

Permissions set at a folder are inherited down through subfolders, unless otherwise changed. Permissions are also cumulative: if a user is a member of a group that has read permission and a member of a group that has write permission, they effectively have both read and write permission.

Moving vs. copying folders and files

When you copy a file, you create a new entity. When you move a file, you simply relocate it and still have but one entity. This distinction is important when it comes to understanding permissions. A copy of a file will generally have the permissions assigned to it that are placed on newly created files in that folder—regardless of what permissions were on the original file.

A moved file, on the other hand, will attempt to keep the same permissions as it had in the original location. Differences will occur if the same permissions cannot exist in the new location—for example, if you are moving a file from an NTFS volume to FAT32, the NTFS permissions will be lost. If, on the other hand, you are moving from a FAT32 volume to an NTFS volume, new permissions will be added that match those for newly created entities.

Folder copy and move operations follow similar guidelines to those with files.

File attributes

Permissions can be allowed or denied individually on a per-folder basis. You can assign any combination of the values shown in Table 6.23.

TABLE 6.23   NTFS directory permissions

NTFS permission	Meaning
Full Control	Gives the user all the other choices and the ability to change permission. The user also can take ownership of the directory or any of its contents.
Modify	Combines the Read & Execute permission with the Write permission and further allows the user to delete everything, including the folder.
Read & Execute	Combines the permissions of Read with those of List Folder Contents and adds the ability to run executables.
List Folder Contents	The List Folder Contents permission (known simply as List in previous versions) allows the user to view the contents of a directory and to navigate to its subdirectories. It does not grant the user access to the files in these directories unless that is specified in file permissions.

TABLE 6.23   NTFS directory permissions *(continued)*

NTFS permission	Meaning
Read	Allows the user to navigate the entire directory structure, view the contents of the directory, view the contents of any files in the directory, and see ownership and attributes.
Write	Allows the user to create new entities within the folder, as well as to change ownership, permissions, and attributes.

Clicking the Advanced button allows you to configure auditing and ownership properties. You can also apply NTFS permissions to individual files. This is done from the Security tab for the file; Table 6.24 lists the NTFS file permissions.

TABLE 6.24   NTFS file permissions

NTFS permission	Meaning
Full Control	Gives the user all the other permissions as well as permission to take ownership and change permission
Modify	Combines the Read & Execute permission with the Write permission and further allows the user to delete the file
Read	Allows the user to view the contents of the file and to see ownership and attributes
Read & Execute	Combines the Read permission with the ability to execute
Write	Allows the user to overwrite the file, as well as to change attributes and see ownership and permissions

By default, the determination of NTFS permissions is based on the *cumulative* NTFS permissions for a user. Rights can be assigned to users based on group membership and individually; the only time permissions do not accumulate is when the Deny permission is invoked.

Shared files and folders

You can share folders, and the files beneath them, by right-clicking on them and choosing Share With (Windows 7) or Sharing And Security (Windows XP) from the context menu. In Windows 7, the context menu asks who you want to share the folder or file with (see Figure 6.5), whereas in Windows XP, the Sharing tab asks whether you want to place the folder or file in the Shared Documents folder or choose a name by which to share it (see Figure 6.6).

FIGURE 6.5   Sharing a folder in Windows 7

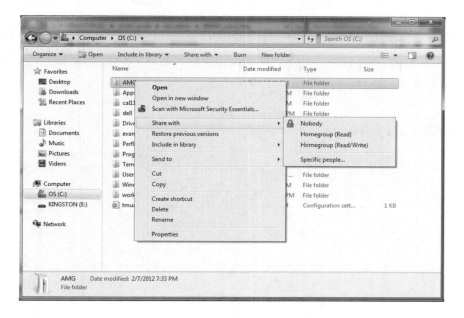

FIGURE 6.6   Sharing a folder in Windows XP

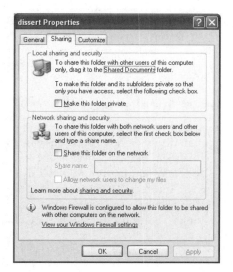

In Windows 7, the options you see on the context menu will depend on the type of network you are connected to—a domain, a workgroup, or a HomeGroup (the one shown in Figure 6.5). If you turn on password-protected sharing (the default), the person accessing the share has to give a username and password to access the shared entity.

The Advanced Sharing settings will come up if you try to share something in one of the Public folders or make other changes. This interface, shown in Figure 6.7, can also be accessed through the Network and Sharing Center applet in the Control Panel and is used to change network settings relevant to sharing.

FIGURE 6.7   Advanced Sharing in Windows 7

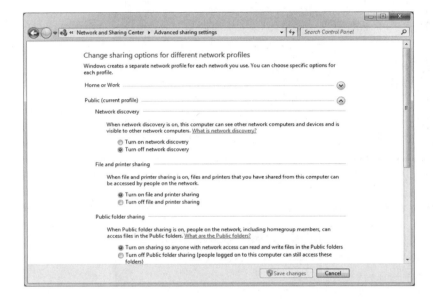

Administrative shares vs. local shares

Administrative shares are created on servers running Windows on the network for administrative purposes. These shares can differ slightly based on which OS is running but always end with a dollar sign ($) to make them hidden. There is one for each volume on a hard drive (c$, d$, and so on) as well as admin$ (the root folder— usually c:\windows), and print$ (where the print drivers are located). These are created for use by administrators and usually require administrator privileges to access.

Local shares, as the name implies, are those that are created locally and are visible with the icon of a hand beneath them.

Permission propagation

As mentioned in the discussion of permissions earlier, permissions are cumulative. A user who is a member of two groups will effectively have the permissions of both groups combined.

Inheritance

Inheritance is the default throughout the permission structure unless a specific setting is created to override this. A user who has read and write permissions in one folder will have that in all the subfolders unless a change has been made specifically to one of the subfolders.

System files and folders

System files are usually flagged with the Hidden attribute, meaning they don't appear when a user displays a directory listing. You should not change this attribute on a system file unless absolutely necessary. System files are required for the OS to function. If they are visible, users might delete them (perhaps thinking they can clear some disk space by deleting files they don't recognize). Needless to say, that would be a bad thing!

User authentication

One of the big problems that larger systems must deal with is the need for users to access multiple systems or applications. This may require a user to remember multiple accounts and passwords. The purpose of a *single sign-on (SSO)* is to give users access to all the applications and systems they need when they log on. This is becoming a reality in many environments, including Kerberos, Microsoft Active Directory, Novell eDirectory, and some certificate model implementations.

Single sign-on is both a blessing and a curse. It's a blessing in that once users are authenticated, they can access all the resources on the network and browse multiple directories. It's a curse in that it removes the doors that otherwise exist between the user and various resources.

In the case of Kerberos, a single token allows any "Kerberized" applications to accept a user as valid. The important thing to remember in this process is that each application that wants to use SSO must be able to accept and process the token presented by Kerberos.

Active Directory (AD) works off a slightly different method. A server that runs AD retains information about all access rights for all users and groups in the network. When a user logs on to the system, AD issues the user a globally unique identifier (GUID). Applications that support AD can use this GUID to provide access control.

Using AD simplifies the sign-on process for users and lowers the support requirements for administrators. Access can be established through groups, and it can be enforced through group memberships. Active Directory can be implemented using a Windows Server (such as Windows Server 2008). All users will then log into the Windows domain using their centrally created AD account.

On a decentralized network, SSO passwords are stored on each server and can represent a security risk. It's important to enforce password changes and make certain passwords are updated throughout the organization on a frequent basis.

While single sign-on is not the opposite of multifactor authentication, they are often mistakenly thought of that way. One-, two-, and three-factor authentication merely refers to the number of items a user must supply to authenticate. Authentication can be based on something users have (a smart card), something they know (a password), something unique (biometric), and so forth. After factor authentication is done, single sign-on can still apply throughout the user's session.

Exam Essentials

Know the difference between single sign-on and multifactor authentication. Single sign-on is the concept of having the user be authenticated on all services they access after logging in once. Multifactor authentication is not the opposite single sign-on, but merely requires more than one entity to be authenticated, for security purposes.

Know the NTFS permissions. Permissions can be allowed or denied individually on a per-folder and per-file basis. Know the values shown in Tables 6.24 and 6.25.

1.9 Explain the basics of client-side virtualization

Virtualization is the current rage due to the cost savings and performance it provides. Virtualization can be implemented through open source (such as Xen and VirtualBox) as well as proprietary (such as VMware) solutions, allowing you to take a single physical device and make it appear to users as if it is a number of standalone entities. In the world of Microsoft solutions, Microsoft Virtual PC 2007 for Windows Vista and Windows XP is popular, as is Windows Virtual PC for Windows 7.

The virtual desktop is often called a virtual desktop interface (VDI). That term encompasses the software and hardware needed to create the virtual environment.

Purpose of Virtual Machines

Traditionally, workstations can have multiple operating systems installed on them but run only one at a time. By running virtualization software, the same workstation can be running Window 7 along with Windows Server 2008 and Red Hat Enterprise Linux (or almost any other operating system) at the same time, allowing a developer to test code in various environments as well as cut and paste between them within a *virtual machine* (VM).

From a networking standpoint, each of the virtual desktops will typically need full network access and configuring the permissions for each can sometimes be tricky.

Remote administration often uses virtual desktops, allowing a remote administrator to work on the workstation with or without the knowledge of the user sitting in front of the machine.

Resource requirements

The resource requirements for virtualization are largely based on what environments you are creating. The hardware on the machine must have enough memory, hard drive space, and processor capability to support the virtualization. You also need the software to make virtualization possible (discussed in the next section).

Emulator requirements

XP Mode has been mentioned earlier in this chapter and is a free emulator from Microsoft that you can download and use as a virtual emulator. A number of others are also available. In most cases, the motherboard and associated BIOS settings need no alteration to provide services to these virtual machines. Some of the newer virtualization products, however (such as Microsoft's Hyper-V, and Windows 7 Virtual PC), require that the motherboard support *hardware-assisted virtualization*. The benefit derived from using hardware-assisted virtualization is it allows the *hypervisor* (the virtualization product) to dynamically allocate memory and CPU to the VMs as required.

VMware Player allows you to work in multiple environments on one system. For more information, go to www.vmware.com/products/player.

Security requirements

Tales of security woes that can occur with attackers jumping out of one virtual machine and accessing another have been exaggerated. Although such threats are possible, most software solutions include sufficient protection to reduce the possibility to a small one.

Most virtualization-specific threats focus on the hypervisor (the software that allows the virtual machines to exist). If the hypervisor can be successfully attacked, the attacker can gain root-level access to all virtual systems. While this is a legitimate issue—and one that has been demonstrated as possible in most systems (including VMware, Xen, and Microsoft Virtual Machine)—it is one that has been patched each time it has appeared. The solution to most virtualization threats is to always apply the most recent patches and keep the systems up-to-date.

Network requirements

Network access is not a requirement in every virtual environment (for example, if you were decoding an application that would only run locally) but is often needed in most. During implementation of the virtualization, you can configure the network functionality for the machine (known as internal), or combine elements of the network together to provide network virtualization (known as external). The difference between internal and external implementations is usually based on which software package you are using.

Hypervisor

The hypervisor is the software that allows the virtual machines to exist.

Exam Essentials

Be familiar with virtualization terminology.   The hypervisor is the software that allows the virtual machines to exist. The virtual desktop is often called a virtual desktop interface (VDI), encompassing the software and hardware needed to create the virtual environment.

Know security concerns related to virtualization.   Most virtualization-specific threats focus on the hypervisor. If the hypervisor can be successfully attacked, the attacker can gain root-level access to all virtual systems.

Review Questions

1. What is the maximum amount of RAM supported by 32-bit editions of Windows Vista?

2. What is the virtual client (emulating Windows XP Professional with Service Pack 3) included with Windows 7 Professional, Enterprise, and Ultimate?

3. What is WinPE used for?

4. What utility will list at the command line all running processes (and their process ID numbers) similar to what you see in the GUI by using Task Manager?

5. Which BOOTREC option is used to write a new boot sector?

6. In Windows 7 Professional, Print _____ allows you to manage multiple printers and print servers from a single interface.

7. What keyboard key combination can be pressed to get the Task Manager directly in Windows?

8. What is the executable used for Remote Desktop Connection?

9. With Windows 7, the Security Center was rolled into what utility?

10. What is the name of the software that allows virtual machines to exist?

Chapter

7

Security

COMPTIA A+ 220-802 EXAM OBJECTIVES COVERED IN THIS CHAPTER:

✓ **2.1 Apply and use common prevention methods.**

- Physical security
    - Lock doors
    - Tailgating
    - Securing physical documents/passwords/shredding
    - Biometrics
    - Badges
    - Key fobs
    - RFID badge
    - RSA token
    - Privacy filters
    - Retinal
- Digital security
    - Antivirus
    - Firewalls
    - Antispyware
    - User authentication/strong passwords
    - Directory permissions
- User education
- Principle of least privilege

✓ **2.2 Compare and contrast common security threats.**

- Social engineering
- Malware
- Rootkits

- Phishing
- Shoulder surfing
- Spyware
- Viruses
  - Worms
  - Trojans

✓ **2.3 Implement security best practices to secure a workstation.**

- Setting strong passwords
- Requiring passwords
- Restricting user permissions
- Changing default user names
- Disabling guest account
- Screensaver required password
- Disable autorun

✓ **2.4 Given a scenario, use the appropriate data destruction/disposal method.**

- Low level format vs. standard format
- Hard drive sanitation and sanitation methods
  - Overwrite
  - Drive wipe
- Physical destruction
  - Shredder
  - Drill
  - Electromagnetic
  - Degaussing tool

✓ **2.5 Given a scenario, secure a SOHO wireless network.**

- Change default user-names and passwords
- Changing SSID
- Setting encryption

- Disabling SSID broadcast
- Enable MAC filtering
- Antenna and access point placement
- Radio power levels
- Assign static IP addresses

✓ **2.6 Given a scenario, secure a SOHO wired network.**

- Change default usernames and passwords
- Enable MAC filtering
- Assign static IP addresses
- Disabling ports
- Physical security

Given the ever-increasing need for security knowledge in the real world, CompTIA expects those who become A+ certified to have a basic knowledge and understanding of the principles behind it. The subobjectives in this category do a good job of providing a thorough overview of the topic.

2.1 Apply and use common prevention methods

A great many of the security issues that plague networks today can be solved through the implementation of basic security elements. Some of those elements are physical (locked doors) and others digital (antivirus software), but all share the goal of keeping out problems.

This objective is divided into four topic areas: physical security, digital security, user education, and the principle of least privilege. As you study for the exam, know what types of physical security elements you can add to an environment to secure. Know as well what types of digital security you should implement to keep malware at bay. Understand that the first line of defense is the users, and you need to educate them to understand why security is important. You should follow the principle of least privilege to prevent users from inadvertently causing harm.

Physical security

Physical security is a grab bag of elements that can be added to an environment to aid in securing it. It ranges from key fobs to retinal scanners. In this section, we will examine the list of components in the order given by CompTIA.

Lock doors

One of the easiest ways to prevent those intent on creating problems from physically entering your environment is to lock your doors and keep them out. A key aspect of access control involves *physical barriers*. The objective of a physical barrier is to prevent access to computers and network systems. The most effective physical barrier implementations require that more than one physical barrier be crossed to gain access. This type of approach is called a *multiple-barrier system*.

Ideally, your systems should have a minimum of three physical barriers. The first barrier is the external entrance to the building, referred to as a *perimeter*, which is protected by burglar alarms, external walls, *fencing*, surveillance, and so on. An *access list* should exist to specifically identify who can enter and be verified by a guard or someone in authority. The second barrier is the entrance into the building and could rely on such items as *ID badges* to gain access. The third barrier is the entrance to the computer room itself (and could require fobs, or keys). Each of these entrances can be individually secured, monitored, and protected with alarm systems.

Think of the three barriers this way: 1. outer (the fence), 2. middle (guards, locks, and mantraps, oh, my), 3. inner (key fobs).

Although these three barriers won't always stop intruders, they will potentially slow them down enough that law enforcement can respond before an intrusion is fully developed. Once inside, a truly secure site should be dependent on a physical token for access to the actual network resources.

Tailgating

Tailgating is the term used for someone being so close to you when you enter a building that they are able to come in right behind you without needing to use a key, a card, or any other security device. Many social engineering intruders needing physical access to a site will use this method of gaining entry. Educate users to beware of this and other social engineering ploys and prevent them from happening.

Mantraps are a great way to stop tailgating.

Securing physical documents/passwords/shredding

It is amazing the information that can be gleaned from physical documents even in the age when there is such a push to go paperless. *Dumpster diving* is a common physical access method. Companies normally generate a huge amount of paper, most of which eventually winds up in dumpsters or recycle bins. Dumpsters may contain information that is highly sensitive in nature (such as passwords after a change and before the user has the new one memorized). In high-security and government environments, sensitive papers should be either shredded or burned. Most businesses don't do this. In addition, the advent of "green" companies has created an increase in the amount of recycled paper, which can often contain all kinds of juicy information about a company and its individual employees.

Biometrics

Biometric devices use physical characteristics to identify the user. Such devices are becoming more common in the business environment. Biometric systems include hand scanners, retinal scanners, and soon, possibly, DNA scanners. To gain access to resources, you must pass a physical screening process. In the case of a hand scanner, this may include identifying finger-prints, scars, and markings on your hand. Retinal scanners compare your eye's retinal pattern to a stored retinal pattern to verify your identity. DNA scanners will examine a unique portion of your DNA structure in order to verify that you are who you say you are.

With the passing of time, the definition of *biometric* is expanding from simply identifying physical attributes about a person to being able to describe patterns in their behavior. Recent advances have been made in the ability to authenticate someone based on the key pattern they use when entering their password (how long they pause between each key, the amount of time each key is held down, and so forth). A company adopting biometric technologies needs to consider the controversy they may face (some authentication methods are considered more intrusive than others). The error rate also needs to be considered and an acceptance of the fact that errors can include both false positives and false negatives.

Badges

Badges can be any form of identification intended to differentiate the holder from everyone else. This can be as simple as a name badge or photo ID.

Smart cards are difficult to counterfeit, but they're easy to steal. Once a thief has a smart card, they have all the access the card allows. To prevent this, many organizations don't put any identifying marks on their smart cards, making it harder for someone to utilize them. Many modern smart cards require a password or PIN to activate the card, and employ encryption to protect the card's contents.

Key fobs

Key fobs are named after the chains that used to hold pocket watches to clothes. They are security devices that you carry with you that display a randomly generated code that you can then use for authentication. This code usually changes very quickly (every 60 seconds is probably the average), and you combine this code with your PIN for authentication.

RFID badges

A *smart card* is a type of badge or card that gives you access to resources, including buildings, parking lots, and computers. It contains information about your identity and access privileges. Each area or computer has a card scanner or a reader in which you insert your card. RFID (Radio Frequency Identification) is the wireless, no-contact, technology used with these cards and their accompanying reader.

The reader is connected to the workstation and validates against the security system. This increases the security of the authentication process, because you must be in physical possession of the smart card to use the resources. Of course, if the card is lost or stolen, the person who finds the card can access the resources it allows.

RSA tokens

Physical tokens are anything that a user must have on them to access network resources and are often associated with devices that enable the user to generate a one-time password authenticating their identity. SecurID, from RSA, is one of the best known examples of a physical token; learn more at www.rsa.com/node.aspx?id=1156.

Privacy filters

Privacy filters are either film or glass add-ons that are placed over a monitor that prevent the data on the screen from being readable when viewed from the sides. Only the user sitting directly in front of the screen is able to read the data.

Retinal

As mentioned a bit earlier, retinal scanners are one form of biometric devices that can be used to identify a user. As the name implies, matches are made based on identification of an individual's retina (such as blood vessels). Though highly reliable, the equipment needed is rather expensive.

Digital security

Whereas physical security under this objective focused on keeping individuals out, digital security focuses mostly on keeping harmful data/malware out. The areas of focus are antivirus software, firewalls, antispyware, user authentication/strong passwords, and directory permissions. Each of these is addressed in the sections that follow.

AntiVirus

The primary method of preventing the propagation of malicious code involves the use of *antivirus software*. Antivirus software is an application that is installed on a system to protect it and to scan for viruses as well as worms and Trojan horses. Most viruses have characteristics that are common to families of virus. Antivirus software looks for these characteristics, or fingerprints, to identify and neutralize viruses before they impact you.

More than 200,000 known viruses, worms, bombs, and other malware have been defined. New ones are added all the time. Your antivirus software manufacturer will usually work very hard to keep the definition database files current. The definition database file contains all of the known viruses and countermeasures for a particular antivirus software product. You probably won't receive a virus that hasn't been seen by one of these companies. If you keep the virus definition database files in your software up-to-date, you probably won't be overly vulnerable to attacks.

 The best method of protection is to use a layered approach. Antivirus software should be at the gateways, at the servers, and at the desktop. If you want to go one step further, you can use software at each location from different vendors to make sure you're covered from all angles.

Firewalls

Firewalls are one of the first lines of defense in a network. There are different types of firewalls, and they can be either standalone systems or included in other devices such as routers or servers. You can find firewall solutions that are marketed as hardware only and others that are software only. Many firewalls, however, consist of add-in software that is available for servers or workstations.

Although solutions are sold as "hardware only," the hardware still runs some sort of software. It may be hardened and in ROM to prevent tampering, and it may be customized—but software is present nonetheless.

The basic purpose of a firewall is to isolate one network from another. Firewalls are becoming available as appliances, meaning they're installed as the primary device separating two networks. *Appliances* are freestanding devices that operate in a largely self-contained manner, requiring less maintenance and support than a server-based product.

Firewalls function as one or more of the following:

- Packet filter
- Proxy firewall
- Stateful inspection firewall

To understand the concept of a firewall, it helps to know where the term comes from. In days of old, dwellings used to be built so close together that if a fire broke out in one, it could easily destroy a block or more before it could be contained. To decrease the risk of this happening, firewalls were built between buildings. The firewalls were huge brick walls that separated the buildings and kept a fire confined to one side. The same concept of restricting and confining is true in network firewalls. Traffic from the outside world hits the firewall and isn't allowed to enter the network unless otherwise invited.

The firewall shown in Figure 7.1 effectively limits access from outside networks, while allowing inside network users to access outside resources. The firewall in this illustration is also performing proxy functions.

FIGURE 7.1   A proxy firewall blocking network access from external networks

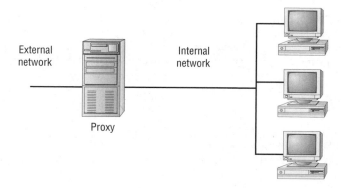

The following list discusses three of the most common functions that firewalls perform:

> Although firewalls are often associated with outside traffic, you can place a firewall anywhere. For example, if you want to isolate one portion of your internal network from others, you can place a firewall between them.

Packet Filter Firewalls   A firewall operating as a *packet filter* passes or blocks traffic to specific addresses based on the type of application. The packet filter doesn't analyze the data of a packet; it decides whether to pass it based on the packet's addressing information. For instance, a packet filter may allow web traffic on port 80 and block Telnet traffic on port 23. This type of filtering is included in many routers. If a received packet request asks for a port that isn't authorized, the filter may reject the request or simply ignore it. Many packet filters can also specify which IP addresses can request which ports and allow or deny them based on the security settings of the firewall.

Packet filters are growing in sophistication and capability. A packet filter firewall can allow any traffic that you specify as acceptable. For example, if you want web users to access your site, then you configure the packet filter firewall to allow data on port 80 to enter. If every network were exactly the same, firewalls would come with default port settings hard-coded, but networks vary, so the firewalls don't include such settings.

Proxy Firewalls   A *proxy firewall* can be thought of as an intermediary between your network and any other network. Proxy firewalls are used to process requests from an outside network; the proxy firewall examines the data and makes rule-based decisions about whether the request should be forwarded or refused. The proxy intercepts all the packages and reprocesses them for use internally. This process includes hiding IP addresses.

The proxy firewall provides better security than packet filtering because of the increased intelligence that a proxy firewall offers. Requests from internal network users are routed through the proxy. The proxy, in turn, repackages the request and sends it along, thereby isolating the user from the external network. The proxy can also offer caching, should the same request be made again, and can increase the efficiency of data delivery.

A proxy firewall typically uses two network interface cards (NICs). This type of firewall is referred to as a *dual-homed* firewall. One of the cards is connected to the outside network, and the other is connected to the internal network. The proxy software manages the connection between the two NICs. This setup segregates the two networks from each other and offers increased security. Figure 7.2 illustrates a dual-homed firewall segregating two networks from each other.

The proxy function can occur at either the application level or the circuit level. *Application-level proxy* functions read the individual commands of the protocols that are being served. This type of server is advanced and must know the rules and capabilities of the protocol used. An implementation of this type of proxy must know the difference between GET and PUT operations, for example, and have rules specifying how to execute them. A *circuit-level proxy* creates a circuit between the client and the server and doesn't deal with the contents of the packets that are being processed.

FIGURE 7.2   A dual-homed firewall segregating two networks from each other

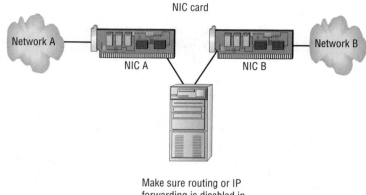

Make sure routing or IP
forwarding is disabled in
the operating system.

A unique application-level proxy server must exist for each protocol supported. Many proxy servers also provide full *auditing*, *accounting*, and other usage information that wouldn't normally be kept by a circuit-level proxy server.

Stateful Inspection Firewalls   The last section on firewalls focuses on the concept of stateful inspection. *Stateful inspection* is also referred to as *stateful packet filtering*. Most of the devices used in networks don't keep track of how information is routed or used. After a packet is passed, the packet and path are forgotten. In stateful inspection (or stateful packet filtering), records are kept using a state table that tracks every communications channel. Stateful inspections occur at all levels of the network and provide additional security, especially in connectionless protocols such as *User Datagram Protocol (UDP)* and *Internet Control Message Protocol (ICMP)*. This adds complexity to the process. Denial-of-service (DoS) attacks present a challenge because flooding techniques are used to overload the state table and effectively cause the firewall to shut down or reboot.

Antispyware

Just as antivirus software seeks out and stops viruses from entering/spreading, so too is the purpose of antispyware software. One thing separating spyware from most other malware is that it almost always exists to provide commercial gain. The operating systems from Microsoft are the ones most affected by spyware, and Microsoft has released Windows Defender to combat the problem.

User authentication/strong passwords

You can set up many different parameters and standards to force the people in your organization to conform. In establishing these parameters, it's important that you consider the capabilities of the people who will be working with these policies. If you're working in an environment where people aren't computer savvy, you may spend a lot of time helping them remember and recover passwords. Many organizations have had to reevaluate their security guidelines after they've invested great time and expense to implement high-security systems.

Setting authentication security, especially in supporting users, can become a high-maintenance activity for network administrators. On one hand, you want people to be able to authenticate themselves easily; on the other hand, you want to establish security that protects your company's resources. In a Windows server domain, password policies can be configured at the domain level using Group Policy objects. Variables you can configure include password complexity, length, and time between allowed changes.

A good password includes both upper- and lowercase letters as well as numbers and symbols. Be wary of popular names or current trends that make certain passwords predictable. For example, during the first release of *Star Wars*, two of the most popular passwords used on college campuses were C3PO and R2D2. This created a security problem for campus computer centers. Educate users to not use personal information that one could easily guess about them, such as their pet names, anniversary, or birthdays.

Directory Permissions

As a user, there is not much that can be done to improve or change the security of the directory services deployed. However, you *can* ensure that you don't become a tool for an attacker bent on compromising your organization's security:

 As for the permission on directories themselves, that is governed by NTFS, which was discussed in Chapter 6, "Operating Systems."

- Ensure that your client is using the most secure form of authentication encryption supported by both your client and the authentication servers.

- Use encrypted software and protocols whenever possible, even for internal communications.

- Change your password according to the company's password policy.

- Use a company-established minimum character password that is unique for each account. While many companies set the minimum at 8 characters, it is not uncommon to see this set at 16.

- Never write your password down, or if you do, divide it up into several pieces and store each in a different secure location (such as a home safe, a gun cabinet, a chemical supply locker, or safety deposit box).

- Never share your password or your logon session with another person; this includes your friends, spouse, and children.

- Verify that your client always interacts with an authentication server during the network logon process and does not use cached credentials.

- Allow all approved updates and patches to be installed onto your client.

- Ensure that all company data is copied back to a central file server before disconnecting from a logon session.

- Back up any personal data onto verified removable media.

- Never walk away from a logged-on workstation.

- Employ a password-protected screensaver.

- Don't use auto-logon features.

- Be aware of who is around you (and may be watching you) when you log on and when you work with valuable data.

- Never leave a company notebook, mobile phone, or PDA in a position where it can be stolen or compromised while you are away from the office. Cable locks should be used to keep notebooks securely in place whenever you are off site.

The protection of a directory service is based on the initial selection of network operating system and its deployment infrastructure. After these foundational decisions are made, you need to fully understand the technologies employed by your selected directory services system and learn how to make the most functional, yet secure, environment possible. This will usually require the addition of third-party security devices, applications, services, and solutions.

User education

The most effective method of preventing viruses, spyware, and harm to data is education. Teach your users not to open suspicious files and to open only those files that they're reasonably sure are virus-free. They need to scan every disk, email, and document they receive before they open them. You should also have all workstations scheduled to be automatically scanned on a regular basis.

Principle of least privilege

The concept of least privilege is a simple one: When assigning permissions, give users only the permissions they need to do their work and no more. This is especially true with administrators. Users who need administrative-level permissions should be assigned two accounts: one for performing nonadministrative, day-to-day tasks and the other to be used only when performing administrative tasks that specifically require an administrative-level user account. Those users should be educated on how each of the accounts should be used.

The biggest benefit to following this policy is the reduction of risk. The biggest headache with following this policy is trying to deal with users who may not understand it. A manager, for example, may assert that he should have more permission than those who report to him, but giving those permissions to him also opens up all the possibilities for inadvertently deleting files, crippling accounts, and so forth.

A least privilege policy should exist, and be enforced, throughout the enterprise. Users should have only the permissions and privileges needed to do their jobs, and no more. The ISO standard 27002 (which updates 17799) sums it up well: "Privileges should be allocated to individuals on a need-to-use basis and on an event-by-event basis, i.e. the minimum requirement for their functional role when needed." Adopting this as the policy for your organization is highly recommended.

Exam Essentials

Be able to describe why antivirus software is needed.   Antivirus software looks at a virus and takes action to neutralize it based on a virus definition database. Virus definition database files are regularly made available on vendor sites.

Understand the need for user education.   Users are the first line of defense against most threats, whether physical or digital. They should be trained on the importance of security and how to help enforce it.

2.2 Compare and contrast common security threats

While the first objective looks at ways to minimize threats, this objective explores what those threats are. As such, it is both a continuation of the earlier discussion and a complement to it.

A number of important topics are discussed in this section that fall into the realm of two broad categories: social engineering and malware. We'll look at both malware and then several different types of attacks, as well as some of the reasons your network is vulnerable. This list is far from inclusive as new variants of each are being created by miscreants on a regular basis. The list is, however, everything CompTIA expects you to know for the exam.

Social engineering

Social engineering is a process in which an attacker attempts to acquire information about your network and system by social means, such as by talking to people in the organization. A social-engineering attack may occur over the phone, by email, or by a visit. The intent is to acquire access information, such as user IDs and passwords. When the attempt is made through email or instant messaging, this is known as *phishing* (discussed later) and often is made to look as if it is coming from sites where users are likely to have accounts (eBay and PayPal are popular).

These types of attacks are relatively low-tech and are more akin to con jobs. Take the following example. Your help desk gets a call at 4:00 a.m. from someone purporting to be the vice president of your company. She tells the help desk personnel that she is out of town to attend a meeting, her computer just failed, and she is sitting in a Kinko's trying to get a file from her desktop computer back at the office. She can't seem to remember her password and user ID. She tells the help desk representative that she needs access to the information right away or the company could lose millions of dollars. Your help desk rep knows how important this meeting is and gives the vice president her user ID and password over the phone.

Another common approach is initiated by a phone call or email from your software vendor, telling you that they have a critical fix that must be installed on your computer system. If this patch isn't installed right away, your system will crash and you'll lose all your data. For some reason, you've changed your maintenance account password and they can't log on. Your systems operator gives the password to the person. You've been hit again.

Malware

We've all been battling malicious, invasive software since we bought our first computers. This software can go by any number of names—virus, malware, and so on—but if you aren't aware of their presence, these uninvited intruders may damage the data on your hard disk, destroy your operating system, and possibly spread to other systems.

You want to make certain that your systems, and the data within them, are kept as secure as possible. The security prevents others from changing the data, destroying it, or inadvertently harming it.

Rootkits

Rootkits have become the software exploitation program du jour. Rootkits are software programs that have the ability to hide certain things from the operating system. With a rootkit, there may be a number of processes running on a system that don't show up in Task Manager, or connections may be established/available that don't appear in a Netstat display—the rootkit masks the presence of these items. The rootkit does this by manipulating function calls to the operating system and filtering out information that would normally appear.

Unfortunately, many rootkits are written to get around antivirus and antispyware programs that aren't kept up-to-date. The best defense you have is to monitor what your system is doing and catch the rootkit in the process of installation.

Phishing

Phishing is a form of social engineering in which you simply ask someone for a piece of information that you are missing by making it look as if it is a legitimate request. An email might look as if it is from a bank and contain some basic information, such as the user's name. In the email, it will often state that there is a problem with the person's account or access privileges. They will be told to click a link to correct the problem. After they click the link—which goes to a site other than the bank's—they are asked for their username, password, account information, and so on. The person instigating the phishing can then use the values entered there to access the legitimate account.

One of the best counters to phishing is to simply mouse over the Click Here link and read the URL. Almost every time it is pointing to an adaptation of the legitimate URL as opposed to a link to the real thing.

The only preventive measure in dealing with social engineering attacks is to educate your users and staff to never give out passwords and user IDs over the phone or via email, or to anyone who isn't positively verified as being who they say they are.

When you combine phishing with Voice over IP (VoIP), it becomes known as *vishing* and is just an elevated form of social engineering. While crank calls have been in existence since the invention of the telephone, the rise in VoIP now makes it possible for someone to call you from almost anywhere in the world, without the worry of tracing, caller ID, and other features of the land line, and pretend to be someone they are not in order to get data from you.

Two other forms of phishing to be aware of are *spear phishing* and *whaling* and they are very similar in nature. With spear phishing, the person conducting it uses information that the target would be less likely to question because it appears to be coming from a trusted source. As an example, instead of Wells Fargo sending the user a message telling you to click here to fix a problem with your account, the message that comes in appears to be from your spouse and it says to click here to see that video of your children from last Christmas. Because it appears far more likely to be a legitimate message, it cuts through the user's standard defenses like a spear and has a higher likelihood of being clicked on. Generating the attack requires much more work on the part of the miscreant and often involves using information from contact lists, friend lists from social media sites, and so on.

Whaling is nothing more than phishing, or spear phishing, for big users. Instead of sending out a To Whom It May Concern message to thousands of users, the whaler identifies one person from whom they can gain all the data they want—usually a manager or owner—and targets the phishing campaign at them.

Shoulder surfing

One form of social engineering is known as *shoulder surfing* and involves nothing more than watching someone when they enter their sensitive data. They can see you entering a password, typing in a credit card number, or entering any other pertinent information. The best defense against this type of attack is simply to survey your environment before entering personal data.

Spyware

Spyware differs from other malware in that it works—often actively—on behalf of a third party. Rather than self-replicating, like viruses and worms, spyware is spread to machines by users who inadvertently ask for it. The users often don't know they have asked for it, but have done so by downloading other programs, visiting infected sites, and so on.

The spyware program monitors the user's activity and responds by offering unsolicited pop-up advertisements (sometimes known as *adware*), gathers information about the user to pass on to marketers, or intercepts personal data such as credit card numbers.

Viruses

Viruses can be classified as polymorphic, stealth, retroviruses, multipartite, armored, companion, phage, and macro viruses. Each type of virus has a different attack strategy and different consequences.

 Estimates for losses due to viruses are in the billions of dollars. These losses include financial loss as well as lost productivity.

The following sections will introduce the symptoms of a virus infection, explain how a virus works, and describe the types of viruses you can expect to encounter and how they generally behave. We'll also discuss how a virus is transmitted through a network and look at a few hoaxes.

Symptoms of a Virus/Malware Infection

Many viruses will announce that you're infected as soon as they gain access to your system. They may take control of your system and flash annoying messages on your screen or destroy your hard disk. When this occurs, you'll know that you're a victim. Other viruses will cause your system to slow down, cause files to disappear from your computer, or take over your disk space.

 Because viruses are the most common malware, the term *virus* is used in this section.

You should look for some of the following symptoms when determining if a virus infection has occurred:

- The programs on your system start to load more slowly. This happens because the virus is spreading to other files in your system or is taking over system resources.

- Unusual files appear on your hard drive, or files start to disappear from your system. Many viruses delete key files in your system to render it inoperable.

- Program sizes change from the installed versions. This occurs because the virus is attaching itself to these programs on your disk.

- Your browser, word-processing application, or other software begins to exhibit unusual operating characteristics. Screens or menus may change.

- The system mysteriously shuts itself down or starts itself up and does a great deal of unanticipated disk activity.

- You mysteriously lose access to a disk drive or other system resources. The virus has changed the settings on a device to make it unusable.

- Your system suddenly doesn't reboot or gives unexpected error messages during startup.

This list is by no means comprehensive. What is an absolute, however, is the fact that you should immediately quarantine the infected system. It is imperative that you do all you can to contain the virus and keep it from spreading to other systems within your network, or beyond.

How Viruses Work

A virus, in most cases, tries to accomplish one of two things: render your system inoperable or spread to other systems. Many viruses will spread to other systems given the chance and then render your system unusable. This is common with many of the newer viruses.

If your system is infected, the virus may try to attach itself to every file in your system and spread each time you send a file or document to other users. Figure 7.3 shows a virus spreading from an infected system either through a network or by removable media. When you give removable media to another user or put it into another system, you then infect that system with the virus.

FIGURE 7.3   Virus spreading from an infected system using the network or removable media

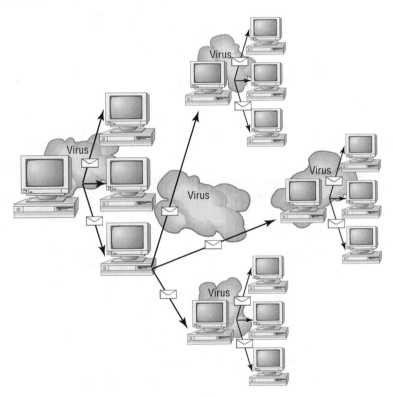

Most viruses today are spread using email. The infected system attaches a file to any email that you send to another user. The recipient opens this file, thinking it's something you legitimately sent them. When they open the file, the virus infects the target system. The virus might then attach itself to all the emails the newly infected system sends, which in turn infects the recipients of the emails. Figure 7.4 shows how a virus can spread from a single user to literally thousands of users in a very short time using email.

FIGURE 7.4   An email virus spreading geometrically to other users

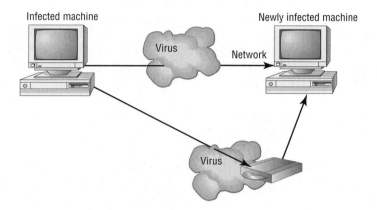

Types of Viruses

Viruses take many different forms. The following sections briefly introduce these forms and explain how they work. These are the most common types, but this isn't a comprehensive list.

The best defense against a virus attack is up-to-date antivirus software installed and running. The software should be on all workstations as well as the server.

Armored Virus   An *armored virus* is designed to make itself difficult to detect or analyze. Armored viruses cover themselves with protective code that stops debuggers or disassemblers from examining critical elements of the virus. The virus may be written in such a way that some aspects of the programming act as a decoy to distract analysis while the actual code hides in other areas in the program.

From the perspective of the creator, the more time it takes to deconstruct the virus, the longer it can live. The longer it can live, the more time it has to replicate and spread to as many machines as possible. The key to stopping most viruses is to identify them quickly and educate administrators about them—the very things that the armor intensifies the difficulty of accomplishing.

Companion Virus   A *companion virus* attaches itself to legitimate programs and then creates a program with a different filename extension. This file may reside in your system's temporary directory. When a user types the name of the legitimate program, the companion virus executes instead of the real program. This effectively hides the virus from the user. Many of the viruses that are used to attack Windows systems make changes to program pointers in the Registry so that they point to the infected program. The infected program may perform its dirty deed and then start the real program.

Macro Virus   A *macro virus* exploits the enhancements made to many application programs. Programmers can expand the capability of applications such as Microsoft Word and Excel. Word, for example, supports a mini-BASIC programming language that allows files to be manipulated automatically. These programs in the document are called *macros*. For example, a macro can tell your word processor to spell-check your document automatically when it opens. Macro viruses can infect all the documents on your system and spread to other systems via email or other methods. Macro viruses are the fastest-growing exploitation today.

Multipartite Virus   A *multipartite virus* attacks your system in multiple ways. It may attempt to infect your boot sector, infect all of your executable files, and destroy your application files. The hope here is that you won't be able to correct all the problems and will allow the infestation to continue. The multipartite virus in Figure 7.5 attacks your boot sector, infects application files, and attacks your Word documents.

Phage Virus   A *phage virus* alters other programs and databases. The virus infects all of these files. The only way to remove this virus is to reinstall the programs that are infected. If you miss even a single incident of this virus on the victim system, the process will start again and infect the system once more.

FIGURE 7.5   A multipartite virus commencing an attack on a system

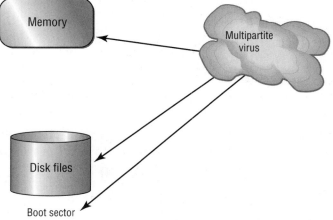

Polymorphic Virus   *Polymorphic viruses* change form in order to avoid detection. These types of viruses attack your system, display a message on your computer, and delete files on your system. The virus will attempt to hide from your antivirus software. Frequently, the virus will encrypt parts of itself to avoid detection. When the virus does this, it's referred to as *mutation*. The mutation process makes it hard for antivirus software to detect common characteristics of the virus. Figure 7.6 shows a polymorphic virus changing its characteristics to avoid detection. In this example, the virus changes a signature to fool antivirus software.

FIGURE 7.6   The polymorphic virus changing its characteristics

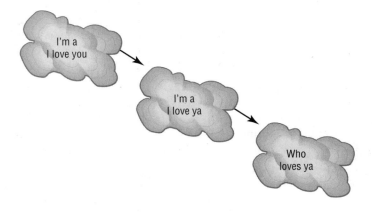

    A *signature* is an algorithm or other element of a virus that uniquely identifies it. Because some viruses have the ability to alter their signature, it is crucial that you keep signature files current, whether you choose to manually download them or configure the antivirus engine to do so automatically.

Retrovirus   A *retrovirus* attacks or bypasses the antivirus software installed on a computer. You can consider a retrovirus to be an anti-antivirus. Retroviruses can directly attack your antivirus software and potentially destroy the virus definition database file. Destroying this information without your knowledge would leave you with a false sense of security. The virus may also directly attack an antivirus program to create bypasses for itself.

Stealth Virus   A *stealth virus* attempts to avoid detection by masking itself from applications. It may attach itself to the boot sector of the hard drive. When a system utility or program runs, the stealth virus redirects commands around itself in order to avoid detection. An infected file may report a file size different from what is actually present in order to avoid detection. Figure 7.7 shows a stealth virus attaching itself to the boot sector to avoid detection. Stealth viruses may also move themselves from fileA to fileB during a virus scan for the same reason.

FIGURE 7.7   A stealth virus hiding in a disk boot sector

Virus Transmission in a Network

Upon infection, some viruses destroy the target system immediately. The saving grace is that the infection can be detected and corrected. Some viruses won't destroy or otherwise tamper with a system; they use the victim system as a carrier. The victim system then infects servers, file shares, and other resources with the virus. The carrier then infects the target system again. Until the carrier is identified and cleaned, the virus continues to harass systems in this network and spread.

Present Virus Activity

New viruses and threats are released on a regular basis to join the cadre of those already in existence. From an exam perspective, you need only be familiar with the world as it existed at the time the questions were written. From an administrative standpoint, however, you need to know what is happening today.

To find this information, visit the CERT/CC Current Activity web page at www.us-cert .gov/current/current_activity.html. Here you'll find a detailed description of the most current viruses as well as links to pages on older threats.

Worms

A *worm* is different from a virus in that it can reproduce itself, it's self-contained, and it doesn't need a host application to be transported. Many of the so-called viruses that have made the news were actually worms. However, it's possible for a worm to contain or deliver a virus to a target system.

By their nature and origin, worms are supposed to propagate, and they use whatever services they're capable of to do that. Early worms filled up memory and bred inside the RAM of the target computer. Worms can use TCP/IP, email, Internet services, or any number of possibilities to reach their target.

Trojans

Trojan horses are programs that enter a system or network under the guise of another program. A Trojan horse may be included as an attachment or as part of an installation program. The Trojan horse can create a back door or replace a valid program during installation. It then accomplishes its mission under the guise of another program. Trojan horses can be used to compromise the security of your system, and they can exist on a system for years before they're detected.

The best preventive measure for Trojan horses is to not allow them entry into your system. Immediately before and after you install a new software program or operating system, back it up! If you suspect a Trojan horse, you can reinstall the original programs, which should delete the Trojan horse. A port scan may also reveal a Trojan horse on your system. If an application opens a TCP or IP port that isn't supported in your network, you can track it down and determine which port is being used.

Exam Essentials

Know the characteristics and types of viruses used to disrupt systems and networks. Several different types of viruses are floating around today. The most common ones are polymorphic viruses, stealth viruses, retroviruses, multipartite viruses, and macro viruses.

Know the various types of social engineering. Social-engineering variants include shoulder surfing (watching someone work) and phishing (tricking someone into believing they are communicating with a party other than the one they are communicating with). Variations on phishing include vishing and whaling as well as spear phishing.

2.3 Implement security best practices to secure a workstation

In the previous objectives, the importance of user education has been mentioned. The user represents the weakest link in the security chain, whether the harm comes to them in the form of malware, social engineering, or simply avoidable mistakes. The workstation represents the digital arm of the user and must be properly and adequately secured to keep the user—and the network—protected.

A number of best practices are involved with securing a workstation. While a checklist could take many pages, depending on your environment, CompTIA has identified seven that should appear on any roster:

- Set strong passwords
- Require passwords
- Restrict user permissions
- Change default usernames

- Disable the guest account
- Make the screensaver require a password
- Disable AutoRun functionality

The following sections will explore these best practices in more detail.

Setting strong passwords

One of the strongest ways to keep a system safe is to employ strong passwords and educate your users in the best security practices. Many password-generation systems are based on a one-way hashing approach. You can't take the hash value and reverse it to guess the password. In theory, this makes it harder to guess or decrypt a password.

Passwords should be as long as possible. Most security experts believe a password of 10 characters is the minimum that should be used if security is a real concern. If you use only the lowercase letters of the alphabet, you have 26 characters with which to work. If you add the numeric values 0 through 9, you'll get another 10 characters. If you go one step further and add the uppercase letters, you'll then have an additional 26 characters, giving you a total of 62 characters with which to construct a password.

 Most vendors recommend that you use nonalphabetical characters such as #, $, and % in your password, and some go so far as to require it.

If you used a 4-character password, this would be $62 \times 62 \times 62 \times 62$, or approximately 14 million password possibilities. If you used 5 characters in your password, this would give you 62 to the fifth power, or approximately 920 million password possibilities. If you used a 10-character password, this would give you 62 to the tenth power, or 8.4×10^{17} (a very big number) possibilities. As you can see, these numbers increase exponentially with each position added to the password. The 4-digit password could probably be broken in a fraction of a day, whereas the 10-digit password would take considerably longer and consume much more processing power.

If your password used only the 26 lowercase letters from the alphabet, the 4-digit password would have 26 to the fourth power, or 456,000 password combinations. A 5-character password would have 26 to the fifth power, or over 11 million, and a 10-character password would have 26 to the tenth power, or 1.4×10^{14}. This is still a big number, but it would take considerably less time to break it.

 To see tables on how quickly passwords can be surmised, visit www.lockdown.co.uk/?pg=combi&s=articles.

Mathematical methods of encryption are primarily used in conjunction with other encryption methods as part of authenticity verification. The message and the hashed value of the message can be encrypted using other processes. In this way, you know that the message is secure and hasn't been altered.

Requiring passwords

Make *absolutely* certain you require passwords (such a simple to thing to overlook in a small network) for all accounts, and change the default passwords on system accounts.

Restricting user permissions

When assigning user permissions, follow the principle of least privilege (discussed earlier): give users only the bare minimum they need to do their job. Assign permissions to groups, rather than users, and make users members of groups (or remove them from them) as they change roles or positions.

Changing default usernames

Default accounts represent a huge weakness in that every miscreant knows they exist. When an operating system is installed, whether on a workstation or a server, there are certain accounts created and since the wrongdoer already knows the account name, it simplifies the process of getting into an account by requiring them to only supply the password. The first thing they will try, of course, is the default password if one exists.

Disabling guest account

To secure the system, disable all accounts that are not needed (especially the guest account). Next, rename the accounts if you can (Microsoft won't allow you to rename Administrator). Finally, change the passwords from the defaults and add them to the cycle of passwords that routinely get changed.

Screensaver required password

A screensaver should automatically start after a short period of idle time, and that screensaver should require a password before the user can begin the session again. This method of locking the workstation adds one more level of security.

Disable AutoRun

It is never a good idea to put any media in a workstation that you do not know where it came from or what it is. The reason is that the media (CD, DVD, USB) could contain malware. Compounding matters, that malware could be referenced in the Autorun.inf file, causing it to be summoned when the media is inserted in the machine and requiring no other action. Autorun.inf can be used to start an executable, access a website, or do any of a large number of different tasks. The best way to prevent a user from falling victim to such a ploy is to disable the AutoRun feature on the workstation.

Microsoft has changed (by default, disabled) the AutoRun function on Windows Vista and Windows 7, though running remains the default action for PCs using Windows XP through Service Pack 3. The reason Microsoft changed the default action can be summed up in a single word: security. That text-based Autorun.inf file can not only take your browser to a web page, it can also call any executable file, pass along variable information about the user, or do just about anything else imaginable. Simply put, it is *never* a good idea to take any media that you have no idea where it came from or what it holds and plug it into your system. Such an action opens up the user—and their network—to any number of possible tribulations. An entire business's data could be jeopardized by such a minuscule act if a harmful CD were placed in a computer at work by someone with elevated privileges.

Exam Essentials

Understand the need for good passwords.   Passwords are the first line of defense for protecting an account. A password should be required for every account and strong passwords should be enforced. Users need to understand the basics of password security and work to keep their accounts protected by following company policies regarding passwords.

Disable what you don't need.   All accounts that are not in use—especially the guest account—should be disabled. You should also disable the AutoRun feature to prevent it from running programs or commands without your knowledge that could inflict harm.

2.4 Given a scenario, use the appropriate data destruction/disposal method

Think of all the sensitive data written to a hard drive. The drive can contain information about students, clients, users—anyone and anything. That hard drive can be in a desktop PC, a laptop, or even a printer (many laser printers above consumer grade offer the ability to add a hard drive to store print jobs). If it falls into the wrong hands, you can not only lose valuable data but also risk a lawsuit for not properly protecting privacy. An appropriate data destruction/disposal plan should be in place to avoid any potential problems.

Since data on media holds great value and liability, that media should never be simply tossed away for prying eyes to stumble upon. For purposes of this objective, the media in question is hard drives and there are three key concepts to understand in regard to theme: formatting, sanitation, and destruction. Formatting prepares the drive to hold new information (which can include copying over data already there). Sanitation involves wiping the data on the drive off it, whereas destruction renders the drive no longer usable.

NOTE   While this objective is heavily focused on hard drives, it is also possible to have data stored on portable flash drives, backup tapes, CDs, or DVDs. In the interest of security, we recommend that you destroy them before disposing of them as well.

Low level format vs. standard format

Multiple levels of formatting can be done on a drive. A standard format—accomplished using the operating system's format utility (or similar) can mark space occupied by files as available for new files without truly deleting what was there. Such erasing—if you want to call it that—doesn't guarantee that the information isn't still on the disk and recoverable.

A low-level format (typically only accomplished in the factory) can be performed on the system, or a utility can be used to completely wipe the disk clean. This process helps ensure that information doesn't fall into the wrong hands.

IDE hard drives are low-level formatted by the manufacturer. Low-level formatting must be performed even before a drive can be partitioned. In low-level formatting, the drive controller chip and the drive meet for the very first time and learn to work together. Because IDE drives have their controllers integrated into the drive, low-level formatting is a factory process with these drives. Low-level formatting is not operating system dependent.

WARNING   Never low-level format IDE or SCSI drives! They're low-level formatted from the factory, and you may cause problems by using low-level utilities on these types of drives.

The main thing to remember for the exams is that most forms of formatting included with the operating system do not actually completely erase the data. Formatting the drive and then disposing of it has caused many companies problems when the data has been retrieved by individuals who never should have seen it using applications that are commercially available.

Hard drive sanitation and sanitation methods

A number of vendors offer hard drives with AES (Advanced Encryption Standard) cryptography built in, but these secure hard drives are still better being completely out of the hands of others than trusting their internal security once their usable lifespan has passed for the client. Some vendors include utilities to erase the hard drive, and if it is a PATA/SATA (Parallel ATA or Serial ATA) drive, you can always run hdderase, but you are still taking your chances.

In addition to hdderase, you can find a number of other software "shredders" by doing a quick web search. It is important to recognize and acknowledge that many of these do not meet military or General Services Administration (GSA) specifications and those specifications should be considered guidelines that you also adhere to when dealing with your own, or a client's, data. The only surefire method of rendering the hard drive contents completely eradicated is physical destruction.

Overwrite

Overwriting the drive entails copying over the data with new data. A common practice is to replace the data with 0s. A number of applications allow you to recover what was there prior to the last write operation, and for that reason, most overwrite software will write the same sequence and save it multiple times.

Drive wipe

If it's possible to verify beyond a reasonable doubt that a piece of hardware that's no longer being used doesn't contain any data of a sensitive or proprietary nature, that hardware can be recycled (sold to employees, sold to a third party, donated to a school, and so on). That level of assurance can come from wiping a hard drive or using specialized utilities.

 Degaussing hard drives is difficult and may render the drive unusable.

If you can't be assured that the hardware in question doesn't contain important data, the hardware should be destroyed. You cannot, and should not, take a risk that the data your company depends on could fall into the wrong hands.

Physical destruction

Physically destroying the drive involves rendering the component no longer usable. While the focus is on hard drives, you can also physically destroy other forms of media, such as flash drives and CD/DVDs.

Shredder

When it comes to DVDs and CDs, many commercial paper shredders include the ability to destroy them. Paper shredders, however, are not able to handle hard drives and you need a shredder created for just such a purpose. Jackhammer makes a low-volume model that will destroy eight drives a minute and carries a suggested list price of just under $30,000.

Drill

If you don't have the budget for a hard drive shredder, you can accomplish similar results in a much more time-consuming way with a power drill. The goal is to physically destroy the platters in the drive. Start the process by removing the cover from the drive—this is normally done with a Torx driver (while #8 does not work with all, it is a good one to try first). You can remove the arm with a slotted screwdriver and then the cover over the platters using a Torx driver. Don't worry about damaging or scratching anything—nothing is intended to be saved. Everything but the platters can be tossed away.

As an optional step, you can completely remove the tracks using a belt sander, grinder, or palm sander. The goal is to turn the shiny surface into fine powder. Again, this step is optional, but adds one more layer of assurance that nothing usable remains. Always be careful to wear eye protection and not breathe in any fine particles that you generate during the grinding/destruction process.

Following this, use the power drill to create as small a set of particles as possible. A drill press works much better for this task than trying to hold the drive and drill it with a handheld model.

Even with practice, you will find that manually destroying a hard drive is time consuming. There are companies that specialize in this and can do it efficiently. One such company is Shred-it, which will pick it up from you and provide a chain-of-custody assurance and a Certificate of Destruction upon completion. You can find out more about what they offer here:

www.shredit.com/shredding-service/What-to-shred/
Hard-drive-destruction.aspx

Electromagnetic

A large electromagnet can be used to destroy any magnetic media—hard drive or backup tape set. The most common of these is the degaussing tool, discussed next.

Degaussing tool

Degaussing involves applying a strong magnetic field to initialize the media (this is also referred to as *disk wiping*). This process helps ensure that information doesn't fall into the wrong hands.

Since degaussing uses a specifically designed electromagnet to eliminate all data on the drive, that destruction also includes the factory pre-recorded servo tracks. You can find wand model degaussers priced at just over $500 or desktop units that sell for up to $30,000.

Exam Essentials

Understand the difference between standard and low-level formatting.   Standard formatting uses operating system tools and makes the drive as available for holding data without truly removing what was on the drive (thus the data can be recovered). A low-level format is operating system independent and destroys any data that was on the drive.

Understand how to physically destroy a drive.   A hard drive can be destroyed by tossing it into a shredder designed for such a purpose, or it can be destroyed with an electromagnet in a process known as degaussing. You can also disassemble the drive and destroy the platters with a drill or other tool that renders the data irretrievable.

2.5 Given a scenario, secure a SOHO wireless network

CompTIA wants administrators of SOHO networks to be able to secure those networks in ways that protect the data stored on them. This objective looks at the security protection that can be added to a wireless SOHO network, and the one that follows examines similar procedures for a wired network.

The wireless network is not and never will be secure. Use wireless only when absolutely necessary. If you must deploy a wireless network, here are some tips to make some improvements to wireless security:

- Change the default SSID.
- Disable SSID broadcasts.
- Disable DHCP or use reservations.
- Use MAC filtering.
- Use IP filtering.
- Use the strongest security available on the wireless access point.
- Change the static security keys on a two- to four-week basis.
- When new wireless protection schemes become available (and reasonably priced), consider migrating to them.
- Limit the user accounts that can use wireless connectivity.
- Use a preauthentication system, such as RADIUS.
- Use remote access filters against client type, protocols used, time, date, user account, content, and so forth.
- Use IPSec tunnels over the wireless links.
- Turn down the signal strength to the minimum needed to support connectivity.
- Seriously consider removing wireless from your LAN.

Change default usernames and passwords

Default accounts not only include those created with the installation of the operating system(s), but are also often associated with hardware. Wireless access points, routers, and similar devices often include accounts for interacting with, and administering, those devices. You should always change the passwords associated with those devices and, where possible, change the usernames.

If there are accounts that are not needed, disable them or delete them. Make certain you use strong password policies and protect the passwords with the same security you do for any users or administrators (in other words, don't write the router's password on an address label and stick it to the bottom of the router).

Changing SSID

All radio frequency signals can be easily intercepted. To intercept 802.11.a/b/g/n traffic, all you need is a PC with an appropriate 802.11.a/b/g/n card installed. Many networks will regularly broadcast their name (known as an *SSID broadcast*) to announce their presence. Simple software on the PC can capture the link traffic in the wireless AP and then process this data in order to decrypt account and password information.

Setting encryption

The available types of wireless encryption available (WEP, WPA, WPA2, etc.) were discussed in Chapter 2. Know that you should always enable encryption for any SOHO network you administer and that you should choose the strongest level of encryption you can work with.

Disabling SSID broadcast

One method of "protecting" the network that is often recommended is to turn off the SSID broadcast. The access point is still there and can be accessed by those who know about it, but it prevents those who are just scanning from finding it. This should be considered a *very* weak form of security as there are still other ways, albeit a bit more complicated, to discover the presence of the access point besides the SSID broadcast.

Enable MAC Filtering

Most APs offer the ability to turn on *MAC filtering,* but it is off by default. In the default stage, any wireless client that knows the values looked for can join the network. When MAC filtering is used, the administrator compiles a list of the MAC addresses associated with the users' computers and enters those. When a client attempts to connect, and other values have been correctly entered, an additional check of the MAC address is done. If the address appears in the list, the client is allowed to join; otherwise, they are forbidden from so doing. On a number of wireless devices, the term *network lock* is used in place of MAC filtering, and the two are synonymous.

Adding port authentication to MAC filtering takes security for the network down to the switch port level and increases your security exponentially.

Antenna and access point placement

Antenna placement can be crucial in allowing clients to reach the access point. There isn't any one universal solution to this issue, and it depends on the environment in which the access point is placed. As a general rule, the greater the distance the signal must travel, the more it will attenuate, but you can lose a signal quickly in a short space as well if the building materials reflect or absorb the signal. You should try to avoid placing access points near metal (which includes appliances) or near the ground. Placing them in the center of the area to be served, and high enough to get around most obstacles, is recommended.

On the other end of the spectrum, you have to contend with the problem of the signal traveling outside your intended network (known as "signal leakage") and being picked up in public areas by outsiders. To lessen this problem, use RF absorbent materials on external walls, essentially shielding the surroundings.

Radio power levels

On the chance that the signal is actually traveling too far, some access points include *power-level controls* that allow you to reduce the amount of output provided.

 A great source for information on RF power values and antenna can be found on the Cisco site at www.cisco.com/en/US/tech/tk722/tk809/ technologies_tech_note09186a00800e90fe.shtml.

Assign static IP addresses

While DHCP can be a godsend, a SOHO network is small enough that you can get by without it issuing IP addresses to each host. The advantage to statically assigning the IP addresses is that you can then make certain which host is associated with which IP address and then utilize filtering to limit network access to only those hosts.

Exam Essentials

Know the names, purpose, and characteristics of wireless security.   Wireless networks can be encrypted through WEP and WPA technologies. Wireless controllers use special ID numbers (SSIDs) and must be configured in the network cards to allow communications. However, using ID number configurations doesn't necessarily prevent wireless networks from being monitored, and there are vulnerabilities specific to wireless devices.

Understand the basics of antenna placement and radio power levels.   Antenna placement can be crucial in allowing clients to reach the access point. Place access points near the center of the area to be served and high enough to get around most obstacles. Power-level controls allow you to reduce the amount of output provided.

2.6 Given a scenario, secure a SOHO wired network

Every network needs attention paid to security—so much so, in fact, that CompTIA included similar information in three objectives beneath the same domain. Some of the content here is similar to that in objectives 2.3 and 2.5, but attempts have been made to avoid repetition where possible.

While a wired network can be more secure than a wireless one, there are still a number of procedures you should follow to leave as little to chance as possible. Among them, change the default usernames and passwords to different values and secure the physical environment.

You should also disable any ports that are not needed, assign static IP addresses, and use MAC filtering to limit access to only those hosts you recognize.

Change default usernames and passwords

Make sure the default password is changed after the installation of any network device. Failure to do so leaves that device open for anyone recognizing the hardware to access it using the known factory password.

In Windows, the Guest account is automatically created in Windows with the intent that it is to be used when someone must access a system but lacks a user account on that system. Since it is so widely known to exist, we recommend that you not use this default account and create another one for the same purpose if you truly need one. The Guest account leaves a security risk at the workstation and should be disabled to prevent it from being accessed by those attempting to gain unauthorized access.

Change *every* username and password that you can so they vary from their default settings.

Enable MAC filtering

Limit access to the network to MAC addresses that are known and filter out those that are not. Even in a home network, you can implement MAC filtering with most routers and typically have an option of choosing to only allow computers with MAC addresses that you list, or only deny computers with MAC addresses that you list.

If you don't know a workstation's MAC address, use `ipconfig /all` to find it in the Windows-based world (it is listed as *physical address*), and `ifconfig` in Unix/Linux.

Assign static IP addresses

Static IP addresses should be used (avoiding the use of DHCP) on SOHO networks to keep from issuing them to hosts other than those you recognize and want on the network.

Disabling ports

Disable all unneeded protocols/ports. If you don't need them, remove them or prevent them from loading. Ports not in use present an open door for an attacker to enter.

Many of the newer SOHO router solutions (and some of the personal firewall solutions on end-user workstations) close down the ICMP ports by default. Keep this in mind; it can drive you nuts when you are trying to see if a brand-new station, server, or router is up and running.

Physical security

Just as you would not park your car in a public garage and leave its doors wide open with the key in the ignition, you should educate users to not leave a workstation that they are logged into when they attend meetings, go to lunch, and so forth. They should log out of the workstation or lock it. "Lock when you leave" should be a mantra they become familiar with. Locking the workstation should require a password (usually the same as their user password) in order to resume working at the workstation.

You can also lock a workstation by using an operating system that provides filesystem security. Microsoft's earliest filesystem was referred to as File Allocation Table (FAT). FAT was designed for relatively small disk drives. It was upgraded first to FAT16 and finally to FAT32. FAT32 allows large disk systems to be used on Windows systems.

FAT allows only two types of protection: share-level and user-level access privileges. If a user has write or change access to a drive or directory, they have access to any file in that directory. This is unsecure in an Internet environment.

The New Technology File System (NTFS) was introduced with Windows NT to address security problems. Before Windows NT was released, it had become apparent to Microsoft that a new filesystem was needed to handle growing disk sizes, security concerns, and the demand for more stability. NTFS was created to address those issues.

With NTFS, files, directories, and volumes can each have their own security. NTFS's security is flexible and built in. Not only does NTFS track security in access control lists (ACLs), which can hold permissions for local users and groups, but each entry in the ACL can also specify what type of access is given—such as Read, Write, Modify, or Full Control. This allows a great deal of flexibility in setting up a network. In addition, special file-encryption programs can be used to encrypt data while it is stored on the hard disk.

Microsoft strongly recommends that all network shares be established using NTFS. While NTFS security is important, though, it doesn't matter what filesystem you are using if you leave your workstation logged in and leave, allowing anyone to sit down at your desk and hack away.

 Since NTFS and share permissions are operating system specific, they were discussed in Chapter 6.

Lastly, don't overlook the obvious need for physical security. Adding a cable to lock a laptop to a desk prevents someone from picking it up and walking away with a copy of your customer database. Laptop cases generally include a built-in security slot in which a cable lock can be added to prevent it from being carried away easily, like the one shown in Figure 7.8.

When it comes to desktop models, adding a lock to the back cover can prevent an intruder with physical access from grabbing the hard drive or damaging the internal components. You should also physically secure network devices—routers, access points, and the like. Place them in locked cabinets, if possible. If they are not physically secured, the opportunity exists for them to be stolen or manipulated in such a way to allow someone unauthorized to connect to the network.

FIGURE 7.8 A cable in the security slot keeps the laptop from being carried away easily.

Exam Essentials

Understand why ports should be disabled.   Disable all unneeded protocols and ports. If you don't need them, remove them or prevent them from loading. Ports not in use present an open door for an attacker to enter.

Understand the purpose of MAC filtering.   MAC filtering allows you to limit access to the network to MAC addresses that are known and filter out (deny access to) those that are not.

Review Questions

1. What is tailgating?

2. What is the principle of least privilege?

3. What is the form of social engineering in which you ask someone for a piece of information that you are missing by making it look as if it is a legitimate request?

4. How does a worm differ from a virus?

5. What is the default status of AutoRun in Windows 7 and Windows Vista?

6. _____ involves applying a strong magnetic field to initialize the media.

7. With what feature does the administrator use to compile a list of the MAC addresses associated with the users' computers and enter those into a list and if the address appears in the list, the client is allowed to join the network?

8. What filesystem does Microsoft strongly recommend that you use to establish all network shares?

9. If you don't know a workstation's MAC address, what can you use to find it in the Windows-based world?

10. A _____ format is operating system independent and destroys any data that was on the drive.

Chapter

8

Mobile Devices

COMPTIA A+ 220-802 EXAM OBJECTIVES COVERED IN THIS CHAPTER:

✓ **3.1 Explain the basic features of mobile operating systems.**

- Android vs. iOS
    - Open source vs. closed source/vendor specific
    - App source (app store and market)
    - Screen orientation (accelerometer/gyroscope)
    - Screen calibration
    - GPS and geotracking

✓ **3.2 Establish basic network connectivity and configure email.**

- Wireless/cellular data network (enable/disable)
- Bluetooth
    - Enable Bluetooth
    - Enable pairing
    - Find device for pairing
    - Enter appropriate pin code
    - Test connectivity
- Email configuration
    - Server address
        - POP3
        - IMAP
        - Port and SSL settings
    - Exchange
    - Gmail

✓ **3.3 Compare and contrast methods for securing mobile devices.**

- Passcode locks
- Remote wipes
- Locator applications
- Remote backup applications
- Failed login attempts restrictions
- Antivirus
- Patching/OS updates

✓ **3.4 Compare and contrast hardware differences in regards to tablets and laptops.**

- No field serviceable parts
- Typically not upgradeable
- Touch interface
  - Touch flow
  - Multitouch
- Solid state drives

✓ **3.5 Execute and configure mobile device synchronization.**

- Types of data to synchronize
  - Contacts
  - Programs
  - Email
  - Pictures
  - Music
  - Videos
- Software requirements to install the application on the PC
- Connection types to enable synchronization

In this chapter, we will focus on the exam topics related to mobile devices. We will follow the structure of the CompTIA A+ 220-802 exam blueprint, objective 3, and we will explore the five subobjectives that the prospective exam taker will need to master before taking the exam.

3.1 Explain the basic features of mobile operating systems

Mobile devices can mean laptops and notebooks but in the context of this chapter, mobile devices include smartphones, PDAs, and tablet computers. These devices differ from larger computing devices in the resources they bring to the job, the operating systems they use, and their features. The topics addressed in objective 3.1 include:

- Android vs. iOS

Android vs. iOS

Although certainly not the only operating systems made for today's highly capable mobile devices, the Android and iOS operating systems are the most widely used. In this section the two systems are compared and contrasted.

Open source vs. closed source/vendor specific

The Android operating system (OS) from Google is built on a Linux kernel with a core set of libraries that are written in Java. It is an open source operating system, which means that developers have full access to the same framework APIs used by the core applications.

The Apple iOS is a vendor-specific system made by Apple. Developers must use the software development kit (SDK) from Apple and register as Apple developers.

App source (app store and market)

Applications ("apps") for mobile devices are where all the exciting functionality comes from on mobile devices. There are thousands of developers creating apps that will do everything but wash your car for you. Although many are free, some you must purchase.

Apps for Android systems can be obtained from what was called the Google Android Market (called Google Play as of this writing) or many other sites. Apple tightly controls the sale of apps (again, many are free) by making them only available on the Apple App Store site.

Screen orientation (accelerometer/gyroscope)

Both accelerometers and gyroscopes can be used by mobile devices to determine the movement and tilt of the device. This means the device can tell which way the screen is being held. It uses this information to automatically adjust the display orientation appropriately with no action on the part of the user.

Either can be used, but since they exhibit slightly different characteristics, one works better for some types of movement and the other for other types of movement. The bottom line is that either will work but they work better together.

The iOS operating system in the iPhone uses an accelerometer and a gyroscope to sense the movement and tilt of the device. The Android used only an accelerometer in earlier models, but since a gyroscope improves the performance, the newer models include both.

Screen calibration

For a touch-screen device to operate correctly—that is, for it to properly interpret your touch and react accordingly—it must be calibrated correctly. When you touch an item on the screen and nothing happens or a movement that normally results in an expected reaction does not, the calibration of the device is off.

Many devices contain a built-in calibration tool. When you use the tool, it will ask you to touch the screen in various ways, which results in it relearning how to react to your touch. It can be a long process but will usually result in a solution to the problem. Consult the documentation for the device to locate the calibration tool.

GPS and geotracking

Some devices use cell towers to get GPS information while others (like Android phones) get GPS information directly from satellites. The upside to getting this from a satellite is that no cell phone service is required for the GPS to work. It is worth noting, however, that when GPS is on it is using the battery, so you might want to turn it off when you are not using it. The iPhone uses a combination of GPS, cell towers, and WiFi towers to plot your location.

One issue that has caused some controversy is the issue of geotracking. Both iPhone and Android devices record the location of the device periodically and send this information to a central location. This upsets some users because U.S. Department of Homeland Security officials have disclosed that they retain the right to access this information when they deem necessary.

Exam Essentials

Describe the major differences between the Android and iOS operating systems.   The Android is an open source operating system, and the iOS is a vendor-specific system made by Apple. Apps for Android systems can be obtained from Google Play or many other sites, whereas iOS apps are only available on the Apple App site. Both use accelerometers and gyroscopes to track device orientation.

Identify the function of calibration.   For a touch-screen device to operate correctly it must be calibrated correctly.

3.2 Establish basic network connectivity and configure email

For mobile devices to deliver the functionality that most accept, they must be connected to a network. To use email (one of the most important functions to many users), the device must be set up properly as well. The topics addressed in objective 3.2 include:

- Wireless/cellular data network (enable/disable)
- Bluetooth
- Email configuration

Wireless/cellular data network (enable/disable)

Like most computing devices, mobile devices provide more robust functionality when connected to a network (especially if that network is the Internet). There are two types of networks that can be used to gain access to the Internet: cell phone networks and WiFi networks.

Cell phone networks have in the past been the second choice because the performance is not as good as an 802.11 WiFi connection. With the introduction of 4G Long Term Evolution (LTE) technologies, however, the performance delivered by the cell network may become more competitive.

In either case most mobile devices will have the ability to make an 802.11 connection or use the cell network. If you would like to disable the automatic connection to the cell phone network, or if it somehow got turned off and needs to be turned back on, this can be done through the settings. One example is Settings ➤ Wireless ➤ Mobile ➤ Enable Data (select or deselect this). This is only one navigational example, and you should consult the documentation that came with the device.

Making a WiFi connection is much like doing so with a laptop. In the settings of the device will be a section for WiFi (in iPhone it's called WiFi and in Android it's called Wireless and Networks). When you access it, you will see all the WiFi networks within range. Just as you would do with a laptop, select one and attempt to connect to the WiFi network. If the connection requires a password, you will have to supply it. You also can preconfigure a wireless profile for commonly used secure wireless networks as well as those where the Service Set Identifier (SSID) has been hidden.

Bluetooth

Bluetooth is a short-range wireless technology that is used to create a wireless connection between digital devices. One of its applications is to create connections between mobile devices and items such as speakers, headphones, external GPS units, and keyboards. Before you can take advantage of this technology, the devices must be configured to connect to one another. In this section, we discuss configuring a Bluetooth connection.

Enable Bluetooth

On Android mobile devices, follow these steps:

1. From the Home screen, select the Menu button. From the menu tap Settings ≻ Wireless And Networks ≻ Bluetooth.

2. Once Bluetooth is selected, wait until a check mark appears next to Bluetooth. Bluetooth is now enabled.

   On iOS mobile devices, follow these steps:

1. On the main page, tap on Settings ≻ General ≻ Bluetooth.

2. Tap on the slider, and Bluetooth is enabled.

Enable pairing

Pairing the mobile device with the external device (speaker, headphone, and so forth) will enable the two devices to communicate. The first step is to enable pairing. This is much simpler than it sounds. For either mobile operating system, simply turn the external device on and you are ready for the next step. In some cases, you may need to make the external device discoverable. Check the documentation for the external device to see if this is the case and how you do this.

Find device for pairing

Now that the external device is on and transmitting a signal, the mobile device is ready for pairing.

   On an Android mobile device, follow these steps:

1. On the Settings menu, select Bluetooth Settings. The device will begin to scan for Bluetooth devices in the area.

2. When the external device appears in the list of detected devices, tap on it. If no pin code is required, the devices will pair.

   On an iOS mobile device, when Bluetooth is enabled it automatically starts scanning for Bluetooth devices. When your device appears in the list, select it. If a PIN is required, move on to the next step.

Enter appropriate pin code

Many external devices will ask for a PIN when you select the external device from the list of discovered devices. In many cases, the PIN is 0000, but check the manual with the external device.

Test connectivity

Once the previous steps are complete, test communication between the two devices. If you're using a headset, turn on some sound and see if you can hear it in the headphones.

Email configuration

Email is one of the most important functions that people access on their mobile devices. In this section configuring email on the device is discussed. The following procedures are common examples, and your specific device may differ slightly. Please consult the documentation for your device.

Server address

Before you can access email on your mobile device, you must know the settings for the email server of your email provider. There are two types of email accounts: POP3 and IMAP. If you know that your account is an IMAP account, you should select it in the following steps, because IMAP accounts have more functionality. If you are not sure, select POP3, which will work for either type of account.

You will need the following information to complete this setup:

- The URL of your POP3 server or IMAP server (this server receives the emails sent to you, so it's sometimes called incoming)
- The URL of your SMTP server (this server sends your email to the recipient's email server, so it's sometimes called outgoing)
- The port numbers used for both server types
- The security type used (if any)

POP3

On an Android mobile device, follow these steps:

1. Click on your device's email icon. On the page that follows, select Add Account.
2. Type your email address and password, and click Next.
3. Select POP3.
4. On the next screen, enter your username (your email address), your password, the URL of the POP3 server, the port number, and security type (if one is in use).
5. Enter the URL of your SMTP server, the port number, your username, and password. Also select Require Sign In.

On an iOS mobile device, follow these steps:

1. Select Settings ➤ Mail ➤ Contacts ➤ Calendars ➤ Add Account.
2. Select Other.
3. Select Add Mail Account. Fill in your name, email address, password, and a description. Click Next.

4. Select POP. Verify that the name, address, and description carried over from the last page.

5. Under Incoming Email Server, enter the URL of the POP3 server, your email address, and password.

6. Under Outgoing Mail Server, enter the URL of the SMTP server and your email address.

7. Click Next. Select Save in the upper-right corner.

IMAP

On an Android mobile device, follow these steps:

1. Click on your device's email icon. On the page that follows, select Add Account.

2. Type your email address and password and click Next.

3. Select IMAP.

4. On the next screen, enter your username (your email address), your password, the URL of the IMAP server, the port number, and security type (if one is in use).

5. Enter the URL of your SMTP server, the port number, your username, and password. Also select Require Sign In.

   On an iOS mobile device, follow these steps:

1. Select Settings ➤Mail ➤ Contacts ➤ Calendars ➤ Add Account.

2. Select Other.

3. Select Add Mail Account. Fill in your name, email address, password, and a description. Click Next.

4. Select IMAP. Verify that the name, address, and description carried over from the last page.

5. Under Incoming Email Server, enter the URL of the IMAP server, your email address, and your password.

6. Under Outgoing Mail Server, enter the URL of the SMTP server and your email address.

7. Click Next. Select Save in the upper-right corner.

Port and SSL settings

With either operating system you can (and should) select to use security if your email server supports it. This will encrypt all traffic between the mobile device and the email server. The choices offered are usually SSL or TLS, so you will need to know which of these is in use.

Exchange

In many cases, your work email will be hosted on a Microsoft Exchange server. The setup is not so very different but does require more information:

- Exchange Server address
- Username and password for account
- Domain name for account

On an Android mobile, device follow these steps:

1. Open the Mail application. Enter your email address and password.

2. Click Next and then Click Exchange Account.

3. Enter your domain\username, password, and Exchange Server address.

4. Check Use Secure Connection and Accept All SSL Certificates.

5. After authentication, check the boxes associated with the features you want to include, such as Push, Amount To Sync, Notifications, Sync Contacts, Sync Calendar, and Sync Calendar Amount. Be careful with the (Automatic) Push setting—it will run the battery down.

6. Click Next. On the next screen, you need to give an account name and your name (this will be displayed on outgoing email messages).

On an iOS mobile device, follow these steps:

1. Select Settings ➢ Mail ➢ Contacts ➢ Calendars ➢ Add Account.

2. Select Microsoft Exchange.

3. Fill in your email address, domain, username, password, and description if desired. Click Next.

4. Verify that the address carried over from the last page. Under Server, enter the URL of the Exchange Server or its IP address, and click Next.

5. Finally select the items you would like to sync automatically with the email server, and click Done.

Gmail

A Gmail account is somewhat simpler than the previous setups.

On an Android mobile device, follow these steps:

1. Select the Gmail icon.

2. Select Already Have A Google account.

3. In the Sign In With Your Google Account field, enter your username and password and select Sign In.

On an iOS mobile device, follow these steps:

1. Select Settings ➢ Mail ➢ Contacts ➢ Calendars ➢ Add Account.

2. Select Gmail.

3. Fill in your name, address, password, and description if desired. Click Next.

4. Verify that the address carried over from the last page. Click Next.

5. Select the items you would like to sync automatically with the email server and click Done.

Exam Essentials

Enable Bluetooth and pair a Bluetooth device with a mobile network. Describe the process for both the iOS and Android operating system.

Configure email on a mobile device. Describe the process of configuring email, including both Exchange and Gmail for both the iOS and Android operating system.

3.3 Compare and contrast methods for securing mobile devices

If laptops are easy to steal, smaller mobile devices are even more so. As mobile devices are increasingly used to store valuable data and to perform functions once the domain of laptops and desktops, the need to secure these devices grows. In this section, methods of securing mobile devices will be discussed. The topics addressed in objective 3.3 include:

- Passcode locks
- Remote wipes
- Locator applications
- Remote backup applications
- Failed login attempts restrictions
- Antivirus
- Patching/OS updates

Passcode locks

One of the most basic (but not necessarily the most utilized) security measures you can take is to implement a passcode lock on the device. This is akin to implementing the password you use to log on to your desktop or laptop, but it's amazing how few people use this basic security measure. This can prevent someone from using the mobile device if it is stolen.

Setting the password on an Android phone is done by navigating to Settings Location & Security ➢ Change Screen Lock. On the Change Screen Lock page, you can set the length of time the device remains idle until the screen locks as well as choose a method from None, Pattern, PIN, or Password. Select Password, and then enter the desired password.

On an iOS-based device, navigate to Settings ➢ General ➢ Passcode Lock to set the password and Settings ➢ General ➢ Auto-Lock to set the amount of time before the iPhone locks.

Remote wipes

Remote wipes are instructions sent remotely to a mobile device that erase all the data in cases where the device is stolen. In the case of the iPhone, this feature is closely connected to the locater application (discussed in the next section). To perform a remote wipe on an iPhone (which requires iOS 5), navigate to Settings ➤ iCloud. On this tab, ensure that Find My iPhone is enabled (set to On). Next, use the browser to go to iCloud.com and log in using the Apple ID you use on your phone.

Next select the icon Find My iPhone. The location of the phone will appear on a map. Click on the *i* icon next to the location. On the dialog box that opens, select Remote Wipe. You will be prompted again to ensure that is what you want to do. Select Wipe Phone.

The Android phones do not come with an official remote wipe. You can, however, install an Android app that will do this. Once the app, Android Lost, is installed, it works in the same way the iPhone remote wipe does. In this case, you log into the Android Lost website using your Google login. From the site, you can locate and wipe the device.

Locator applications

Locator applications like the Android Lost app for Android are available where apps are sold for Androids. These apps allow you to locate the device, to lock the device, and even to send a message to the device offering a reward for its return. Finally, they can remote-wipe the device as well. The iOS devices have this feature built in, and it performs all the same functions.

Remote backup applications

Backing up your data with the iPhone can be done by connecting the device to a Mac and using iTunes to manage the content. (The data can also be backed up to a PC that has iTunes.) As users start to use the mobile device as their main tool, this may not be an optimal way to manage backups. New apps like Mozy are available that perform an online backup, which is attractive because the laptop or desktop where you backed up your data is not always close at hand but the Internet usually is.

Android has always taken a cloud approach to backups. There are many Android apps now that can be used to back data up to locations such as Dropbox or Box.net.

Failed login attempts restrictions

Most of us have become accustomed to the lockout feature on a laptop or desktop that locks out an account after a certain number of failed login attempts. This feature is available on a mobile device and can even be set to perform a remote wipe of the device after repeated failed login attempts.

On the iOS, the Erase Data function can be set to perform a remote wipe after 10 failed passcode attempts. After 6 failed attempts, the iPhone locks out users for a minute before another passcode can be entered. And the device increases the lockout time following each additional failed attempt.

The Android does not have this feature built in but does provide the APIs that allow enterprise developers to create applications that will do this.

Antivirus

Mobile devices can suffer from viruses and malware just like laptops and desktops. Major antivirus vendors such as McAfee and Kaspersky make antivirus products for mobile devices that provide the same real-time protection that the products do for desktops. The same guidelines apply for these mobile devices: keep them up-to-date by setting the device to check for updates whenever connected to the Internet.

Patching/OS updates

Security patches and operating system updates are available on an ongoing basis for both the iOS and the Android. For the iPhone, both operating system updates and security patches are available at the Apple support site. Automatic updates can be enabled for the device in iTunes. Use the Check For Updates button located in the middle of iTunes.

An auto-update feature is built into Android, and you can also manually check for patches and updates by navigating to Settings ➤ About Phone ➤ System Updates. Selecting these options will cause the phone to check for, download, and install patches or updates.

Exam Essentials

Describe the options available to secure the data on a mobile device.   These options include passcode locks, remote wipes, locator applications, failed login attempt restrictions, and remote backup applications.

List other security guidelines for mobile devices,   Always keep antivirus definitions up-to-date and set the mobile device to automatically check for OS updates and patches.

3.4 Compare and contrast hardware differences in regards to tablets and laptops

Chapter 3, "Laptops," discussed how laptops differ from desktops. In that chapter you learned that laptops use different form factors for processors, memory, and expansion slots due to size restrictions. With mobile devices such as tablet computers, an even stricter size limitation is imposed. In this section, some of the differences between tablet and laptop hardware will be discussed. The topics addressed in objective 3.4 include:

- No field-serviceable parts
- Typically not upgradeable
- Touch interface
- Solid-state drives

No field serviceable parts

One of the biggest differences between tablet computers and laptops is that, with some exceptions, there are no field-serviceable or field-replaceable units (FRUs) in a tablet as there are in laptops. Batteries and battery packs are items that can be replaced easily by a user, and hard drives (covered later in this section) are not too difficult to replace. But in most other cases, any repairs will not be done by replacing a part but by repairing what's there or replacing the device. This is why most repairs of tablets should be done at a shop that specializes in tablet repairs.

Typically not upgradeable

Another major difference between tablets and laptops is that for the most part upgrades are not possible without replacing the device. An exception to that is memory, which sometimes can be added to a tablet computer. Hard drives can also be upgraded in some instances. In most cases, however, the manufacturer has included the maximum memory and the largest hard drive to enhance the performance of the device out of the box.

Touch interface

Tablets use a touch-screen interface that eliminates the need for a keyboard. Touch-screen monitors use two technologies: touch flow and multitouch. In this section, both are discussed.

Touch flow

Touch flow, or TouchFLO, is a user-interface feature designed by HTC. It is used by dragging your finger up and down or left and right to access common tasks on the screen. This movement is akin to scrolling the screen up and down or scrolling the screen left and right.

Multitouch

Multitouch allows the screen to recognize multiple simultaneous screen touches. This allows for movements such as those used for expanding or enlarging pictures with two fingers and then reducing them back again with the reverse movement.

Solid state drives

Tablet computers usually use solid-state drives. The advantages and disadvantages of these drives were covered in Chapter 1, "Hardware." However, mechanical hard drives are being made for tablets now, and the main advantage to these mechanical drives is the price. These drives are made to use less power than their desktops counterparts, but like any mechanical drive they will make more noise and be more vulnerable to impact due to the moving parts. They are also heavier than SSDs, which adds to the weight of the tablet.

Exam Essentials

Describe the differences between tablets and laptops.   These differences include parts that are not typically field serviceable, hardware that for the most part is not upgradable, solid-state drives instead of mechanical ones, and touch-screen interfaces that use multi-touch and touch flow technology.

3.5 Execute and configure mobile device synchronization

Keeping information in sync between your desktop or laptop and your mobile device is one of the features that many users want to take advantage of. There are many types of information that can be synced, applications that can be installed to perform the synchronization, and a number of connection methods that can be used to do this. In this section, mobile device synchronization is discussed. The topics addressed in objective 3.5 include:

- Types of data to synchronize
- Software requirements to install the application on the PC
- Connection types to enable synchronization

Types of data to synchronize

Users may be interested in maintaining a consistency between the state of data that exists on the laptop or desktop and the state of the same data on a mobile device. In this section, common types of data are discussed.

Contacts

No one wants to enter a long list of contacts into a mobile device when that same list already exists in your email account. Using push synchronization (*push* means it's automatic and requires no effort on the part of the user), you ensure that any changes made to the contact list either on the mobile device or on the desktop will be updated on the other device the next time you make a connection to the email account from the other device. It will also update if the mobile device makes a direct connection to the desktop (covered later in "Connection types to enable synchronization").

Programs

Program data from applications like databases can also be synchronized between servers and mobile devices. A good example is the synchronization of the data entered into handheld devices used by the wait staff in restaurants and the server in the back room of the restaurant. Another example is the synchronization of data from handheld scanners in a warehouse with a server that may or may not be onsite. This seamless automatic updating makes the entire operation more productive.

Email

Even more important to users than their contacts is the state of their email. The mobile device will synchronize the contacts, calendar items, and email each time the mobile device makes contact with the email account. This results in a consistent state between what is seen on the desktop and what is seen on the mobile device. Push synchronization will usually allow you to configure the push schedule, such as every 30 minutes. To preserve battery life, push sync should take place less frequently.

Pictures

Pictures are another item that users frequently want to view from the mobile device without going through the process of manually downloading them to the device. Synchronization allows the pictures stored on the desktop (or even a share on a server) to be available on the mobile device, even the one you just added an hour ago.

Music

Music files can also be included in the sync process. This helps to keep your library available on the mobile device. When you start talking about music and video files (see the next section), a word of a caution is in order. These very large files can quickly add up and fill the hard drive, and also add significantly to your data usage if the sync is happening over a wireless cell phone connection using a data plan. They can also be hard on the battery.

Videos

Video libraries can be kept consistent across devices using synchronization. Be aware of the effect of these large files on your drive space, battery level, and data usage if you are syncing wirelessly through a cell phone network.

Software requirements to install the application on the PC

Some devices come with a sync feature installed, but for the most robust functionality (such as syncing between devices with different operating systems such as iPhone to Android and Android to Blackberry), synchronization applications that will do a much better job than the built-in applications can be purchased either at the Apple App site or in other app marketplaces.

When obtaining one of these, ensure that your device meets all the requirements of the application. These applications will call for certain minimum requirements on the mobile device to operate correctly, so observe these guidelines to ensure a successful installation and operation.

Connection types to enable synchronization

The synchronization process can be carried out over several methods of connection between the devices. In some cases, you can connect the mobile device to the laptop or desktop using a USB connector. In other cases, you can establish a Bluetooth connection from the mobile device and the desktop. Finally, an 802.11 WLAN network can also be used to establish this connection. In some instances, the synchronization application will allow you to introduce a shared folder into the scenario (like Dropbox, for example), which then allows you to use the Internet to sync from the laptop to the Dropbox and then from the Dropbox to the mobile device.

Exam Essentials

Identify the types of data usually synchronized on mobile devices.   This includes but is not limited to contacts, programs, email, music, pictures, and videos.

Describe the connection types available to enable synchronization.   These include USB cables, cell phone networks, Bluetooth connections, and 802.11 networks and shared folders available through the Internet.

Review Questions

1. List the two most widely used mobile operating systems.

2. Which mobile operating system is considered open source?

3. True/False: The iOS uses either accelerometers or gyroscope but not both.

4. For a touch-screen device to operate correctly, it must be _____ correctly.

5. What two types of networks can be used to gain access to the Internet with a mobile device?

6. What is the process called when a Bluetooth device makes a connection to a mobile device?

7. When configuring email on a mobile device, what function does the SMTP server perform?

8. What information is required to configure a mobile device to use an Exchange server?

9. What application is required to perform a remote wipe?

10. What two technologies are used in touch interfaces?

Chapter

9

Troubleshooting

COMPTIA A+ 220-802 EXAM OBJECTIVES COVERED IN THIS CHAPTER:

✓ **4.1 Given a scenario, explain the troubleshooting theory.**

- Identify the problem
    - Question the user and identify user changes to computer and perform backups before making changes
- Establish a theory of probable cause (question the obvious)
- Test the theory to determine cause
    - Once theory is confirmed determine next steps to resolve problem
    - If theory is not confirmed re-establish new theory or escalate
- Establish a plan of action to resolve the problem and implement the solution
- Verify full system functionality and if applicable implement preventive measures
- Document findings, actions and outcomes

✓ **4.2 Given a scenario, troubleshoot common problems related to motherboards, RAM, CPU and power with appropriate tools.**

- Common symptoms
    - Unexpected shutdowns
    - System lockups
    - POST code beeps
    - Blank screen on bootup
    - BIOS time and settings resets
    - Attempts to boot to incorrect device
    - Continuous reboots

- No power
- Overheating
- Loud noise
- Intermittent device failure
- Fans spin – no power to other devices
- Indicator lights
- Smoke
- Burning smell
- BSOD
- Tools
- Multimeter
- Power supply tester
- Loopback plugs
- POST card

✓ **4.3 Given a scenario, troubleshoot hard drives and RAID arrays with appropriate tools.**

- Common symptoms
  - Read/write failure
  - Slow performance
  - Loud clicking noise
  - Failure to boot
  - Drive not recognized
  - OS not found
  - RAID not found
  - RAID stops working
  - BSOD
- Tools
  - Screwdriver
  - External enclosures
  - CHDKS

- CHKDSK
- FORMAT
- FDISK
- File recovery software

✓ **4.4 Given a scenario, troubleshoot common video and display issues.**

- Common symptoms
  - VGA mode
  - No image on screen
  - Overheat shutdown
  - Dead pixels
  - Artifacts
  - Color patterns incorrect
  - Dim image
  - Flickering image
  - Distorted image
  - Discoloration (degaussing)
  - BSOD

✓ **4.5 Given a scenario, troubleshoot wired and wireless networks with appropriate tools.**

- Common symptoms
  - No connectivity
  - APIPA address
  - Limited connectivity
  - Local connectivity
  - Intermittent connectivity
  - IP conflict
  - Slow transfer speeds
  - Low RF signal

- Tools
  - Cable tester
  - Loopback plug
  - Punch down tools
  - Toner probes
  - Wire strippers
  - Crimper
  - PING
  - IPCONFIG
  - TRACERT
  - NETSTAT
  - NBTSTAT
  - NET
  - Wireless locator

✓ **4.6 Given a scenario, troubleshoot operating system problems with appropriate tools.**

- Common symptoms
  - BSOD
  - Failure to boot
  - Improper shutdown
  - Spontaneous shutdown/restart
  - RAID not detected during installation
  - Device fails to start
  - Missing dll message
  - Services fails to start
  - Compatibility error
  - Slow system performance
  - Boots to safe mode
  - File fails to open
  - Missing NTLDR

- - Missing Boot.ini
  - Missing operating system
  - Missing Graphical Interface
  - Graphical Interface fails to load
  - Invalid boot disk
- Tools
  - Fixboot
  - Recovery console
  - Fixmbr
  - Sfc
  - Repair disks
  - Pre-installation environments
  - MSCONFIG
  - DEFRAG
  - REGSRV32
  - REGEDIT
  - Event viewer
  - Safe mode
  - Command prompt
  - Emergency repair disk
  - Automated system recovery

✓ **4.7 Given a scenario, troubleshoot common security issues with appropriate tools and best practices.**

- Common symptoms
  - Pop-ups
  - Browser redirection
  - Security alerts
  - Slow performance
  - Internet connectivity issues
  - PC locks up
  - Windows updates failures

- Rogue antivirus
- Spam
- Renamed system files
- Files disappearing
- File permission changes
- Hijacked email
- Access denied
- Tools
  - Anti-virus software
  - Anti-malware software
  - Anti-spyware software
  - Recovery console
  - System restore
  - Pre-installation environments
  - Event viewer
- Best practices for malware removal
  - Identify malware symptoms
  - Quarantine infected system
  - Disable system restore
  - Remediate infected systems
    - Update anti-virus software
    - Scan and removal techniques (safe mode, pre-installation environment)
  - Schedule scans and updates
  - Enable system restore and create restore point
  - Educate end user

✓ **4.8 Given a scenario, troubleshoot, and repair common laptop issues while adhering to the appropriate procedures.**

- Common symptoms
  - No display
  - Dim display

- Flickering display
- Sticking keys
- Intermittent wireless
- Battery not charging
- Ghost cursor
- No power
- Num lock indicator lights
- No wireless connectivity
- No Bluetooth connectivity
- Cannot display to external monitor
- Disassembling processes for proper re-assembly
  - Document and label cable and screw locations
  - Organize parts
  - Refer to manufacturer documentation
  - Use appropriate hand tools

✓ **4.9 Given a scenario, troubleshoot printers with appropriate tools.**

- Common symptoms
  - Streaks
  - Faded prints
  - Ghost images
  - Toner not fused to the paper
  - Creased paper
  - Paper not feeding
  - Paper jam
  - No connectivity
  - Garbled characters on paper
  - Vertical lines on page
  - Backed up print queue
  - Low memory errors

In this chapter, we will focus on the exam topics related to troubleshooting. We will follow the structure of the CompTIA A+ 220-802 exam blueprint, objective 4, and we will explore the nine subobjectives that the prospective exam taker will need to master before taking the exam.

4.1 Given a scenario, explain the troubleshooting theory

Most of those employed in the IT field who will be seeking CompTIA's A+ certification are regularly in positions where they need to know how to troubleshoot, repair, and maintain computer systems. The sequence of steps involved in troubleshooting are covered in objective 4.1 and are as follows:

1. Identify the problem.

2. Establish a theory of probable cause (question the obvious).

3. Test the theory to determine the cause.

4. Establish a plan of action to resolve the problem and implement the solution.

5. Verify full system functionality and, if applicable, implement preventive measures.

6. Document findings, actions, and outcomes.

Identify the problem

Although it may sound obvious, you can't troubleshoot a problem without knowing what the problem is. In some cases the problem will be obvious. But in others, especially when relying on the description of the problem by the user, it will appear to be one thing on the surface when in actuality the issue the user is experiencing is a symptom of a different, possibly larger problem. In this section, processes that can help bring clarity to the situation are discussed and a cautionary note about this step is covered as well.

Question the user and identify user changes to computer and perform backups before making changes

Identify the problem by questioning the user and identifying user changes to the computer. Before you do anything else, ask the user:

- What the problem is
- When the last time was that the problem didn't exist
- What has changed since

Be sure that you do a backup before you make any changes so that all of your actions can be undone, if necessary.

When performing this step, be wary of accepting the user's diagnosis of the problem at face value. For example, a user may start the conversation with the statement "The email server is down." At this point ask the question, "Is there anything else you cannot do besides open your email?" Ask them to try accessing a shared folder or the Internet. If either of those tasks fails, the problem is probably not the email server but basic network connectivity of their computer.

Establish a theory of probable cause (question the obvious)

As you get answers to your initial questions, theories will begin to evolve as to the root of the problem. Analyze the problem, including potential causes, and make an initial determination of whether it's a software or hardware problem. As you narrow down the problem, determine whether it's hardware or software related so you can act accordingly.

Once you have developed a list of possible causes, develop a list of tests you can perform to test each to narrow the list by eliminating each theory one by one. Don't forget to consider the obvious and make no assumptions. Just because the cable has worked every day for the last five years doesn't mean the person cleaning the office may not have caught the vacuum cleaner on the cable and damaged its connector last night.

Test the theory to determine cause

Test related components, including connections and hardware and software configurations; use Device Manager; and consult vendor documentation. Whatever the problem may be, the odds are good that someone else has experienced it before. Use the tools at your disposal—including manuals and websites—to try to zero in on the problem as expeditiously as possible.

Once theory is confirmed determine next steps to resolve problem

If your theory is confirmed, then determine the next steps you need to take to resolve the problem. In cases where you have determined the device where the problem lies but you have no expertise in that area, escalate the problem to someone as needed. For example, if you have narrowed down the problem to the router and you don't understand or manage the router, escalate the problem to the router administrator.

If theory is not confirmed re-establish new theory or escalate

If your theory is not confirmed, then come up with a new theory, or bring in someone with more expertise (escalate the problem). If you make changes to test one theory, make sure you reverse those changes before you test another theory. Making multiple changes can cause new problems and make the process even more difficult.

Establish a plan of action to resolve the problem and implement the solution

Evaluate the results, and develop an action plan of steps to fully resolve the problem. Keep in mind that it's possible that more than one thing is causing the problem. If that is the case, you may need to solve one problem and then turn your attention to the next.

Once you have planned your work, work your plan. Methodically make the required changes while always having a back-out plan if your changes cause a larger problem.

Verify full system functionality and if applicable implement preventive measures

When the problem is believed to be resolved, verify that the system is fully functional. If there are preventive measures that can be put in place to keep this situation from recurring, take those measures on this machine and all others where the problem may exist. Also keep in mind that times like this are great learning moments to teach users what role they may have played and what actions they may be able to take on their own in the future to prevent the problem, if that is appropriate.

Document findings, actions and outcomes

Document your activities and outcomes. Experience is a wonderful teacher, but only if you can remember what you've done. Documenting your actions and outcomes will help you (or a fellow administrator) troubleshoot a similar problem when it crops up in the future.

In some cases you may think you have solved a problem only to find it occurs again later because you only treated the symptom of a larger problem. When this type of thing occurs, documentation of what has occurred in the past can be very helpful in seeing patterns that otherwise would remain hidden.

Exam Essentials

Know the six main steps in the troubleshooting process.   The six steps are to identify the problem; establish a theory of probable cause; test the theory to determine the cause; establish a plan of action to resolve the problem and implement the solution; verify full system functionality and if applicable implement preventive measures; and document findings, actions, and outcomes.

4.2 Given a scenario, troubleshoot common problems related to motherboards, RAM, CPU and power with appropriate tools

While problems can occur with the operating system with little or no physical warning, that is rarely the case when it comes to hardware problems. Your senses will often alert you that something is wrong based on what you hear, smell, or see. In this section, common issues with the main players are discussed. The topics addressed in objective 4.2 include:

- Common symptoms
- Tools

Common symptoms

Once you have performed troubleshooting for some time, you will notice a pattern. With some exceptions, the same issues occur over and over and usually give you the same warnings each time. In this section, common symptoms or warning signs are covered. When you learn what these symptoms are trying to tell you, it makes your job easier.

Unexpected shutdowns

It doesn't get any more obvious that something is wrong when the computer just shuts down on its own. In some cases, a blue screen on the display with a lot of text precedes this shutdown. If that occurs, the problem is operating system related and may not involve a hardware issue. Operating system issues related to the "Blue Screen of Death" are covered in the section "BSOD" later in this chapter.

One common reason for shutdowns is overheating. Often when that is the case, however, the system reboots itself rather than just shutting down. Reboots are covered later in this section.

Always check the obvious, such as the power cable and the source of power. Check to see if a breaker flipped in the power box as well. Checking these items is an example of starting the process at the physical layer. If the computer is plugged into a power strip or UPS that has a fuse or breaker, check to see if the fuse blew or if the breaker flipped due to a power surge.

System lockups

Sometimes the system just freezes up and will not respond to any keyboard input or mouse clicks. The difference between a blue screen and a system lockup is whether the dump message that accompanies a blue screen is present. With a regular lockup, things just stop working. As with blue screens, lockups have been greatly reduced with more recent versions of the Microsoft operating systems (a notable exception may occur with laptops, which go to hibernate and then occasionally do not want to exit this mode). If lockups occur, you can examine the log files to discover what was happening (such as a driver loading) and take steps to correct it.

From a hardware standpoint, freezes or lockups can be caused by the following:

Memory Problems   A bad or failing memory chip, using memory that's too slow for the system, or using applications that require more memory than is present in the computer. Replace and upgrade the memory as required.

Virus or Malware   If the system freezes and there is still significant hard drive activity occurring, a virus could be present. Scan the system, preferably from an external source such as a memory stick or CD.

Video Driver   Bad video drivers can sometimes cause a lockup. Update the video driver.

POST code beeps

During the boot-up of the system, a power-on self-test (POST) occurs and each device is checked for functionality. If the system boots to the point where the video driver is loaded and the display is operational, any problems will be reported with a numeric error code.

If the system cannot boot to that point, problems will be reported with a beep code. Although each manufacturer's set of beep codes and their interpretation can be found in the documentation for the system or on the website of the manufacturer, one short beep always means everything is OK.

During startup, problems with devices that fail to be recognized properly, services that fail to start, and so on are written to the system log and can also be viewed with Event Viewer. If no POST error code prevents a successful boot, this utility provides information about what's been going on system-wise to help you troubleshoot problems. Event Viewer shows warnings, error messages, and records of things happening successfully. You can access it through Computer Management, or you can access it directly from the Administrative Tools in Control Panel.

Blank screen on bootup

When the screen is blank after boot-up and there are signs that the system has power and some functionality (perhaps you can hear the fan or you see lights on the system), the problem could lie in several areas. Consider these possibilities:

- Make sure the monitor is on. It has a power switch, so check it.

- If you hear the fan but the system doesn't boot, it could be the power to the motherboard. Check and reseat the power cable to the motherboard.

- Make sure the cable from the monitor to the system is connected properly and try changing it out with a known good cable.

- Try a known good video card to rule out a bad card.

BIOS time and settings resets

If you find that you are continually resetting the system time, it could be that the CMOS battery is dying. In the absence of an external time source, the time in the BIOS is where the system gets its cue for date and time. Change the CMOS battery and the problem should be solved.

Attempts to boot to incorrect device

When multiple volumes or partitions exist on the computer, or there are multiple hard drives and maybe CD/DVD and floppy drives as well, there are multiple potential sources for the boot files. If the system delivers an "operating system not found" message, it could be that the system is looking in the wrong location for the boot files.

The boot order is set in the BIOS. Check the boot order and ensure that it is set to boot to the partition, volume, and hard drive where the boot files are located. One thing that you should always check first is if there is no floppy in the floppy drive. When the system is running down the list of potential sources of boot files, in all other cases if it looks in a location and finds no boot files it will move on to the next location in the list. However, if a floppy is in the floppy drive and it checks the floppy drive and no boot files are present, it does not proceed but stops and issues the nonsystem disk message.

Boot problems can also occur with corruption of the boot files or missing components (such as the NTLDR file being "accidentally" deleted by an overzealous user). Luckily, during the installation of the OS, log files are created in the %SystemRoot% or %SystemRoot%\ Debug folder (C:\WINNT and C:\WINNT\DEBUG or C:\Windows and C:\Windows\Debug, depending on the operating system). If you have a puzzling problem, look at these logs to see if you can find error entries there. These are primarily helpful during installation. For routine troubleshooting, you can activate boot logging by selecting Enable Boot Logging from the Windows Advanced Options menu to create an ntbtlog.txt log file in the %systemroot% folder.

Continuous reboots

If the system reboots on its own, consider the following possibilities:

- Electrical problems such as brownouts (not a total loss of power but a sag in the power level) or blackouts can cause reboots.

- Power supply problems can cause reboots as well. The power supply continually sends a Power_Good signal to the motherboard and if this signal is not present momentarily the system will reset.

- Overheating is also a big cause of reboots. When CPUs get overheated, a cycle of reboots can ensue. Make sure the fan is working on the heat sink and the system fan is also working. If required, vacuum the dust from around the vents.

No power

Power problems usually involve the following issues and scenarios:

- Check the power cord and if it's plugged into a power strip or UPS, ensure the strip is plugged in (and if it has a breaker, check to see if it was tripped by a surge). In the case of a UPS, check whether the UPS battery is dead.

- Try replacing the power supply with a known good unit to see if the power supply failed.

Overheating

Under normal conditions, the PC cools itself by pulling in air. That air is used to dissipate the heat created by the processor (and absorbed by the heat sink). When airflow is restricted by clogged ports, a bad fan, and so forth, heat can build up inside the unit and cause problems. Chip creep—the unseating of components—is one of the more common byproducts of a cycle of overheating and cooling of the inside of the system.

Since the air is being pulled into the machine, excessive heat can originate from outside the PC as well, due to a hot working environment. The heat can be pulled in and cause the same problems. Take care to keep the ambient air within normal ranges (approximately 60–90 degrees Fahrenheit) and at a constant temperature.

Replacing slot covers is vital. Computers are designed to circulate air with slot covers in place or cards plugged into the ports. Leaving slots on the back of the computer open alters the air circulation and causes more dust to be pulled into the system.

Loud noise

When it comes right down to it, there are not a lot of moving parts within a PC. When you hear noise, you can begin to readily narrow down the possible culprits. The most common are the fan and the hard drive. No matter what is responsible, you will want to take immediate steps to shut down the machine and start the replacement process. Change each component you suspect with a known good replacement until the noise stops.

Intermittent device failure

One of the most vexing issues to troubleshoot is one that comes and goes. When presented with this type of behavior, consider the following possibilities:

- Try replacing the problem component with a known good one.

- A bad motherboard can cause these types of problems when there are issues with its circuitry. Try replacing the motherboard with a known good motherboard.

Fans spin – no power to other devices

This issue was discussed in the section "Blank screen on bootup."

Indicator lights

Many of the components in the system have an indicator light that should be in a specific state during normal operation. Status lights are often found on the network interface card (NIC) as well as on the front of a desktop model and in the display area of a laptop.

On the NIC, a display other than a green light can indicate that there are problems with the network; more important, though, the lack of any light can indicate that the card itself has gone bad.

The hard drive, CD-ROM, and tape or DVD drive lights will be on when activity is occurring and will blink accordingly. The power light should be a steady green.

Smoke

Smoke is never a good thing. Shut the system down immediately to prevent further damage. This is usually a burning or overheating component, usually the CPU.

Burning smell

A burning smell usually accompanies smoke but could be present after the smoke has ended because the burning component is now dead. Try to identify the damaged component through a visual inspection; if that is not possible, try to determine the damaged component by replacing parts one by one until functionality returns.

BSOD

Once a regular occurrence when working with Windows, blue screens (also known as the Blue Screen of Death) have become much less frequent. Occasionally systems will lock up, and you can usually examine the log files to discover what was happening when this occurred and then take the necessary steps to correct it. For example, if you see that a driver or application was loading before the crash, you can begin to isolate it as a possible problem. The details included in the BSOD error that comes up can help in troubleshooting the problem. It is often easy to query Microsoft's knowledgebase with the first part of the BSOD error to discover the component causing the problem. Often the knowledgebase article gives a detailed explanation of how to fix the problem as well.

In more recent versions of Windows (Vista and Windows 7), information from such crashes is written to XML files by the operating system. When the system becomes stable, a prompt usually appears asking for approval to send this information to Microsoft. The goal that Microsoft has in collecting this data is to be able to identify drivers that cause such problems and work with vendors to correct these issues.

Better-known error messages include the following:

Data_Bus_Error   This error is described on the Microsoft website: "The most common cause of this error message is a hardware problem. It usually occurs after the installation of faulty hardware, or when existing hardware fails. The problem is frequently related to defective RAM, L2 RAM cache, or video RAM. If hardware has recently been added to the system, remove it and test to see if the error still occurs."

Unexpected_Kernel_Mode_Trap   This error is described on the Microsoft website: "If hardware was recently added to the system, remove it to see if the error recurs. If existing hardware has failed, remove or replace the faulty component. Run hardware diagnostics supplied by the system manufacturer, especially the memory scanner, to determine which hardware component has failed. For details on these procedures, see the owner's manual for your computer. Setting the CPU to run at speeds above the rated specification (known as overclocking the CPU) can also cause this error."

Page_Fault_in_nonpaged_area   This error is described on the Microsoft website: "This Stop message usually occurs after the installation of faulty hardware or in the event of failure of installed hardware (usually related to defective RAM, either main memory, L2 RAM cache, or video RAM). If hardware has been added to the system recently, remove it to see if the error recurs. If existing hardware has failed, remove or replace the faulty component. Run hardware diagnostics supplied by the system manufacturer. For details on these procedures, see the owner's manual for your computer."

irql_not_less_or_equal   This error is described on the Microsoft website: "This Stop message indicates that a kernel-mode process or driver attempted to access a memory address to which it did not have permission to access. The most common cause of this error is an incorrect or corrupted pointer that references an incorrect location in memory. A pointer is a variable used by a program to refer to a block of memory. If the variable has an incorrect value in it, the program tries to access memory that it should not. When this occurs in a user-mode application, it generates an access violation. When it occurs in kernel mode, it generates a STOP 0x0000000A message. If you encounter this error while upgrading to a newer version of Windows, it might be caused by a device driver, a system service, a virus scanner, or a backup tool that is incompatible with the new version."

machine_check_exception   This error is described on the Microsoft website: "This behavior occurs because your computer processor detected and reported an unrecoverable hardware error to Windows XP. To do this, the processor used the Machine Check Exception (MCE) feature of Pentium processors or the Machine Check Architecture (MCA) feature of some Pentium Pro processors. The following factors may cause this error message:

- System bus errors
- Memory errors that may include parity or Error Correction Code (ECC) problems
- Cache errors in the processor or hardware
- Translation Lookaside Buffers (TLB) errors in the processor
- Other CPU-vendor specific detected hardware problems
- Vendor-specific detected hardware problems

Tools

There are troubleshooting tools that you should be familiar with that can aid you. In this section some of the most important tools are discussed.

Multimeter

Multimeters were discussed in Chapter 1, "PC Hardware." But just to review, these can be used to check voltages found on power plugs coming from the power supply to ensure the proper voltage is being delivered to the hard drive, motherboard, and other components. If that is not the case, components will not function properly and could be damaged.

Power supply tester

Inexpensive devices called power supply testers can go a bit beyond simply checking the voltage of the power cables. One of the things these devices can check is the proper operation of the Power_Good signal. If this signal is not working correctly, the computer will not boot from the power button but will do so when you press Ctrl+Alt+Del.

Loopback plugs

Loopback plugs are used to test the functionality of various types of ports, but their most common use is to test a network card. These plugs send a signal out of the card and then loop it back into the same card to test its operation. They look like an RJ-45 connector without the cable.

POST card

POST cards are plugged into one of the slots in the computer and when the computer is booting, the card will generate error codes on an LED. These codes serve a similar purpose as the beep codes discussed in the section "POST code beeps." In some cases the system is incapable of generating the codes.

Exam Essentials

Describe the common symptoms of hardware problems. These symptoms include unexpected shutdowns, lockups, and reboots, POST code beeps, blank screens on boot-up, loss of system timekeeping, attempts to boot to an incorrect device, overheating, loss of power, loud noises, intermittent device failures, smoke, a burning smell, and Blue Screens of Death.

Identify tools used in troubleshooting. These tools include but are not limited to multimeters, power supply testers, loopback plugs, and POST cards.

4.3 Given a scenario, troubleshoot hard drives and RAID arrays with appropriate tools

Hard drives must be operational for the system to function, and hard drive arrays such as RAID introduce an additional level of complexity. In this section, issues with hard drives and RAID arrays are discussed. The topics addressed in objective 4.3 include:

- Common symptoms
- Tools

Common symptoms

Hard drives and RAID arrays typically exhibit symptoms before they fail. Learning to read these clues is critical to troubleshooting. In this section, the most common of these clues and symptoms are discussed.

Read/write failure

Read/write failures occur when areas of the hard drive require repeated attempts before successful reads or writes occur. This is because these areas are at least partially damaged, although perhaps not enough for these areas to be marked as bad sectors.

Slow performance

Another symptom of hard drive issues is slow access to the drive. Oddly, one of the potential causes of this is insufficient memory. When this is the case, it causes excessive paging. Another cause can be a drive that needs to be defragmented. A fragmented drive results in it taking much longer for all of the parts of a file to be located before the file will open. Other issues that cause slow performance are controller cards that need updating, improper data cables, and slower devices sharing the same cable with the hard drive.

Loud clicking noise

A loud clicking noise, sometimes referred to as the "click of death," is caused by the read/write heads making contact with the platters. After that happens, both the heads and the platters become damaged and the system becomes unable to establish a successful starting point to read the drive. This is serious damage and cannot be repaired. Back up all of the data if that's still possible (which at that point may not be the case). If the drive is beyond readable, the only option to recover the data is with the help of a professional data recovery service. At that point you must balance the cost of the recovery with the value of the data. This is a case where regular backups save the day!

Failure to boot

A failure of the system to boot can be caused by a number of issues. Among them are:

- Failure of the system to locate the boot files. See the section "Attempts to boot to incorrect device."

- If you are presented with an "IDE drive not ready" at startup, the drive may not be spinning up fast enough to be read during startup. Enable or increase the hard disk predelay time.

- If you receive the "Immediately back up all your data and replace your hard drive. A fault may be imminent" message, take it seriously. This means the drive is using Self-Monitoring, Analysis, and Reporting Technology (SMART) to predict a failure.

- The hard drive data or power cable may have become unseated. Sometimes even if the cable appears to be seated fine, reseating it can have a positive effect. Also ensure that the data cable has not been reversed.

Drive not recognized

If the system does not recognize the drive, the problem could be the following:

- The hard drive data or power cable may have become unseated. Sometimes even if the cable appears to be seated fine, reseating it can have a positive effect. Also ensure that the data cable has not been reversed.

- If you just added a drive, ensure that both drives have not been set to master or slave and that the boot drive is set as master on the first channel.

- If the system uses serial ATA and you just added a drive, ensure that all of the onboard SATA ports are enabled.

- If you just added a drive, ensure that there is no conflict between the new drive and another device.

- If you receive the "No boot device available, strike F1 to retry boot, F2 for setup utility" message, it could be incorrect drive geometry (probably not the case if this drive has been functioning properly before), bad CMOS battery, or inability to locate the active partition or master boot record.

OS not found

When you receive the "operating system not found" message, it's usually a software error rather than a hardware error. It could be that the master boot record cannot be located or the active partition cannot be located. These issues can be corrected in Windows by rebooting the computer into Recovery mode and executing one of several commands at the command line of the Recovery environment. See the section on the Recovery Console in Chapter 6, "Operating Systems."

RAID not found

RAID can either be software or hardware based. When hardware-based RAID is implemented, a RAID controller card is installed into a slot and the RAID drives connect to that controller card. When the RAID array cannot be located, usually it's a problem with the controller card.

One item to check if you just installed the RAID controller card is that RAID is set in the BIOS. It is also possible that the computer has a built-in RAID controller. If that is the case, there will be ports for the drives in the motherboard. Ensure that the two hard drives (or three) are connected to the same port group.

If the RAID system has been operational, check all of the cables connecting the drives to the motherboard, reseating them to ensure a good connection. Also ensure the BIOS is still set to RAID.

If there is no onboard RAID controller and the controller card is installed in a slot, ensure that the card is seated properly (maybe even try reseating it). Also ensure that all of the drives are securely connected to the ribbon cable coming from the controller card.

RAID stops working

In some cases, one of the drives in the RAID array will cease to function and, depending on the type of RAID, can cause the entire array to be unavailable.

If this is a RAID 1 or a mirrored set, you should still be able to access the other drive. To determine which drive is bad, remove each drive one by one and reboot until you have identified the bad drive. Replace the bad drive and use the RAID software to rebuild the array.

If this is a RAID 5 array, follow the same procedure. The bad news is that if more than one drive has failed you will not be able to rebuild the array. You will need to create the array again after replacing the bad drives and then restore the data from backup.

Once the bad drives have been replaced, the system may rearrange the drives such that the system cannot locate the drive with the operating system. Use the RAID setup program that you access during boot-up to set the boot order of the drives in the array with the drive with the operating system first in the list.

BSOD

When presented with a Blue Screen of Death (BSOD), it's often difficult to interpret the problem. Always try rebooting, which in many cases causes it to go away. When dealing with the ambiguity of the BSOD, it is often useful to ask yourself these questions:

- Did I just make any changes?
- Is there any component that has been exhibiting symptoms of a problem?

If you just changed a hard drive, made a hard drive configuration change, installed a new driver, or have been dealing with hard drive issues, you have reason to suspect that as the source of the BSOD. Try reversing the change you made and rebooting; if that helps, it indicates something faulty or detrimental about your change.

If you have multiple drives, try removing them one by one and observe the effect on the BSOD. Once you have located the drive causing the BSOD, begin to consider what the problem with the drive is or simply replace it, if no possible remedy comes to mind.

Tools

Troubleshooting and working on hard drives requires some tools, both hardware and software. In this section, tools used in the process of troubleshooting hard drives are covered. The types of external enclosures encountered in the process of getting at the hard drives physically are also discussed.

Screwdriver

Screws of various sizes and types hold many parts of the PC together, from the case itself to internal hard drives in their drive bays. The following types of screwdrivers should be a part of your tool kit when dealing with hard drive issues:

- Phillips screwdriver (nonmagnetic)

- Hex driver (looks like a screw driver with a head like a socket wrench). The most common size is the 3/16″ but you may also need the 1/4″ ones as well.

- Magnetic screwdrivers. These can be used, but you should be careful to avoid touching them to anything on the board or touching the hard drive.

External enclosures

Before you can get to the hard drives, you have to open the external enclosure. Enclosure designs have evolved over the years, but one of the most common types and the approach to opening it are covered in this section.

Unfasten the computer's cover by removing any retaining screws at the back of the computer. Some cases don't have screws; instead, they have a sliding bar or latches that release the cover. Many of today's PCs can be completely disassembled without a single tool.

Then, remove the cover by sliding or lifting it. The exact procedure varies greatly depending on the case; Figure 9.1 shows an example for a desktop-style case.

 Don't remove all the screws at the back of the computer! Some of these **WARNING** screws hold vital components (such as the power supply) to the case, and removing them will cause those components to drop into the computer.

CHKDSK

CHKDSK is an older MS-DOS utility that is used to correct logical errors in the FAT filesystem. The most common switch for the chkdsk command is /F, which fixes the errors that it finds. Without /f, chkdsk is an information-only command.

FIGURE 9.1   Removing the enclosure

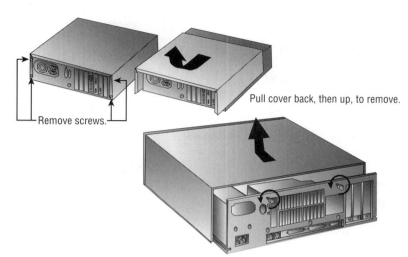

Remove screws.

Pull cover back, then up, to remove.

format

When implementing a new hard drive and creating new partitions or volumes, you must format the partition or volume before data can be written to it. You can do this for both FAT and NTFS partitions by using the Disk Management utility or by using the formatting function that is available during the installation of an operating system.

Another older option is to use the format command. It is executed at the command line and will not only format the volume or partition but will also erase all data, so you should be aware of that end result as well. To format the C: drive, you execute format c:.

fdisk

Another command whose thunder has been stolen by other methods is fdisk. It is used to view partition information and to create and delete volumes or partitions. Once you have executed the command, the menu shown in Figure 9.2 will be displayed. Here you can view, create, and delete using the menu. Something to note about this command is that changes you make will not be acted on until you reboot the computer.

File recovery software

In some cases, a hard drive cannot be saved but the data can be recovered. Data recovery companies can recover data from some of the most damaged hard drives you can imagine, but the cost is high. Before going to those lengths to recover data from damaged drives or simply to recover data that may have been inadvertently deleted, consider using data recovery software. Popular examples are Data Rescue, Advanced Disk Recovery, and Recover My Files.

FIGURE 9.2 Using fdisk

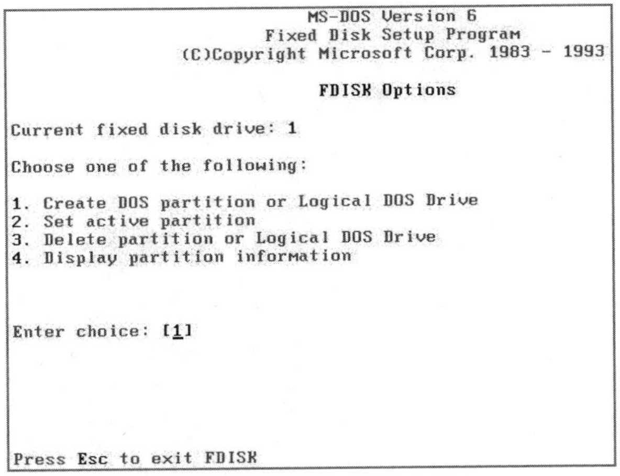

```
                    MS-DOS Version 6
                 Fixed Disk Setup Program
           (C)Copyright Microsoft Corp. 1983 - 1993

                      FDISK Options

Current fixed disk drive: 1

Choose one of the following:

1. Create DOS partition or Logical DOS Drive
2. Set active partition
3. Delete partition or Logical DOS Drive
4. Display partition information



Enter choice: [1]




Press Esc to exit FDISK
```

Exam Essentials

Identify the most common symptoms of hard drive issues.   These include but are not limited to read/write failures, slow performance, loud clicking noises, boot failures, unrecognizable drives, missing operating systems, and Blue Screens of Death.

List symptoms of RAID array issues.   These include missing arrays and RAID arrays that stop functioning.

Describe hardware troubleshooting tools.   These include screwdrivers of various types and their proper use in opening the external enclosures and drive bays.

Use software troubleshooting tools.   Utilize tools such as CHKDSK, format, fdisk, and file recovery software.

4.4 Given a scenario, troubleshoot common video and display issues

Video and display problems may not rate at the top of the priority list for technicians (unless the display is not functioning at all), but to a user, problems with their display may seem like a huge issue. In this section, common video- and display-related symptoms and their possible sources are discussed. The topics addressed in objective 4.4 include:

- Common symptoms

Common symptoms

Display monitors can exhibit a wide range of symptoms when video-related problems arise. Some are as obvious as no signal whatsoever, whereas other symptoms can be so slight as to almost defy detection. In this section, common symptoms are discussed and some approaches to dealing with these issues are suggested.

VGA mode

When a display ceases to function at the resolution level supported by the video card and reverts to 16-bit VGA mode (Lo-resolution in Windows 7 and Vista), the problem is almost always video drivers. If the issue arises during the installation of a new video card, then the driver was not found in the cache of drivers provided with the operating system.

Even if the video card is plug-and-play, the driver must be present. If it is not, the computer will not be able to use the card and will revert to using VGA mode (Lo-resolution in Windows 7 and Vista). Another common problem associated with drivers is not having the current version—as problems are fixed, the drivers are updated, and you can often save a great deal of time by downloading the latest drivers from the vendor's site early in the troubleshooting process.

The easiest way to see or change drivers in Windows Vista and Windows 7 is to click the Driver tab in the Properties dialog box for the device. For example, to see the driver associated with the hard drive in Windows 7, double-click the hard drive in Device Manager (Start ➢ Settings ➢ Control Panel ➢ System, and then click Device Manager in the Task list), and choose the Driver tab. Among other things, this shows the driver provider, date, version, and signer. You can choose to view details about it, update it, roll it back to a previous driver, or uninstall it. If the installation of the device resulted in VGA mode (Lo-resolution in Windows 7 and Vista), then you need to select Update Driver and point the system to the CD or local folder where the correct driver is located.

No image on screen

When there is no image on the screen, the display is either dead or it is not receiving the signal from the computer. Check the cable from the back of the PC to the monitor and ensure it is tightly screwed in place, and reseat the cables if required.

To eliminate the video card as the problem, connect a known good display to the computer and see if the same problem exists. If so, then the problem is not the display. If it works fine, the problem is the display. Displays do die and usually are not cost effective to repair. The usual solution is to replace the display.

If the card is the problem, try reseating it. If that provides no relief, insert a known good card. Operating in the same fashion as you did with the display, you can determine whether the video card is the problem.

Overheat shutdown

When the video card is overheating, it can cause display problems and shutdowns. Overheating video cards usually exhibit symptoms like garbled output on the display or artifacts (covered later in this section). It also can result in flickers and flashes. In some cases, the display will cease functioning after being on a few seconds. After you restart the computer, the display again works for a few seconds and then fails.

When overheating is the problem, you must find the reason for the overheating. Clean all the dust out of the inside of the case and inspect all fans to ensure they are functioning—especially the fan on the video card if one is present. If the problem has been present for some time, the card may have become damaged. Try using a different card and see if the problem goes away. You may need to replace the video card.

Dead pixels

Pixels are the very small dots on the screen that are filled with a color and as a group presents the image you see on the screen. Two conditions can occur with the pixels: stuck pixels and bad or dead pixels.

Stuck pixels have been filled with a color and are not changing as required to display changes in the image. Dead pixels are simply black with no color in them.

When there are very few of these and they are not clustered in the same spot, you may not even be able to notice them. When they build to the point where they are noticeable, they cannot be fixed. You may be able to get some satisfaction from the manufacturer depending on how old the monitor is and the policy of the vendor.

Artifacts

Artifacts are visual anomalies that appear on the screen. They might be pieces of images left over from a previous image or a "tear in the image" (it looks like the image is divided into two parts and the parts don't line up).

Artifacts can be generated whenever hardware components such as the processor, memory chip, or cabling malfunction causing data corruption. It may be caused by physical damage, but the first thing to check is overheating of the graphics processor or video card. Use the same techniques described in the section "Overheat shutdown."

Color patterns incorrect

When the image displayed uses incorrect color patterns or is garbled, the root of the problem could depend on when the condition presents itself. If the screen looks fine during the POST but then goes bad when Windows starts to load, it probably is due to an incorrect setting of the video card. For example, it may be set to do something the card is incapable of doing. Restart in Safe mode (which will cause the system to use the VGA driver) and check all of the settings of the card while ensuring that it is not set for a resolution level for which the card is not capable. You may also try updating the driver if a new one is available.

If this problem occurs from the moment you turn the system on, the problem is hardware and you should check the monitor, cable, and card, replacing each with a known good piece until you isolate the bad component.

Dim image

If the image is fine but dim, first check the brightness setting, usually found in the front of the monitor. If this is a laptop, remember there are Function keys that when hit inadvertently will dim the screen as well. Check that.

If it is a CRT, then the display is probably dying and needs replacing.

If it is an LCD, the backlight may be going bad. You learned earlier that these are pencil-sized lights that go behind the screen. They can be replaced on a laptop by following the procedure for opening the laptop lid (where the display resides) and replacing the backlight. Keep in mind that opening the case voids the warranty, so if you still have warranty left, make use of that option.

If it is the backlight on a desktop LCD, the backlight can be replaced for about $20, so it makes a repair worth doing if you want to open up the monitor. Use the documentation or the vendor website for details on opening the case.

Flickering image

When the image is flickering, check the cables and ensure they are seated properly. If that doesn't help, try different cables as it could be a problem with the cable itself.

Another possible reason is a mismatch between the resolution settings and the refresh rate. If this is the problem, it will only occur when using the higher resolutions. You should increase the refresh rate to support the higher resolutions.

Distorted image

This behavior can be caused by problems with power. Try replacing the power cable, and if that doesn't help, try plugging the monitor into a different wall outlet. Sometimes other devices on the same line (air conditioner, refrigerator, and so forth) can cause problems for the supply of power to the monitor.

Discoloration (degaussing)

An issue only with CRT displays, discoloration can be caused by the buildup of magnetism in the display. Exposure to a magnetic field can cause swirls and fuzziness even in high-quality monitors. The earth generates magnetic fields, as do unshielded speakers and power surges. Most monitors have metal shields that can protect against magnetic fields. But eventually these shields can become polluted by taking on the same magnetic field as the earth, so they become useless.

To solve this problem, these monitors have a built-in feature known as Degauss; it removes the effects of the magnetic field by creating a stronger magnetic field with opposite polarity that gradually fades to a field of zero. A special Degauss button or feature in the monitor's onscreen software activates it. You need only press it when the picture starts to deteriorate. The image will shake momentarily during the Degauss cycle and then return to normal.

BSOD

As with all Blue Screens of Death (BSODs), you should always ask yourself, "What did I just change?" When caused by display problems, BSODs are usually related to changes to the settings of the display that are not supported or by changing the video driver to one that is causing the BSOD. Reverse the action that may have caused the BSOD.

If this removes the BSOD and allows the system to function, you know what caused the problem. Using the documentation and the vendor website, investigate what there is about the change you made that is problematic; if the problem is a driver update, roll back to the old driver until you have a chance to obtain a driver that does not result in a BSOD.

Exam Essentials

List the common symptoms of display problems and the appropriate troubleshooting technique for each. These include but are not limited to reversion to VGA mode, no image, overheating, dead pixels, artifacts, incorrect color patterns, dim, flickering or distorted image, discoloration (degaussing), and BSOD. Resolution techniques include updating drivers, degaussing, changing resolution settings and replacing the monitor.

4.5 Given a scenario, troubleshoot wired and wireless networks with appropriate tools

At one time wireless networks were considered an extravagant and insecure addition to the enterprise network, but now users expect wireless access. No longer is it a business advantage; it is now a business requirement. In this section, troubleshooting both wired and wireless networks is covered. The topics addressed in objective 4.5 include:

- Common symptoms
- Tools

Common symptoms

Network problems, usually manifesting themselves as an inability to connect to resources, can arise from many different sources. In this section, some common symptoms of networking issues are discussed.

No connectivity

When no connectivity can be established with the network, your troubleshooting approach should begin at the Physical layer and then proceed up the OSI model. As components at each layer are eliminated as the source of the problem, proceed to the next higher layer. A simple yet effective set of steps might be as follows:

1. Check the network cable to ensure it is the correct cable type (crossover or straight through) and that it is functional. If in doubt, try a different cable.

2. Ensure that the NIC is functional and the TCP/IP protocol is installed and functional by pinging the loopback address 127.0.0.1. If required, install or reinstall TCP/IP and/or replace or repair the NIC.

3. Check the local IP configuration and ensure that the IP address, subnet mask, and gateway are correct. If the default gateway can be pinged, the computer is configured correctly for its local network and the problem lies beyond the router or with the destination device. If pings to the gateway are unsuccessful, ensure that the IP configurations of the router interface and the computer are compatible and in the same subnet.

When dealing with a wireless network, ensure that the wireless card is functional. The wireless card is easily disabled with a key stroke on a laptop and should be the first thing to check. If the network uses a hidden SSID, ensure that the station in question is configured with the correct SSID.

APIPA address

Automatic Private IP Addressing (APIPA) is a TCP/IP feature Microsoft added to their operating systems. If a DHCP server cannot be found, the clients automatically assign themselves an IP address, somewhat randomly, in the 169.254.*x.x* range with a subnet mask of 255.255.0.0. This allows them to communicate with other hosts that have similarly configured themselves, but they will be unable to connect to the Internet or to any machines or resources that have DHCP-issued IP addresses.

If the network uses DHCP for IP configuration and the computer with the connectivity issue has an APIPA address, the problem is one of these three things:

- The DHCP server is out of IP addresses.

- The DHCP server is on the other side of a router and there is no functional DHCP relay present or no IP helper address configured on the router—all of which is to say the DHCP request is not reaching the DHCP server.

- The computer has a basic connectivity issue preventing it from connecting to the network (see the section "No connectivity").

Limited connectivity

In some cases, the computer has connectivity to some but not all resources. When this is the case, issues that may reside on other layers of the OSI model should come under consideration. These include:

Authentication Issues   Does the user have the permission to access the resource?

DNS Issues   You may be able to ping the entire network using IP addresses, but most access is done by name, not IP address. If you can't ping resources by name, DNS is not functional, meaning either the DNS server is down or the local machine is not configured with the correct IP address of the DNS server.

Remote Problem   Don't forget that establishing a connection is a two-way street, and if the remote device has an issue, communication cannot occur. Always check the remote device as well. Any interconnecting device between the computer and resource, such as a switch or router, should also be checked for functionality.

Local connectivity

When a computer can communicate only on its local network or subnet, the problem is usually one of the following:

Incorrect Subnet Mask   Sometimes an incorrect mask will prevent all communication, but in some cases it results in successful connections locally but not remotely (outside the local subnet). The subnet mask value should be the same mask used on the router interface connecting to the local network.

Incorrect Default Gateway Address   If the computer cannot connect to the default gateway, it will be confined to communicating with devices on the local network. This IP address should be that of the router interface connecting to the local network.

Router Problem   If all users on the network are having connectivity problems, you likely have a routing issue that should be escalated to the proper administrators.

Intermittent connectivity

When a connectivity issue comes and goes, it can be a hardware issue or a software issue. The following hardware components should be checked for functionality:

Network Cable   A damaged cable can cause intermittent connectivity.

Network Interface Card   If the NIC is not properly seated or has worked its way partially out of its slot, it can cause connections that come and go.

Interference   On a wireless network, cordless phones, microwave ovens, and other wireless networks can interfere with transmissions. Also users who stray too far from the access point can also experience a signal that comes and goes.

Software issues that can cause intermittent connectivity include:

DHCP Issues   When the DHCP server is down or out of IP addresses, the problem will not manifest itself to those users who already have an IP address until their lease expires and they need a new address. In this case, some users will be fine and others will not, and then users who were fine earlier in the day may have problems later when their IP address lease expires.

DNS Problems   If the DNS server is down or malfunctioning, it will cause problems for DNS clients who need name resolution requests answered. For users who have already connected to resources in the last hour before the outage, connectivity to those resources will still be possible until the name-to-IP address mapping is removed from the client DNS resolver cache.

IP conflict

IP addresses conflicts are somewhat rare when DHCP is in use, but they can still happen. DHCP servers and clients both check for IP duplication when the DHCP client receives an IP address, but the process doesn't always work. Moreover, if someone with a statically configured IP address connects to the network with the same address as another machine, a conflict will exist.

Regardless of how the conflict occurs, it must be resolved because until it is, one or possibly both computers with the same address will not be able to network. You can determine the MAC address of the computer with which you are experiencing the conflict by using the ping command followed by the arp -d command.

Slow transfer speeds

Slow transmission on the network can be caused by hardware and software issues. Some of the physical issues that can cause slow performance are:

Interference   Both wireless and wired networks can be affected by interface from electromagnetic interference (EMI) and radio frequency interference (RFI). EMI will degrade network performance. This can be identified by the poor operation present. Be sure to run cables around (not over) ballasts and other items that can cause EMI. RFI is a similar issue introduced by radio waves. Wireless networks suffer even more from both of these issues.

Incorrect Cabling   The network can only go as fast as its weakest link. Using CAT 3 cabling, for example, will only allow the network to operate at 10 Mbps even if all of the network cards are capable of 10 Gbps.

Malfunctioning NIC   Network interface cards (NICs) can malfunction and cause a broadcast storm. These broadcast packets fill the network with traffic that slows performance for all. Use a protocol analyzer to determine the MAC address of the offending computer.

From a software standpoint, the following issues can result in less than ideal performance:

Router Misconfiguration   If the router is not configured correctly, it can cause slow performance due to less than optimal routing paths. Escalate the issue to the appropriate administrators.

Switch Misconfiguration   An improperly implemented redundant switch network can result in switching loops that cause slow performance. Escalate the issue to the appropriate administrators.

Low RF signal

In a wireless network, the signal coming from the access point has a distance limit. With some variation by standard, this is about 300 feet. However, this distance is impacted by obstructions and interference in the area. The WLAN design should include a site survey that identifies these issues and locates access points (APs) and antenna types in such a way as to mitigate these effects.

It is also useful to know that APs and some client radios have a setting to control signal strength. It is not a normal practice to change the setting in a laptop wireless card, but it may be necessary to change the transmit level on an AP. In many cases, it is actually beneficial to reduce the transmit level of an AP in situations where it is interfering with other APs in your network or you want to limit the range of the signal to prevent it leaving the building. This is especially true in high-density areas where several APs are collocated in the same area for increased throughput.

Tools

There are a number of tools at your disposal when troubleshooting. Some of these tools have already been discussed, and some are new to the discussion. In this section, some of the main ones are covered.

Cable tester

Commonly used with network cabling, cable testers are used to verify that the cable you are using is good. You can perform many of the same tests with a multimeter. Although trading a known good cable for a suspected bad cable is also acceptable, a cable tester can help determine exactly what's wrong with the cable.

Loopback plug

Also called wrap plugs, loopback plugs take the signal going out and essentially echo it back. This allows you to test parallel, serial, and network ports to make certain they're working correctly. This is a good way to eliminate or implicate the NIC as a problem.

Punch down tools

A punch-down tool is used when you are securing cables to the patch panel that have been run from the wall outlets into the switch room. A wire is pre-positioned into a slotted post, and then the punch-down tool is pressed down on top of the wire, over the post. Once the required pressure is reached, the internal spring is triggered, and the blade pushes the wire into the slot, cutting the insulation and securing the wire. A punch-down tool is shown in Figure 9.3.

FIGURE 9.3   Punch-down tool

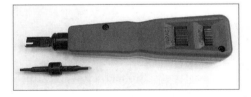

WIKIPEDIA COMMONS/ADAMANTIOS

Toner probes

Toner probes (also called tone generators) are used to locate the correct cable coming into a patch panel from the wall outlet when connections have either not been labeled or the labels have been removed from the patch panel. They are two-piece units (sometimes called Fox and Hound) where one end sends a signal and the other end is used to locate the wires that contain the signal in the switch room. A set is displayed in Figure 9.4.

FIGURE 9.4 Toner probe

WIKIPEDIA COMMONS/ADAMANTIOS

Wire strippers

Wire strippers are used to prepare the end of a cable for the attachment of a connector. They are used to remove the plastic covering and any shielding to get to the wire pairs contained in a twisted pair wire. This functionality is often included with the crimper (see the next section).

Crimper

A crimper is used to attach a connector to a cable by securing each wire (8 of them in a twisted-pair wire) to the proper connector in an RJ-45 connector. It usually also includes a stripper as well. A coaxial crimper is shown in Figure 9.5.

FIGURE 9.5 Crimper

WIKIPEDIA COMMONS/TRÅDLÖST IMAGEBANK

ping

The ping command makes use of the ICMP protocol to test connectivity between two devices. ping is one of the most useful commands in the TCP/IP protocol. It sends a series of packets to another system, which in turn sends back a response. The ping utility can be extremely useful for troubleshooting problems with remote hosts.

The ping command indicates whether the host can be reached and how long it took for the host to send a return packet. On a LAN, the time is indicated as less than 10 milliseconds. Across WAN links, however, this value can be much greater. When the -a parameter is included, it will also attempt to resolve the hostname associated with the IP address. An example of a successful ping is shown in Figure 9.6.

FIGURE 9.6   Ping

```
C:\Users\tmcmillan>ping 10.88.2.103

Pinging 10.88.2.103 with 32 bytes of data:
Reply from 10.88.2.103: bytes=32 time<1ms TTL=128
Reply from 10.88.2.103: bytes=32 time<1ms TTL=128
Reply from 10.88.2.103: bytes=32 time<1ms TTL=128
Reply from 10.88.2.103: bytes=32 time<1ms TTL=128

Ping statistics for 10.88.2.103:
    Packets: Sent = 4, Received = 4, Lost = 0 (0% loss),
Approximate round trip times in milli-seconds:
    Minimum = 0ms, Maximum = 0ms, Average = 0ms
```

ipconfig

The ipconfig command is used to view the IP configuration of a device and, when combined with certain switches or parameters, can be used to release and renew the lease of an IP address obtained from a DHCP server and to flush the DNS resolver cache. Its most common use is to view the current configuration. Figure 9.7 show its execution with the /all switch, which results in a display of a wealth of information about the IP configuration.

ipconfig can be used to release and renew a configuration obtained from a DHCP server by issuing first the ipconfig /release command, followed by the ipconfig /renew command.

It is also helpful to know that when you have just corrected a configuration error (such as an IP address) on a destination device, you should ensure that the device registers its new IP address with the DNS server by executing the ipconfig /registerdns command.

It may also be necessary to clear incorrect IP address to hostname mappings that may still exist on the devices that were attempting to access the destination device. This can be done by executing the ipconfig /flushdns command.

tracert

The tracert command (called traceroute in Linux and UNIX) is used to trace the path of a packet through the network. Its best use is in determining exactly where in the network the packet is being dropped. It will show each hop (router) the packet crosses and how long it takes to do so. A partial display of a traced route to www.msn.com is shown in Figure 9.8.

FIGURE 9.7   Using ipconfig

```
C:\Users\tmcmillan>ipconfig/all

Windows IP Configuration

   Host Name . . . . . . . . . . . . : tmcmillan
   Primary Dns Suffix  . . . . . . . : alpha.kaplaninc.com
   Node Type . . . . . . . . . . . . : Hybrid
   IP Routing Enabled. . . . . . . . : No
   WINS Proxy Enabled. . . . . . . . : No
   DNS Suffix Search List. . . . . . : alpha.kaplaninc.com
                                       kaplaninc.com

Ethernet adapter Local Area Connection:

   Connection-specific DNS Suffix  . : alpha.kaplaninc.com
   Description . . . . . . . . . . . : Broadcom NetXtreme 57xx Gigabit Controlle
r
   Physical Address. . . . . . . . . : 00-1A-A0-E1-95-AB
   DHCP Enabled. . . . . . . . . . . : Yes
   Autoconfiguration Enabled . . . . : Yes
   Link-local IPv6 Address . . . . . : fe80::ada3:8b73:a66e:6bc0%10(Preferred)
   IPv4 Address. . . . . . . . . . . : 10.88.2.103(Preferred)
   Subnet Mask . . . . . . . . . . . : 255.255.254.0
   Lease Obtained. . . . . . . . . . : Monday, January 30, 2012 9:38:37 AM
   Lease Expires . . . . . . . . . . : Tuesday, January 31, 2012 9:38:37 AM
   Default Gateway . . . . . . . . . : 10.88.2.6
   DHCP Server . . . . . . . . . . . : 10.88.10.48
   DHCPv6 IAID . . . . . . . . . . . : 234887840
   DHCPv6 Client DUID. . . . . . . . : 00-01-00-01-14-EE-0F-98-00-1A-A0-E1-95-AB

   DNS Servers . . . . . . . . . . . : 10.88.10.48
                                       10.75.139.18
   NetBIOS over Tcpip. . . . . . . . : Enabled
```

FIGURE 9.8   Using tracert

```
C:\Users\tmcmillan>tracert www.msn.com

Tracing route to us.co1.cb3.glbdns.microsoft.com [70.37.131.153]
over a maximum of 30 hops:

  1    11 ms     1 ms     1 ms  10.88.2.6
  2     2 ms     2 ms     1 ms  208-47-7-130.dia.static.qwest.net [208.47.7.130]
  3     7 ms     7 ms     7 ms  frp-edge-04.inet.qwest.net [205.168.14.213]
  4     7 ms     7 ms     7 ms  frp-core-02.inet.qwest.net [205.171.22.49]
  5    22 ms    22 ms    22 ms  chx-edge-03.inet.qwest.net [67.14.38.1]
  6    22 ms    22 ms    23 ms  63-234-10-14.dia.static.qwest.net [63.234.10.14]
  7    23 ms    23 ms    23 ms  xe-0-1-2-0.ch1-16c-1b.ntwk.msn.net [207.46.43.20
4]
  8    24 ms    24 ms    24 ms  xe-0-1-0-0.ch1-96c-1a.ntwk.msn.net [207.46.46.13
3]
  9    34 ms    34 ms    34 ms  ge-2-1-0-0.ash-64cb-1b.ntwk.msn.net [207.46.45.1
4]
 10    38 ms    38 ms    38 ms  ge-4-0-0-0.nyc-64cb-1b.ntwk.msn.net [207.46.46.5
7]
 11    39 ms    38 ms    38 ms  xe-3-1-0-0.ewr-96cbe-1b.ntwk.msn.net [207.46.47.
2]
 12    39 ms     *       39 ms  xe-3-0-0-0.ewr-96cbe-1a.ntwk.msn.net [207.46.43.
250]
 13
```

netstat

The netstat (network status) command is used to see what ports are listening on the TCP/IP-based system. The -a option is used to show all ports, and /? is used to show what other options are available (the options differ based on the operating system you are using). When executed with no switches the command displays the current connections, as shown in Figure 9.9.

FIGURE 9.9   Using netstat

```
C:\Users\tmcmillan>netstat

Active Connections

  Proto  Local Address          Foreign Address          State
  TCP    10.88.2.103:51273      64.94.18.154:https        ESTABLISHED
  TCP    10.88.2.103:51525      sratl060:microsoft-ds     ESTABLISHED
  TCP    10.88.2.103:51529      gmonsalvatge:microsoft-ds ESTABLISHED
  TCP    10.88.2.103:51573      sjc-not18:http            ESTABLISHED
  TCP    10.88.2.103:51716      schexv02:2785             ESTABLISHED
  TCP    10.88.2.103:51720      schvoip01:epmap           ESTABLISHED
  TCP    10.88.2.103:51721      schvoip01:1297            ESTABLISHED
  TCP    10.88.2.103:51722      schvoip01:1299            ESTABLISHED
  TCP    10.88.2.103:51824      69.31.116.27:http         CLOSE_WAIT
  TCP    10.88.2.103:51965      dcalpsch2:1026            ESTABLISHED
  TCP    10.88.2.103:53865      cs219p3:5050              ESTABLISHED
  TCP    10.88.2.103:53871      sip109:http               ESTABLISHED
  TCP    10.88.2.103:62522      ord08s08-in-f22:https     ESTABLISHED
  TCP    10.88.2.103:62567      ord08s08-in-f22:https     CLOSE_WAIT
  TCP    10.88.2.103:62682      by2msg3010613:http        ESTABLISHED
  TCP    10.88.2.103:63554      baymsg1020213:msnp        ESTABLISHED
  TCP    10.88.2.103:63770      v-client-2b:https         CLOSE_WAIT
  TCP    10.88.2.103:63771      ec2-174-129-205-197:https CLOSE_WAIT
  TCP    10.88.2.103:63772      v-client-2b:https         CLOSE_WAIT
  TCP    10.88.2.103:63773      65.55.121.231:http        ESTABLISHED
  TCP    10.88.2.103:63774      168.75.207.20:http        ESTABLISHED
  TCP    10.88.2.103:63777      65.55.17.30:http          ESTABLISHED
  TCP    10.88.2.103:63779      70.37.131.11:http         ESTABLISHED
  TCP    10.88.2.103:63781      65.124.174.56:http        ESTABLISHED
  TCP    10.88.2.103:63788      69.31.76.41:http          ESTABLISHED
  TCP    10.88.2.103:63791      207.46.140.46:http        ESTABLISHED
  TCP    10.88.2.103:63792      64.4.21.39:http           ESTABLISHED
  TCP    127.0.0.1:2002         tmcmillan:51543           ESTABLISHED
  TCP    127.0.0.1:19872        tmcmillan:51571           ESTABLISHED
  TCP    127.0.0.1:51543        tmcmillan:2002            ESTABLISHED
  TCP    127.0.0.1:51549        tmcmillan:51550           ESTABLISHED
  TCP    127.0.0.1:51550        tmcmillan:51549           ESTABLISHED
  TCP    127.0.0.1:51571        tmcmillan:19872           ESTABLISHED
  TCP    127.0.0.1:53869        tmcmillan:53870           ESTABLISHED
  TCP    127.0.0.1:53870        tmcmillan:53869           ESTABLISHED
  TCP    127.0.0.1:63557        tmcmillan:63574           ESTABLISHED
  TCP    127.0.0.1:63574        tmcmillan:63557           ESTABLISHED

C:\Users\tmcmillan>
```

nbtstat

Microsoft networks use an interface called Network Basic Input/Output System (NetBIOS) to resolve workstation names with IP addresses. The nbtstat command can be used to view NetBIOS information. In Figure 9.10 it has been executed with the -n switch, which will display the NetBIOS names that are currently known to the local machine. In this case, this local machine is only aware of its own NetBIOS names.

FIGURE 9.10   Using nbtstat

```
C:\Users\tmcmillan>nbtstat -n

Local Area Connection:
Node IpAddress: [10.88.2.103] Scope Id: []

           NetBIOS Local Name Table

    Name              Type         Status
    TMCMILLAN   <00>  UNIQUE       Registered
    ALPHA       <00>  GROUP        Registered
    TMCMILLAN   <20>  UNIQUE       Registered
    ALPHA       <1E>  GROUP        Registered

VMware Network Adapter VMnet1:
Node IpAddress: [192.168.21.2] Scope Id: []
```

net

The net command is one of the most powerful on the Windows-based network, as illustrated by net use. The options that can be used with the command differ slightly based on the Windows operating system you are using; you can view a full list by typing **net /?**.

The net use command is used on Windows-based clients to connect or disconnect from shared resources. You can see what options are available by typing **/?** or see what is currently shared by typing **net use** without any other parameters, as shown in Figure 9.11.

FIGURE 9.11   Typing net use lets you see what is currently shared.

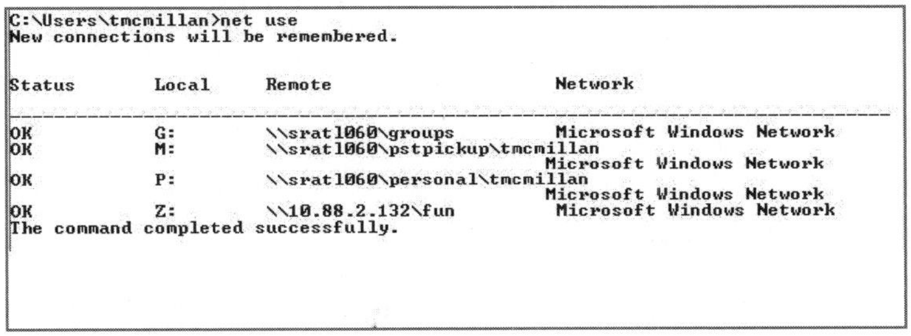

```
C:\Users\tmcmillan>net use
New connections will be remembered.

Status       Local      Remote                    Network
-------------------------------------------------------------------------------
OK           G:         \\srat1060\groups          Microsoft Windows Network
OK           M:         \\srat1060\pstpickup\tmcmillan
                                                   Microsoft Windows Network
OK           P:         \\srat1060\personal\tmcmillan
                                                   Microsoft Windows Network
OK           Z:         \\10.88.2.132\fun          Microsoft Windows Network
The command completed successfully.
```

Wireless locator

A wireless locator is used to view any wireless networks that are in the area. It works the same as the wireless location utility built into any laptop or other device, but it is small and easily attached to a key chain for use when needed. It simply picks up the signal from all networks broadcasting in the area and displays them on a screen. It can be helpful in determining the networks in the area and the channels they are using. That way, you can set your APs so as not to interfere with—or be interfered with by—the other networks.

Exam Essentials

Identify common symptoms of network issues and their potential causes.   Examples include limited, intermittent, local only or no connectivity, APIPA addresses, IP conflict, slow transfer speeds, and low RF signal.

Identify hardware tools available to diagnose and repair network cables.   These include but are not limited to cable testers, loopback plugs, punch-down tools, toner probes, wire strippers, crimpers, and wireless locators.

Identify commands that let you identify network issues.   These include ping, ipconfig, tracert, netstat, nbtstat, and net.

4.6 Given a scenario, troubleshoot operating system problems with appropriate tools

Because it's software and there are so many places where things can go wrong, the operating system can be one of the most confusing components to troubleshoot. Sometimes it seems a miracle that they even work at all considering the hundreds of files that work together to make the system function. In this section, common operating system issues and their solutions are covered. The topics addressed in objective 4.6 include:

- Common symptoms
- Tools

Common symptoms

What follows in this section can seem like a daunting list of symptoms the operating system can exhibit. With a proper plan of action and good backup (always have a backup!), you can approach any of these problems with confidence. In many cases today, technicians have ceased to spend significant amounts of time chasing operating system issues since most important data is kept on servers and computers can be reimaged so quickly troubleshooting doesn't warrant the effort. Nevertheless, you should know these basic symptoms and the approach to take when they present themselves.

BSOD

Once a regular occurrence when working with Windows, blue screens (also known as the Blue Screen of Death) have become less common. Occasionally, systems will lock up; you can usually examine the log files to discover what was happening when this occurred and take steps to correct it. Remember, when dealing with a blue screen always ask yourself "What did I just install or change?" In many cases, the change is involved in the BSOD. Also keep in mind that (as the instructions on the blue screen will tell you) a simple reboot will often fix the problem. Retaining the contents of the BSOD can help troubleshoot the issue. In most instances, the BSOD error can be located in Microsoft's knowledgebase to help with troubleshooting.

Failure to boot

Booting problems can occur with corruption of the boot files or missing components. Common error messages include an invalid boot disk, inaccessible boot drive, missing NTLDR file, or bootmgr is missing (some of which are discussed in more detail later in this section). Luckily, during the installation of the operating system, log files are created in the %SystemRoot% and %SystemRoot%\Debug folders (C:\WINNT for older systems and C:\Windows for Windows 7 and

Windows Vista). If you have a puzzling problem, look at these logs and see if you can find error entries there. With Windows 7, for example, the following files are some of the log files created:

netsetup.log   This file differs from all the others in that it's in the Debug folder and not just %SystemRoot%. Entries in it detail the workgroup and domain options given during installation.

setupact.log   Known as the action log, this file is a chronological list of what took place during the setup. There is a tremendous amount of information here; of key importance is whether errors occurred. The last lines of the file can show which operation was transpiring when the installation failed, or whether the installation ended with errors. Like all the log files created during setup, this file is in ASCII text format and can be viewed with any viewer (WordPad, Word, and so on).

setuperr.log   The error log, as this file is commonly called, is written to at the time errors are noted in other log files. For example, an entry in setupact.log may show that an error occurred, and additional information on it will be found in setuperr.log. Not only are the errors here, but also the severity of each is given.

You can configure problems with system failure to write dump files (debugging information) for later analysis when they occur by going to the System applet in Control Panel, choosing the Advanced tab, and clicking Settings under Startup And Recovery (Windows XP). For Windows 7 or Vista, click Start ➢ Control Panel ➢ System and then click the Advanced System Settings option. The Advanced tab of the System Properties dialog box should open. Then click the Settings button in the Startup And Recovery section. Here, in addition to choosing the default operating system, you can configure whether events should be written to the system log, whether an alert should be sent to the administrator, and the type of memory dump to be written.

Improper shutdown

Although not nearly the danger it once was, when the system is improperly shut down, either from a loss of power or by being forced to shut down without all programs closing, problems can result. For certain, anything that is still residing in memory and not saved to the disk will be lost (although Word may save you with its auto-recovery feature).

In other cases, though, important files may be corrupted or lost. In fact, if some files are lost the computer may not even boot after the shutdown. If the system does boot and you have any doubts about the integrity of important system files, execute the command **sfc/ scannow**. This program (called the system file checker) will check the file structure. Another good command to execute if you have any doubts is chkdsk/R. This command will check the disk for errors and repair them if possible.

Spontaneous shutdown/restart

Some restarts are a function of hardware. (See the section on restarts in Chapter 1). In other cases it's software related. If the system is automatically restarting, there is the possibility that it has a virus or is unable to continue current operations (in other words, it has become unstable). To solve issues with viruses, Trojans, and the like, install virus detection software on every client (as well as on the server), keep the definitions current, and run them often.

If the problem is with the system being unstable, examine the log files and try to isolate the problem. Reboot in Safe Mode (discussed in more detail in the "Tools" section) and correct any incompatibility issues. You can also deselect the Automatically Restart On Startup And Recovery option of the System applet (Advanced tab) in Control Panel to prevent the system from rebooting.

Occasionally, systems reboot when they have been updated. This is a necessary process, and users are always given warning before the reboot is to occur. If no one is present to choose to reboot later (it's the middle of the night, for example), the reboot will take place. Users who leave files open overnight in an unsaved state are at risk of losing work because of this process.

RAID not detected during installation

When installing an operating system to a machine that is using a RAID controller, often-times (okay, almost all the time) the system cannot access the hard drive because the driver for the RAID controller is not present in the drive cache. In Windows the program will alert you that no hard drive can be found, and in earlier versions of Windows you will be prompted to press F6 to point the system to the proper driver. In Windows Vista and Windows 7, choose to repair the system on the first installation screen and then on the next screen select Load Driver.

Place the driver on a floppy (if the system still has a floppy drive) or a memory stick and then load the driver. After that, the RAID array will most likely appear as a single drive. Create a partition and install into it.

Device fails to start

Usually when devices fail to start and you have eliminated a hardware issue, the problem involves drivers. Drivers are associated with devices, and you can access them by looking at the properties for the device. The following, for example, are the three most common tabs of an adapter's Properties dialog box (tabs that appear are always dependent on the type of device and its capabilities):

General   This tab displays the device type, manufacturer, and location. It also includes information regarding whether the device is currently working properly and a Troubleshooter button to walk you through diagnostics.

Driver Access   This tab displays information on the current driver and digital signer. Three command buttons allow you to see driver details and uninstall or update the driver.

Resources   This tab shows the system resources in use (I/O, IRQ, and so on) and whether there are conflicts.

The most common driver-related device issue is device failure when a new driver is installed. If this occurs, you can use the Roll Back Driver option in Device Manager or boot into the Last Known Good Configuration.

Missing dll message

One of the more useful error messages you can receive is one indicating a missing DLL file. It's useful because it tells you exactly what's missing. DLL files are shared by various components. If they are missing or corrupted, you will receive an error message whenever you do something that requires the file. Make note of the name of the DLL and its location.

You can download DLL files from the Internet or copy them from another machine. Place them in the same location and the problem should be fixed. When you receive the error message, locate the missing DLL by searching for it. If it's gone completely, search for it on another system and copy it. Then just paste it into the proper location (that should be the `system32` folder on the drive where the operating system is installed).

Services fail to start

Sometimes when the system is started you receive a message that tells you a service failed to start. When that occurs, use the event log to determine the service that failed. Then to interact with service, access the Administrative Tools section of Control Panel and choose Services. This starts up the Services console. You can right-click any service and choose to start, stop, pause, resume, or restart it. You can also double-click the service to access its properties and configure such things as the startup type, dependencies, and other variables.

If the service refuses to start, it could be that a service on which it depends will not start. To determine what services must be running for the problem service to start, select the Dependencies tab of the service's Properties dialog box, as shown in Figure 9.12.

In the figure you can see that the Remote Desktop service depends on both the RPC and the Terminal Device Driver services to function. Try starting these services first. In some cases, you may need to trace the dependencies up several levels to get things going.

Compatibility error

Some applications that function on an older operating system like Windows 2000 or Windows XP experience problems when running on Windows Vista or Windows 7. The problem is even more acute if the application was made to run on Windows NT or Windows 95/98.

When an application will not function for this reason, there are two solutions. It may even require using both measures listed here to make the application function:

- Set the application to operate in the mode for which it was created. In the Properties dialog box of each application is the Compatibility tab. There you can use a drop-down box to select Windows XP mode, Windows 95 mode, or whatever is required. The Compatibility tab is shown in Figure 9.13.

- Set the application to run as an administrator. Some older applications must run in the security context of an administrator to function, which is not generally allowed anymore in Windows Vista and Windows 7. You may have to check the Run As Administrator box as well. The box is near the bottom of the Compatibility tab, as shown in Figure 9.13.

FIGURE 9.12 Service dependencies

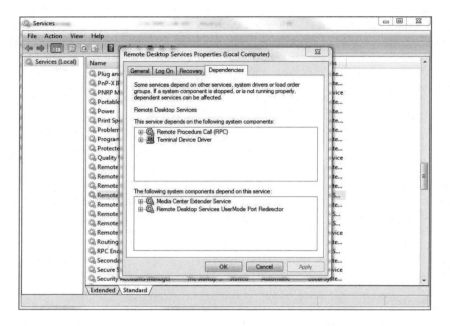

FIGURE 9.13 Compatibility tab

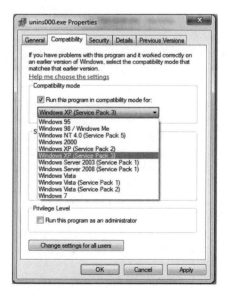

Slow system performance

Slow system performance can come from many issues. For the purposes of this discussion, we are going to focus on performance that deteriorates after being acceptable as opposed to system performance that is poor from the outset (which could be a matter of insufficient resources such as RAM). Here is a list of possibilities:

- The first thing to check is the presence of a virus. If the system seems to have an overabundance of disk activity, scan it for viruses, using a virus program that resides externally on a CD/DVD or memory stick.

- Defragment the hard drive. The more fragmented it is, the slower the disk access will be.

- Check the space on the hard drive. When the partition or volume where the operating system is located becomes full, performance will suffer. This is why it is a good idea to store data and applications on a different partition from that holding the system files.

- Ensure the latest updates are installed. In many cases, updates help to solve performance problems so make sure they are current.

Boots to safe mode

In many cases a system will not boot in regular mode but will do so in Safe Mode. Safe Mode loads the operating system but none of the drivers, with the exception of those absolutely essential to the system and those required for use of the keyboard, mouse, and the basic display (VGA mode).

If the system will start in Safe Mode but not otherwise, it is most likely a bad driver that is causing the system to hang during the boot-up. One option to try for a quick fix is to perform a System Restore procedure to a point in time before the driver problem occurred. You can also use the Roll Back Driver feature to revert back to the older but functional driver as well. The problem with this approach is that you have not identified the problem driver and the issue may emerge again later.

If you go to Device Manager and check the status of all the devices, you should see a device that has a problem. Try updating the driver; that may be a better long-term solution. Another option is to look in the system log in Event Viewer and the problem driver may be specified in a message there as well.

 Adding the /sos option to the operating system option in the boot.ini file will show the drivers as they're loaded in Windows 2000 and XP. When the problem driver is encountered the process will stop, allowing you to determine the name and location of the problem driver.

File fails to open

Files will sometimes not open when you click on them. In some cases it's a problem of file association, which means the system doesn't know which application to use to open the file. Right-click on the file and choose Open With. Then select the program to open the file. At that point you may realize that the program required to open the file is not present, and you may have to install it.

If this occurs with EXE files, the culprit is usually a virus. Remove the virus first. If the EXE files still fail to function, there are EXE file association fixes available that can reassociate the files with the proper program.

Missing NTLDR

The NTLDR file loads the operating system files for Windows XP and 2000. In Windows Vista and Windows 7, BOOTMGR performs this operation. If it is not present, the system will not boot.

The good news is that this file can be copied from any other system to the operating system drive. In Windows XP:

1. Insert the Windows XP installation CD into the computer.

2. When prompted to press any key to boot from the CD, press any key.

3. Once in the Windows XP setup menu, press the R key to repair Windows.

4. Log into the problematic Windows installations (if there are more than one) by pressing the number of the installation in the list presented. The number will be 1 if it is the only installation.

5. Enter the administrator password.

6. Copy the `ntldr` and the `ntdetect.com` files to the root directory of the primary hard disk. Where the CD-ROM drive letter is E and your root directory is on the C drive, execute the following commands. Insert the proper drive letters for your CD-ROM and the root directory of your installation.

   ```
   copy e:\i386\ntldr c:\
   copy e:\i386\ntdetect.com c:\
   ```

7. Once both of these files have been successfully copied, remove the CD from the computer and reboot.

Missing *boot.ini*

The `boot.ini` file in Windows XP and Windows 2000 holds information about which OSs are installed on the computer. In Windows Vista, the Boot Configuration Data (BCD) file holds this information. When the `boot.ini` file is missing, the system will not boot because the operating system files cannot be found.

The `boot.ini` file unfortunately is not a file you can copy from another system (unless that system is installed exactly the same, which may be the case if the computers were imaged). For this reason, it is always a good idea to put the `boot.ini` file on an external drive or memory stick in case it becomes missing; then you can boot to the device, get the system running, and then copy the `boot.ini` file back to its proper location on the operating system drive.

Missing operating system

The "no operating system found" message can result from a number of issues. Among them are:

- Nonsystem disk in the floppy drive
- Incorrect boot device order in the BIOS
- Corrupted or missing boot sector
- Corrupted boot files

In short, the operating system is not actually missing; the system is missing a file that can either locate it or load it. Follow the steps in this section with respect to the `ntldr` and `boot.ini` files.

Missing Graphical Interface

The graphical user interface (GUI) is the method by which a person communicates with a computer. GUIs use a mouse, touchpad, or another mechanism (in addition to the keyboard) to interact with the computer to issue commands. A missing GUI and a GUI that fails to load (see the next section) usually results from a bad driver or something that is preventing the operating system from loading to the point where the GUI can load.

When the GUI is missing, try booting into Safe Mode. If the GUI appears for Safe Mode, you know it is a driver problem and can proceed with determining the offending driver as discussed in the section "Boots to Safe Mode."

Graphical Interface fails to load

The approach to troubleshooting a GUI that won't load is basically the same as for a missing GUI since a GUI that won't load manifests itself as a GUI that is missing. Be aware that inappropriate or misinformed edits to the Registry can also delete files required for the GUI.

Sometimes restoring the Registry from a backup can solve the problem. Since the GUI will not be available, you must use the command line or the Recovery Console (discussed in the upcoming section "Recovery console").

Invalid boot disk

The "invalid boot disk" message indicates that the disk or drive to which the system is attempting to boot has no boot files on it. This could be for the following reasons:

- There is a floppy in the floppy drive with no boot files.
- The boot order in the BIOS is missing the drive or disk where boot files are located.
- A nonbootable CD or DVD is in the CD-ROM or DVD drive.

However, it is also worth noting that in some cases a USB device plugged into one of the USB ports can cause the system to fail to boot to the drive where the boot files are located. This makes sense if the device is seen by the system as a USB storage device (a potential boot device), but it has been reported to have occurred with devices like a wireless USB mouse as well.

Tools

A number of tools are available for troubleshooting operating system problems, some of which have been mentioned in passing in the earlier sections on common symptoms.

Fixboot

The Recovery Console is a Windows XP/2000 command-line utility used for troubleshooting. From it, you can format drives, stop and start services, and interact with files. The latter is extremely important because many boot and command-line utilities bring you into a position where you can interact with files stored on FAT or FAT32, but not NTFS.

The Recovery Console can work with files stored on all three filesystems. One of the most useful commands that can be executed from the command line of the console is the `fixboot` command. This command writes a new boot sector. If the computer will not boot, this command is a good option to try.

Recovery console

The Recovery Console isn't installed on a system by default. To install it, use the following steps:

1. Place the Windows CD in the system.

2. From a command prompt, change to the `i386` directory of the CD.

3. Type `winnt32 /cmdcons`.

4. A prompt appears, alerting you to the fact that 7 MB of hard drive space is required and asking if you want to continue. Click Yes.

Upon successful completion of the installation, the Recovery Console (Microsoft Windows 2000 Recovery Console, for example) is added as a menu choice at the bottom of the startup menu. To access it, you must choose it from the list at startup. If more than one installation of Windows 2000 or Windows NT exists on the system, another boot menu will appear, asking which you want to boot into, and you must make a selection to continue.

To perform this task, you must give the administrator password. You'll then arrive at a command prompt. You can give a number of commands from this prompt, two of which are worth special attention: `exit` restarts the computer, and `help` lists the commands you can give.

Fixmbr

Another useful command that can be executed from within the Recovery Console is `fixmbr`. It checks and fixes (if possible) the master boot record. If the computer will not boot, this command is another one you should try.

SFC

The System File Checker (SFC) utility was discussed in the earlier section "Improper shutdown." The purpose of this utility is to keep the operating system alive and well. SFC automatically verifies system files after a reboot to see if they were changed to unprotected copies. If an unprotected file is found, it's overwritten by a stored copy of the system file from %systemroot%\system32\dllcache. (%systemroot% is the folder into which the operating system was installed.)

Repair disks

The Windows Backup and Recovery Tool wizard allows you to create an emergency repair disk (ERD), in Windows 2000 only. As the name implies, this is a disk you can use to repair a portion of the system in the event of a failure.

When you choose this option, the tab changes to the Backup tab, and a prompt tells you to install a blank, formatted floppy disk. A check box inquires whether you want to save the Registry as well. (The default is no.) If you don't choose to save the Registry, the following files are placed on the floppy disk:

- SETUP.LOG
- CONFIG.NT
- AUTOEXEC.NT

This doesn't leave you much to work with. The disk isn't bootable and contains only three minor configuration utilities.

If you check the box to include the Registry in the backup, the floppy disk contains the preceding files plus the following:

- SECURITY._
- SOFTWARE._
- SYSTEM._
- DEFAULT._
- SAM._
- NTUSER.DAT
- USRCLASS.DAT

The user profile (NTUSER.DAT) is for the default user; the files with the ._ extension are compressed files from the Registry. The compression utility used is EXPAND.EXE, which offers you the flexibility of restoring any or all files from any Microsoft operating system, including this utility (Windows 95/98, Windows NT, and so on). Because this floppy contains key Registry files, it's important that you label it appropriately and store it in a safe location, away from users who should not have access to it.

 During the process of creating the floppy, the Registry files are also backed up (in uncompressed state) to %systemroot%\repair\RegBack.

As before, the floppy isn't bootable, and you must bring the system up to a point (booted) where the floppy can be accessed before it's of any use.

ERD does not exist in Windows Vista or Windows 7. The System Restore tab lets you disable or enable and configure the new System Restore feature in Windows XP, Vista, and Windows 7 (using the System Protection tab in Windows 7). If you have a system crash, it can restore your data back to the restore point. You can turn on System Restore for all drives on your system or for individual drives. Note that turning off System Restore on the system drive (the drive on which the OS is installed) automatically turns it off on all drives.

Pre-installation environments

Windows Preinstallation Environment (Windows PE) is a minimal operating system with limited services, built on the Windows Vista or Windows 7 kernel. It is used to prepare a computer for Windows installation, to copy disk images from a network file server, and to initiate Windows Setup. It is also the environment in use when operating in the Windows Recovery environment.

It can be used as a platform to repair issues with a system by booting to a disk with PE on it, somewhat like booting to a disk with DOS and system files on it. It includes much more functionality than a DOS boot disk but can be used in the same way to boot and access a drive with an operating system that will not boot.

msconfig

The MSCONFIG utility helps you troubleshoot startup problems by allowing you to selectively disable individual items that normally are executed at startup. There is no menu command for this utility, so in Windows XP, for example, you use Start ➢ Run, type **msconfig**, and press Enter. It works in most versions of Windows, although the interface window is slightly different among versions. Figure 9.14 shows an example in Windows Vista.

FIGURE 9.14   MSCONFIG

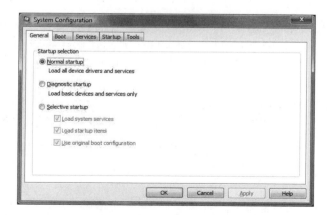

defrag

One of the biggest factors affecting hard drive performance over time is fragmentation. The more files are read, added to, and rewritten, the more fragmentation is likely to occur. The Disk Defragmenter utility (the `defrag` command) is the best tool for correcting fragmentation.

Disk Defragmenter reorganizes the file storage on a disk to reduce the number of files that are stored noncontiguously. This makes file retrieval faster, because the read/write heads on the disk have to move less.

There are two versions of Disk Defragmenter: a command-line version and a Windows version that runs from within Windows. The Windows version is located on the System Tools submenu on the Start menu (Start ➢ All Programs ➢ Accessories ➢ System Tools ➢ Disk Defragmenter).

Before doing any operation, you should run Analyze. This will check the volume and recommend an action, as shown in Figure 9.15. If you choose View Report, you can see the files that are most fragmented in successive order.

FIGURE 9.15   Using Disk Defragmenter in XP

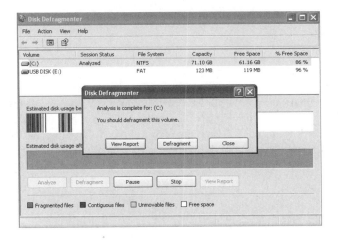

The available XP switches for the command-line version (`defrag.exe`) include the following:

-a   Analyze only

-f   Force defragmentation even if disk space is low

-v   Verbose output

REGSRV32

REGSRV32 (Microsoft Register Server) is a command-line utility in Windows operating systems for registering and unregistering DLLs and ActiveX controls in the Registry.

Many DLL files must be registered with the system to run. If you replace a missing DLL, you may need to also need to register the file. An example of registering a DLL looks like this:

```
regsvr32 shmedia.dll
```

REGEDIT

Windows configuration information is stored in a special configuration database known as the *Registry*. This centralized database contains environmental settings for various Windows programs.

Windows 2000, XP, Vista, and Windows 7 have two applications that can be used to edit the registry: REGEDIT and REGEDT32 (note the spelling with no i). In Windows XP and Vista, REGEDT32 opens REGEDIT. They work similarly, but each has slightly different options for navigation and browsing. In addition, REGEDT32 allows you to configure security-related settings for Registry keys, such as assigning permissions.

Registry edits are immediate and generate no warning message like you might get when making a change in Control Panel. Proceed with care, as a mistake could render the system useless.

Event viewer

During startup, problems with devices that fail to be recognized properly, services that fail to start, and so on are written to the system log and can be viewed with Event Viewer. This utility provides information about what's been going on system-wise to help you troubleshoot problems. Event Viewer shows warnings, error messages, and records of things happening successfully. It's found in NT versions of Windows only (Windows NT and later). You can access it through Computer Management, or you can access it directly from the Administrative Tools in Control Panel.

Safe mode

To access Safe Mode, you must press F8 when the OS menu is displayed during the boot process. A menu of Safe Mode choices appears, and you can select the mode you want to boot into. This is the mode to boot into if you suspect driver problems and want to load with a minimal set while you diagnose the problem.

Command prompt

A complete discussion of the command prompt is found in objective 1.3 in Chapter 6.

Emergency repair disk

Emergency repair disks were discussed in the earlier section "Repair disks."

Automated system recovery

In Windows XP and later systems, the ERD has been replaced with Automated System Recovery (ASR), which is accessible through the Backup utility. It's possible to automate the process of creating a system recovery set by choosing the ASR Wizard on the Tools menu of the Backup utility (Start ➢ All Programs ➢ Accessories ➢ System Tools ➢ Backup). This wizard walks you through the process of creating a disk that can be used to restore parts of the system in the event of a major system failure.

The default name of this file is backup.bkf; it requires a floppy disk. The backup set contains all the files necessary for starting the system, whereas the floppy becomes a bootable pointer to that backup set and can access or decompress it.

 A weakness of this tool is its reliance on a bootable floppy in a day when many new systems no longer include a 3.5″ drive.

Exam Essentials

Identify the most common symptoms of operating system and system boot problems.   These include BSODs, boot failures, problems from improper shutdowns, spontaneous shutdowns/restarts, undetected RAID drives, devices that fail to start, missing DLL messages, services failures, compatibility errors, slow system performance, files that fail to open, missing items (NTLDR, boot.ini, operating system, GUI), and invalid boot disk.

Describe the use of troubleshooting tools for operating system problems.   Among these tools are fixboot, Recovery Console, fixmbr, sfc, preinstallation environments, msconfig, defrag, regsrv32, regedit, Event Viewer, Safe Mode, the command prompt, emergency repair disks, and Automated System Recovery.

4.7 Given a scenario, troubleshoot common security issues with appropriate tools and best practices

System issues in many cases have security breaches at the root of the cause. It has become almost a given that any problem that cannot be traced to any other cause should be attacked by first scanning for viruses and malware. This section discusses common symptoms of security-related failures and tools that can be used to mitigate the damage. The topics addressed in objective 4.7 include:

- Common symptoms
- Tools
- Best practices for malware removal

Common symptoms

Crazy things start to happen when malware is introduced to a computer. In this section, some of the strange behaviors of computers that are infected are discussed.

Pop-ups

Although relatively benign when compared with malware in general, pop-ups are annoying to users. They also use system resources as they open and in some cases can introduce additional malware when they open.

Fortunately most browsers now contain pop-up blockers that can prevent unwanted pop-ups. In some cases users want pop-ups to be allowed—in fact, some website functions fail when a pop-up blocker is enabled. For that reason, users can use the Pop-up Blocker Settings of Internet Explorer to allow pop-ups for certain websites, as shown in Figure 9.16. Other browsers usually have a similar setting.

FIGURE 9.16   Pop-up Blocker Settings

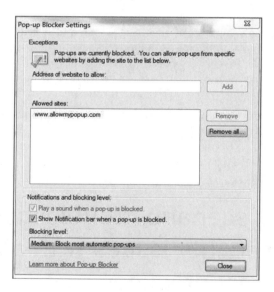

Browser redirection

A browser redirection is one of the most serious security problems. Browser hijacking software is external code that changes your Internet Explorer settings. It may include changing your home page or adding or removing items from your favorites. Some sites will be added that point to dubious content. In most cases, the home page will revert back to the unwanted destination even if you change it manually because the hijacker made Registry changes to your system. To prevent this from occurring:

- Avoid suspect sites.
- Use and update an antivirus program regularly.
- Tighten your browser security settings.

Once you are a victim, you may have to apply antivirus software from an external source.

Security alerts

Sometimes you can tell by security warnings that the site you are on is attempting to attack your computer. This is true if you have a personal firewall like Windows Firewall. It can also occur when you have the phishing filter enabled in Internet Explorer. You will know when the system asks you if you want to allow access to your machine from the site. Unless you initiated a download, don't allow it.

Slow performance

A reduction in performance is one of the classic signs of malware infection. When no other reason can be isolated for the slowing of a system, scanning for malware is always recommended. All types of malware eat up significant system resources, starving the normal processes of the computer of the power they need.

Internet connectivity issues

Some malware will affect your Internet access. It may disallow you from accessing certain sites or it may only allow access to a small number of sites. It has been reported that viral programs block access for certain programs and browsers while still allowing others to function. When access is denied, the following message is generated:

```
Unable to connect to HTTP Proxy. Your proxy may be misconfigured or
offline. -336
```

Moreover, this occurred even after the virus was supposedly cleaned from the system.

PC locks up

It is quite common for the system to lock up when the malware is attacking. You may notice when this occurs that the hard drive is very busy, although nothing appears to be going on. In some cases you can use Task Manager to end the process that is locking everything up and in other cases you simply must shut the computer down to break out of the lockup.

Windows Updates failures

Malware may take certain measures to protect itself. One of these is to block you from accessing Windows Update. You never notice this because these updates can be set to run automatically so when they fail it may not be obvious that they did.

Another action the malware can take along the same lines is to disable your antivirus software. For this reason, anytime your antivirus program notifies you that it is not functional or cannot update itself, you should consider this possibility and get it back up and running (if you can) as soon as possible.

Rogue antivirus

If you receive messages (again usually at a suspect website) warning you that your system is infected, it will also usually offer to clean the system. At a minimum they are trying to sell you antimalware software through the bogus warning.

Worse, though, is that executing the "cleaning" sometimes results in the introduction of malware to the system—which was the whole point of the message to begin with. In general, pay no attention to these messages and try to close them and exit the website that generated them as quickly as possible.

Spam

A sudden increase in spam may indicate that adware has been installed on the machine. This type of malware monitors your activities so that it can more accurately target spam email. This is not particularly dangerous, but you have to wonder if that malware got on your system what *else* might lurking in your computer.

Renamed system files

Many viruses will rename system files and adopt the name of the system file. This can help the virus escape detection when scanning occurs, since most virus definitions identify the virus by the name of the file that introduced the virus. This renaming of the system file can cause big problems when the file is required and the virus file is incapable of providing the required functionality.

Files disappearing

Another symptom of a viral infection is the deletion of files in the system. Many viruses delete key files in your system to render it inoperable. This could be one of the ways it renders any existing antivirus programs inoperable. It also can be a part of disabling Internet access either completely or selectively.

File permission changes

If the malware is a rootkit or Trojan horse, it can change permissions to key files. The permissions would then allow access to remote systems. This can help to enhance the functionality of backdoors, which allow the computer to be controlled remotely.

Hijacked email

Viruses may also make changes to the email client that sends a copy of all emails to another system. Depending on the content of email, this can make the user open to identity theft and can also be used in corporate espionage. It is especially harmful if the account is an IT administrator passing key enterprise security details through email.

Access denied

This can be a symptom of the file permission changes discussed in Chapter 7. It can also be a message you get when you try to access the Internet in general or try to access specific sites such as those used for security updates and antivirus definitions.

Tools

Fortunately there are tools at your disposal to help you in the fight against malware of all types. In this section, the major items in this toolbox are discussed.

Anti-virus software

The first line of defense against malware of all types is antivirus software kept up-to-date with the latest antivirus engine and definition files. Antivirus software is an application that is installed on a system to protect it and to scan for viruses as well as worms and Trojan horses. Most viruses have characteristics that are common to families of viruses. Antivirus software looks for these characteristics, or fingerprints, to identify and neutralize viruses before they impact you.

More than 200,000 known viruses, worms, bombs, and other malware have been defined. New ones are added all the time. Your antivirus software manufacturer will usually work very hard to keep the definition database files current. The definition database file contains all of the known viruses and countermeasures for a particular antivirus software product. You probably won't receive a virus that hasn't been seen by one of these companies. If you keep the virus definition database files in your software up-to-date, you probably won't be overly vulnerable to attacks.

Anti-malware software

Since all type of harmful software discussed in this section are classified as malware, antimalware software is any that identifies and protects your system from viruses, worms, Trojans, and spyware.

Anti-spyware software

Although not as dangerous as other types of malware, spyware, typically in the form of adware, can be very annoying. It tracks user activities for the purpose of targeting spam and pop-ups that offer products and services based on the collected data. The problem with spyware is that it starts up whenever the system starts and remains running, eating up resources. If the computer has five instances of adware running, each program is using resources.

Antispyware programs can identify and delete these programs. Although not a good idea with antivirus software, using multiple antispyware programs is recommended because one always seems to find programs the other misses. (This is not good with antivirus software because the two programs will see each other as viruses.)

Recovery console

The malware may not allow you to take steps such as deleting the programs while in the GUI. Oftentimes you can boot to the Recovery Console (Windows 2000) and delete the files you need to.

In many cases you can identify the files in question by using Task Manager to view the processes that are running. However, identifying them and deleting them may be another matter. Using the Recovery Console, you may be able to do this once you know the names of the files or programs.

System restore

The Recovery Console that existed in Windows 2000 and Windows XP has been removed from Vista and Windows 7. In its place is the System Recovery Options menu that appears on the installation disk. While renamed, it serves the same purpose of allowing you to troubleshoot startup problems or restore your system.

To access this feature, restart your system using the installation disk. At the language settings, choose your language and click Next. On the following menu, choose Repair Your Computer. Choose which operating system you are having a problem with (if more than one is installed) and click Next. The System Recovery Options menu will open and you can then choose any tool from the menu and run it. The tools available on the System Recovery Options menu are listed in Table 9.1. The most useful ones for removing malware are the command prompt and the Windows Complete PC Recovery. When the PC Recovery Tool has been used to make a backup of the entire PC, the tool can be used to re-create the entire computer without the virus!

TABLE 9.1   System Recovery options

Tool	Purpose
Command Prompt	Offers access to the tools that were available in the Recovery Console
Startup Repair	Used to fix problem with startup, such as missing operating system files
System Restore	Allows you to restore the system to a saved restore point
Windows Complete PC Restore	Copies all the files from a backup and overwrites anything currently on the system
Windows Memory Diagnostic Tool	Checks the memory for errors

Pre-installation environments

Preinstallation environments like Windows PE were discussed in the tools section of "Given a scenario, troubleshoot operating system problems with appropriate tools." Just as you can use this tool to access the hard drive when a system won't boot, you can also use it to access and delete viral programs using the same identification and removal techniques discussed in the topic "Recovery console" in this section.

Event viewer

Many times a viral program is intelligent enough to prevent its activities from being recorded in Event Viewer, but it is still worth the effort to see if there are events recorded that are related to its operation. You may be able to determine its name and what it's doing. Information you glean here could be helpful in identifying and removing the malware.

Best practices for malware removal

Over time best practices have been developed through trial and error that help minimize both the chances of getting viruses and reduce the effort involved in getting rid of malware. Some of these practices are discussed in this section.

Identify malware symptoms

First identify the symptoms the malware is producing as clearly as you can. This can help identify the exact virus in some cases. In many scenarios identifying the symptoms can help establish the severity of the infection, which is good to determine when IT resources are stretched thin and battles must be chosen.

Quarantine infected system

The infected system should be quarantined—removed from the network to prevent a spread of the infection to other systems. This is why it is a good practice to keep data on servers so that when user systems need to be quarantined a new machine can be quickly imaged for the user to reduce the impacts on productivity while the infected machine is cleaned.

Disable system restore

System Restore is a useful tool in many cases, but when a virus infection occurs, it can be an ally of the virus. Virus scanners cannot clean infections from restore points, making reinfection possible. If a system restore is performed after running an antispyware utility, viral objects may reappear. Disable System Restore before attempting to clean a system. When you do this, you will delete all restore points in the system, including any that may have an infection.

Remediate infected systems

Once the infected system has been quarantined, you must take steps to clean it. This two-step process is discussed in this section.

Update anti-virus software

Before scanning the system with antivirus software, update the software and the engine if necessary. Definition files can change daily and the virus may be so new that it is not contained in your current definitions file even if it is only a week old.

Scan and removal techniques (safe mode, pre-installation environment)

Although you can run the scan and removal from the GUI, it is a best practice to do this either after booting to Safe Mode or from a preinstallation environment like Windows PE. Viruses that evade detection in the GUI are not as easily able to do so in either of these environments.

Schedule scans and updates

The antivirus software can be scheduled to perform a scan of the system. You should set this up to occur when the system is not in use, like at night. The scanning process will go faster then and will not affect users. Also, set the software to automatically check for and install any updates to the definition files and to the engine when available.

Enable system restore and create restore point

Although it is recommended that you disable System Restore before cleaning an infection, it is a good idea to create a restore point after an infection is cleaned. This gives you a clean restore point going forward in case the system becomes infected again at some point.

Educate end user

In many cases users are partly responsible for the virus infection. After an infection occurs is a great time to impress on users the principles of secure computing. They should be reminded that antivirus software and firewalls can only go so far in protecting them and that they should exercise safe browsing habits and refrain from opening any attachments in email from unknown sources, regardless of how tempting.

Exam Essentials

Identify the symptoms of malware infection.   Some of the symptoms are pop-ups, browser redirection, security alerts, slow performance, Internet connectivity issues, lockups, Windows Update failures, spam, renamed and disappearing system files, file permission changes, hijacked email, and access denied messages.

List the tools available to prevent and address virus infections.   Among the tools used for prevention and removal are antivirus, antimalware, and antispyware software; Recovery Console; System Restore; preinstallation environments; and Event Viewer.

Implement best practices for malware removal.   According to best practices, the steps to address malware removal are:

- Identify malware symptoms.
- Quarantine infected system.

- Disable System Restore.
- Remediate infected systems.
- Update antivirus software.
- Scan and remove the malware.
- Enable System Restore and create restore point.
- Educate end users.

4.8 Given a scenario, troubleshoot, and repair common laptop issues while adhering to the appropriate procedures

Laptop computers have their own unique sets of issues that may not be encountered with desktop computers. In this section, we discuss common issues and their solutions. Laptops require a different set of procedures for opening the case while protecting the integrity of the unit. The topics addressed in objective 4.8 include:

- Common symptoms
- Disassembling processes for proper reassembly

Common symptoms

Not all laptop issues are unique to laptops. Laptops suffer from many of the same issues as desktop machines. However, some problems are unique to laptops or at least more prone to occur with laptops, as you will learn in this section.

No display

The backlight is the light in the laptop that powers the LCD screen. It can go bad over time and need to be replaced, and it can also be held captive by the inverter. The inverter takes the DC power the laptop is providing and boosts it up to AC to run the backlight. If the inverter goes bad, you can replace it on most models (it's cheaper than the backlight).

Before going to the trouble of opening the case, however, ensure that the screen has not been inadvertently dimmed to the off position with the Fn keys or that the system has not been set to direct the output to an external monitor.

Dim display

As with a blank display, the backlight and inverter can cause dimming problems, but in most cases the screen has been dimmed inadvertently with the Fn keys. It is also possible that the switch on the laptop that tells the system the lid is closed may be held down by some obstruction. Check that as well.

Flickering display

Flickering screens can be caused by video drivers. The first thing to try is updating the driver. Another cause can be a low screen-refresh rate. Make sure the rate is set according to the documentation. Keep in mind that if you set it incorrectly, another symptom that may appear is more than one image displaying with the top image appearing transparent.

Flickering can also be caused by a loose connection. You may remember that a cable connects the display to the motherboard. Open the lid as described in Chapter 8, "Mobile Devices," and reseat the cable.

Sticking keys

Problems with keyboards can range from collecting dust (in which case you need to blow it out) to their springs wearing out. In the latter case, you can replace the keyboard (they cost about 10 times more than desktop keyboards) or choose to use an external one (provided the user isn't traveling and having to lug another hardware element with them). As you can imagine, spilled liquids are often the cause of sticking keys.

Intermittent wireless

Most laptops today include an internal wireless card. This is convenient, but it can be susceptible to interference (resulting in a low signal strength) between the laptop and the access point. Do what you can to reduce the number of items blocking the signal between the two devices, and you'll increase the strength of the signal. It is also possible that the cable that connects the antenna to the laptop needs to be reseated. Open the lid as described in Chapter 8.

Battery not charging

Most NiCad batteries build up memory and that memory can prevent a battery from offering a full charge. The biggest issue with DC power problems is a battery's inability to power the laptop as long as it should. If a feature is available to fully drain the battery, you should use it to eliminate the memory (letting the laptop run on battery on a regular basis greatly helps). If you can't drain the battery and eliminate the memory effect, you should replace the battery.

Ghost cursor

A second, or ghost, cursor can be caused when the laptop has a track pad that is too sensitive. Some laptops and tablets also vent warm air through the keyboard and when the lid gets left down, it heats up the track pad and causes this type of cursor behavior. Updating the driver for the touchpad has been known to help this problem. Another approach is to disable the touchpad completely and use an external mouse.

No power

In the absence of AC power, the laptop will attempt to run off the battery. This solution is good for a time, but AC power must be available to keep the battery charged and the laptop running. Most laptops have an indicator light showing whether AC power is being received, and the AC cord typically has an indicator light on it as well to show that it's receiving power. If no lights are lit on the cord or the laptop indicating that AC power is being received, try a different outlet or a different cord. Also try reseating the cord in the power adapter. The cord between the wall and the adapter is removable (to interchange for different countries' outlet types), and sometimes it works loose from the brick.

The presence of AC can affect the action of the NIC. To conserve power, the NIC is often configured not to be active when running on DC power (see Figure 9.17). In some laptop models you can access this dialog box through Start ➢ Control Panel ➢ Internal NIC Configuration. If power problems arise, ensure that this setting is enabled.

FIGURE 9.17   NIC settings

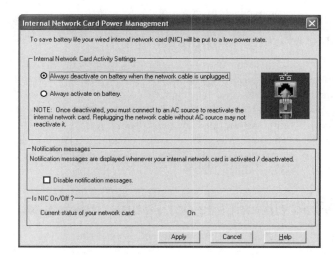

In Windows XP/Vista/7 use Device Manager to set "Allow the computer to turn off this device to save power" in the Properties ➢ Power Management tab. Then use the Power Options to set the NIC to Maximum Power Saving.

Num lock indicator lights

Sometimes the Num Lock indicator light does not function. This can be a hardware issue but many times it is a case of not understanding the exact process for enabling and disabling Num Lock. In many laptops you simply hit the key once to turn it on and again to turn it off. However, on some devices you must also use the Fn key simultaneously. Spilling liquids on the laptop can also cause these problems and usually requires taking the laptop in for service to clean the internal parts.

No wireless connectivity

When there is no wireless connectivity, it is usually one of two things:

- Wireless capability is disabled (enabling and disabling this function is usually done with a key combination or a Fn key) as this is very easy to disable inadvertently. This can also be a hardware switch on the side, front, or back of the case.

- The wireless antenna is bad or the cable needs to be reseated.

No Bluetooth connectivity

Bluetooth is also enabled and disabled with a key combination and can also be disabled easily. The first thing to try is to reenable it. The second thing to try is to reseat the antenna cable. If all else fails, try a new antenna. Like the WLAN NIC, this can also be a hardware switch on the side, front, or back of the case.

Cannot display to external monitor

It's always possible that a hardware issue is causing an external monitor to not work when connected to a laptop but, again, in most cases the problem is an incomplete understanding of the key combination to use to send the output to the external monitor.

On some laptops you need to use the Fn key in combination with keys on the top row; on other laptops you simply use the top row keys. Before spending too much time troubleshooting, consult the documentation and ensure you are using the correct procedure. In some models this can also be controlled from the video control panel or from within PowerPoint or other presentation software.

Disassembling processes for proper re-assembly

Disassembling a laptop in such a way that you end up with no leftover parts after the reassembly can be more of a challenge than with desktop machines. In this section, best practices for this process are discussed.

Document and label cable and screw locations

With a desktop computer there is often plenty of empty space in the case. In a laptop, space is at a premium, and because of that every screw is crucial! To avoid playing a guessing game about which screw goes where, you should create a map that tells you not only where each screw goes (and organize the screws by whatever naming convention you choose), but also where each cable plugs. You should create this roadmap as you disassemble the laptop and follow it carefully when reassembling it. Taking photos with your phone as you work can also suffice.

Organize parts

As you disassemble the device, organize the parts in such a way that you can reverse your steps when it comes time to reassemble the laptop. Keep screws of the same type together and be careful about making assumptions about screws that appear to be the same kind. Keep all screws that hold a particular component in place together in the same place, perhaps in a cup or on a paper plate.

Another helpful idea is to maintain the parts in the same sequence in which they were taken off the laptop. This will help you remember which part must go back on before another, which may not be as obvious as you think when the time comes to put the laptop back together.

Refer to manufacturer documentation

There is no better source of information about the idiosyncrasies of disassembling and reassembling a particular laptop model than the manufacturer documentation. No, it's not cheating to look at that! Each model's documentation has certain small tips that can save much time and grief.

Use appropriate hand tools

Laptop tools were discussed in Chapter 1. The important message beyond what is provided there is to use the correct tools. If you render a screw useless by trying to take it out with the wrong kind of screwdriver, you will be wishing you had just bought the correct tool.

Exam Essentials

Identify common symptoms of laptop issues.   Some of the symptoms include a dim, flickering, or blank display; sticking keys; intermittent or nonexistent wireless or Bluetooth connectivity; battery and power issues; ghost cursors; problems with Num Lock indicator lights; and inability to use an external monitor.

Describe proper disassembly and reassembly procedures.   Use the following guidelines:

- Document and label cable and screw locations.
- Organize parts.
- Refer to manufacturer documentation.
- Use appropriate hand tools.

4.9 Given a scenario, troubleshoot printers with appropriate tools

In the real world, you'll find that a large portion of all service calls relate to printing problems. This section will give you some general guidelines and common printing solutions to resolve printing problems. The topics addressed in objective 4.9 include:

- Common symptoms
- Tools

Common symptoms

There is no single shared device in the network that more users come in contact with and use every day than the printer. You may have to troubleshoot the common symptoms in this section on a daily basis, depending on your environment. Your ability to get a down printer working will make you more valuable to your employer.

Streaks

With laser printers, streaks usually indicate that the fuser is not fusing the toner properly on the paper. It could also be that the incorrect paper is being used. If you can pick up a sheet from a laser printer, run your thumb across it, and have the image come off on your thumb, you have a fuser problem. The fuser isn't heating the toner and fusing it onto the paper. This could be caused by a number of things—but all of them can be taken care of with a fuser replacement. For example, if the halogen light inside the heating roller has burned out, that will cause the problem. The solution is to replace the fuser. The fuser can be replaced with a rebuilt unit, if you prefer. Rebuilt fusers are almost as good as new fusers, and some even come with guarantees. Plus, they cost less.

 The whole fuser may not need to be replaced. You can order fuser components from parts suppliers and then rebuild them. For example, if the fuser has a bad lamp, you can order a lamp and replace it in the fuser.

Another, similar problem happens when small areas of smudging repeat themselves down the page. Dents or cold spots in the fuser heat roller cause this problem. The only solution is to replace either the fuser assembly or the heat roller.

If an ink cartridge becomes damaged or develops a hole, it can put too much ink on the page, and the letters will smear. In this case the solution is to replace the ink cartridge. (However, a very small amount of smearing is normal if the pages are laid on top of each other immediately after printing.) Because damage is possible in the process, you need to be careful when refilling cartridges, and many manufacturers do not suggest using refilled cartridges at all.

With inkjet or dot-matrix printers, streaks can mean the printhead needs cleaning. If cleaning doesn't help, try replacing the cartridge (inkjet) or the ribbon (dot matrix).

Faded prints

In laser printers, faded output is usually an indication that the toner cartridge is just about empty. You can usually remove it, shake it, and replace it, and then get a bit more life out of it before it is completely empty, but it is a signal that you are very near the end.

Another possibility is that the ink cartridge has dried out from lack of use. That's why the manufacturers include a small suction pump inside the printer that primes the ink cartridge before each print cycle. If this priming pump is broken or malfunctioning, this problem will manifest itself, and the pump will need to be replaced.

For dot matrix printers, faded printing mean you need to replace the ribbon, which is the source of ink in those printer types.

Ghost images

A problem unique to laser printers, *ghosting*, means you can see light images of previously printed pages on the current page. This is caused by one of two things: bad erasure lamps or a broken cleaning blade. If the erasure lamps are bad, the previous electrostatic discharges aren't completely wiped away. When the electrophotographic (EP) drum rotates toward the developing roller, some toner sticks to the slightly discharged areas. A broken cleaning blade, on the other hand, causes old toner to build up on the EP drum and consequently present itself in the next printed image.

Replacing the toner cartridge solves the second problem. Solving the first problem involves replacing the erasure lamps in the printer. Because the toner cartridge is the least expensive cure, you should try that first. Usually, replacing the toner cartridge will solve the problem. If it doesn't, you'll then have to replace the erasure lamps.

Toner not fused to the paper

In laser printers when the toner does not fuse properly to the paper (as discussed in the section "Streaks"), it will streak and smudge. See the section "Streaks" for more information.

Creased paper

Creased paper is a sign of a paper jam inside the printer that, although not grinding the entire operation to halt (see the section on "Paper jam" later in this section), is mangling your paper. Approach this problem with the same techniques described in the section "Paper jam."

Paper not feeding

When the paper is not feeding into the printer it means the pickup rollers have hardened and lost their ability to pick up the paper. Replacing these rollers usually fixes the problem.

In some cases it's not the rollers but the paper-feed sensor. It is designed to tell the printer when it is out of paper. Always try cleaning the sensor first before replacing it. High humidity can also cause the paper to not feed properly.

Paper jam

Laser printers today run at copier speeds. As a result, their most common problem is paper jams. Paper can get jammed in a printer for several reasons. First, feed jams happen when the paper feed rollers get worn. The solution to this problem is easy: replace the worn rollers.

 WARNING   If your paper-feed jams are caused by worn pickup rollers, there is something you can do to get your printer working while you're waiting for the replacement pickup rollers. Scuff the feed rollers with a pot scrubber pad (or something similar) to roughen up the feed rollers. This trick works only once. After that, the rollers aren't thick enough to touch the paper.

Another cause of feed jams is related to the drive of the pickup roller. The drive gear (or clutch) may be broken or have teeth missing. Again, the solution is to replace it. To determine if the problem is a broken gear or worn rollers, print a test page, but leave the paper tray out. Look into the paper feed opening with a flashlight, and see if the paper pickup rollers are turning evenly and don't skip. If they turn evenly, the problem is more than likely worn rollers.

Worn exit rollers can also cause paper jams. These rollers guide the paper out of the printer into the paper-receiving tray. If they're worn or damaged, the paper may catch on its way out of the printer. These types of jams are characterized by a paper jam that occurs just as the paper is getting to the exit rollers. If the paper jams, open the rear door and see where the paper is. If the paper is very close to the exit roller, the exit rollers are probably the problem.

The solution is to replace all the exit rollers. You must replace all of them at the same time, because even one worn exit roller can cause the paper to jam. Besides, they're inexpensive. Don't be cheap and skimp on these parts if you need to have them replaced.

Paper jams can be the fault of the paper. If your printer consistently tries to feed multiple pages into the printer, the paper isn't dry enough. If you live in an area with high humidity, this could be a problem. Some solutions are pretty far out but may work (like keeping the paper in a Tupperware-type airtight container or microwaving it to remove moisture). The best all-around solution, however, is humidity control and keeping the paper wrapped until it's needed. Keep the humidity around 50 percent or lower (but above 25 percent if you can, in order to avoid problems with electrostatic discharge). Poor paper quality can also cause this problem.

Finally, a metal, grounded strip called the static eliminator strip inside the printer drains the corona charge away from the paper after it has been used to transfer toner from the EP cartridge. If that strip is missing, broken, or damaged, the charge will remain on the paper and may cause it to stick to the EP cartridge, causing a jam. If the paper jams after reaching the corona assembly, this may be the cause.

No connectivity

A number of software issues can cause printer problems. Sometimes it's difficult to tell exactly where in the process the computer and the printer communication is breaking down. It could be that you are not establishing a connection with the printer, or it could be an incorrect setting or driver is preventing successful printing.

To determine whether it is a connectivity problem, ping the IP address of the printer. If you cannot ping the printer by IP address, that problem must be solved or all other troubleshooting of settings and drivers will be wasted effort. Use this simple test to rule out a network connectivity problem.

If the printer is connected directly to the computer (locally connected), then check the cables. If they check out, ensure that the printer port is enabled and that the correct driver for the printer is installed.

Garbled characters on paper

Many problems with a printer that won't work with the operating system or that prints the wrong characters can be traced to problems with its software. Computers and printers can't talk to each other by themselves. They need interface software to translate software commands into commands the printer can understand.

For a printer to work with a particular operating system, a driver must be installed for it. This driver specifies the page description language (PDL) the printer understands, as well as information about the printer's characteristics (paper trays, maximum resolution, and so on). For laser printers, there are two popular PDLs: Adobe PostScript (PS) and Hewlett-Packard Printer Control Language (PCL). Almost all laser printers use one or both of these.

If the wrong printer driver is selected, the computer will send commands in the wrong language. If that occurs, the printer will print several pages of garbage (even if only one page of information was sent). This "garbage" isn't garbage at all, but the printer PDL commands printed literally as text instead of being interpreted as control commands.

Vertical lines on page

Vertical lines can appear in either of two forms.

Vertical Black Lines on the Page

With laser printers, a groove or scratch in the EP drum can cause the problem of vertical black lines running down all or part of the page. Because a scratch is lower than the surface, it doesn't receive as much (if any) of a charge as the other areas. The result is that toner sticks to it as though it were discharged. Because the groove may go around the circumference of the drum, the line may go all the way down the page.

Another possible cause of vertical black lines is a dirty charge corona wire. A dirty charge corona wire prevents a sufficient charge from being placed on the EP drum. Because the EP drum has almost zero charge, toner sticks to the areas that correspond to the dirty areas on the charge corona wire.

The solution to the first problem is, as always, to replace the toner cartridge (or EP drum, if your printer uses a separate EP drum and toner). You can also solve the second problem with a new toner cartridge, but in this case that would be an extreme solution. It's easier to clean the charge corona with the brush supplied with the cartridge.

When dealing with inkjet printers, vertical black lines on the page can mean the print head needs cleaning or that the print cartridge needs to be replaced.

Vertical White Lines on the Page

With laser printers, vertical white lines running down all or part of the page are relatively common problems on older printers, especially ones that see little maintenance. They're caused by foreign matter (more than likely toner) caught on the transfer corona wire. The dirty spots keep the toner from being transmitted to the paper (at those locations, that is), with the result that streaks form as the paper progresses past the transfer corona wire.

The solution is to clean the corona wires. Some printers come with a small corona-wire brush to help in this procedure. To use it, remove the toner cartridge and run the brush in the charge corona groove on top of the toner cartridge. Replace the cartridge and use the brush to brush away any foreign deposits on the transfer corona. Be sure to put it back in its holder when you're finished.

For inkjet printers, clean the print head first (or run the built-in cleaning cycle), and then try replacing the cartridge. This behavior is usually due to dust or debris.

Backed up print queue

Sometimes the printer will not print and all attempts to delete print jobs or clear the print queue fail. It's almost as if the printer is just frozen. When this occurs, the best thing to do is restart the print spooler service on the computer that is acting as the print server. Unfortunately, all users will have to resend their print jobs after this, but at least the printer will be functional again.

Low memory errors

A printer can have several types of memory errors. The most common is insufficient memory to print the page. Sometimes you can circumvent this problem by doing any of the following:

- Turn off the printer to flush out its RAM, and then turn it back on and try again.
- Print at a lower resolution. (Adjust this setting in the printer's properties in Windows.)
- Change the page being printed so it's less complex.
- Try a different printer driver if your printer supports more than one PDL. (For example, try switching from PostScript to PCL, or vice versa.) Doing so involves installing another printer driver.
- Upgrade the memory, if the printer allows.

Access denied

Printers are considered resources just like files and folders and as such can have permissions attached to them. When a user receives an access denied message, the user lacks the print permission. Typically a printer that has been shared will automatically give all users the print permission, but when permissions have been employed to control which users can print to a particular printer, that default has been altered.

When checking permissions, keep in mind that in Windows, users may have permissions derived from their personal account and from groups of which they are a member. You must ensure that users have not been explicitly denied print permission through their accounts or through any groups of which they are members. A single Deny will prevent them from printing, regardless of what other permissions they may have to the printer.

Also, *print availability* or *print priority* can affect access to the printer. Print availability is used to permit certain users to only print during certain times. With print priority, print jobs from certain users or groups are assigned a higher priority than other users or groups. These settings, usually set by an administrator, can prevent or delay successful printing.

Printer will not print

If your printer isn't spitting out print jobs, it may be a good idea to print a test page and see if that works. The test page information is stored in the printer's memory, so there's no formatting or translating of jobs required. It's simply a test to make sure your printer hears your computer. In addition to the Windows Print Test Page button, try the built-in test function on the printer if your printer has one. While going through Windows tests the driver and connectivity, printing directly at the printer tests the print device itself.

When you install a printer, one of the last questions it asks you is if you want to print a test page. If there's any question, go ahead and do it. If the printer is already installed, you can print a test page from the printer Properties window. Just click the Print Test Page button and it should work. If nothing happens, double-check your connections and stop and restart the print spooler. If garbage prints, there is likely a problem with the printer's memory or the print driver.

In many cases, a printer will not print either because the printer is not on, it doesn't have power, or the print queue is stopped or paused. Printing a test page will identify these issues before they affect users.

Color prints in wrong print color

Incorrect colors or colors that are faint or washed out are almost always the result of a dirty print head. Head cleaning is a crucial operation that should be carried out at least once a month under normal usage. This is a procedure carried out in the Properties or Preferences of the printer (which may vary by printer).

You should not perform this procedure if the ink cartridges are low because it takes ink to do this. Check that first and, if they are low, replace any cartridges that need it and the run the head-cleaning procedure.

Unable to install printer

Installing a printer and attaching to a shared printer are two different operations in the Windows environment. Users with no administrative rights can attach to an existing shared printer, but installing a printer on the machine (which means that machine will function as the print server for that device) requires administrative permissions in the local machine. When an inability to install occurs, verify that you are logged into the computer with an administrator account.

Error codes

Many laser printers include LCD displays for interaction with the printer. When error codes appear, refer to the manufacturer's manuals or website for information on how to interpret the codes and solve the problem causing them.

Tools

Tools are available in the crusade to keep the printers working. In this section, some of the most important tools that should be present in your toolkit are discussed.

Maintenance kit

For many printers, the scheduled maintenance includes installing maintenance kits. Maintenance kits typically include a fuser, transfer roller, pickup rollers (for the trays), separation rollers, and feed rollers.

After installing the maintenance kit, you need to reset the maintenance counter as explained in the vendor's documentation.

Toner vacuum

Sometime accidents occur and toner gets spilled on the floor or carpet. You should never vacuum this up with a regular household vacuum cleaner. Toner particles may create static-electric charges when they rub against other particles or the interior of the vacuum or its hoses because of their electrostatic properties. If there is dust in the vacuum, static discharge can ignite it and create a small explosion. This may damage the vacuum cleaner or, worse, start a fire.

For spills into the printer, a special type of vacuum cleaner with an electrically conductive hose and a high efficiency (HEPA) filter may be needed for effective cleaning. These are called electrostatic discharge-safe (ESD-safe) or toner vacuums. Similar vacuums should be used for cleanup of larger toner spills.

Compressed air

Although compressed air is a good approach for cleaning out the inside of the case of a desktop computer, it's generally not a good idea to use compressed air to clean a printer. Most manufactures warn against this. If you insist on using compressed air, blow the dust out of the printer and not into it. A lint-free cloth is the best for removing dust when you can get at it.

Printer spooler

The print spooler service controls the print queue. This service can be stopped and started to solve many software related problems. Locate this service in the Services console and right-click it; you can first start and then stop the service. This can also be done at the command line using the `net stop spooler` and `net start spooler` commands.

Exam Essentials

Identify the most common symptoms of printing problems. These include streaks, faded prints, ghost images, incompletely fused toner, creased paper, paper jams and feeding issues, no connectivity, garbled characters, vertical lines, print queue issues, low memory errors, permission issues, total print failure, and incorrect print colors.

List the tools used to address printer issues. These tools include maintenance kits, toner vacuums, compressed air, and the printer spooler.

Review Questions

1. List three questions you should always ask a user about their problem.

2. What is the final step in the standard troubleshooting method?

3. True/False: Overheating can result in restarts.

4. When are POST beep codes issued?

5. What should be the first step when smoke appears?

6. What is the first thing to try when a Blue Screen of Death appears?

7. What sound indicates that the read/write heads are hitting the hard drive surface?

8. Magnetic screwdrivers should not be allowed to come in contact with the _____ or the _____.

9. What is the main use of the fdisk command?

10. What procedure can help to eliminate the buildup of magnetism in the display?

Appendix A

Answers to Review Questions

Chapter 1: PC Hardware

1. Port settings (parallel, serial, USB), drive types, boot sequence, date and time, and virus/security protections.

2. POST performs diagnostics, including checking the CPU, checking the RAM, and checking for the presence of a video card.

3. The multiplier.

4. Chipset.

5. Molex.

6. Error detection.

7. FireWire.

8. 650–700 MB.

9. False; only two devices can be placed in an IDE ribbon cable.

10. 34-pin ribbon cable.

Chapter 2: Networking

1. The default port for DNS is 53.

2. CAT6 transmits data at speed up to 10 Gbps.

3. IPv4 uses 32-bit addresses. IPv6 uses a 128-bit addressing scheme.

4. It is estimated that the 802.11n speeds might be able to reach 600 Mbps.

5. When MAC filtering is implemented, you identify each host by this number and determine specifically which addresses are allowed access the network.

6. WPA requires the use of TKIP (Temporal Key Integrity Protocol).

7. In a mesh network design, each computer on the network connects to every other, creating a point-to-point connection between every device on the network.

8. A Domain Name System (DNS) server translates hostnames to IP addresses.

9. The default subnet mask value for a host with a Class B address is 255.255.0.0.

10. DSL uses existing phone lines with a modem and a network card. A standard RJ-45 connector is used to connect the network card to the DSL modem, and a phone cord with RJ-11 connectors is used to connect the DSL modem to the phone jack.

Chapter 3: Laptops

1. ExpressCard.

2. ExpressCard/34 (34 mm wide) and ExpressCard/54 (54 mm wide, in an L shape).

3. Type I.

4. CardBus.

5. SoDIMM.

6. The advantages are reduced heat, lower power consumption, less noise, and better reliability since you have no moving parts.

7. T-8 Torx screwdriver.

8. Data connector.

9. False. Laptops use 2.5″ drives, which have lower capacity, lower cache, and lower velocity compared to 3.5″ drives.

10. In the display case.

Chapter 4: Printers

1. USB, parallel, serial, and Ethernet all represent wired printers. Wireless printers include Bluetooth, 802.11x, and infrared (IrDA).

2. The ability to print on multipart forms.

3. It applies a uniform negative charge to the drum.

4. Cleaning, conditioning, writing, developing, transferring, fusing.

5. Fuser.

6. USB is fully plug-and-play, it allows several printers to be connected at once without adding additional ports or using up additional resources, and it is faster.

7. Clean the ink jets; one or more is clogged.

8. False. A completely blank page results from the primary (charging) corona malfunctioning.

9. Because the heat from the laser printer's fuser could melt it.

10. A scratch on the drum.

Chapter 5: Operational Procedures

1. The EPA (Environmental Protection Agency) keeps a copy of material safety data sheets.

2. Toner. You must be careful not to spill it and send used cartridges to recycling centers.

3. True. An ESD strap should connect to the ground of an electrical outlet.

4. A high-voltage capacitor inside the monitor retains a charge even long after the monitor has been unplugged.

5. Class C.

6. Send a message to all users notifying them that the system will be going down and give an estimate of how long the users will be affected. The estimate should include time to address any other issues that you fear may crop up.

7. One of the first questions you should ask the user is if they have ever printed to that printer. This can then be followed up with questions as to how recently they did so and what has changed since then.

8. You should adhere to policies of the company you work for on this matter. Some companies do not mind customers having the mobile number for a technician, whereas others want all calls to come to a central location so the calls can be processed more efficiently. Whichever situation applies, you should carefully explain it to your customer and let them know the rules of response time, escalation, and other issues.

9. This is known as chain of custody.

10. True. Once they begin, law enforcement professionals are required to pursue an investigation.

Chapter 6: Operating Systems

1. Four GB of RAM is the most supported for any 32-bit version.

2. Windows XP Mode is included with Windows 7 Professional, Enterprise, and Ultimate and is a virtual client emulating Windows XP Professional with Service Pack 3.

3. Windows Preinstallation Environment (WinPE) which is a stub operating system often used to install the operating system or for troubleshooting.

4. TASKLIST will list all running processes (and their process ID numbers) at the command line.

5. The BOOTREC option /Fixboot is used to write a new boot sector.

6. In Windows 7 Professional, Print Management allows you to manage multiple printers and print servers from a single interface.

7. To get to the Task Manager directly in Windows, press Ctrl+Shift+Esc.

8. Remote Desktop Connection is the MSTSC.EXE utility.

9. The Security Center was rolled into the Action Center in Windows 7. This interface shows the status of, and allows you to configure, the firewall, Windows Update, virus protection, spyware and unwanted software protection, Internet security settings, UAC, and network access protection, as well as backup, troubleshooting, and Problem Reports and Solutions.

10. The hypervisor is the software that allows virtual machines to exist.

Chapter 7: Security

1. Tailgating is the term used for someone being so close to you when you enter a building that they are able to come in right behind you without needing to use a key, a card, or any other security device.

2. The principle of least privilege is that when you assign permissions, give users only the permissions they need to do their work and no more.

3. Phishing.

4. A worm is different from a virus in that it can reproduce itself, it's self-contained, and it doesn't need a host application to be transported.

5. Microsoft has changed the AutoRun function on Windows Vista and Windows 7 (though running remains the default action for PCs running Windows XP through Service Pack 3) so that it is now disabled by default.

6. Degaussing involves applying a strong magnetic field to initialize the media (this is also referred to as disk wiping).

7. With MAC filtering, the administrator compiles a list of the MAC addresses associated with the users' computers and enters those. When a client attempts to connect, and other values have been correctly entered, an additional check of the MAC address is done. If the address appears in the list, the client is allowed to join; otherwise, they are forbidden from doing so.

8. Microsoft strongly recommends that all network shares be established using NTFS.

9. If you don't know a workstation's MAC address, use ipconfig /all to find it in the Windows-based world.

10. A low-level format is operating system independent and destroys any data that was on the drive.

Chapter 8: Mobile Devices

1. Android and iOS.

2. Android.

3. False.

4. Calibrated.

5. Cell phone networks and Wi-Fi networks.

6. Pairing.

7. It sends your email to the recipient's email server so it's sometimes called outgoing.

8. Exchange server address, username, and password for the account and domain name for the account.

9. Locator application.

10. Touch flow and multitouch.

Chapter 9: Troubleshooting

1. Ask these questions:

   What is the problem?

   When was the last time that the problem didn't exist?

   What has changed since?

2. Document the issue and the results.

3. True.

4. During startup.

5. Shut the machine down.

6. Restarting the machine.

7. A loud clicking noise.

8. Motherboard or hard drive.

9. It is used to view partition information and to create and delete volumes or partitions.

10. Degaussing.

Appendix

B

About the Additional Study Tools

IN THIS APPENDIX:

✓ Additional study tools

✓ System requirements

✓ Using the study tools

✓ Troubleshooting

Additional Study Tools

The following sections are arranged by category and summarize the software and other goodies you'll find on the companion website. If you need help with installing the items, refer to the installation instructions in the "Using the Study Tools" section of this appendix.

> The additional study tools can be found at www.sybex.com/go/aplusrg2e. Here, you will get instructions on how to download the files to your hard drive.

Sybex Test Engine

The files contain the Sybex test engine, which includes four total bonus practice exams (two each for exams 220-801 and 220-802).

Electronic Flashcards

These handy electronic flashcards are just what they sound like. One side contains a question, and the other side shows the answer.

PDF of Glossary of Terms

We have included an electronic version of the Glossary in PDF format. You can view this with Adobe Reader.

Adobe Reader

We've also included a copy of Adobe Reader so you can view the PDF files that accompany the book's content. For more information on Adobe Reader or to check for a newer version, visit Adobe's website at www.adobe.com/products/reader/.

System Requirements

Make sure your computer meets the minimum system requirements shown in the following list. If your computer doesn't match up to most of these requirements, you may have problems using the software and files. For the latest and greatest information, please refer to the ReadMe file located in the downloads.

- A PC running Microsoft Windows 98, Windows 2000, Windows NT4 (with SP4 or later), Windows Me, Windows XP, Windows Vista, or Windows 7
- An Internet connection

Using the Study Tools

To install the items, follow these steps:

1. Download the zip file to your hard drive, and unzip to an appropriate location. Instructions on where to download this file can be found here: www.sybex.com/go/aplusrg2e.
2. Click the Start.exe file to open the study tools file.
3. Read the license agreement, and then click the Accept button if you want to use the study tools.

The main interface appears. The interface allows you to access the content with just one or two clicks.

Troubleshooting

Wiley has attempted to provide programs that work on most computers with the minimum system requirements. Alas, your computer may differ, and some programs may not work properly for some reason.

The two likeliest problems are that you don't have enough memory (RAM) for the programs you want to use or you have other programs running that are affecting installation or running of a program. If you get an error message such as "Not enough memory" or "Setup cannot continue," try one or more of the following suggestions and then try using the software again:

Turn off any antivirus software running on your computer.   Installation programs sometimes mimic virus activity and may make your computer incorrectly believe that it's being infected by a virus.

Close all running programs.   The more programs you have running, the less memory is available to other programs. Installation programs typically update files and programs, so if you keep other programs running, installation may not work properly.

Have your local computer store add more RAM to your computer.   This is, admittedly, a drastic and somewhat expensive step. However, adding more memory can really help the speed of your computer and allow more programs to run at the same time.

Customer Care

If you have trouble with the book's companion study tools, please call the Wiley Product Technical Support phone number at (800) 762-2974. 74, or email them at `http://sybex` `.custhelp.com/`.

Index

C

U

X